Story Central Plus

Teacher Edition 3 with Teacher Resources

Dave Tucker

Macmillan Education Limited
4 Crinan Street
London N1 9XW

Companies and representatives throughout the world

Story Central Plus level 3 Teacher Edition ISBN 978-1-380-06106-5
Story Central Plus Level 3 Teacher Edition with Student eBook, Reader eBook, CLIL eBook, Digital Activity Book, Teacher Resource Center, and Test Generator
ISBN 978-1-380-06104-1

Story Central is a registered trademark published by Macmillan Education Limited
This edition published 2021
First edition entitled "Story Central" published 2015 by Macmillan Education Limited.

Teacher Edition credits:
Designed by Red Phoenix Design
Page make-up by Mo Choy Design Ltd and Composure
Illustrated by Steven Wood (Advocate Art)
Cover design by Wild Apple Design Ltd

Student Book credits:
Text © Angela Llanas and Libby Williams 2021
Design and illustration © Macmillan Education Limited 2021
Additional material written by Mo Choy Design Ltd
The authors have asserted their rights to be identified as the authors of this work in accordance with the Copyright, Designs and Patents Act 1988.

Designed by Liz Adcock and Pronk Media, Inc.
Illustrated by Aardvart pp 64, 65; Robin Boyden (Pickled Ink) pp 24 -25, 27; Paco Cavero (Sylvie Poggio Artist Agency) pp 31, 59, 87; Russ Daff (Beehive Illustration) pp 15, 22, 92; Nikki Dyson (Advocate Art) pp 108 -109, 111; Pablo Gallego (Beehive Illustration) pp 9, 13b, 17t, 23, 27b, 41b, 45, 51, 66, 67b, 73, 79, 81, 83b, 85, 93, 107, 83b, 121, 125b, 127; Ria Maria Lee (The Bright Agency) pp 18, 19, 20, 46, 47, 48, 74, 75, 76, 102, 103, 104, 130, 131, 132; Ayesha Lopez (Advocate Art) pp 52 -53, 55; Andrew Painter pp 66 -67, 69; Carl Pearce pp 10 11,13, 17m; Louise Redshaw (Plum Pudding) pp 36 -37, 38, 39t; Stephen Reed (The July Group) pp 94 -95, 96, 97; Shahab Shamshirsaz (Sylvie Poggio Artist Agency) pp 80 -81, 83; Michelle Simpson (Advocate Art) pp 32, 33, 34, 35, 60, 61, 62, 88, 89, 90, 116, 117, 118; Laszlo Veres (Beehive Illustration) pp 8, 44, 50, 73b, 120; Steven Wood (Advocate Art) pp 4 -129 (border design and main character artwork) 4 -5, 6 -7, 10, 14, 24l, 28, 36l, 40, 52l, 56, 66l, 70, 80l, 84, 94l, 98, 108l, 112, 122l, 126.
Cover design by Wild Apple Design Ltd and Roberto Martinez
Cover artwork by Steven Wood (Advocate Art)
Cover photographs by Paul Bricknell
Picture research by Composure
The authors and publishers would like to thank the following for permission to reproduce their photographs: Alamy Stock Photo/Aflo Co., Ltd. (tl)p. 15, Alamy Stock Photo/Andrey Kuzmin (cbl)p. 64, Alamy Stock Photo/ClassicStock (tr)p. 71, Alamy Stock Photo/Heritage Image Partnership Ltd p. 71, Alamy Stock Photo/Image Professionals GmbH (tr)p. 64, Alamy Stock Photo/Image Source (tr)p. 29, Alamy Stock Photo/Jake Lyell (tr)p. 15, Alamy Stock Photo/Martin Wierink (bc)p. 8, Alamy Stock Photo/moodboard (cl)p. 85, Alamy Stock Photo/National Geographic Image Collection (tc)p. 15, Alamy Stock Photo/PCN Photography (2)p. 92, Alamy Stock Photo/PhotoStock-Israel (ctl)p. 64, Alamy Stock Photo/Piero Cruciatti p. 105, Alamy Stock Photo/Roger Sedres p. 103, Alamy Stock Photo/Science History Images (bl)p. 99, Alamy Stock Photo/Simon Price (t)p. 49, Alamy Stock Photo/Stuart Pearce (1)p. 120, Alamy Stock Photo/World History Archive (tl)p. 99; Getty Images/Ericka McConnell p. 127, Getty Images/4x6 (6)p. 92, Getty Images/Adam Taylor p. 37, Getty Images/alxpin p. 91, Getty Images/Atlantide Phototravel (bl)p. 78, Getty Images/Bernd Vogel (6)p. 120, Getty Images/Bob Thomas/Contributor p. 100, Getty Images/Carlo A p. 119, Getty Images/Cavan Images (bl)p. 36, Getty Images/Comstock (tr)p. 36, Getty Images/Daniel Milchev (4)p. 120, Getty Images/David Madison (4)p. 92, Getty Images/David Woo (cbr)p. 64, Getty Images/DEA / G. DAGLI ORTI p. 43, Getty Images/Dean Mitchell p. 61, Getty Images/Dorling Kindersley p. 74, Getty Images/FabioFilzi (bc) p. 78, Getty Images/Fraser Hall (tl)p. 79, Getty Images/Friedrich Schmidt (br)p. 78, Getty Images/fuchs-photography p. 77, Getty Images/Fuse (tr)p. 8, (tc)p. 85, (7)p. 92, Getty Images/Gandee Vasan (3)p. 92, Getty Images/General Photographic Agency/Stringer (tc) p. 71, Getty Images/guenterguni (ctr)p. 78, Getty Images/Hannah Peters / Staff (cr)p. 99, Getty Images/Image Source (cc)p. 64, Getty Images/Image Source/Zero Creatives (bl)p. 121, Getty Images/izusek (bcr)p. 36, Getty Images/John Elk (tl)p. 64, Getty Images/John Giustina (bl)p. 113, Getty Images/Jose Luis Pelaez Inc (br)p. 8, (tr)p. 113, Getty Images/Juanmonino (bc)p. 64, Getty Images/Julie Thurston (br)p. 64, Getty Images/mareciok (bcl)p. 36, Getty Images/Maskot (bl)p. 64, Getty Images/Medioimages/Photodisc (br)p. 36, Getty Images/Michelle McMahon (c)p. 29, Getty Images/monticelllo (cr)p. 8, Getty Images/Olix Wirtinger/Corbis (tl)p. 36, Getty Images/OSTILL (tl)p. 113, Getty Images/Paul Burns (5)p. 92, Getty Images/Rana Faure (br)p. 113, Getty Images/Reed Kaestner (2) p. 120, Getty Images/Rob Lewine (cc)p. 121, Getty Images/Robert Recker (tcr)p. 36, Getty Images/Rubberball/Nicole Hill (tcl)p. 36, Getty Images/SolStock p. 63, Getty Images/Stephen Shepherd (cl)p. 8, Getty Images/Thomas Koehler (cbr)p. 78, Getty Images/Wysiati (tc)p. 79; Macmillan Education Limited/CORBIS (br)p. 49, Macmillan Education Limited/DigitalStock/Corbis (tr)p. 79, Macmillan Education Limited/DigitalVision/Punchstock (8)p. 92, Macmillan Education Limited/FLPA/Alamy Stock Photo (br)p. 90, Macmillan Education Limited/Hero Images (7)p. 120, Macmillan Education Limited/jamesteohart (tr)p. 90, Macmillan Education Limited/Jose Luis Pelaez Inc (bl)p. 8, Macmillan Education Limited/Martin Lindsay/Alamy Stock Photo (tc)p. 133, Macmillan Education Limited/National Geographic Image Collection/Alamy Stock Photo (tr)p. 78, Macmillan Education Limited/PHOTODISC (cc)p. 78, Macmillan Education Limited/Purestock p. 21, Macmillan Education Limited/SensorSpot (tl)p. 29, Macmillan Education Limited/stevecoleimages,Steve Cole - christie & cole studio inc. p. 64, Macmillan Education Limited/SUPERSTOCK (tl)p. 133, Macmillan Education Limited/thinkomatic (1)p. 92, Macmillan Education Limited/Torfinn (tr)p. 133, Macmillan Education Limited/VisionsofAmerica/Joe Sohm (cr)p. 90; Shutterstock/Jacek Chabraszewski (5)p. 120, Shutterstock/R.Filip (ctr)p. 64, Shutterstock/ricochet64 (cc)p. 99; Superstock/Michael DeYoung/Blend Images (3)p. 120.
Commissioned photographs by MMStudios pp. 16, 30, 44, 58, 72, 86, 100, 114, 128.
Prop artwork by Carla Drury

Reader credits:
Text, design and illustration © Macmillan Education Limited 2021
Written by Angela Llanas and Libby Williams
Stories adapted by Jenny Mason
The authors have asserted their rights to be identified as the authors of this work in accordance with the Copyright, Designs and Patents Act 1988.

Page Design and art editing by Wild Apple Design Ltd
Storyboard layouts by Carrie Webb (Red Phoenix Design)
You Have to Listen! illustrated by Peter Francis (MB Artists); The Magic Money Tree illustrated by Carl Pearce; Coppelia illustrated by Stephanie Dehennin (MB Artists); Cinderella Goes to the Party illustrated by Coen Hamelink (Bright Agency); Journey into the Past illustrated by Victor Tavares (Beehive Illustration); Goanna and the Moon illustrated by Laura Watkins (Bright Agency); The Champion illustrated by Russ Daff (Beehive Illustration); Sneaky Snake illustrated by Aardvart; Holly's Vacation illustrated by Caroline Romanet (Advocate Art).

Activity Book credits:
Text, design and illustration © Macmillan Education Limited 2021
Written by Sue Clarke
Additional material written by Tracy Traynor
The author has asserted her right to be identified as the author of this work in accordance with the Copyright, Designs and Patents Act 1988.

Designed by Liz Adcock
Illustrated by Aardvart p. 64; Robin Boyden (Pickled Ink) pp.10, 12, 15, 19, 23, 28, 31, 33, 35, 38, 43, 44, 46, 52, 59, 60, 62, 67, 70, 79, 82, 90, 92; Russ Daff (Beehive Illustration) p. 56; Peter Francis (MB Artists) p. 8; Coen Hamelink (Bright Agency) p. 32; Andy Hamilton pp. 5 -6, 11, 13, 21, 25, 29 -30, 37, 39, 45, 50, 53, 58, 61, 69, 77, 84, 86, 94, 95; Andy Keylock (Beehive Illustration) p. 76; Andrew Painter pp. 83, 89, 92, 98, 100, 101; Carl Pearce p. 16 -17; Caroline Romanet (Advocate Art) p. 72; Jorge Santillan (Beehive Illustration) pp. 7, 9, 14, 18 -20, 22, 26, 27, 34, 36, 42, 51, 54 -55, 63, 65 -66, 68, 71, 73 -74, 80, 83, 85, 86, 87, 88, 91, 93, 95, 100, 101, 104, 97; Victor Tavares (Beehive Illustration) p. 40; Laura Watkins (Bright Agency) p.48; Steven Wood (Advocate Art) pp. 3 -77.
Cover design by Wild Apple Design Ltd. and Roberto Martinez.
Cover illustration Steven Wood (Advocate Art)
Picture research by Composure

Printed and bound in Singapore

2021
80

Contents

Contents

Competencies

me	act	think	learn	communicate

Activities that encourage children to accept responsibility and reflect on the consequences of lifestyle choices.	Activities that develop societal understanding and identification of children's own circumstances in a wider context.	Activities that develop critical thinking skills to reflect upon, manipulate, process, and interpret information.	Activities that foster learner autonomy and allow children to demonstrate and put into practice learning strategies.	Activities that promote interpersonal and collaborative skills, develop teamwork, and allow children to express opinions and ideas.

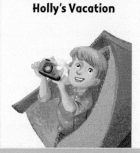

Philosophy and Methodology

Philosophy

1 Language is power.

Story Central Plus empowers children to communicate effectively and develop their knowledge of the world around them through stories. The course enables children to become critical and active readers, writers, and storytellers through its strong focus on literacy development.

2 An empowered teacher empowers children and changes lives.

Story Central Plus provides teachers with all the support they need to deliver effective and inspiring lessons. Children will respond to the meaningful texts and activities, ensuring that both teachers and children feel a real sense of achievement. Children will develop the skills they need to participate fully in their lives both inside and outside the classroom.

3 The child is not a blank slate.

Children bring their culture, beliefs, and a rich inner world to the classroom. Our materials respect this and recognize that it is key to engaging and interesting children in learning English.

4 Nurturing critical and creative thinking helps children become well-rounded and innovative adults.

Story Central Plus actively encourages creative, divergent, and playful thinking, and consistently supports the acquisition of academic knowledge.

Methodology

Literacy

Reading and writing skills are developed throughout the course. Each chapter is based around a story. An extract from the story is introduced in Student Book Lesson 3, allowing opportunities to develop reading skills and encouraging children to think creatively as they analyze the language in a meaningful context, and predict story developments. The full story is given in the beautifully illustrated Reader. Use of the Reader is fully integrated and the story links together the chapter theme and target language, providing language-rich input and enabling holistic learning. Activities engage children's interest and imagination as they are encouraged to read for pleasure. After children have read the story, their writing skills are developed through personal responses and creative writing. A love of literature is further fostered by the Oral Storytelling Videos.

Critical Literacy

Story Central Plus takes children beyond understanding texts. The material and activities help them analyze and respond, as they develop the skills of questioning and interpreting the information they encounter. Children are encouraged to discuss the story's meaning and how the values expressed relate to their lives and the world around them. Children are supported in expressing their opinions through presentations, role play, and extended writing. These essential skills will empower them to use language effectively later in life.

Critical and Creative Thinking

Critical and creative thinking are actively encouraged. Children are given every opportunity to figure things out for themselves and share their ideas. Vocabulary is presented in context, requiring them to use textual and visual clues to process and deduce meaning. Prediction, reflection, and drawing conclusions all play an important part in developing an imaginative and reflective response.

A Cool Place to Hang Out With Friends!

Story Central is a cool club where kids hang out with their friends and read great books. They also share ideas and stories, plan events, do homework, and drink milkshakes! In Story Central you can explore, discover, learn, research, and interact. It's the sort of place where kids really want to be!

Children will love getting to know the fun characters who hang out in Story Central. They appear in Lesson 3 and Lesson 6 in every chapter.

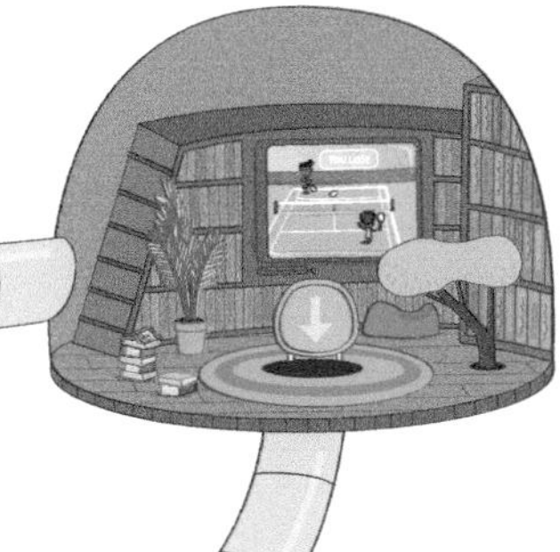

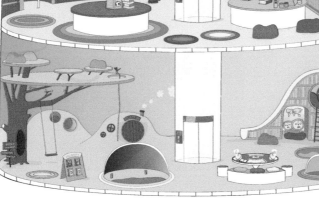

Level 3 Characters

Jason is a college student who works part-time in Story Central. He studies English and loves writing stories!

Felicity is an independent nine-year-old girl who likes taking the lead. She is independent and fun-loving! She loves reading.

Cheng is Felicity's best friend. He's also nine years old and he really enjoys sports. He always has a lot of good ideas!

Miguel is ten years old and loves hanging out with Felicity and Cheng at Story Central. He's really into gadgets!

Component Overview

For the Student

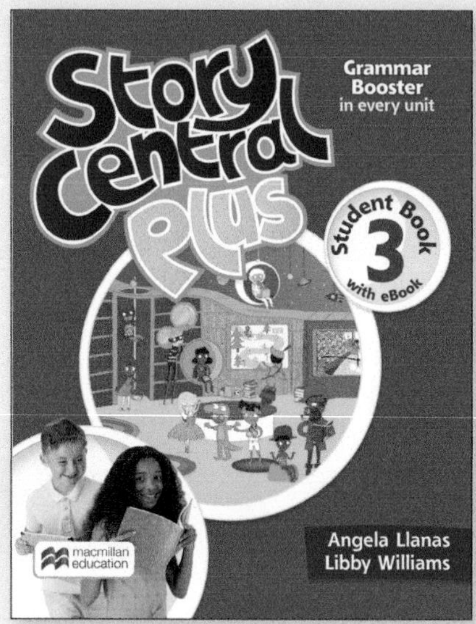

Student Book

Consists of 9 thematic chapters, featuring a story extract, literacy development, competency coverage, CLIL content, and project work. Focuses on developing critical thinking, creativity, communication, and collaboration. NEW! Grammar Booster section per chapter presents and provides further grammar practice of the target grammar.

Reader

Consists of 9 stories of different genres and styles. Focuses on promoting critical literacy and reading skills through developing a love of reading.

Activity Book

Consists of follow-on lessons for every Student Book lesson. Focuses on consolidating key language and skills, and developing creative use of language in writing. NEW! Exam Booster section per chapter provides Cambridge YLE practice activities.

eBooks

The Student Book has an access code which provides access to eBooks for the Student Book, Reader, and CLIL Book. The eBooks have embedded audio, video, and a set of tools to interact with the pages to provide flexibility for remote learning and give students more ways to read and learn.

The Inks Vocabulary Practice App

The Inks Apps provide a fun way for students to practice the vocabulary words they've learned for better retention. They're free and available to download from the App Store and Google Play.

Digital Activity Book

These books provide students an interactive way to practice. Students' answers are sent automatically to the gradebook so teachers and caregivers can monitor progress.

For the Teacher

Teacher Edition

Consists of teaching notes for each lesson of the Student Book, Reader, and Activity Book, and suggestions on when and how to use digital components. Focuses on providing clear and concise support for lesson planning and teaching.

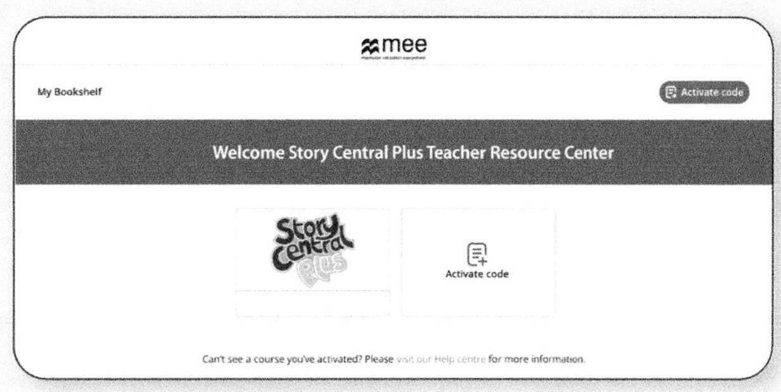

Teacher Resource Center

Consists of the class audio, and additional resources and ideas to extend lessons and learning, and give further practice of key language. Focuses on giving teachers flexibility and the means to deliver dynamic and varied lessons.

Test Generator

Pre-written tests for each chapter, mid-year, and end-of-year are available to download from the Teacher Resource Center. In addition, the Test Generator allows teachers to customize and create new tests from a bank of activities.

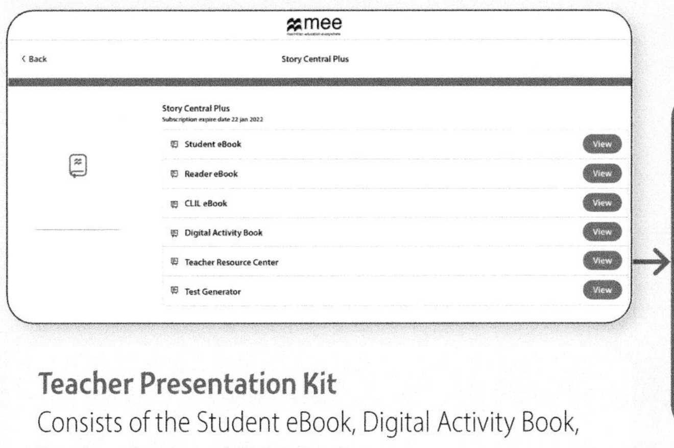

Teacher Presentation Kit

Consists of the Student eBook, Digital Activity Book, Reader eBook and CLIL eBook.

Student eBook

This eBook provides a digital version of the Student Book with integrated audio, video and answer keys.

Digital Activity Book

This eBook provides an interactive version of the Activity Book that is linked to a gradebook.

Oral Storytelling Videos bring the stories to life with mesmerising narration set in *Story Central Plus*. These are available for Chapters 1, 3, 5, 7, and 9.

Music Videos will get children dancing! They can copy the actions modeled on screen for the songs from Chapters 2, 4, 6, and 8.

Reader eBook

This eBook provides a digital version of the Reader with embedded audio and Storytelling Videos.

CLIL eBook

This eBook provides a digital version of the CLIL Book with embedded audio.

Teaching with *Story Central Plus*

Lesson 1 Vocabulary

High-impact openers introduce the chapter theme to create interest and engage children.

Vocabulary is introduced through visual clues to develop **critical thinking skills**, encouraging children to deduce meaning.

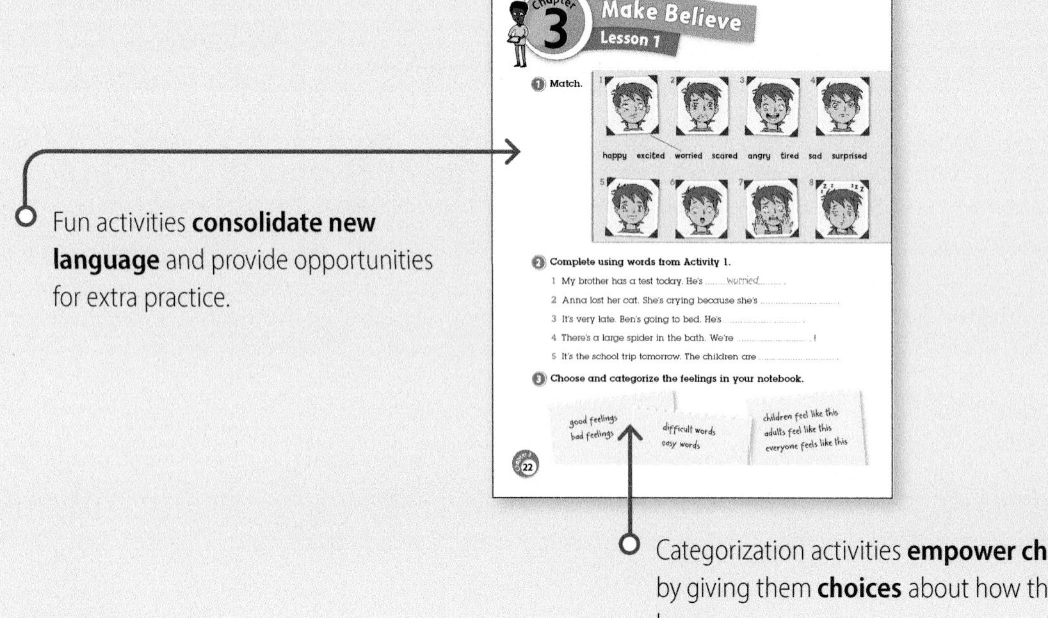

Fun activities **consolidate new language** and provide opportunities for extra practice.

Categorization activities **empower children** by giving them **choices** about how they learn.

Lesson 2 Grammar

Grammar is presented clearly and accessibly, recycling Lesson 1 vocabulary.

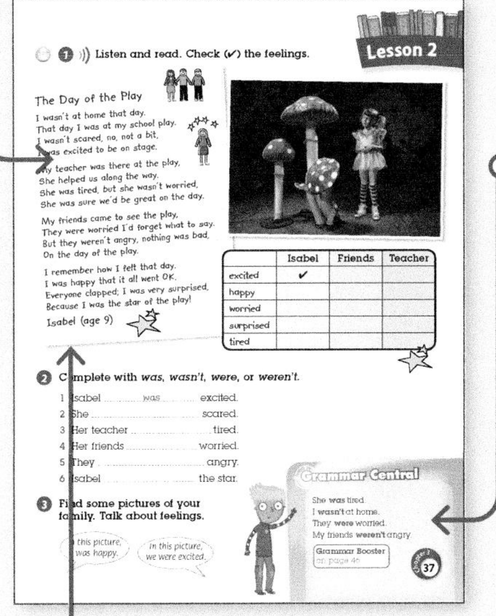

Lesson 2

1 Listen and read. Check (✔) the feelings.

The Day of the Play

I wasn't at home that day.
That day I was at my school play.
I wasn't scared, no, not a bit,
I was excited to be on stage.

My teacher was there at the play,
She helped us along the way.
She was tired, but she wasn't worried,
She was sure we'd be great on the day.

My friends came to see the play,
They were worried I'd forget what to say.
But they weren't angry, nothing was bad,
On the day of the play.

I remember how I felt that day.
I was happy that it all went OK.
Everyone clapped; I was very surprised,
Because I was the star of the play!

Isabel (age 9)

	Isabel	Friends	Teacher
excited	✔		
happy			
worried			
surprised			
tired			

2 Complete with *was, wasn't, were,* or *weren't.*

1 Isabel ..... was ..... excited.
2 She ..... scared.
3 Her teacher ..... tired.
4 Her friends ..... worried.
5 They ..... angry.
6 Isabel ..... the star.

3 Find some pictures of your family. Talk about feelings.

In this picture, I was happy.

In this picture, we were excited.

Grammar Central

She **was** tired.
I **wasn't** at home.
They **were** worried.
My friends **weren't** angry.

Grammar Booster on page 46

37

Grammar Central highlights new grammar structures, providing a useful reference for activities.

Listening activities are available to stream or download from the Teacher Resource Center and in the Student eBook.

Further grammar practice in the Activity Book consolidates language.

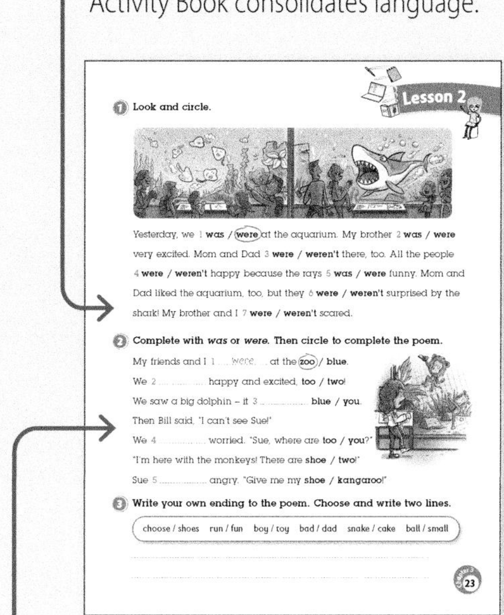

Lesson 2

1 Look and circle.

Yesterday, we 1 was / were at the aquarium. My brother 2 **was / were** very excited. Mom and Dad 3 **were / weren't** there, too. All the people 4 **were / weren't** happy because the rays 5 **was / were** funny. Mom and Dad liked the aquarium, too, but they 6 **were / weren't** surprised by the shark! My brother and I 7 **were / weren't** scared.

2 Complete with *was* or *were.* Then circle to complete the poem.

My friends and I 1 ..... were ..... at the **zoo / blue.**
We 2 ..... happy and excited, **too / two!**
We saw a big dolphin – it 3 ..... **blue / you.**
Then Bill said, "I can't see Sue!"
We 4 ..... worried. "Sue, where are **too / you?**"
"I'm here with the monkeys! There are **shoe / two!**"
Sue 5 ..... angry. "Give me my **shoe / kangaroo!**"

3 Write your own ending to the poem. Choose and write two lines.

choose / shoes run / fun boy / toy bad / dad snake / cake ball / small

23

Writing activities provide well-supported and progressive development of writing skills.

NEW! Grammar Booster sections in the Student Book at the end of each chapter provide four pages of extra support. They include detailed grammar boxes and scaffolded practice for lessons 2 and 6, a review page that combines the grammar points in both lessons and a challenge page. These pages offer support for different language proficiency levels in the classroom. They can be assigned to individual children or the entire class.

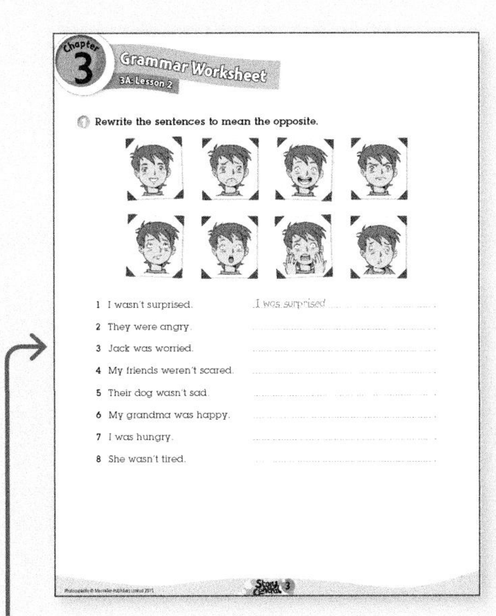

Chapter 3 Grammar Worksheet

3A: Lesson 2

1 Rewrite the sentences to mean the opposite.

1 I wasn't surprised. I was surprised
2 They were angry.
3 Jack was worried.
4 My friends weren't scared.
5 Their dog wasn't sad.
6 My grandma was happy.
7 I was hungry.
8 She wasn't tired.

Story Central 3

Supplementary **grammar worksheets** can be downloaded from the Teacher Resource Center to further consolidate learning in class or as homework.

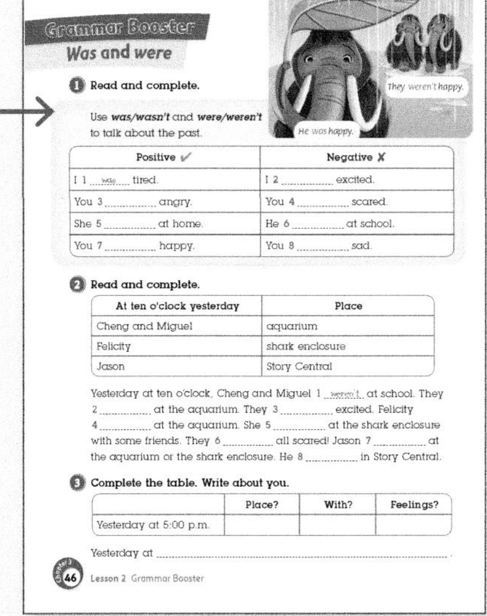

Grammar Booster

Was and were

1 Read and complete.

Use **was/wasn't** and **were/weren't** to talk about the past.

He was happy.

They weren't happy.

Positive ✔	Negative ✘
I 1 ..... was ..... tired.	I 2 ..... excited.
You 3 ..... angry.	You 4 ..... scared.
She 5 ..... at home.	He 6 ..... at school.
You 7 ..... happy.	You 8 ..... sad.

2 Read and complete.

At ten o'clock yesterday	Place
Cheng and Miguel	aquarium
Felicity	shark enclosure
Jason	Story Central

Yesterday at ten o'clock, Cheng and Miguel 1 ..... weren't ..... at school. They 2 ..... at the aquarium. They 3 ..... excited. Felicity 4 ..... at the aquarium. She 5 ..... at the shark enclosure with some friends. They 6 ..... all scared! Jason 7 ..... at the aquarium or the shark enclosure. He 8 ..... in Story Central.

3 Complete the table. Write about you.

	Place?	With?	Feelings?
Yesterday at 5:00 p.m.			

Yesterday at .....

46 Lesson 2 Grammar Booster

Lesson 3 Reading: Story Extract

Children predict what the story is about before reading, to develop **visual literacy**.

A **functional dialogue** featuring the Story Central characters teaches useful language for the classroom.

Comprehension questions about the story extract check understanding.

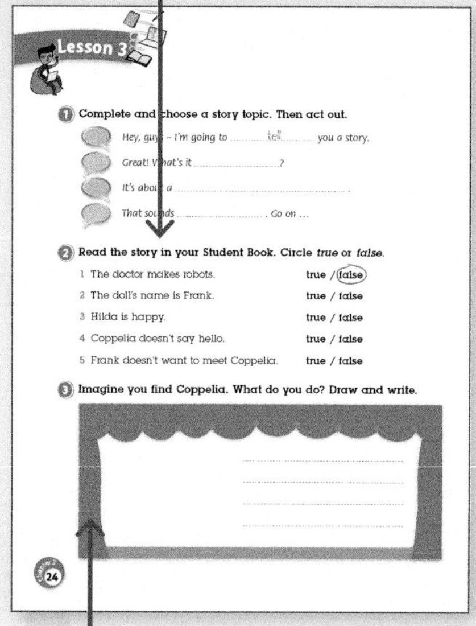

Comprehension develop reading skills and strategies.

The **story extract** (beginning, middle, or end) engages children but leaves plenty to the imagination.

A **prediction activity** asks children to use their **imagination** to figure out what will happen in the story.

Reader

Children read the whole story in their Reader.

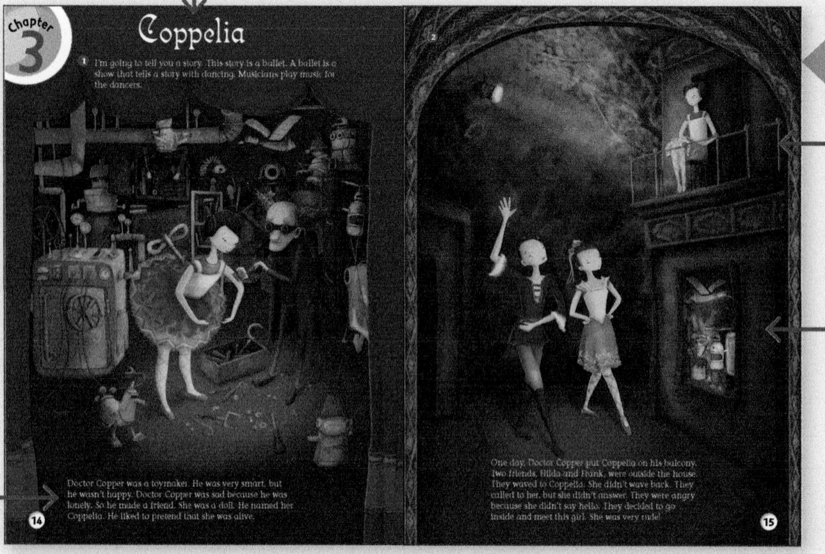

A wide variety of story genres and narrative styles gives a **rich literary experience**.

Beautiful illustrations motivate children to **read for pleasure** and develop **a lifelong love of reading**.

Extensive language input allows **holistic language learning**, with the focus on overall understanding.

Lesson 4 Reading Comprehension and Critical Literacy

After reading the story in the Reader, children answer comprehension questions which help develop **reading strategies**.

The **I Can Read!** feature focuses awareness on text conventions.

Graphic organizer activities develop **study skills**.

Children practice the Student Book **I Can Read and Write!** text conventions.

Lesson 4 Time to Think

1 Read the story in your Reader.

2 Circle T (true) or F (false).

Reading Report

1 Doctor Copper had a lot of friends. T F
2 Coppelia was a doll. T F
3 Hilda was inside the magical machine. T F
4 Frank and Hilda escaped. T F
5 At the end of the story, Doctor Copper was happy. T F

3 Imagine that Coppelia can talk. Write what she says.

4 Talk about the story.

Does the story remind you of another story?

I Can Read and Write!

The word because can tell us more information, e.g. Doctor Copper was sad because he was lonely. Find more examples of because in the story. What does it tell us about the characters' feelings?

40

Lesson 4 Time to Think

1 How did the characters feel? Complete.

1 Doctor Copper was ....sad........ because ....he was lonely........
2 Hilda .... because Coppelia ....
3 Doctor Copper .... because he thought ....
4 Frank and Hilda .... because ....

2 Match.

1 Mom was surprised — a because it was my party.
2 My brother was worried — b because it was his test.
3 My teacher was happy — c because we made a cake.
4 I was excited — d because we did our homework.

3 Design a friend for Coppelia. Write in your notebook about a different toy that came to life. Use the Story Builder.

Story Builder

He/She was a ...
He/She was big/old ...
Coppelia wasn't ... She was ...
They were ...

4 Connect to Me

Which storybook character would you like to come to life?

I'd like .... to come to life because ....

25

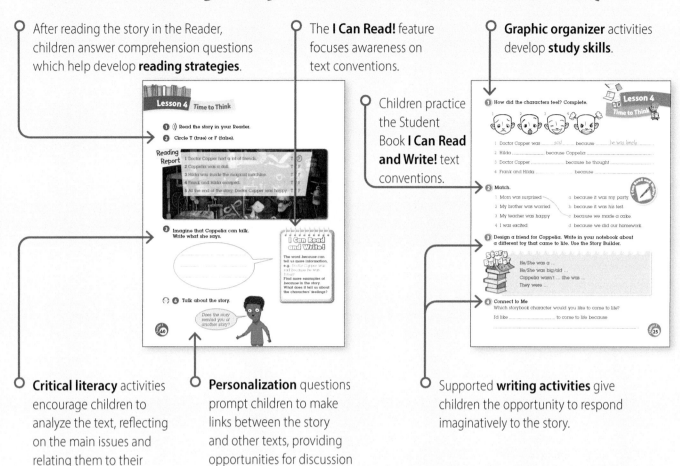

Critical literacy activities encourage children to analyze the text, reflecting on the main issues and relating them to their own lives.

Personalization questions prompt children to make links between the story and other texts, providing opportunities for discussion and self-expression.

Supported **writing activities** give children the opportunity to respond imaginatively to the story.

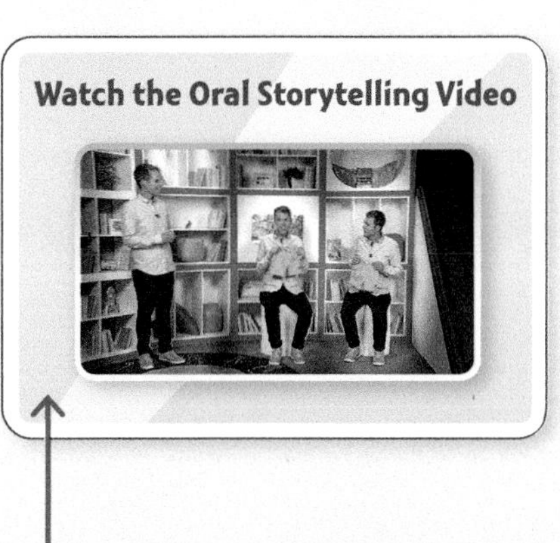

In the **Oral Storytelling Videos** professional storytellers act out and bring to life the Reader stories for Chapters 1, 3, 5, 7, and 9 (available in the Student eBook and the Reader eBook.).

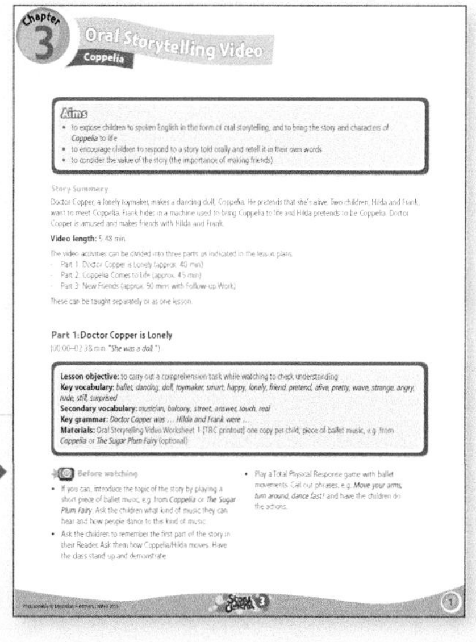
Chapter 3 Oral Storytelling Video

Coppelia

Aims

Story Summary

Video length:

Part 1: Doctor Copper is Lonely

Lesson objective:

Key vocabulary:

Secondary vocabulary:

Key grammar:

Materials:

Before watching

Teaching notes and worksheets for the Oral Storytelling Videos provide activity ideas for before, during, and after watching (downloadable from the Teacher Resource Center). A **Literacy Handbook** gives support and ideas for developing literacy skills with young learners.

Lesson 5 Vocabulary, Song, and Phonics

Catchy **songs** present new vocabulary in a fun, memorable, and motivating context.

Vocabulary is introduced through textual and visual clues to develop **critical thinking skills** (deduction of meaning).

Word work activities consolidate vocabulary and help develop strategies for memorizing vocabulary.

Speaking activities give practice in a meaningful context to develop fluency.

Spelling tips are covered in **Spelling Central**, with a chant and activity to give practice.

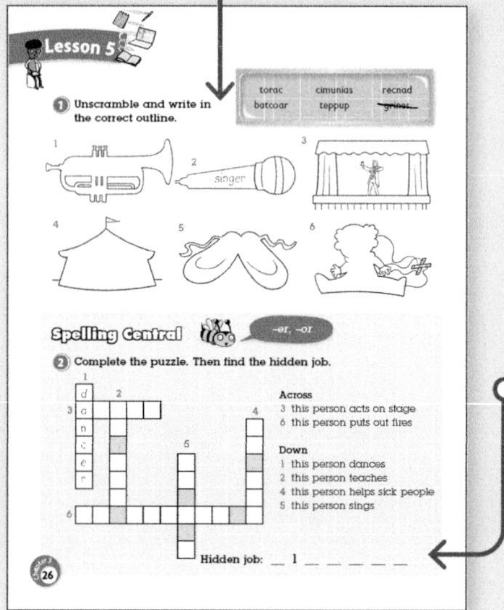

Children identify and practice the spellings from the Student Book **Spelling Central** feature.

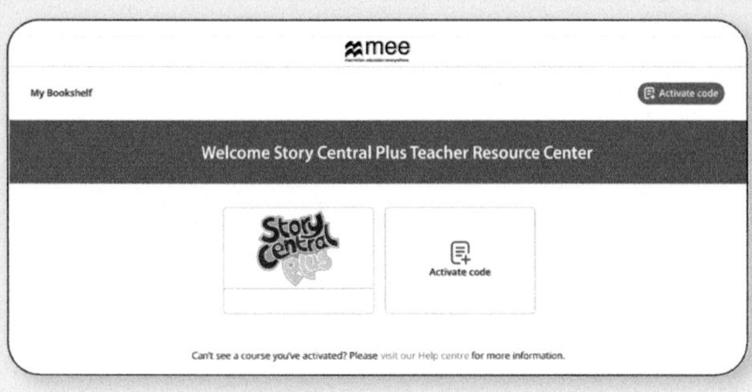

Supplementary **phonics worksheets** can be downloaded from the Teacher Resource Center to further consolidate learning in class or as homework.

Music Videos for Chapters 2, 4, 6, and 8 encourage children to move to the music and the actions consolidate the learning of the target vocabulary (available in the Student eBook).

The lively clan of The Inks on the **Student's App** provide children with motivating and challenging games to practice the chapter vocabulary from Lesson 1 and Lesson 5 outside the classroom. *The Inks* Apps are free and available on the App Store and Google Play.

Lesson 6 Grammar and Reading

The Story Central characters present new **grammar** in a lively, meaningful context which recycles the vocabulary from the chapter.

Grammar practice activities give staggered support.

Lesson 6

1 Listen and read. What are the children doing?

Story Central Saturday Show

2 Look at the story. Complete the questions and then answer.

1 When was the show? It was last week.
2 Who .... the acrobat? ....
3 .... the singers? ....
4 .... Cheng a good actor? ....

Grammar Central

When was the show?
It was last week.
Who were the singers?
Was he good?
Yes, he was. / No, he wasn't.

Grammar Booster on page 47

42

Grammar Central highlights new grammar structures and provides a useful reference.

Lesson 6

1 Match.

1 When was it? — a My friends, Megan and Stephan.
2 Where was it? — b It was last week.
3 Who were the actors? — c They were great!
4 Were they good? — d It was in the school hall.

2 Circle.

Bobby: Look at this! It's a recording of the game.
Jason: 1 When / Where was the game?
Bobby: It was last week – on Saturday.
Jason: 2 Where / Who was the game?
Bobby: It was at the stadium.
Jason: Who 3 was / were the players?
Bobby: My brother was on the team.
Jason: 4 Was / Were he good?
Bobby: No, he 5 was / wasn't.

3 Write questions about a sports game. Then ask and answer.

1 When .... ?
2 Where .... ?
3 .... ?
4 .... ?

27

Children are given the opportunity for controlled **written practice** of the new structures.

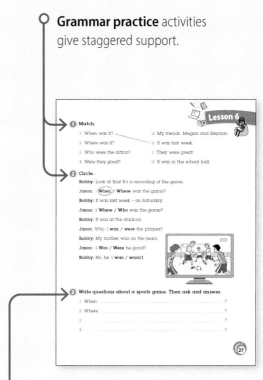

A **guided writing** activity consolidates grammar and progressively develops writing skills.

NEW! Grammar Booster sections in the Student Book at the end of each chapter provide four pages of extra support. They include detailed grammar boxes and scaffolded practice for lessons 2 and 6, a review page that combines the grammar points in both lessons and a challenge page. These pages offer support for different language proficiency levels in the classroom. They can be assigned to individual children or the entire class.

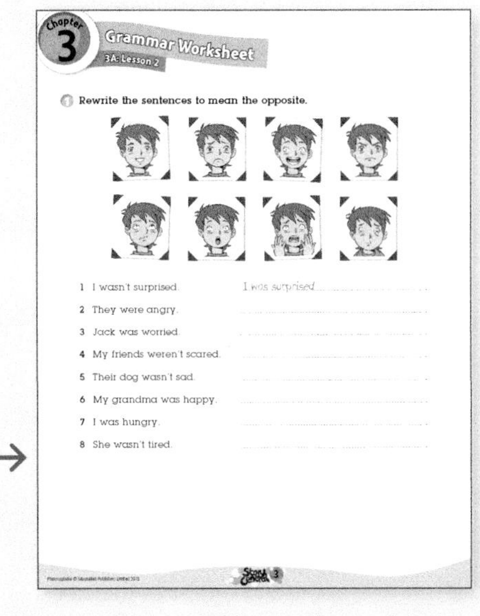

Chapter 3 Grammar Worksheet

3A: Lesson 2

Rewrite the sentences to mean the opposite.

1 I wasn't surprised. I was surprised.
2 They were angry.
3 Jack was worried.
4 My friends weren't scared.
5 Their dog wasn't sad.
6 My grandma was happy.
7 I was hungry.
8 She wasn't tired.

Supplementary **grammar worksheets** can be downloaded from the Teacher Resource Center to further consolidate learning in class or as homework.

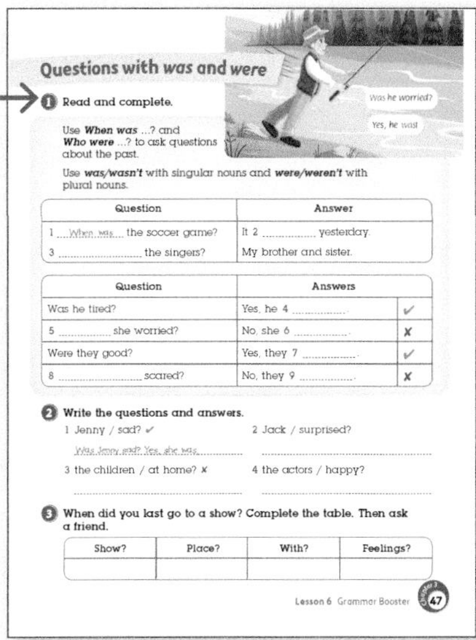

Questions with *was* and *were*

1 Read and complete.

Use **When was** ...? and **Who were** ...? to ask questions about the past.

Use **was/wasn't** with singular nouns and **were/weren't** with plural nouns.

Question	Answer
1 When was the soccer game?	It 2 .... yesterday.
3 .... the singers?	My brother and sister.

Question	Answers	
Was he tired?	Yes, he 4	✓
5 .... she worried?	No, she 6	✗
Were they good?	Yes, they 7	✓
8 .... scared?	No, they 9	✗

2 Write the questions and answers.

1 Jenny / sad? ✓ Was Jenny sad? Yes, she was.
2 Jack / surprised?
3 the children / at home? ✗
4 the actors / happy?

3 When did you last go to a show? Complete the table. Then ask a friend.

Show?	Place?	With?	Feelings?

Lesson 6 Grammar Booster 47

Lesson 7 CLIL

The **CLIL** focus gives the opportunity to find out about other curricular areas (such as science, math, social science) through English.

Children use their **Find Out More!** research to complete a mini-project extending the CLIL topic.

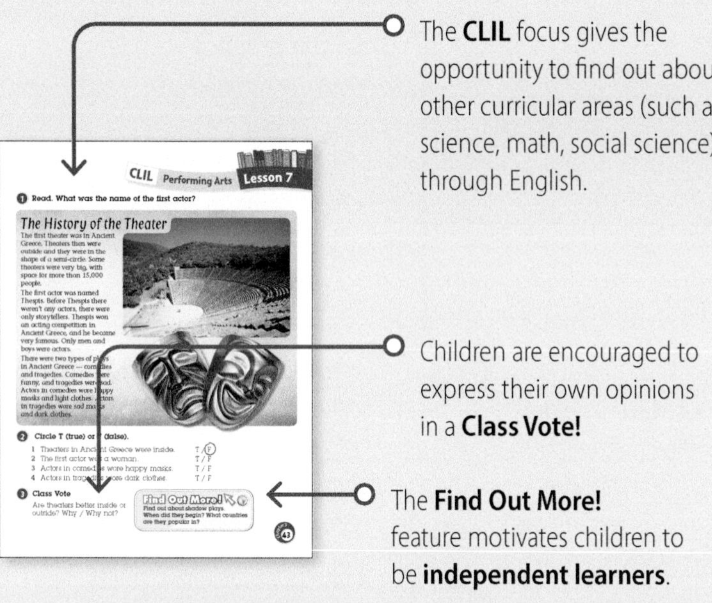

CLIL Performing Arts Lesson 7

1 Read. What was the name of the first actor?

The History of the Theater

The first theater was in Ancient Greece. Theaters then were outside and they were in the shape of a semi-circle. Some theaters were very big, with space for more than 15,000 people.

The first actor was named Thespis. Before Thespis there weren't any actors, there were only storytellers. Thespis won an acting competition in Ancient Greece, and he became very famous. Only men and boys were actors.

There were two types of plays in Ancient Greece — comedies and tragedies. Comedies were funny, and tragedies were sad. Actors in comedies wore happy masks and light clothes. Actors in tragedies wore sad masks and dark clothes.

2 Circle T (true) or F (false).

1 Theaters in Ancient Greece were inside. T / F
2 The first actor was a woman. T / F
3 Actors in comedies wore happy masks. T / F
4 Actors in tragedies wore dark clothes. T / F

3 Class Vote

Are theaters better inside or outside? Why / Why not?

Find Out More! Find out about shadow plays. When did they begin? What countries are they popular in?

43

Children are encouraged to express their own opinions in a **Class Vote!**

The **Find Out More!** feature motivates children to be **independent learners**.

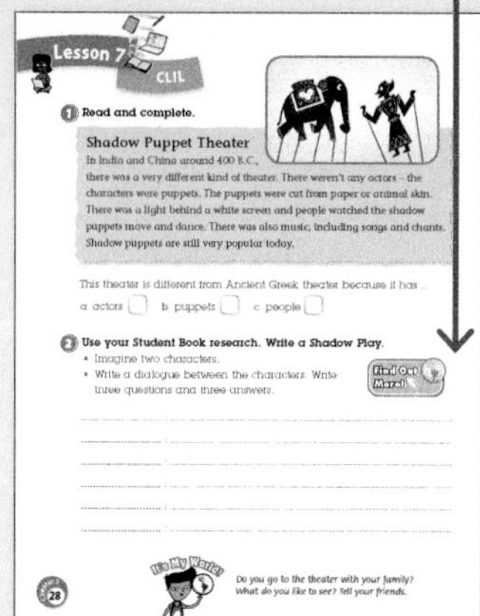

Lesson 7 CLIL

1 Read and complete.

Shadow Puppet Theater

In India and China around 400 B.C., there was a very different kind of theater. There weren't any actors - the characters were puppets. The puppets were cut from paper or animal skin. There was a light behind a white screen and people watched the shadow puppets move and dance. There was also music, including songs and chants. Shadow puppets are still very popular today.

This theater is different from Ancient Greek theater because it has ...

a actors b puppets c people

2 Use your Student Book research. Write a Shadow Play.

- Imagine two characters.
- Write a dialogue between the characters. Write three questions and three answers.

It's My World! Do you go to the theater with your family? What do you like to see? Tell your friends.

28

Lesson 8 Project

Children do a **craft experiment, or presentation** that relates to the chapter theme.

An interactive speaking task—a **fun game** for children to complete in pairs—rounds off the chapter.

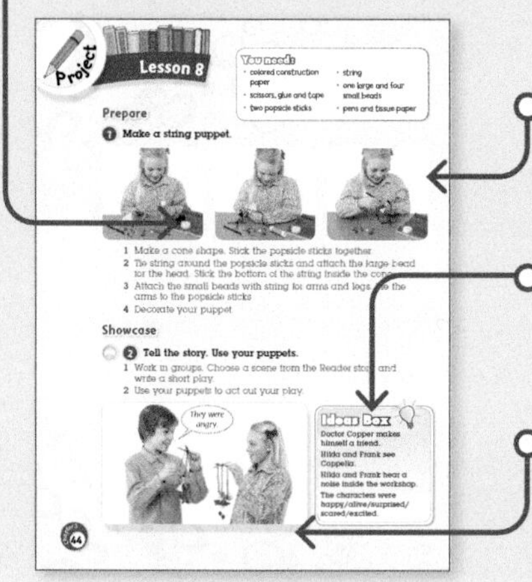

Project Lesson 8

You need: colored construction paper; scissors, glue and tape; two popsicle sticks; string; one large and four small beads; pens and tissue paper

Prepare

1 Make a string puppet.

1 Make a cone shape. Stick the popsicle sticks together.
2 Tie string around the popsicle sticks and attach the large bead for the head. Stick the bottom of the string inside the cone.
3 Attach the small beads with string for arms and legs. Tie the arms to the popsicle sticks.
4 Decorate your puppet.

Showcase

2 Tell the story. Use your puppets.

1 Work in groups. Choose a scene from the Reader story and write a short play.
2 Use your puppets to act out your play.

Ideas Box

Doctor Copper makes himself a friend.
Rikko and Frank see Coppelia.
Rikko and Frank hear a noise inside the workshop.
The characters were happy/angry/surprised/scared/excited.

44

Photographs provide clear, step-by-step instructions.

An Ideas Box gives children useful language that they can use in their presentation.

Children then **present** their project to the class.

Lesson 8

1 Play "The Performers Game."

Take turns. Flip a coin. Move one space for heads. Move two spaces for tails. Color the grid - the person with the most correct answers wins!

29

The **CLIL eBook** expands the CLIL topics from the Student Book with **additional real-world content and practice activities.**

Chapter 3 Graphic Organizers

Complete the Fact File with your Find Out More! research.

Shadow Plays

Stick/Draw a picture of a shadow play.

They began in ...

They're popular in ...

They use ...

Complete the Fact File with your Find Out More! research.

Shadow Plays

Stick/Draw a picture of a shadow play.

They began in ...

They're popular in ...

They use ...

Each CLIL lesson has an optional **graphic organizer** template to help children organize their findings (downloadable from the Teacher Resource Center).

Review

The Review lesson provides **further practice and consolidation** of language from the chapter.

Review

1 Listen and write how the characters feel. Use these words.

~~excited~~ happy worried tired scared surprised

Ben	excited	Tina	
parents		Grandpa	
brother		sisters	

2 Complete the superlative questions. Then write answers.

1 Where .... was .... Ben last night? He was at the circus.
2 His parents .... worried about the acrobats.
3 Was his brother happy? No, he ....
4 Who .... surprised? Tina.
5 Grandpa .... excited. He fell asleep!
6 His sisters .... happy.

3 Think about Chapter 3. Color and complete for you.

I'm not sure OK! Got it!

My favorite page in Chapter 3 is ....

Treasure Hunt! Look back at pages 4 and 5. Find: a character dressed as Coppelia

45

Children reflect on their own progress and color in the appropriate circle to record their progress (**self-evaluation**).

A fun **Treasure Hunt!** activity takes children back to the Welcome section (pp. 4–5) to find an item from the chapter.

New! Exam Booster sections in the Activity Book (pp. 78–104) provides **Cambridge English Young Learners Exams**-style activities practicing the language from each chapter. These help prepare for the Reading and Writing, Listening and Speaking papers of the Cambridge English Exam.

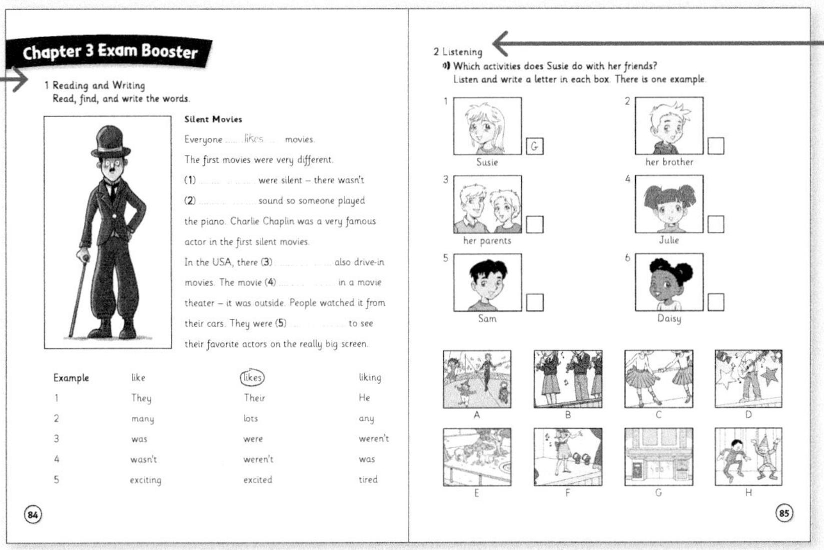

Chapter 3 Exam Booster

1 Reading and Writing
Read, find, and write the words.

Silent Movies

Everyone .... likes .... movies. The first movies were very different. (1) .... were silent – there wasn't (2) .... sound so someone played the piano. Charlie Chaplin was a very famous actor in the first silent movies. In the USA, there (3) .... also drive-in movies. The movie (4) .... in a movie theater – it was outside. People watched it from their cars. They were (5) .... to see their favorite actors on the really big screen.

Example	like	(likes)	liking
1	They	Their	He
2	many	lots	any
3	was	were	weren't
4	wasn't	weren't	was
5	exciting	excited	tired

84

2 Listening
Which activities does Susie do with her friends?
Listen and write a letter in each box. There is one example.

1 Susie G
2 her brother
3 her parents
4 Julie
5 Sam
6 Daisy

A B C D E F G H

85

Class audio for the listening activities are in the Teacher Resource Center.

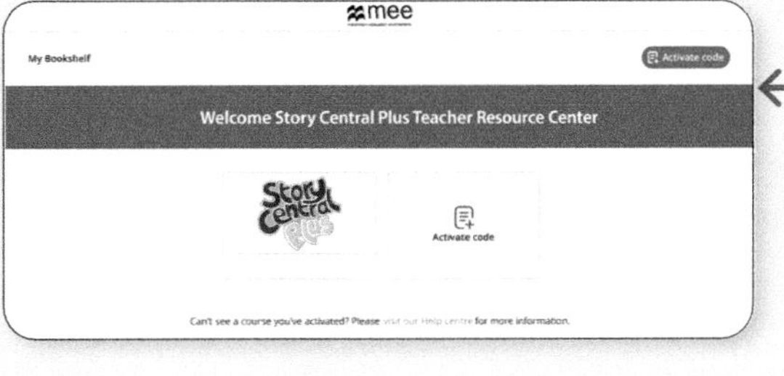

The Teacher Resource Center provides a wealth of assessment support including pre-written chapter, mid-year, and end-of-year tests. **CEYLT** (**Cambridge YLE**)-style speaking prompts and tips are also available.

Festivals worksheets and teaching notes to be used during the year bring the world outside into the classroom and help to foster an understanding of different cultures.

Teacher Edition Overview

Chapter Overview

An **Overview** at the start of every chapter provides a quick reference point to show what is covered. The **Competency Focus** shows where competencies are developed throughout the chapter.
The **Digital Overview** shows the variety of digital resources available for the chapter.

Student Book and Activity Book Lessons

Each lesson opens with the lesson objectives, key language, and any materials required.

A **Warmer** activity introduces children to the lesson topic, activating prior knowledge, and getting the children energized!

Reduced pages for the **Student Book** and the **Activity Book** give easy reference to the components being used.

The **Competency Focus** shows how competencies are developed in the lesson.

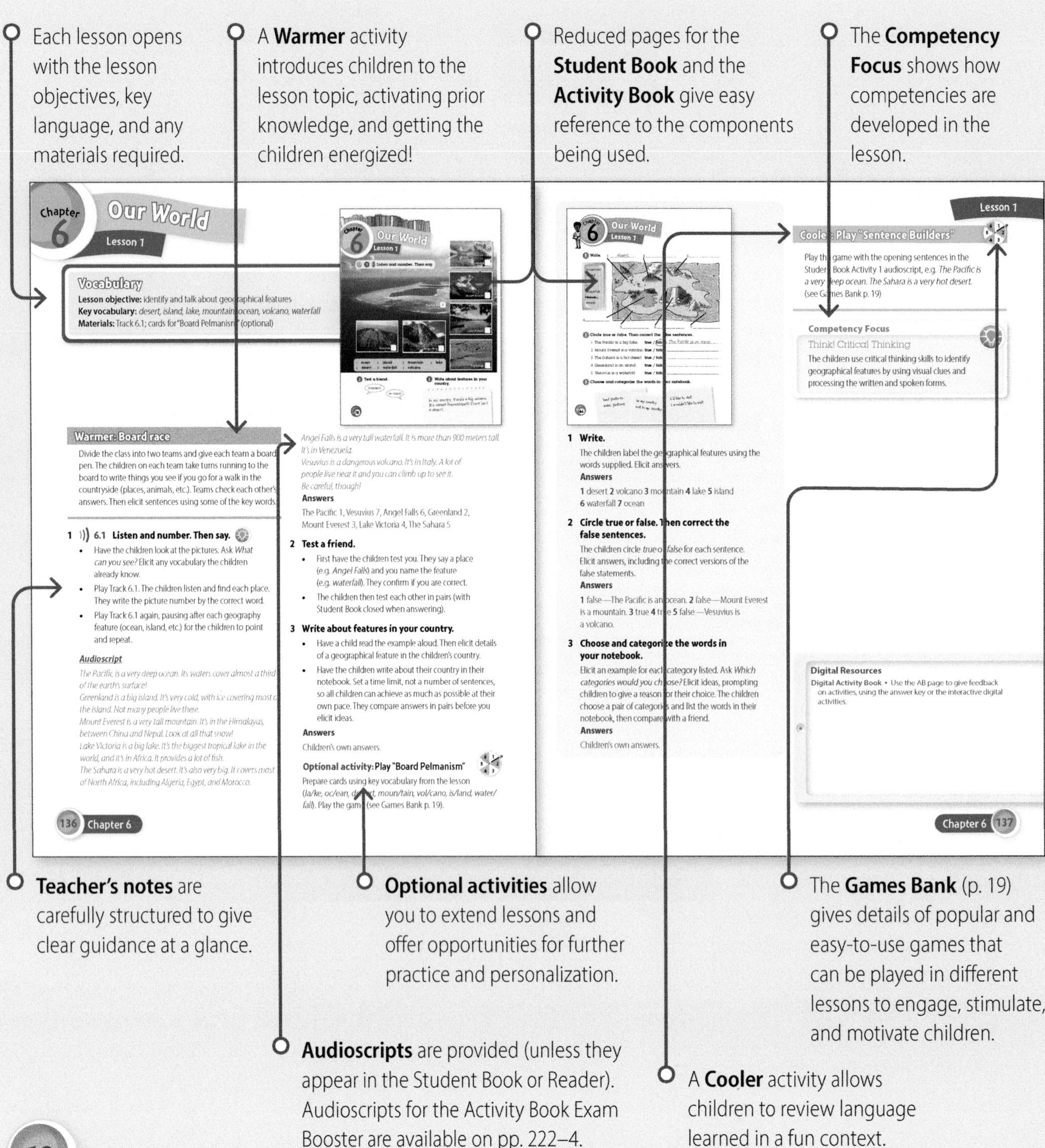

Teacher's notes are carefully structured to give clear guidance at a glance.

Optional activities allow you to extend lessons and offer opportunities for further practice and personalization.

The **Games Bank** (p. 19) gives details of popular and easy-to-use games that can be played in different lessons to engage, stimulate, and motivate children.

Audioscripts are provided (unless they appear in the Student Book or Reader). Audioscripts for the Activity Book Exam Booster are available on pp. 222–4.

A **Cooler** activity allows children to review language learned in a fun context.

Reader

The **Reader** lesson contains a range of additional activities that teachers can use as they please. Teachers can get children to read the Reader story at home or in class.

Story Time helps you get the most out of the Reader component, helping teachers become more effective storytellers in the classroom.

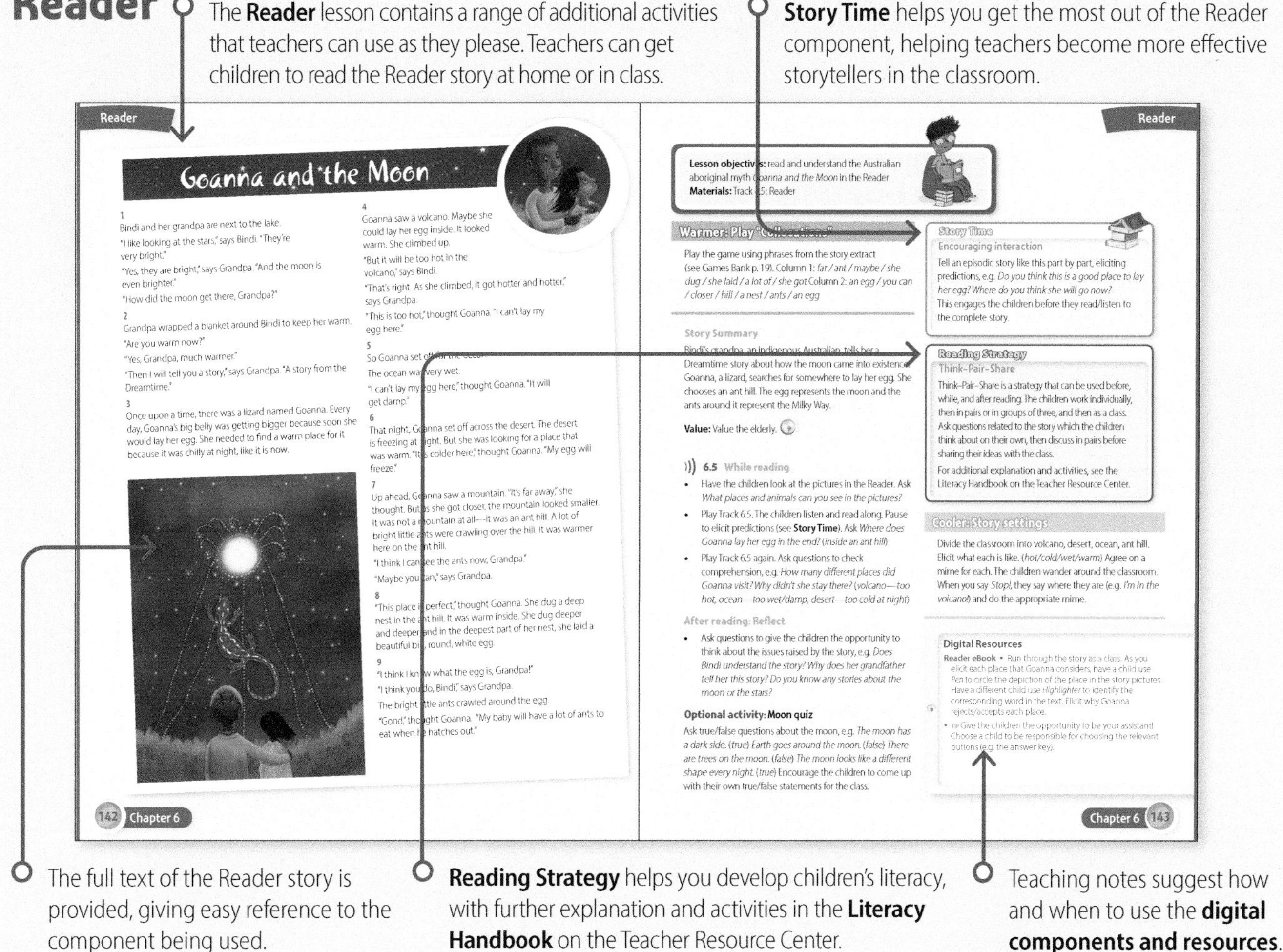

The full text of the Reader story is provided, giving easy reference to the component being used.

Reading Strategy helps you develop children's literacy, with further explanation and activities in the **Literacy Handbook** on the Teacher Resource Center.

Teaching notes suggest how and when to use the **digital components and resources**.

Games Bank

Below are details of popular and easy-to-use games that can be played in different lessons to engage, stimulate and motivate.

Bingo

Draw a grid with nine squares on the board and have the children copy it into their notebooks. The children add a vocabulary item to each square. Call out items. The children cross them off if they have them. When all are crossed off, they shout *Bingo!*

I Spy

Divide the children into two teams. Have a child from the first team look around the class and secretly choose one object. They say *I spy with my little eye something beginning with (C)!* The other team guesses the object. Teams take turns.

Ready, Set, Draw!

Divide the children into teams. Secretly give a child from each team a word to draw. The first team to identify the word correctly wins a point.

Simon Says

Have the children stand. Say actions for them to mime. They can only mime when you say *Simon says (swim)*. If you say just *Swim*, they stand still. If a child does the wrong mime, they sit down. The last child standing is the winner.

Spelling Bee

Divide the class into two teams. Say a word. The children from each team take turns writing it on the board. Each correctly spelled word wins a point.

The Chain Game

Have the class stand. Start off a chain, e.g. *I went to the store and I bought apples.* Each child repeats the chain so far and adds an item, e.g. *I went to the store and I bought apples and oranges.* If a child makes a mistake or can't think of an item, they sit down. The last child standing wins.

The Shark Game

Draw on the board six steps leading down to water. On the top step, draw a stick person. In the water, draw a shark. Think of a word and draw a line to represent each letter. The children take turns calling out a letter. If it's correct, write the letter on the corresponding line. If it's wrong, erase the stick person and move him down one step, closer to the shark. If the children guess the word correctly, the class wins a point.

Story Central

Lesson objectives: remember Story Central and sing a song
Key language: *welcome, fun, books, friends, learning, characters, costume, share, poems, mysteries, history, sing, violin*
Materials: Track 0.2

Warmer: Welcome back to Story Central!

Have the children look at pp. 4–5 of the Student Book. Ask *How many … ?* questions to focus their attention, e.g. *How many rugs are in the picture? (seven) How many people are wearing blue hats? (two) How many people are eating? (one) How many planets are in the picture? (five)*

1))) 0.2 Listen and sing.

- Play Track 0.2. Have the children listen and point to the features mentioned in the picture.
- Play Track 0.2 again and have the children repeat after each line. Agree on mimes for each part.
- Play Track 0.2 again for the children to sing along and mime.

Optional activity: Play "Disappearing Words"

Play the game using words from the song. Have the children close their book and tell you all the words they can remember (choose up to 20) (see Games Bank p. 19).

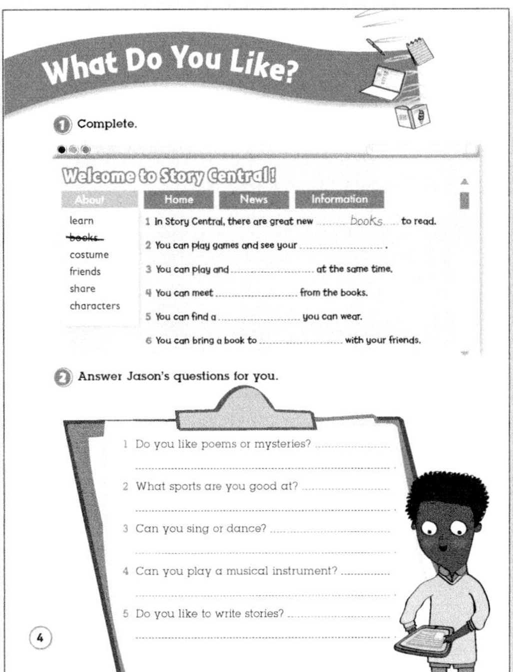

What Do You Like?

1 Complete.

Welcome to Story Central!

About | Home | News | Information

learn
~~books~~
costume
friends
share
characters

1 In Story Central, there are great new ......books...... to read.
2 You can play games and see your ....
3 You can play and .... at the same time.
4 You can meet .... from the books.
5 You can find a .... you can wear.
6 You can bring a book to .... with your friends.

2 Answer Jason's questions for you.

1 Do you like poems or mysteries? ....
2 What sports are you good at? ....
3 Can you sing or dance? ....
4 Can you play a musical instrument? ....
5 Do you like to write stories? ....

4

1 Complete.

The children complete the Story Central website using the words supplied, then compare answers in pairs. Elicit answers and check with the class.

Answers

1 books **2** friends **3** learn **4** characters **5** costume **6** share

2 Answer Jason's questions for you.

Have the children ask you the questions first. Give your answers. They write their own answers and then practice asking and answering with a friend. Invite pairs to ask and answer for the class.

Answers

Children's own answers.

Cooler: Story Central characters

Divide the class into pairs. Give the pairs a minute to look at pp. 4–5 of the Student Book. Ask them to think up a sentence describing their favorite person in the picture. Encourage the children to give as much detail as possible, using adjectives in their descriptions and giving reasons for their choice. Elicit sentences.

Digital Resources

Student eBook, Digital Activity Book • All SB and AB pages can be shown on the board. Use them for "heads-up" teaching and reference throughout the lesson. For "heads-up" teaching activities, ask the children to close their book so that you have their full attention.

- The tool bar across the top of the screen helps you navigate to different units and books. It also contains tools to use on the screen, e.g. *Pen*, *Highlighter*, etc.

What Do You Like?

Lesson objectives: review vocabulary and grammar from Story Central 2
Key language: *story, moon, doll, money,* descriptions, activities; *My name's …, I have … hair and … eyes. I'm wearing … I like to … I don't like to …*
Materials: Tracks 0.3 and 0.4

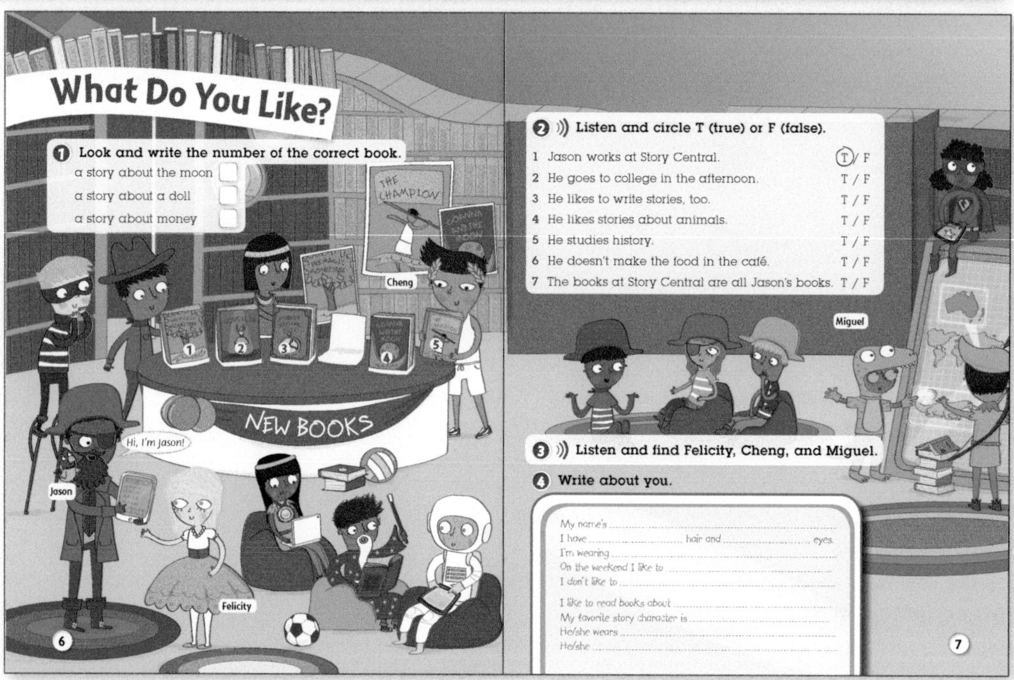
What Do You Like?

1 Look and write the number of the correct book.
a story about the moon
a story about a doll
a story about money

2 Listen and circle T (true) or F (false).
1 Jason works at Story Central. T / F
2 He goes to college in the afternoon. T / F
3 He likes to write stories, too. T / F
4 He likes stories about animals. T / F
5 He studies history. T / F
6 He doesn't make the food in the café. T / F
7 The books at Story Central are all Jason's books. T / F

3 Listen and find Felicity, Cheng, and Miguel.

4 Write about you.
My name's …
I have … hair and … eyes.
I'm wearing …
On the weekend I like to …
I don't like to …
I like to read books about …
My favorite story character is …
He/she wears …
He/she …

Warmer: Choose a book

Have the children look at the covers of the books on Student Book p. 6. Elicit which book they would like to read. Take a vote by a show of hands. Say they will read all of them!

1 Look and write the number of the correct book.

- Have the children write the number of each book described. Elicit answers and check with the class.

Answers

4, 2, 1

2 0.3 Listen and circle T (true) or F (false).

- Point to Jason (on p. 6, in pirate costume). Ask *How old is he? What do you think he does?*
- Give the children time to read the sentences.
- Play Track 0.3 twice. The children listen and circle true or false for each sentence.
- Elicit answers, including the correct versions of false sentences.

Audioscript

Jason: *Hi, I'm Jason Griffin. I work here at Story Central. I go to college in the morning, and work here in the afternoon. I like to write stories and I read a lot of books.*
I like stories about people and animals. So, do you have any questions?
Boy 1: *What do you study at college?*
Jason: *I study English.*
Girl 1: *Do you make the food in the café, too?*
Jason: *No, I don't. A chef makes the food in the café.*
Boy 2: *Are all of these your books?*
Jason: *Ha, ha! No, they're not my books. I just work here. But I can help you choose a book to read. What do you like? Write it here.*

Answers

1 T **2** F **3** T **4** T **5** F **6** T **7** F

3)) 0.4 Listen and find Felicity, Cheng, and Miguel.

- Explain that Jason is going to talk about Felicity, Cheng, and Miguel, the other main characters.
- Play Track 0.4 twice for the children to listen and find the characters. Elicit answers.

Audioscript

Jason: *Today Felicity, Cheng, and Miguel are helping me. Here's Felicity—she's wearing a white and pink dress and pink shoes. She has long, blond hair. Cheng is putting books on the table. He's wearing a white shirt, white shorts, and sneakers. He likes sports. And Miguel is … I can't find Miguel. What's he wearing?*

Felicity: *Um, I think he's wearing green pants and a green T-shirt. He likes technology and computers.*

4 Write about you.

- Elicit information from different children to model how to complete the profile.
- The children write their text, then read it to a friend.

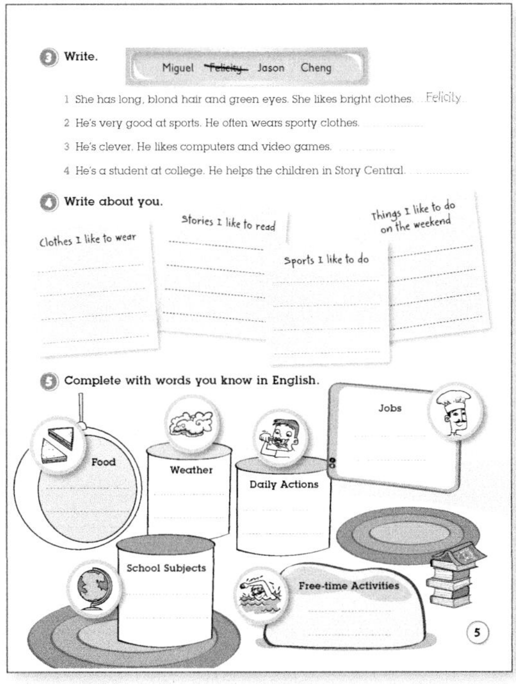

3 Write. Miguel ~~Felicity~~ Jason Cheng

1 She has long, blond hair and green eyes. She likes bright clothes. Felicity

2 He's very good at sports. He often wears sporty clothes. ....

3 He's clever. He likes computers and video games. ....

4 He's a student at college. He helps the children in Story Central. ....

4 Write about you.

Clothes I like to wear

Stories I like to read

Sports I like to do

Things I like to do on the weekend

5 Complete with words you know in English.

Food

Weather

Daily Actions

Jobs

School Subjects

Free-time Activities

5

3 Write.

The children identify the characters described from the names supplied. Elicit answers.

Answers

1 Felicity **2** Cheng **3** Miguel **4** Jason

4 Write about you.

Elicit examples of answers in each category. The children write their own preferences, then tell a friend. Elicit answers.

5 Complete with words you know in English.

You can make this a competition. The children work in pairs to write two examples for each category. Elicit answers. Each pair gets one point for a correct answer, but two points if it is an answer no one else has. The pair with the most points wins.

Cooler: You and me

Ask children to read their text from Student Book, Activity 4 to the class. The other children raise their hand if any detail is the same for them.

Digital Resources

Student eBook • Focus on the characters one by one to elicit what they are dressed up as.

- Encourage the children to imagine a new friend and think up details about them using the prompts in SB Activity 4. Have children use *Pen* to write in a detail each.

Chapter 1 School Trip Overview

The children will:

- use critical thinking skills to identify school rules.
- talk about things they have to/don't have to do.
- read, understand, and act out a story.
- talk about a trip to an aquarium.
- talk about things they can/can't do.
- find out about greetings in different cultures.
- design a brochure for a fun park or aquarium.

Key Vocabulary

School rules: arrive on time, bring a packed lunch, get parents' permission, listen to your teacher, meet at school, wear your school uniform
Areas of an aquarium: aquarium, enclosure, entrance, petting zoo, picnic area, playground, show, ticket office

Key Grammar

- You have to (get your parents' permission).
- We don't have to (wear a school uniform).
- We can (use the computers in Story Central).
- We can't (use cell phones).
- Can we (play soccer in Story Central)?
- Yes, we can. / No, we can't.

Reading Skills

Story: *You Have to Listen!*
Genre: modern story

Literacy Development

- predict story content from title and pictures
- reflect on and personalize the theme of the story
- use pictures for information

Functional Language

- It's a good idea to …
- That's great!
- Thank you.

Spelling

Short vowel before double letter

CLIL: Social sciences—Greetings around the world

The children find out about greetings in different cultures.

Competency Focus

The children will:

use critical thinking skills to identify school rules. (Lesson 1)	apply new grammar to previously learned vocabulary. (Lesson 2)	work in threes to act out a dialogue. (Lesson 3)	personalize the story by thinking about how they might act in a similar situation. (Lesson 4)	develop cultural understanding by finding out about greetings in different countries. (Lesson 7)
predict the content of a story. (Lesson 3)	talk about things they can/can't do. (Lesson 6)	work in groups to act out the story. (Lesson 8)	evaluate their own progress in the chapter. (Review)	
identify and name areas of an aquarium. (Lesson 5)				

Digital Overview

Teacher Presentation

Student eBook and Digital Activity Book

- Oral Storytelling Video 1.1: *You Have to Listen!*
- Interactive versions of AB activities
- Integrated audio and answer key for all activities

Teacher resources for planning, lesson delivery, and homework

Teacher Resource Center

- Class Planner Chapter 1
- Worksheets to print out (including notes and answers):
  - Grammar Worksheet 1A: What is it? It's a/an …
  - Grammar Worksheet 1B: What color is it? It's …
  - Oral Storytelling Video Worksheet 1: *You Have To Listen!*
  - Phonics Worksheet 1
  - CLIL Graphic Organizer 1
  - Test Chapter 1
- Test Generator
- Literacy Handbook

Watch the Oral Storytelling Video

Children's resources for learning and practicing at home

Student eBook and Reader eBook

- Oral Storytelling Video 1.1: *You Have to Listen!*

The Inks Student's App

Vocabulary games: School rules and areas of an aquarium

Chapter 1

School Trips

Lesson 1

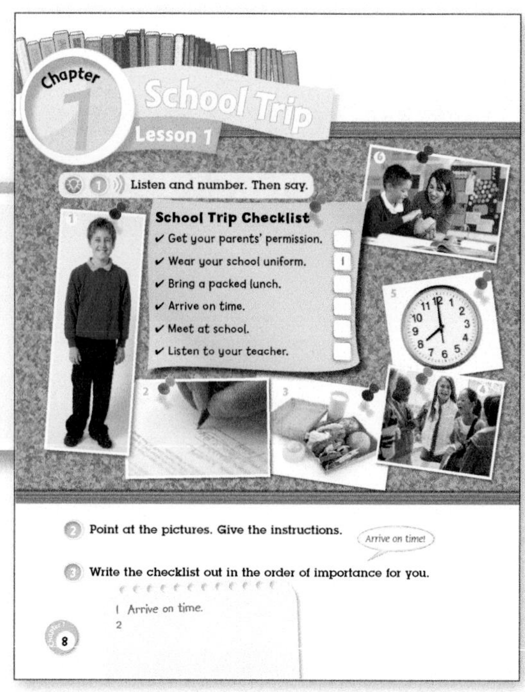

Vocabulary

Lesson objective: identify and talk about rules for a school trip
Key vocabulary: *arrive on time, bring a packed lunch, get your parents' permission, listen to your teacher, meet at school, wear your school uniform*
Materials: Track 1.1

Warmer: Play "School Trips"

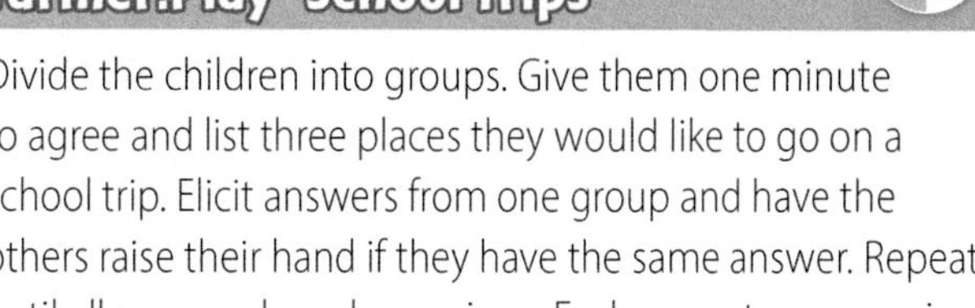

Divide the children into groups. Give them one minute to agree and list three places they would like to go on a school trip. Elicit answers from one group and have the others raise their hand if they have the same answer. Repeat until all answers have been given. Each correct answer wins one point—or two if no other group has it.

1 1.1 Listen and number. Then say.

- Have the children look at the pictures. Ask *Where do you think the children are going for their school trip? Do they look happy?*
- Play Track 1.1. The children listen and find each rule. They write the number of each picture next to the appropriate rule on the list.
- Play Track 1.1 again and have the children point to the correct picture for each rule. Then say the rules for the class to repeat.

Audioscript

OK. Settle down, everyone. It's the school trip on Wednesday. Don't forget to wear your school uniform. Remember your blue sweater. Don't forget to get your parents' permission. Ask your mom and dad to sign the permission slip. Bring a packed lunch … what about sandwiches, an apple, and milk? Meet at school, in our classroom. Arrive on time—8 o'clock please. That's 8 o'clock in the morning, not in the evening! Always listen to your teacher. That way you won't miss any important information. It's going to be a lot of fun, so don't be late!

Answers

Get your parents' permission. **2,** Wear your school uniform. **1,** Bring a packed lunch. **3,** Arrive on time. **5,** Meet at school. **4,** Listen to your teacher. 6

2 Point at the pictures. Give the instructions.

- Point to each picture in Activity 1 and say the instruction for the children to repeat. Say the picture numbers to elicit the instructions.
- The children continue the activity in pairs, taking turns pointing and responding.

Optional activity: Finish the phrase

Say *Get …* to elicit *Get your parents' permission.* Repeat with *Listen …* (*to your teacher*). Have the children work in pairs, taking turns prompting and saying the whole phrase.

3 Write the checklist out in the order of importance for you.

- Ask *Bring a packed lunch—is it important?* Elicit ideas, e.g. *Yes, because you'll be hungry on the trip.* Repeat with the other points on the list.
- Have the children write the phrases in order (from most to least important) in their notebook. Explain that there are not right or wrong answers but they do need to think about the reasons for their choices. They compare lists in pairs. Elicit ideas and reasons.

Chapter 1 School Trip
Lesson 1

1 Match. Then look and number.

School Trip Rules

2	a Get	to your teacher.
	b Wear	at school in your classroom.
	c Bring	your parents' permission.
	d Listen	your school uniform.
	e Meet	on time.
	f Arrive	a packed lunch.

2 Choose and categorize the verbs in your notebook.

do every day
do for trips
both

easy phrases
hard phrases

verb + a person/place/thing
verb + at/on/to + a person/place/thing

3 Complete the instructions. Use the verbs from Activity 1.

1 Arrive on time, at 8:30.
2 .... to your trainer.
3 .... your soccer ball.
4 .... your parents' permission to travel.
5 .... at the sports club.
6 .... your sneakers.

Chapter 1 6

1 Match. Then look and number.

The children match the sentence halves, then write the picture number by each sentence. Elicit answers.

Answers

a Get your parents' permission. 2

b Wear your school uniform. 1

c Bring a packed lunch. 5

d Listen to your teacher. 6

e Meet at school in your classroom. 3

f Arrive on time. 4

2 Choose and categorize the verbs in your notebook.

Remind the children that organizing vocabulary into categories makes it easier to learn. Elicit an example for each category listed. Ask *Which categories would you choose?* Elicit ideas, prompting children to give a reason for their choice. The children choose a pair of categories and list the words in their notebook, then compare with a friend.

Answers

Children's own answers.

3 Complete the instructions. Use the verbs from Activity 1.

The children complete the sentences with the verbs from Activity 1. Elicit answers.

Answers

1 Arrive **2** Listen **3** Bring **4** Get **5** Meet **6** Wear

Cooler: Class vote

Elicit five places for a school trip and write them on the board. The children vote for their two favorite trips by raising their hand. Ask a different child to count the hands each time. Elicit the favorite.

Competency Focus

Think! Critical Thinking

The children use critical thinking skills to identify the rules for a school trip by using visual clues and processing the written and spoken forms.

Digital Resources

Student eBook, Digital Activity Book • All SB and AB pages can be shown on the board. Use them for "heads-up" teaching and reference throughout the lesson.

• All audio is accessible within the SB/AB pages.

Digital Activity Book • TIP Use the AB page to give feedback on activities, using the answer key or interactive activities.

Grammar

Lesson objectives: talk about things we have to or don't have to do
Key grammar: *You have to (get your parents' permission). We don't have to (wear a school uniform).*
Secondary language: *rules, trip*
Materials: Track 1.2; blank paper and colored pens/pencils (optional); Grammar Worksheet 1A [TRC printout] (optional)

Warmer: Play a spelling game

Spell out the following word slowly: *permission, parents, uniform, packed lunch, teacher, arrive.* When the children know the word, they raise their hand and tell you. This can be played as a team game for points.

1 1.2 Listen and check (✓) (have to) or cross (✗) (don't have to).

- Have the children look at the pictures. Ask *What kind of text is this? Where would you find it? (a list of rules; in a school)* Elicit the rules or key words in the rules. If you have something similar in your class, compare the two lists.
- Play Track 1.2. The children listen and write a check for rules with *have to* or a cross for *don't have to.* Pause after each rule if necessary.
- Play Track 1.2 again. Elicit answers.

Audioscript

Dad: *Hey, Karly. So you have your school trip on Wednesday, right?*
Karly: *Yes, Dad. We have our school trip rules here.*
Dad: *Great, Karly. What do you have to do?*
Karly: *We have to get our parents' permission.*
Dad: *OK, well, I can sign your permission slip now.*
Karly: *Thanks, Dad. We don't have to wear our school uniforms.*
Dad: *That's nice. So you can wear your own clothes?*
Karly: *Yes. We have to bring a packed lunch.*
Dad: *OK, so I need to go shopping for food. What about your classes?*
Karly: *Dad! We're on a school trip, so we don't have to go to class!*
Dad: *Oh, yes! Of course. What else?*
Karly: *We have to meet at school.*
Dad: *OK, so we both have to arrive on time in the morning.*
Karly: *Yes, Dad. We have to arrive on time—at 8 o'clock!*
Dad: *OK, so tell me again. You have to get your parents' permission?*
Karly: *Yes, that's you, Dad!*
Dad: *You have to bring a packed lunch … you don't have to wear a school uniform … you have to meet at school … um … and you have to arrive on time?*
Karly: *Correct, Dad. And YOU have to listen!*

Answers

✓, ✗, ✓,
✗, ✓, ✓

2 Look at the pictures. Complete the sentences.

- Have a child read the examples in Activity 1. Elicit the meaning of *have to* (*you need to do it*) and *don't have to* (*you don't need to do it*).
- The children complete the sentences using the checks and crosses as prompts. Elicit answers and check with the class.

Answers

have to, don't have to, have to, don't have to, have to, have to

Grammar Central

You have to get your parents' permission. …

Have the children look at the patterns. Elicit when *have to* and *don't have to* are used. (*when you need to / don't need to*) Elicit rules in the children's own school using *have to / don't have to.*

For extra practice, try the **Grammar Booster** section in the Student Book (p. 18).

Answers p. 18

Activity 1: **1** have to **2** don't have to **3** have to **4** don't have to **5** have to **6** don't have to **7** have to **8** don't have to

Activity 2: **1** have to **2** have to **3** don't have to **4** don't have to **5** have to **6** don't have to

Activity 3: Children's own answers.

3 Talk to a friend.

- Have two children read the example aloud.
- Elicit things the children have to do every day and write them on the board. Repeat with a list of things they don't have to do every day (encourage them to be inventive here, e.g. *bring the teacher some chocolate*).
- The children take turns making a sentence with *have to/don't have to* + a phrase from the board, and responding *True!* or *False!*

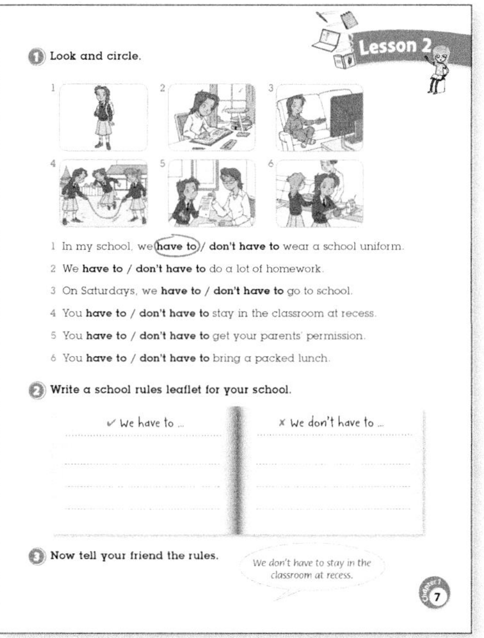

Lesson 2

1 Look and circle.

1 In my school, we **have to** / **don't have to** wear a school uniform.
2 We **have to** / **don't have to** do a lot of homework.
3 On Saturdays, we **have to** / **don't have to** go to school.
4 You **have to** / **don't have to** stay in the classroom at recess.
5 You **have to** / **don't have to** get your parents' permission.
6 You **have to** / **don't have to** bring a packed lunch.

2 Write a school rules leaflet for your school.

✔ We have to … | ✘ We don't have to …

3 Now tell your friend the rules.

We don't have to stay in the classroom at recess.

Chapter 1 7

Optional activity: Opposite school rules

Ask the children to imagine a very different school where everything is the opposite from their own school. Have them work in pairs to make a list of "opposite" school rules with illustrations like those in Activity 1.

1 Look and circle.

The children circle *have to / don't have to* to complete the sentences. Elicit answers.

Answers

1 have to **2** have to **3** don't have to **4** don't have to **5** have to **6** don't have to

2 Write a school rules leaflet for your school.

Elicit one example for each column. The children write their own rules.

Answers

Children's own answers.

3 Now tell your friend the rules.

The children compare their rules in pairs. Elicit rules.

Cooler: Mime the rules

Say rules with *You have to* or *You don't have to.* If you say *You have to …*, the children do the mime; if you say *You don't have to,* they do not do anything.

Competency Focus

Learn

The children use previously acquired vocabulary in a different context with new grammatical structures.

Digital Resources

Digital Activity Book • Children use *Pen* to write AB Activity 2 answers. The class raises their hand if they had the same answer each time.

Teacher Resource Center • Print out Grammar Worksheet 1A for extra practice after SB Activity 2.

Reading: Story Extract

Lesson objectives: accept someone else's suggestion; predict story content from title and pictures; read the extract from *You Have to Listen!* (beginning)
Functional language: *It's a good idea to … That's great! Thank you.*
Secondary language: *bathing suit, funny, sign, slide*
Materials: Tracks 1.3 and 1.4

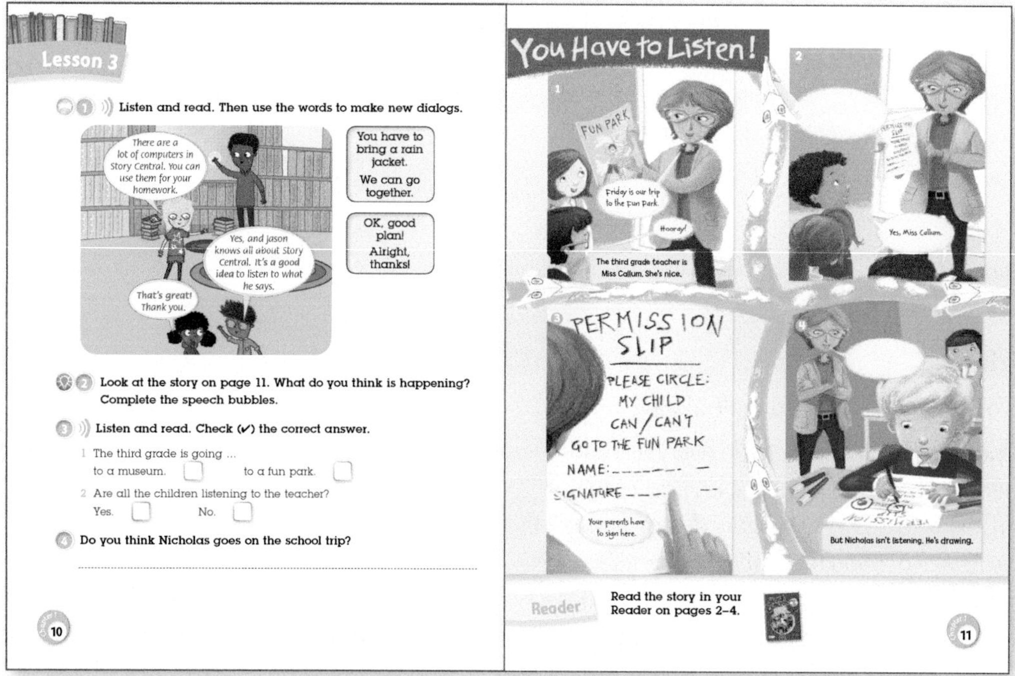
Lesson 3

1 Listen and read. Then use the words to make new dialogs.

You have to bring a rain jacket.
We can go together.

OK, good plan!
Alright, thanks!

2 Look at the story on page 11. What do you think is happening? Complete the speech bubbles.

3 Listen and read. Check (✓) the correct answer.

1 The third grade is going …
to a museum. ☐ to a fun park. ☐

2 Are all the children listening to the teacher?
Yes. ☐ No. ☐

4 Do you think Nicholas goes on the school trip?

10

You Have to Listen!

Reader Read the story in your Reader on pages 2–4.

11

Warmer: You have to listen!

Ask *Do you listen all the time? What happens when you don't?* Elicit ideas on what does or might go wrong if you do not listen.

Functional language

1 1.3 Listen and read. Then use the words to make new dialogs.

- Have the children look at the pictures and dialogue. Ask *Where are they?* (*Story Central*)
- Play Track 1.3. The children listen and read along. Ask *Who can help you at Story Central?* (*Jason*)
- Play Track 1.3 again, pausing for the children to repeat.
- Divide the class into groups of three and have the children practice the dialogue. Encourage them to adapt the dialogue with different things they can use computers for—play games, watch videos, etc.

Before reading

2 Look at the story on page 11. What do you think is happening? Complete the speech bubbles.

- Have the children look at the pictures. Ask *Where are they? (at school) What's the teacher talking about? (a trip to the Fun Park)*
- Have the children use the title and pictures to imagine what the teacher is saying and complete the speech bubbles. Elicit suggestions.

Answers (suggested)

You have to get your parents' permission. Are you listening to me, Nicholas?

3 1.4 Listen and read. Check (✓) the correct answer.

- Play Track 1.4 twice. The children listen and check the correct options. Elicit answers.

Answers

1 to a fun park. **2** No.

4 Do you think Nicholas goes on the school trip?

- Have the children write their prediction. Elicit ideas including reasons, but do not confirm. Say they will have to read the story to find out.

Answers

Children's own answers.

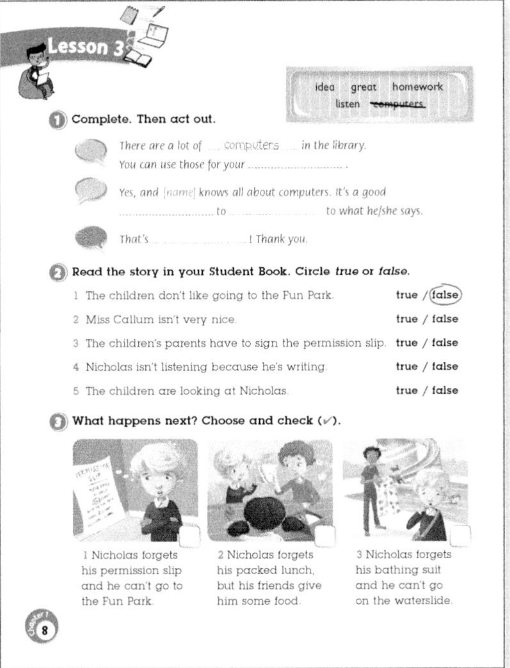

Lesson 3

idea great homework listen ~~computers~~

1 Complete. Then act out.

There are a lot of computers in the library. You can use those for your ....

Yes, and [name] knows all about computers. It's a good .... to .... to what he/she says.

That's ....! Thank you.

2 Read the story in your Student Book. Circle *true* or *false*.

1 The children don't like going to the Fun Park. true / (false)
2 Miss Callum isn't very nice. true / false
3 The children's parents have to sign the permission slip. true / false
4 Nicholas isn't listening because he's writing. true / false
5 The children are looking at Nicholas. true / false

3 What happens next? Choose and check (✓).

1 Nicholas forgets his permission slip and he can't go to the Fun Park.
2 Nicholas forgets his packed lunch, but his friends give him some food.
3 Nicholas forgets his bathing suit and he can't go on the waterslide.

Chapter 1 8

1 Complete. Then act out.

The children complete the dialogue using the words supplied. Elicit answers. Then they act out the dialogue in threes. Have threes act out for the class.

Answers

computers / homework / [name] / idea / listen / great

2 Read the story in your Student Book. Circle true or false.

Read the example and elicit why the answer is false. (*They are all happy!*) The children read the Student Book story extract again and circle true or false for each sentence. Elicit answers, including the correct versions of the false statements.

Answers

1 false **2** false **3** true **4** false **5** true

3 What happens next? Choose and check (✓).

The children look at the pictures, read the sentences, and check what they think happens next in the story. Elicit ideas and have a class vote.

Answers

Children's own answers.

Read the story extract, pausing before key language to elicit the next word. You can play this as a team game for points.

Competency Focus

Collaborate and Communicate

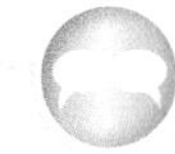

The children act out an authentic dialogue together, putting into practice new functional language.

Think! Critical Thinking

The children apply reading skills (exploiting pictures and text clues) to understand the story.

Digital Resources

Student eBook, Digital Activity Book • Choose the audio/answer key buttons on the page; the materials appear in a pop-up window.

- Hover over each icon in the tool bar to reveal the function of each button.

You Have to Listen!

1
Miss Callum: Friday is our trip to the Fun Park.
Ben: Hooray!
The third grade teacher is Miss Callum. She's nice.

2
Miss Callum: You have to get your parents' permission.
Children: Yes, Miss Callum.

3
Miss Callum: Your parents have to sign here.

4
Miss Callum: Are you listening to me, Nicholas?
But Nicholas isn't listening. He's drawing.

5
Miss Callum: You have to listen, Nicholas!
Nicholas: Sorry, Miss Callum.
Miss Callum is explaining about the form. But Nicholas just plays with it.

6
Miss Callum: Nicholas! Your parents have to sign that form!
Nicholas: Um … Why?
Miss Callum: You see. You're not listening!
The other children think their friend Nicholas is very funny.

7
Miss Callum: We're having a picnic so you have to bring a packed lunch, but you don't have to wear your school uniform. Are you listening, Nicholas?
Nicholas: Excuse me?

8
Miss Callum: You have to meet at the school bus at 8:30 in the morning. You have to arrive on time! What time is the bus leaving on Friday, Nicholas?
Nicholas: Um … nine o'clock?
Miss Callum: EIGHT THIRTY!

9
Miss Callum: And remember—you have to bring your bathing suits!
Everyone is listening to Miss Callum. Everyone except Nicholas.

10
Friday comes. Nicholas is late! He wasn't listening. Everyone arrives on time except him.
Miss Callum: Where's Nicholas?

11
Lisa: We have to stop! Nicholas is coming!
Nicholas: Please wait for me!
Luckily, Nicholas's friend Lisa stops the bus.

12
Amy: Can we see the sharks first?
Miss Callum: Yes, we'll go to the aquarium before lunch, and then we can go on the waterslide.

13
Nicholas: I'm glad I don't have to do that!

14
Miss Callum: Lunchtime!
Nicholas: Oh …
Nicholas doesn't have a packed lunch! He wasn't listening!

15
The other children share their lunches with Nicholas.
Tom: You can eat one of my sandwiches.

16
Nicholas is wearing his uniform, and he doesn't have a bathing suit. He wasn't listening!
Miss Callum: Go and put on your bathing suit.
Nicholas: Oh …
Miss Callum: I'm sorry, you have to wear a bathing suit, Nicholas. You can't go on the slide in your school uniform.

17
Keenan: I have two. You can wear these!
Nicholas: Um …
Nicholas really wants to go on the slide. So, he wears Keenan's swimming shorts.

19
Nicholas: Thanks, Keenan. I think it's a good idea to listen to you, Miss Callum.

20
Nicholas: How can I say sorry to Miss Callum, and thank my friends for helping me?

21
On Monday, Nicholas takes a cake to school.
Miss Callum: What does that say?
Nicholas: It says, "I have to listen!"

Lesson objective: read and understand the modern story *You Have to Listen!* in the Reader
Materials: Track 1.5; Reader; Oral Storytelling Video Worksheet 1 [TRC printout] (optional)

Warmer: Missing vowels

Write on the board *school trip, listen, packed lunch, picnic, bathing suit, water slide* with all the vowels missing (e.g. *schl trp*). The children complete the words in their notebook. Then elicit what happens in the story extract.

Story Summary

Nicholas doesn't listen to his teacher, Miss Callum. On the school trip, he doesn't arrive on time or bring a packed lunch or a bathing suit. Luckily, his friends are nice and they share. Nicholas thanks his class with a cake.

Value: Share with others. 

1.5 While reading

- Have the children look at the pictures in the Reader. Ask *What places can you see? What are the children doing?*
- Play Track 1.5. The children listen and read along. Ask *What are Nicholas's friends like?* (*nice*)
- Play Track 1.5 again. Ask questions to check comprehension, e.g. *Was Nicholas listening to the teacher?* (*no*) *How do you know?* (*he doesn't do what he has to*) *How does he feel at the end of the story?* (*sorry he didn't listen / he wants to say thank you*)
- Read the story aloud and have the children respond emotionally (see **Story Time**).

After reading: Reflect

- Ask questions to give the children the opportunity to think about the issues raised by the story, e.g. *Why doesn't Nicholas pay attention? Do you think he is happy being like this? Does he want to change? Is it easy to change your personality/behavior?*

Optional activity: Scanning

To help improve the children's skill in scanning a text, ask *Where does the teacher talk about time?* (*picture 8*) Repeat with different questions, e.g. *Where does the teacher say what they'll do after lunch?* (*picture 12*), etc.

Story Time

Responding emotionally to the story

Responses to the story which do not use words are an easy and fun way for the children to be involved and engaged. When something good happens, have them clap or say *Yay!* When something bad happens, have them say *Boo!*

Reading Strategy

Which Question?

The Which Question? strategy helps the children tackle different types of questions: "Look" questions are found by spotting words in the text, "Think" questions require critical skills, and "Up to you" questions help personalize the story.

For additional explanation and activities, see the Literacy Handbook on the Teacher Resource Center.

Cooler: I'm at the Fun Park!

Have the children imagine they are at the Fun Park with Nicholas and his class. Ask them to draw a simple picture of them doing an activity, e.g. sliding down the water slide or looking at a shark. Invite children to present their drawing and talk about it, e.g. *I'm going very fast!*

Digital Resources

Reader eBook • Display the Reader story. Review the story extract. Then elicit predictions on what will happen before the children read the rest of the story.
• Oral Storytelling Video 1.1 gives the story with a different ending. Watch it together at the end of the lesson, then discuss the differences.

Teacher Resource Center • Print out Oral Storytelling Video Worksheet 1 to help you get the most from the video.

Reading Comprehension and Critical Literacy

Lesson objectives: focus on extra information provided in pictures; reflect on the story theme and relate it to personal behavior
Materials: Track 1.5; Reader; Oral Storytelling Video Worksheet 1 [TRC printout] (optional)

Lesson 4 Time to Think

1 Read the story in your Reader.

2 Match the phrases to make sentences.

Reading Report

1 The main character is	a his bathing suit.
2 The third grade is	b Nicholas.
3 They have to meet	c a packed lunch.
4 Everyone has to take	d listen to the teacher.
5 Nicholas doesn't take	e going to the fun park.
6 The children have to	f at 8:30.

3 Choose picture 5, 15, or 17 in your Reader. How do you think Nicholas feels? Write words for the cake. it.

I Can Read and Write! The pictures in a story can tell us more information. What do you learn about Nicholas from the pictures?

4 Talk about the story.

Do you know someone like Nicholas? What can you say to help?

12

Note: Please ensure that your class has read the Reader story before you do this lesson.

Warmer: Board race

Divide the class into two teams and give each team a board pen. The children on each team take turns running to the board to write a name, place, object, or activity from the story. Teams check eath other's answers. Then elicit sentences using some of the key words.

1 1.5 Read the story in your Reader.

- Have the children read the story. (Alternatively, play Track 1.5 and have them read along.) Elicit whether they were correct in their predictions in Lesson 3 Activity 4.
- Check comprehension by asking *What silly things did Nicholas do?* (*he didn't listen, he almost missed the bus, he wore his school uniform, he forgot his lunch and bathing suit*) *What nice things did his friends do?* (*Lisa stopped the bus, his friends gave him lunch. Keenan lent him swimming shorts.*)

2 Match the phrases to make sentences.

- Have the children match the sentences halves. Elicit answers and check with the class.

Answers

1 b **2** e **3** f **4** c **5** a **6** d

I Can Read and Write!

Point out that pictures are important in a story because they give us more information. Point to picture 5 in the Reader and ask *What do we learn about Nicholas here?* (*He likes making things.*) Repeat with picture 9 (*He likes drawing/cakes.*) and picture 11 (*He really wants to go on the trip.*), etc.

3 Choose picture 5, 15, or 17 in your Reader. How do you think Nicholas feels? Write words for the cake.

- Elicit how Nicholas feels in picture 5 and why. (*bad—because the teacher is telling him off*) Then brainstorm adjectives and write them on the board.
- The children choose one of the three story pictures and write appropriate adjective(s) in the cake. Elicit answers, e.g. *In picture 5, Nicholas feels …*

Answers

Children's own answers.

Optional activity: Interpret more pictures

Have the children look at Miss Callum in the Reader pictures. Elicit how she feels in each picture (e.g. picture 1 *excited*).

4 Talk about the story. 

- Have a child read Jason's questions. Ask *Do you know someone like Nicholas?* Have the children answer *yes* or *no* without naming the person.

- Ask *What can you say to help?* Elicit ideas to help people like Nicholas using *have to*, e.g. *You have to listen to your teacher. You have to make a list of important things you need to do.*, etc. Decide with the class which is the best idea.

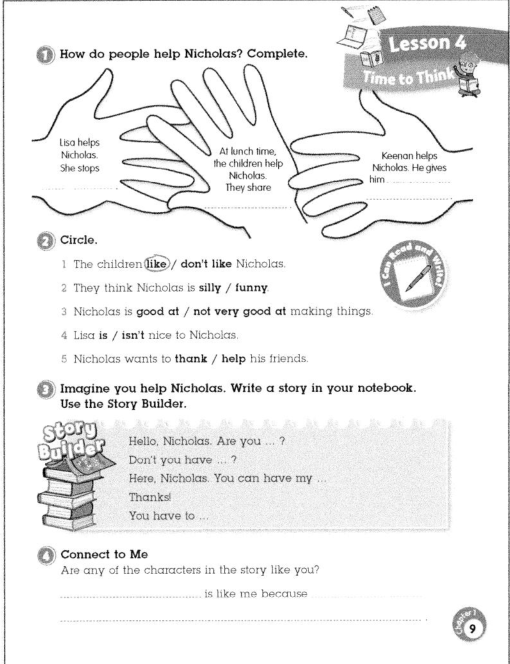
Lesson 4
Time to Think

1 How do people help Nicholas? Complete.

Lisa helps Nicholas. She stops ....

At lunch time, the children help Nicholas. They share ....

Keenan helps Nicholas. He gives him ....

2 Circle.

1 The children like / don't like Nicholas.
2 They think Nicholas is silly / funny.
3 Nicholas is good at / not very good at making things.
4 Lisa is / isn't nice to Nicholas.
5 Nicholas wants to thank / help his friends.

I Can Read and Write!

3 Imagine you help Nicholas. Write a story in your notebook. Use the Story Builder.

Story Builder

Hello, Nicholas. Are you ... ?
Don't you have ... ?
Here, Nicholas. You can have my ...
Thanks!
You have to ...

4 Connect to Me

Are any of the characters in the story like you?

.... is like me because ....

....

Chapter 1 9

1 How do people help Nicholas? Complete.

The children complete the sentences, looking back at the story as necessary. Elicit answers.

Answers

1 the bus **2** their food **3** his bathing suit

2 Circle.

The children practice the **I Can Read and Write!** feature by circling the correct words. Elicit answers in the form of complete sentences.

Answers

1 like **2** funny **3** good at **4** is **5** thank

3 Imagine you help Nicholas. Write a story in your notebook. Use the Story Builder.

Use the **Story Builder** prompts to elicit ideas. The children write a story in their notebook, then swap with a friend to check. Have children read out their story for the class.

4 Connect to Me

Elicit ideas on how the story characters are like the children. The children write their own response, then compare with a friend. Elicit responses.

Answers

Children's own answers.

Cooler: True or False?

Say true/false sentences about the story, e.g. *Nicholas always listens to Miss Callum.* (*false*) *Nicholas tries to catch the bus on his bicycle.* (*true*) Ask the children to shout *True!* or *False!* accordingly. Elicit the correct versions of the false statements.

Competency Focus

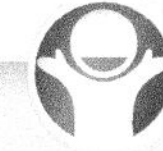

Me: Critical Literacy

The children use critical literacy skills to reflect on the story theme and imagine how they would behave in a similar situation.

Digital Resources

Reader eBook • Display the Reader on the board. Say key items for children to circle using *Pen*, e.g. the characters, important things like packed lunch/bathing suit/cake.

- If you haven't already, watch Oral Storytelling Video 1.1 (version of the story with a different ending).

Teacher Resource Center • If you haven't already, print out Oral Storytelling Video Worksheet 1 to do the support activities.

Vocabulary, Song, and Phonics

Lesson objectives: identify and name areas of an aquarium; practice short vowel sounds before double consonants
Key vocabulary: *aquarium, enclosure, entrance, petting zoo, picnic area, playground, show, ticket office*
Secondary language: *first, next, then*
Materials: Tracks 1.6 and 1.7; Phonics Worksheet 1 [TRC] (optional)

Lesson 5

Song

1 Listen and draw the route on the map. Then sing.

The School Trip

Hey, hey, hey,
We're on our way,
To the Ocean Aquarium,
With the school today.

We're at the entrance,
It's time to pay,
Here's the ticket office,
The dolphin show is this way.

First to the sharks,
In their enclosures, OK?
Then to the petting zoo,
To touch starfish and rays.

Next to the picnic area,
We're hungry as can be,
And then to the playground,
Come and play with me!

2 Talk to a friend about your day at the Ocean Aquarium.

I'm buying my ticket at the ticket office. I'm at the shark enclosure.

3 Write a plan for a day at the Ocean Aquarium.

First, go to the ....
Next, see the ....

4 Listen and say the chant.

The parrot is at the ticket office and the rabbit is at the petting zoo.

5 Find it!
How many can you find on the page?
words with a double letter

Spelling Central
A double letter often makes a short vowel sound,
e.g. parrot, parent.

13

Warmer: Pre-teach vocabulary

Point to the picture on Student Book p. 13 to pre-teach the vocabulary. Agree on a mime for each word. Say words from Lesson 1 and Lesson 5 and have the children say *Aquarium!* each time the word is from the new word set.

1 1.6 Listen and draw the route on the map. Then sing.

- Give the children time to look at the map. Point to the places and elicit the words.
- Play Track 1.6 twice. The children listen and draw the route on the map. Ask *What's first on the map? What's next?* to elicit answers.
- Play Track 1.6 again for the children to sing along.

Answers

entrance, ticket office, show, enclosures, petting zoo, picnic area, playground

Optional activity: Interesting animals

Write the animals from the song on the board: *dolphin, shark, starfish, ray.* Elicit what children know about each animal (e.g. what they eat, how fast they move, where they live, etc.). Have a class vote to find out the most interesting animal.

2 Talk to a friend about your day at the Ocean Aquarium.

- Have a child read the example. Ask the children to imagine they are at the Ocean Aquarium. Ask *Where are you now? What are you doing?* Elicit ideas.
- The children talk about their day at the Ocean Aquarium in pairs. Ask pairs to perform for the class.

3 Write a plan for a day at the Ocean Aquarium.

- Elicit answers using the sentence openings supplied, e.g. *the dolphin show, the petting zoo, the picnic area, the playground / dolphins, sharks, starfish, rays,* etc.
- Have the children write a plan for their day at the aquarium.
- The children compare their plans in pairs. Ask pairs to tell the class their plans.

Answers

Children's own answers.

Spelling Central

Short vowel + double letter

Point out that the vowels before double consonants are short. Write on the board *parrot / parent, hopping / hoping.* Read out the words and have the children repeat after you. Point out the short vowel sounds in *parrot/hopping* and the long vowel sounds in *parent/hoping.*

4 1.7 Listen and say the chant.

- Have the children look at the picture. Ask *What can you see?*
- Play Track 1.7. The children listen and read along. Elicit the words with double consonants.
- Play Track 1.7 again, pausing for the children to repeat.

5 Find it!

- Set a time limit for the children to find words with double consonants on the page. Elicit answers.

Answers

5—school, office, petting, parrot, rabbit

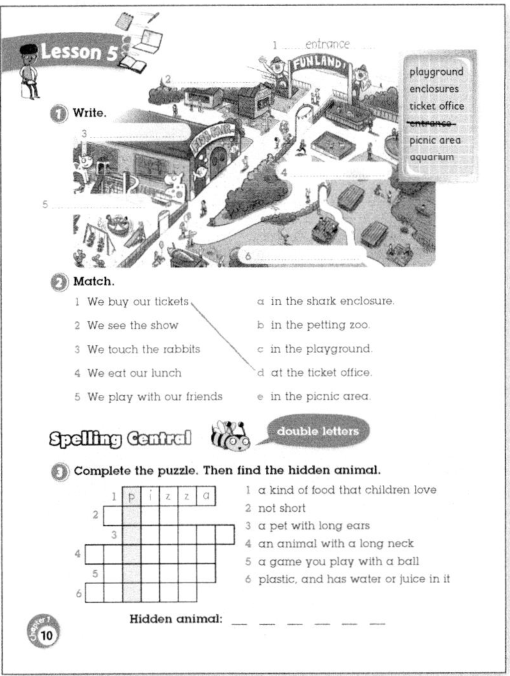

Lesson 5

1 Write.

1 entrance

2

3

4

5

6

playground
enclosures
ticket office
~~entrance~~
picnic area
aquarium

2 Match.

1 We buy our tickets — a in the shark enclosure.
2 We see the show — b in the petting zoo.
3 We touch the rabbits — c in the playground.
4 We eat our lunch — d at the ticket office.
5 We play with our friends — e in the picnic area.

Spelling Central — double letters

3 Complete the puzzle. Then find the hidden animal.

1 p i z z a

1 a kind of food that children love
2 not short
3 a pet with long ears
4 an animal with a long neck
5 a game you play with a ball
6 plastic, and has water or juice in it

Hidden animal: _ _ _ _ _ _

Chapter 1 10

1 Write.

The children label the picture. Elicit answers.

Answers

1 entrance **2** ticket office **3** aquarium **4** enclosures **5** playground **6** picnic area

2 Match.

Have a child read out the example. The children match the sentences, then compare answers in pairs. Elicit answers.

Answers

1 d **2** a **3** b **4** e **5** c

3 Complete the puzzle. Then find the hidden animal.

To practice the **Spelling Central** feature, the children can complete the puzzle in pairs. As soon as they finish and find the animal, they raise their hand. Elicit answers.

Answers

1 pizza **2** tall **3** rabbit **4** giraffe **5** soccer **6** bottle

Hidden animal: parrot

Have the children tell you their plan for the aquarium trip from Student Book Activity 3. Write four sentences on the board. Have the children read them out. Now erase a word from each sentence, and have the children read them again, remembering the missing words. Continue until the children say the sentences without any text on the board.

Competency Focus

Think! Critical Thinking

The children use critical thinking skills to produce a visual representation by identifying written and spoken forms of new language.

Digital Resources

Student eBook • When on the SB page, choose the audio button to see the song lyrics highlighted as the audio plays.

- TIP Children use *Highlighter* to identify the words which illustrate the spelling feature on the page (here, words with double letters).

Teacher Resource Center • For phonics practice, print out Phonics Worksheet 1.

Grammar and Reading

Lesson objective: talk about things using *can/can't*
Key grammar: *We can (use the computers in Story Central). We can't (use cell phones). Can we (play soccer in Story Central)? Yes, we can. / No, we can't.*
Secondary language: *share, sign (them) out, take out*
Materials: Tracks 1.6 and 1.8; Grammar Worksheet 1B [TRC printout] (optional)

Lesson 6

1 Listen and read. What are the children doing?

Yes, We Can!

2 Look at the Respect Rules for Story Central. Write *Yes, we can* or *No, we can't.*

1 Can we use the computers? Yes, we can.
2 Can we take computers out? ....
3 Can we play soccer inside? ....
4 Can we take video games out? ....
5 Can we eat? ....

3 Write another rule for Story Central.

....

Grammar Central

We can use the computers in Story Central.
We can't use cell phones.
Can we play soccer inside Story Central?
Yes, we can. / No, we can't.

Grammar Booster on page 19

14

Warmer: What was the last word?

1.6

Divide the class into two teams. Give one child from each team a board pen. Play the Lesson 5 song, pausing after key vocabulary (words in red). (Alternatively, read the text aloud.) The children run to the board and write the last word. Repeat, with a different child responding each time.

1 **1.8** **Listen and read. What are the children doing?**

- Have the children look at the story. Ask *How does Felicity feel in Pictures 2 and 3? (She's happy in Picture 2 and worried in Picture 3.)*
- Play Track 1.8. The children listen and read along. Then ask *What are the children doing? (They're writing Respect Rules for Story Central.)*
- Play Track 1.8 again, pausing for the children to repeat.

2 **Look at the Respect Rules for Story Central. Write *Yes, we can* or *No, we can't.***

- Have two children read the example. Ask *Where do we see this in the story? (Picture 4)* Have the children write the answers, referring to the story.
- Elicit answers.

Answers

1 Yes, we can. **2** No, we can't. **3** No, we can't. **4** Yes, we can. **5** Yes, we can.

Grammar Central

We can use the computers in Story Central. …

Ask *Which sentence talks about something it's OK to do? (We can …) Which sentence talks about something it's not OK to do? (We can't …) How do you ask if it's OK to do something? (Can we …?)*

Ask questions about their own class to elicit *Yes, we can. / No, we can't.*

For extra practice, try the **Grammar Booster** section in the Student Book (p. 19–21).

Answers p. 19

Activity 1: **1** can **2** can't **3** can **4** can't **5** can **6** can't **7** Can **8** can **9** Can **10** can't

Activity 2: **1** can eat in his bedroom, eat in his mom and dad's bedroom

2 can't eat in her bedroom, can play ball inside

Activity 3: Children's own answers.

p. 20

Activity 1: **1** have to **2** to **3** Can **4** can **5** can't **6** Can **7** can't **8** have to **9** have to **10** don't

Activity 2: **1** d **2** e **3** a **4** c **5** b

p. 21

Activity 1: **1** have to **2** don't have to **3** Can we **4** have to hold **5** like **6** do **7** do they eat **8** they have **9** don't **10** can play

Activity 2: wash their hands

3 Write one more rule for Story Central.

- Brainstorm ideas for more rules for Story Central, e.g. *We can drink water. We can't draw in our books.*, etc. Write these in two columns on the board under the headings *We can …* and *We can't …*
- Have the children choose and write one more rule for Story Central. Ask children to read out their rule.

Answers

Children's own answers.

Optional activity: Our English rules

Elicit the rules for your English lessons and write them on the board in note form. Have the children work in pairs to write and illustrate rules for the English classroom. These can be used as a wall display.

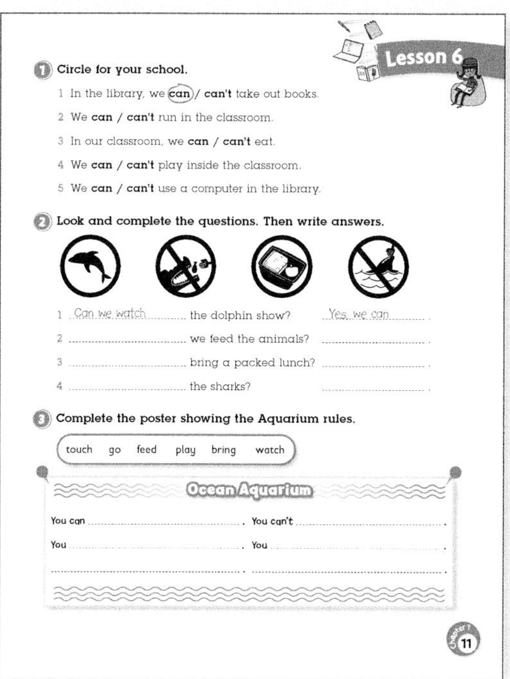

Lesson 6

1 Circle for your school.

1 In the library, we **can** / **can't** take out books.
2 We **can** / **can't** run in the classroom.
3 In our classroom, we **can** / **can't** eat.
4 We **can** / **can't** play inside the classroom.
5 We **can** / **can't** use a computer in the library.

2 Look and complete the questions. Then write answers.

1 Can we watch .... the dolphin show? Yes, we can.
2 .... we feed the animals? ....
3 .... bring a packed lunch? ....
4 .... the sharks? ....

3 Complete the poster showing the Aquarium rules.

touch go feed play bring watch

Ocean Aquarium

You can .... You can't ....
You .... You ....
....

Chapter 1 11

1 Circle for your school.

The children circle *can/can't* to complete rules for their school. Elicit answers. Accept contradicting answers if children can justify them. (They might need to use L1.)

Answers

Children's own answers.

2 Look and complete the questions. Then write answers.

Have a child read the example. The children read and complete the questions, then look at the pictures and write the answers. Elicit answers by asking pairs to read out a question and answer.

Answers

1 Can we watch; Yes, we can.
2 Can; No, we can't.
3 Can we; Yes, we can.
4 Can we touch; No, we can't.

3 Complete the poster showing the Aquarium rules.

The children write the rules for the Aquarium, using the words supplied. Elicit answers.

Answers

Children's own answers.

Cooler: Put in order

Write on the board *soccer, video games, phones, food, books, computers*. Have the children work in pairs to order the words as they are mentioned in the Story Central rules in the story. Set a time limit. Then have the children check in their book. Elicit the full rules in order.

Competency Focus

The children demonstrate and consolidate their understanding of the new language by reading the text and completing the activity.

Digital Resources

Student eBook • Minimize the page. Use *Timer* to give the children working in pairs two minutes to recall the five Story Central rules. Children use *Highlighter* to identify the answers in the text.

• Show Grammar Central. Use *Highlighter* to focus on key grammar structures.

Teacher Resource Center • For extra grammar practice, print out Grammar Worksheet 1B.

CLIL: Social Sciences—Greetings around the world

Lesson objective: find out about greetings in different cultures
Materials: large pieces of paper with *Yes* and *No* (Warmer); CLIL Graphic Organizer 1 [TRC printout] (optional)

CLIL Social Sciences Lesson 7

1 Read. Can people say hello without speaking?

Greetings From Around the World

In every country, there are different ways of saying hello. Children in the United States can say "Hello" or "Good morning" to their teacher and friends. Greetings in some countries are very different.

Children in Japan bow to the teacher when they come into school in the morning. When children bow, they put their feet together and look down to show respect.

Maori children in New Zealand say hello by pressing their noses together! This greeting is called a "Hongi."

In some African countries, the children and the teacher clap their hands to say hello in the morning.

How do children say hello in your country? Are there any greeting rules in your school?

2 Answer the questions.

1 Where do children bow to their teachers?
2 Where do people clap their hands to say hello?
3 How do Maori children say hello?

3 Class Vote

Are school rules important? Why / Why not?

Find Out More!
Choose another country.
How do people there say hello and goodbye?

15

Warmer: Yes or no?

Write *Yes* and *No* on pieces of paper and stick them on different sides of the classroom. Ask *Can you …?* questions, e.g. *Can you play soccer in the classroom? Can you take your books home?* The children point to *Yes* or *No* and call out *Yes, we can.* or *No, we can't.* If there is space, the children can line up in the middle and jump to the left or right side to answer. Continue, with children making the questions.

1 Read. Can people say hello without speaking?

- Ask *What do you say when you see your friends in the morning? Do you use your hands to say hello?*
- Ask *Can people say hello without speaking?* and elicit ideas. (*Yes, you can say hello by pressing noses together/by bowing/by clapping hands.*) Have the children read the text. Elicit the ways of saying hello by pointing to the pictures in the text.
- Ask *What's your favorite way of saying hello?* Have a class vote and practice them all together as a class.

2 Answer the questions.

- Have the children write the answers.
- Elicit answers.

Answers

1 Japan **2** Africa **3** by pressing their noses together

Optional activity: Formal and informal language

Brainstorm different ways of saying hello in English, e.g. *Hi, hello, hiya, yo!, Good morning/afternoon/evening.* Ask them which they think is most appropriate (1) when talking to a friend and (2) when talking to an important person (*Yo!, What's up?, Hi* are more informal; *Hello, How are you?, Good morning/afternoon/evening* are more polite).

3 Class Vote

- Ask *Are school rules important?* Elicit examples of school rules (help phrase them with *can/can't* or *have to*). Give the class a minute to think, then take a vote with a show of hands. Write the result on the board.
- Then ask the children to talk in pairs about why they voted that way. (They might need L1 to do this.) Ask pairs to share their ideas with the class. Point out that it is important to explain the reasons for your opinions.

Find Out More!  

Elicit which country children are going to choose to find out how people say hello there, asking them to give reasons for their choice. (Prompt as necessary, e.g. *Brazil, China, Russia, Saudi Arabia, Greece.*) Suggest appropriate resources, e.g. Internet, library books, etc. The children will need to complete this research before doing the follow-up activity in the Activity Book. (It could be set as homework.)

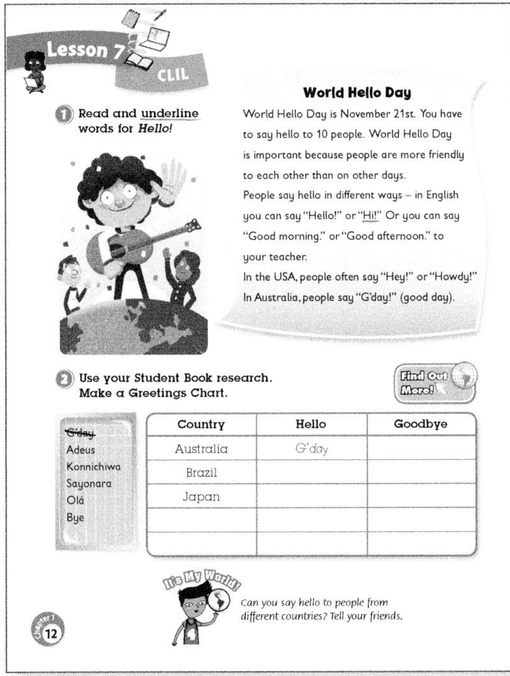
Lesson 7 CLIL

1 Read and underline words for *Hello!*

World Hello Day

World Hello Day is November 21st. You have to say hello to 10 people. World Hello Day is important because people are more friendly to each other than on other days.
People say hello in different ways – in English you can say "Hello!" or "Hi!" Or you can say "Good morning." or "Good afternoon." to your teacher.
In the USA, people often say "Hey!" or "Howdy!" In Australia, people say "G'day!" (good day).

2 Use your Student Book research. Make a Greetings Chart.

Find Out More!

~~G'day~~
Adeus
Konnichiwa
Sayonara
Olá
Bye

Country	Hello	Goodbye
Australia	G'day	
Brazil		
Japan		

It's My World!

Can you say hello to people from different countries? Tell your friends.

12

1 Read and underline words for *Hello!*

Have the children underline all the ways of saying hello in the text. Point out that there are seven. Elicit answers.

Answers

Hello, Hi!, Good morning, Good afternoon, Hey!, Howdy!, G'day

2 Use your Student Book research. Make a Greetings Chart.

Elicit greetings the children found in their Student Book research and write them on the board. Divide the class into groups of four. The children pool the information learned from their research in the Student Book and the Activity Book. Working individually, they complete the table using the words supplied. Then they complete the other two rows with greetings from two different countries of their choice. Elicit answers.

Answers

Australia: g'day, bye
Brazil: olá, adeus
Japan: konnichiwa, sayonara

It's My World!

Have the children work in small groups to see how many languages they can say *hello* or *goodbye* in. Elicit and list on the board.

Cooler: Cultures in the classroom

Divide the class into three groups: *Maori, Japanese, African.* Tell the children when you say *Go!* they have to walk around the class. When you clap and say *Greet!*, they have to greet the people near them in the correct way according to their culture (i.e. pressing noses, bowing, or clapping). Repeat three times.

Competency Focus

Act

The children carry out research to find out about greetings in different cultures. They relate what they learn to their world, both inside and outside the classroom.

Digital Resources

Student eBook • Display the SB page on the board to do Activity 1, points 1 and 2, for a "heads-up" introduction to the topic. This helps the children engage.

• TIP Store Internet links and other ideas in *Add personal note* for easy access during the lesson.

Teacher Resource Center • Print out CLIL Graphic Organizer 1 for the children to use in collating their Find Out More! research.

CLIL eBook • The children can use the CLIL eBook to expand their knowledge of the lesson topic.

Project

Lesson objectives: review language from Chapter 1; write a brochure for a Fun Park or Aquarium; plan a trip to a Fun Park or Aquarium
Materials: large colored construction paper, colored pencils or markers, aquarium/fun park brochures, scissors, glue; two game pieces and a coin for each pair

Project

Lesson 8

You need:
- large colored construction paper
- colored pencils or markers
- aquarium / fun park brochures
- scissors and glue

Prepare

1 **Design a brochure for a fun park or aquarium.**

1 Fold your construction paper into three.
2 Include a name for your park, a map of the park, special shows, picnic areas, and rules for visitors.
3 Decorate your brochure.

Showcase

2 **Plan a trip to your fun park or aquarium.**

1 Decide what to do there, and what the class need to bring.
2 Tell the class about the trip. Be prepared to answer questions from your class.

Ideas Box
The name of my aquarium / fun park is ...
There is / are ...
You have to / don't have to ...
It's a good idea to ...
Yes, you can. / No, you can't.

Chapter 1 16

Warmer: Hello! mingle

Elicit some of the different ways and languages the children used to say hello in the last lesson. Give them two minutes to mingle and say hello to as many different friends as they can, using different languages and gestures.

Prepare

1 Design a brochure for a fun park or aquarium.

- Distribute the materials. Read through the instructions together and ensure the children are clear on what to do.
- Ask *What information is necessary in a brochure?* Brainstorm ideas for the categories listed in sentence 2, and ideas on how to decorate their brochure.
- Have the children follow the instructions to make their brochure. They could work in pairs. Give support as necessary.

Alternative craft activity

The children work in groups to create their brochure. Allocate roles to cover writing the heading and notes, drawing the map, drawing and coloring rides, and adding further decoration to the brochure.

Showcase

2 Plan a trip to your fun park or aquarium.

- Explain to the class that they will plan a trip, then tell the class about it. The children decide on the activities and rules and plan their trip in pairs, using the **Ideas Box** for support.
- Organize the pairs into groups. Each pair will tell the others in the group about their trip. Encourage the children listening to ask questions, e.g. *Can I/we …? Do we have to …?*
- Have pairs present their trip to the class.

Optional activity: Browse the brochures

Have the brochures visible on the children's desks or on the walls. Give the children five minutes to walk around and look at the brochures and find (a) a very pretty brochure, (b) a great name for a park, (c) a good set of rules, and (d) interesting shows. Elicit their opinions.

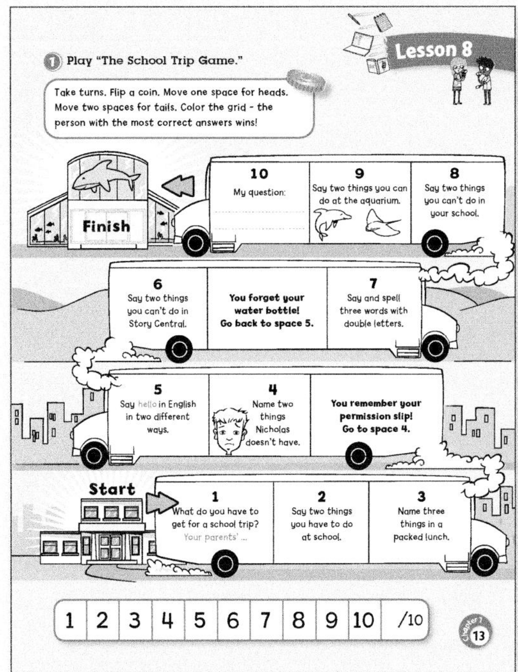

1 Play "The School Trip Game."

Have the children write a new question in the blank space. Divide the class into pairs and give each pair a coin (or something else they can flip, e.g. an eraser with 1 and 2 written on opposite sides). Explain that they play the game on one shared book, but color the squares at the bottom of the page in their own book when they get a question correct. If they land on an unnumbered space, they follow the instructions. The child with the most correct answers wins.

Answers

1 permission **2** You have to go to class. You have to arrive on time., etc. **3** sandwich, fruit (apple, banana, etc.), drink (juice, water) **4** a packed lunch, a bathing suit **5** Good morning! Hey! **6** You can't play soccer. You can't use a cell phone. **7** parrot, rabbit, carrot **8** You can't run. You can't eat in the classroom., etc. **9** You can watch the dolphins. You can touch the starfish., etc. **10** Children's own answers.

Cooler: Imaginary binoculars

Say *I'm in an aquarium.* Hold imaginary binoculars to your eyes and say excitedly *I can see sharks!* Hand the "binoculars" to the next child and say *Can you see it/them?* and encourage them to say *No, but I can see …* The children work in small groups, handing the binoculars to each other and describing what they can see.

Competency Focus

Collaborate and Communicate

By acting out the story, the children consolidate their understanding in a fun and engaging way. They also demonstrate their ability to work with friends and use interpersonal skills.

Digital Resources

Student eBook • For the craft activity, display the SB page on the board and show the pictures, stage by stage, as you talk the class through the process.

Digital Activity Book • For "The School Trip Game" in AB Activity 1, you can use *Timer*. Set a time limit. The child who has most correct answers when the time is up wins.

Language Review

Lesson objective: review language from Chapter 1

Materials: Tracks 1.9 and AB 1.1

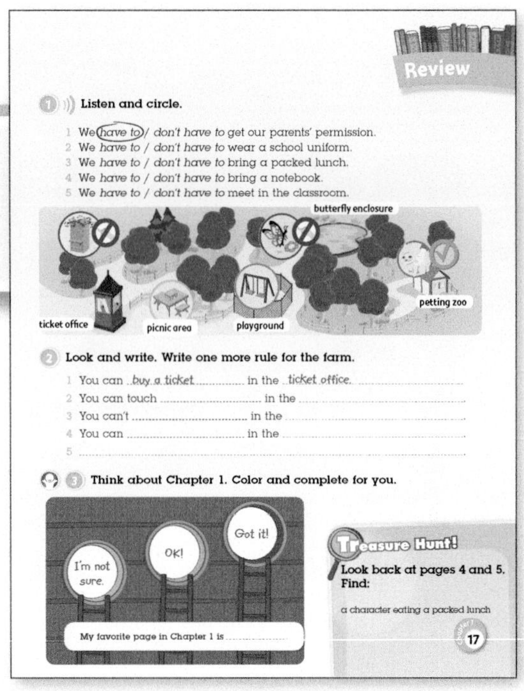

Review

1 Listen and circle.

1 We have to / don't have to get our parents' permission.
2 We have to / don't have to wear a school uniform.
3 We have to / don't have to bring a packed lunch.
4 We have to / don't have to bring a notebook.
5 We have to / don't have to meet in the classroom.

2 Look and write. Write one more rule for the farm.

1 You can buy a ticket in the ticket office.
2 You can touch .... in the ....
3 You can't .... in the ....
4 You can .... in the ....
5 ....

3 Think about Chapter 1. Color and complete for you.

My favorite page in Chapter 1 is ....

Treasure Hunt!

Look back at pages 4 and 5. Find:

a character eating a packed lunch

17

Warmer: Play "The Shark Game"

Play the game with a selection of vocabulary from Chapter 1 (see Games Bank p. 19).

1 1.9 Listen and circle.

- Have the children look at the picture. Ask *What can you see?*
- Play Track 1.9 twice. Have the children circle the correct option for each sentence. Elicit answers.

Answers

1 have to **2** don't have to **3** have to **4** have to **5** don't have to

Audioscript

Miss Green: *Now listen, class. It's the school trip to Green Farm tomorrow. Don't forget your permission slip. You have to get your parents' permission.*
Lucy: *Do we have to wear a school uniform?*
Miss Green: *No, you don't. You can wear a T-shirt and jeans.*
Lucy: *OK. And do we have to bring a packed lunch? Can we have a picnic?*
Miss Green: *Yes, Lucy, we can have a picnic, so please bring a packed lunch. And you have to bring your notebook to write about the animals.*
Lucy: *Yes, Miss Green.*
Miss Green: *And don't be late. We have an early start, so arrive at 7:45 a.m. And don't forget … meet at the school entrance, not in the classroom. OK class, that's all!*

2 Look and write. Write one more rule for the farm.

- Have the children look at the picture in Activity 1. Ask one child to read out the example sentence. Elicit suggestions for the second sentence. Then have the children continue the activity individually.

Answers

1 You can buy a ticket in the ticket office. 2 You can touch the rabbit in petting corner. 3 You can't touch the bees. 4 You can eat in the picnic area. 5 You can't touch the butterfly. / You can play in the playground

3 Think about Chapter 1. Color and complete for you.

- Have the children look back at Chapter 1. Elicit their favorite parts. The children then color the circle which represents how they feel about their own progress (self-evaluation).
- Have the children complete the sentence about their favorite page. Elicit responses.

Treasure Hunt!

Have the children look at pp. 4–5 to find a character eating a packed lunch. They hold up their Student Book and point to the right place on the page.

Cooler: Play "Sentence Builders"

Play the game with four sentences from Student Book Activity 1 audioscript (see Games Bank p. 19).

Competency Focus

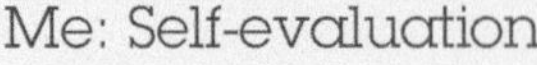

Me: Self-evaluation

The children reflect on the chapter and express their opinions about their own progress. This encourages them to evaluate and make decisions about how they learn and what they need to revisit.

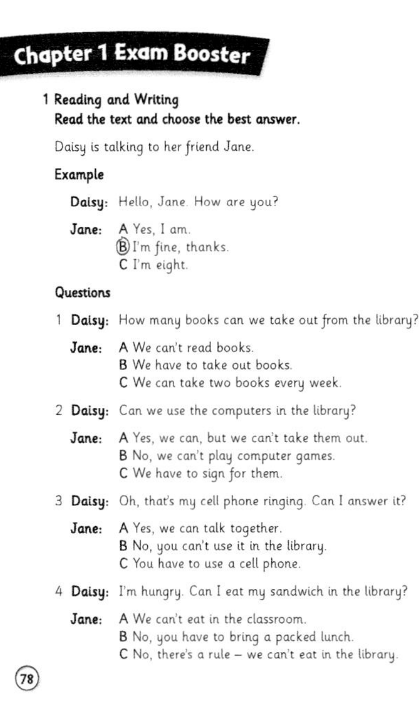

Chapter 1 Exam Booster

1 Reading and Writing
Read the text and choose the best answer.

Daisy is talking to her friend Jane.

Example

Daisy: Hello, Jane. How are you?

Jane: A Yes, I am.
Ⓑ I'm fine, thanks.
C I'm eight.

Questions

1 **Daisy:** How many books can we take out from the library?

Jane: A We can't read books.
B We have to take out books.
C We can take two books every week.

2 **Daisy:** Can we use the computers in the library?

Jane: A Yes, we can, but we can't take them out.
B No, we can't play computer games.
C We have to sign for them.

3 **Daisy:** Oh, that's my cell phone ringing. Can I answer it?

Jane: A Yes, we can talk together.
B No, you can't use it in the library.
C You have to use a cell phone.

4 **Daisy:** I'm hungry. Can I eat my sandwich in the library?

Jane: A We can't eat in the classroom.
B No, you have to bring a packed lunch.
C No, there's a rule – we can't eat in the library.

78

2 Listening
Listen and draw lines. There is one example.

79

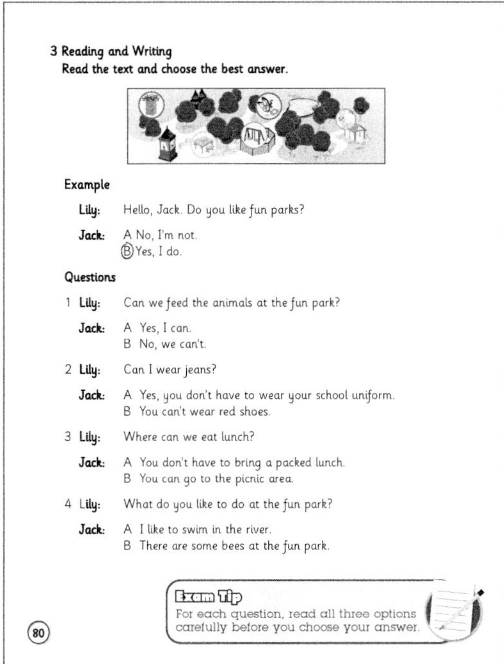

3 Reading and Writing
Read the text and choose the best answer.

Example

Lily: Hello, Jack. Do you like fun parks?

Jack: A No, I'm not.
Ⓑ Yes, I do.

Questions

1 **Lily:** Can we feed the animals at the fun park?

Jack: A Yes, I can.
B No, we can't.

2 **Lily:** Can I wear jeans?

Jack: A Yes, you don't have to wear your school uniform.
B You can't wear red shoes.

3 **Lily:** Where can we eat lunch?

Jack: A You don't have to bring a packed lunch.
B You can go to the picnic area.

4 **Lily:** What do you like to do at the fun park?

Jack: A I like to swim in the river.
B There are some bees at the fun park.

Exam Tip
For each question, read all three options carefully before you choose your answer.

80

1 Reading and Writing. Read the text and choose the best answer.

The children read the dialogue and choose the best response from the three options each time.
Check answers.

Answers

1 c **2** a **3** b **4** c

2 AB 1.1 Listening. Listen and draw lines. There is one example.

Play Track AB 1.1 twice. The children listen and match the names to the characters pictured. Check answers.

Answers (Audioscript on p. 222)

Lines drawn between:
Tom—boy wearing school uniform
Paul—boy holding a soccer ball
Lucy—girl carrying bag with bathing suit
Anna—girl showing packed lunch
Ben—boy at back not listening

3 Reading and Writing. Read the text and choose the best answer.

The children read the dialogue and choose the best response from the two options each time.
Check answers.

Answers

1 b **2** a **3** b **4** a

Digital Resources

Teacher Resource Center • Print out Test Chapter 1 to use at the end of this lesson. The Test Generator also allows you to create customized tests.

Student's App • Encourage the children to play the games on their smartphone/tablet as a fun way to review the chapter vocabulary. (*The Inks* Apps are free and available on the App Store and Google Play.)

Chapter 2

The Store and More

Overview

The children will:

- use critical thinking skills to identify food items.
- ask about and give prices using *how much*.
- read, understand, and act out a story.
- talk about fruit and vegetables in a market.
- ask and answer about food using *some/any*.
- develop math skills.
- make a money box.

Key Vocabulary

Food: black olives, bread, cucumber, egg, green pepper, mayonnaise, mustard, red onion, tomato, turkey
Fruit and vegetables: apples, bananas, cabbages, carrots, grapes, melons, oranges, pears, potatoes, strawberries

Key Grammar

- How much is the (bread)? It's (one seventy-five).
- How much are the (eggs)? They're (two dollars).
- Are there any (sandwiches)?
- There are some (sandwiches).
- There aren't any (cookies).
- Is there any (fruit)?
- There is some (fruit).
- There isn't any (cake).

Reading Skills

Story: *The Magic Money Tree*
Genre: modern fable

Literacy Development

- predict story content from title and pictures
- reflect on and personalize the theme of the story
- focus on the use of " " for showing direct speech

Functional Language

- What would you like?
- Can I have …, please?
- Sure. Here you go.

Spelling

Regular plurals (*–s, –es, –ies*)

CLIL: Math—At the market

The children develop their math abilities with food prices.

Competency Focus

The children will:

use critical thinking skills to identify food items. (Lesson 1)	apply new grammar to previously learned vocabulary. (Lesson 2)	work in pairs to act out a dialogue. (Lesson 3)	personalize the story by thinking about how they might act in a similar situation. (Lesson 4)	develop a wider understanding of their own culture by finding out about national food. (Lesson 7)
predict the content of a story. (Lesson 3)	talk about food. (Lesson 6)	work in groups to act out the story. (Lesson 8)	evaluate their own progress in the chapter. (Review)	
identify and talk about fruits and vegetables. (Lesson 5)				

Digital Overview

Teacher Presentation

Student eBook and Digital Activity Book

- Music Video 2.1 (2.2): *In the Market*
- Interactive versions of AB activities
- Integrated audio and answer key for all activities

Teacher resources for planning, lesson delivery, and homework

Teacher Resource Center

- Class Planner Chapter 2
- Worksheets to print out (including notes and answers):
  - Grammar Worksheet 2A: How much is/are …? It's/They're …
  - Grammar Worksheet 2B: Are there any …? There are some/aren't any …
  - Phonics Worksheet 2
  - CLIL Graphic Organizer 2
  - Festival Worksheet: Halloween
  - Test Chapter 2
- Test Generator
- Literacy Handbook

Watch the Music Video

Children's resources for learning and practicing at home

Student eBook

- Music Video 2.1 (2.2): *In the Market*

The Inks Student's App

Student's App

Vocabulary games: Food, fruit, and vegetables

Chapter 2 The Store and More

Lesson 1

Vocabulary

Lesson objective: identify and talk about food items
Key vocabulary: *black olives, bread, cucumber, egg, green pepper, mayonnaise, mustard, red onion, tomato, turkey*
Materials: Track 2.1; alphabet sheets (Warmer)

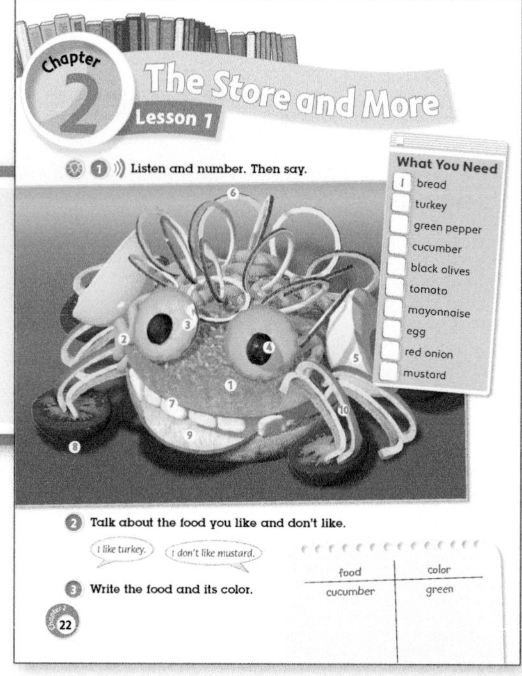

Warmer: A–Z of food

Prepare two sheets of paper with the alphabet listed vertically. Divide the class into two teams. Give each team an alphabet sheet. The teams have two minutes to write a food name starting with each letter, with the children on each team taking turns. (More than one food per letter is allowed.) Elicit answers. Each correct answer wins a point.

1 2.1 Listen and number. Then say. 

- Have the children look at the pictures and say the foods. Ask *What can you make with this food?*
- Play Track 2.1 and have them listen and find each food. They write the picture number of each food by the word in the list.
- Play Track 2.1 again, pausing after each food for the children to point and repeat.

Audioscript

Dad: *Hey, look at this fun face sandwich! Do you want one for lunch?*
Boy: *Yes, please!*
Dad: *Then we need bread for the face. Oh, and turkey for the mouth.*
Boy: *And green pepper for the legs!*
Dad: *Some cucumber for the eyes, with a black olive—no, two black olives.*
Boy: *And tomato for the feet!*
Dad: *We can use some mayonnaise for teeth.*
Boy: *Yes, it's white. And we need one egg cut in half for the ears.*
Dad: *How about red onion slices for curly hair?*
Boy: *Yes, and we can use yellow mustard for the hair, too.*
Dad: *OK, then, so we have to go to the store!*

Answers

bread 1, turkey 9, green pepper 10, cucumber 3, black olive 4, tomato 8, mayonnaise 7, egg 5, red onion 6, mustard 2

2 Talk about the food you like and don't like.

- Hold up your Student Book and point to different foods, saying, e.g. *Mm—I like black olives! But, ugh! I don't like green peppers.*
- The children continue this in pairs, taking turns saying what they like/don't like and responding *Me, too! / Not me!*

3 Write the food and its color.

- Say foods to elicit the color, e.g. *turkey. (pink)*
- The children write the list of foods and colors in their notebook, then compare lists in pairs. Elicit answers.

Answers

cucumber—green, bread—brown/white, turkey—pink, pepper—green, olives—black, tomato—red, mayonnaise—white, egg—white/yellow, onion—red, mustard—yellow

Optional activity: Make a sandwich!

Talk through and mime making a sandwich, using *Cut … Put the … on the … Spread some … Eat it!* Do it in stages: (1) the children mime with you, (2) they speak and mime with you, (3) they speak and mime while you just mime, (4) they speak and mime without you.

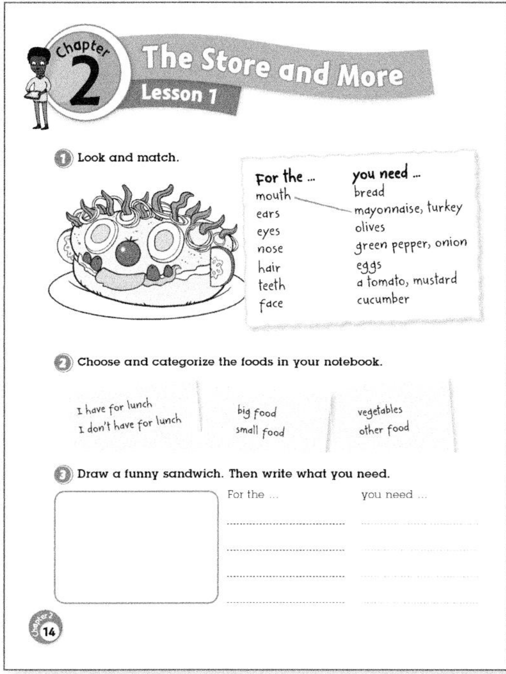

Chapter 2 The Store and More

Lesson 1

1 Look and match.

For the …	you need …
mouth	bread
ears	mayonnaise, turkey
eyes	olives
nose	green pepper, onion
hair	eggs
teeth	a tomato, mustard
face	cucumber

2 Choose and categorize the foods in your notebook.

I have for lunch / I don't have for lunch

big food / small food

vegetables / other food

3 Draw a funny sandwich. Then write what you need.

For the … you need …

14

1 Look and match.

The children look at the picture and match the body parts and food. Elicit answers.

Answers

mouth—mayonnaise, turkey; ears—cucumber; eyes—eggs; nose—a tomato, mustard; hair—green pepper, onion; teeth—olives; face—bread

2 Choose and categorize the foods in your notebook.

Elicit an example for each category listed. Ask *Which categories would you choose?* Elicit ideas, prompting children to give a reason for their choice. The children choose a pair of categories and list the words in their notebook, then compare with a friend.

Answers

Children's own answers.

3 Draw a funny sandwich. Then write what you need.

The children draw a sandwich similar to the one in Activity 1 and write about it. They compare drawings in pairs or small groups.

Answers

Children's own answers.

Cooler: Play "The Chain Game"

Play the game to review food (see Games Bank p. 19). Start the chain with *I went to the store and I bought apples.*

Competency Focus

Think! Critical Thinking

The children use critical thinking skills to identify food items by using visual clues and processing the written and spoken forms.

Digital Resources

Student eBook • Use *Timer* to time the A–Z Warmer game.

• Call out the food in the SB Activity 1 picture in random order. Children use *Pen* to circle each one.

Digital Activity Book • To give feedback on AB Activity 3, invite a child to draw a funny sandwich using *Pen*. The other children write the ingredients.

Grammar

Lesson objectives: ask and answer about food prices
Key grammar: *How much is the (bread)? It's (one seventy-five) [$1.75]. How much are the (eggs)? They're (two dollars) [$2.00].*
Secondary language: *Excuse me. We need …*
Materials: Track 2.2; Grammar Worksheet 2A [TRC printout] (optional)

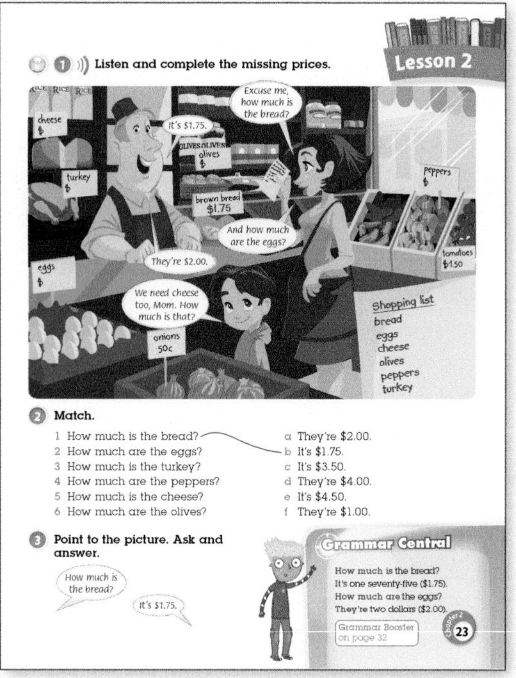
Listen and complete the missing prices.

Lesson 2

Match.

1 How much is the bread?
2 How much are the eggs?
3 How much is the turkey?
4 How much are the peppers?
5 How much is the cheese?
6 How much are the olives?

a They're $2.00.
b It's $1.75.
c It's $3.50.
d They're $4.00.
e It's $4.50.
f They're $1.00.

Point to the picture. Ask and answer.

Grammar Central

How much is the bread?
It's one seventy-five ($1.75).
How much are the eggs?
They're two dollars ($2.00).

Grammar Booster on page 32

Chapter 2

23

Warmer: Split words

Write split words on the board (in random order): *tur/key, pep/per, cucum/ber, toma/to, oli/ves, mayo/nnaise, on/ion, mus/tard*. Ask children to draw a line between parts to make a food word and say the word. Have a class vote (hands raised for yes/no) on whether the children like each food item.

1 2.2 Listen and complete the missing prices.

- Have the children look at the picture. Ask *Where is this?* (*a store*) *What are the boy and his mom buying?* (*fruit and vegetables*) *What food can you see?* (*see picture*)
- Point out that some prices are missing. Play Track 2.2 twice and have the children write the prices, then check their answers. Elicit answers and ask children to write them on the board.

Audioscript

Mom: *Excuse me, how much is the bread?*
Assistant: *It's $1.75.*
Mom: *And how much are the eggs?*
Assistant: *They're $2.00.*
Boy: *We need cheese too, Mom. How much is that?*
Assistant: *Um … $3.50.*
Mom: *How much are the olives?*
Assistant: *They're $4.00.*
Mom: *OK, and how much are the peppers?*
Assistant: *They're $1.00 each.*
Mom: *We need turkey. How much is the turkey?*
Assistant: *It's $4.50.*

Answers

bread $1.75, eggs $2.00, cheese $3.50, olives $4.00, peppers $1.00, turkey $4.50

2 Match.

- Have the children look at the picture in Activity 1 again and draw lines to match the questions and answers. Elicit answers and check with the class.

Answers

1 b **2** a **3** e **4** f **5** c **6** d

Grammar Central

How much is the bread? …

Have the children look at the patterns. Elicit which form is used to ask about one thing (*How much is …?*) and about more than one thing (*How much are …?*). Repeat for the answers. (*It's …, They're …*) Elicit singular and plural questions using the picture in Activity 1 to check understanding. Have the class repeat the questions and answers.

For extra practice, try the **Grammar Booster** section in the Student Book (p. 32).

Answers p. 32

Activity 1: **1** How much is **2** How much is **3** It's **4** How much are **5** How much are **6** They're

Activity 2: **1** mayonnaise **2** It's **3** are **4** is **5** It's **6** is

Activity 3: Children's own answers.

3 Point to the picture. Ask and answer.

- Have two children read the example. Ask one more question about the picture and elicit the answer.
- The children take turns in pairs asking and answering about the prices in the picture.

Optional activity: Chant

Demonstrate how to chant/rap the questions and answers. Have the children chant/rap in their pairs.

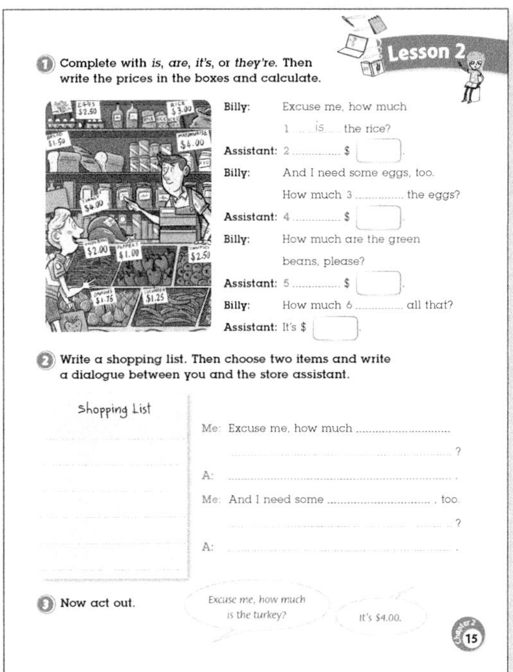

Lesson 2

1 Complete with *is*, *are*, *it's*, or *they're*. Then write the prices in the boxes and calculate.

Billy: Excuse me, how much 1 ...is... the rice?
Assistant: 2 .... $.
Billy: And I need some eggs, too. How much 3 .... the eggs?
Assistant: 4 .... $.
Billy: How much are the green beans, please?
Assistant: 5 .... $.
Billy: How much 6 .... all that?
Assistant: It's $.

2 Write a shopping list. Then choose two items and write a dialogue between you and the store assistant.

Shopping List

Me: Excuse me, how much ....?
A: ....
Me: And I need some ...., too. ....?
A: ....

3 Now act out.

Excuse me, how much is the turkey?
It's $4.00.

Chapter 2 15

1 Complete with is, are, it's, or they're. Then write the prices in the boxes and calculate.

The children complete the dialogue using *is*, *are*, *it's*, or *they're*. Then they look at the picture to write the prices and calculate the total cost. Elicit answers.

Answers

1 is **2** It's, $3.00 **3** are **4** They're, $2.50 **5** They're, $2.00 **6** is, $7.50

2 Write a shopping list. Then choose two items and write a dialogue between you and the store assistant.

Point out to the children that they can use the dialogue in Activity 1 as a model. They choose and list items, then write a dialogue they have with a store assistant when they purchase the items.

Answers

Children's own answers.

3 Now act out.

The children act out their dialogues in pairs. Invite pairs to act out for the class.

Cooler: Play "Change Places"

Explain the game: you will ask questions and if a child's answer is *Yes*, they stand up and move to a different seat. Ask *Do you like . . . ?* questions about food from Student Book pp. 18–19 (you can also include review of food items they already know).

Competency Focus

Learn

The children use previously acquired vocabulary in a different context with new grammatical structures.

Digital Resources

Student eBook • Show the SB Grammar Central box. Use *Highlighter* to focus on key grammar structures.

Teacher Resource Center • For extra grammar practice, print out Grammar Worksheet 2A.

Reading: Story Extract

Lesson objectives: make offers and requests; predict story content from title and pictures; read the extract from *The Magic Money Tree* (beginning)

Functional language: *What would you like? Can I have . . .? Sure. Here you go.*

Materials: Tracks 2.3 and 2.4; a handful of coins in your pocket (Warmer)

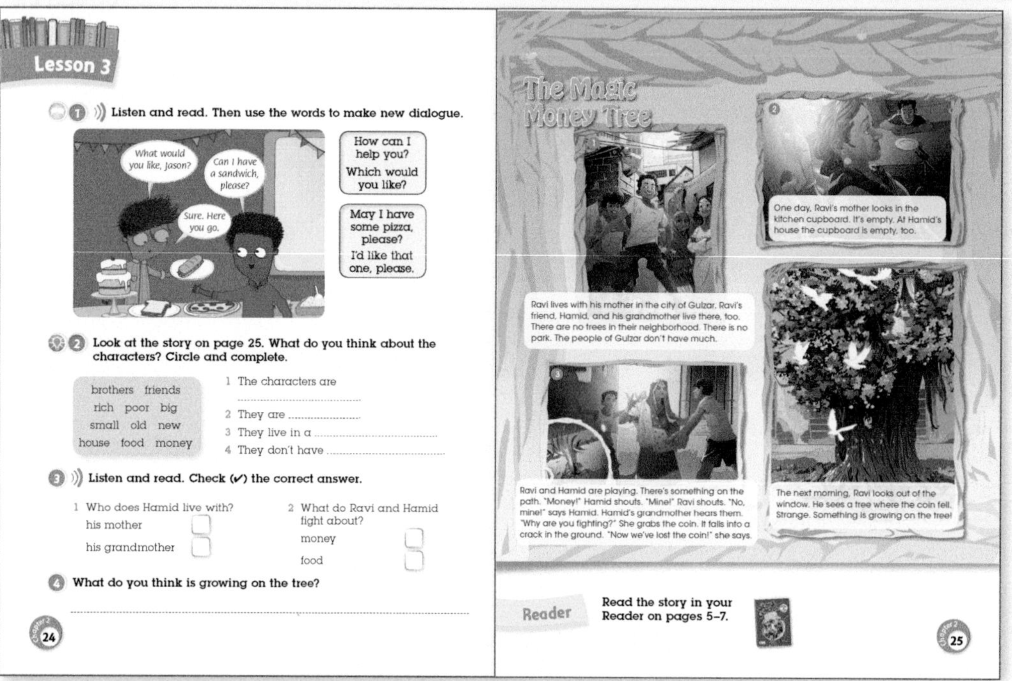

Lesson 3

1 Listen and read. Then use the words to make new dialogue.

How can I help you?
Which would you like?

May I have some pizza, please?
I'd like that one, please.

2 Look at the story on page 25. What do you think about the characters? Circle and complete.

brothers friends
rich poor big
small old new
house food money

1 The characters are ....
2 They are ....
3 They live in a ....
4 They don't have ....

3 Listen and read. Check (✓) the correct answer.

1 Who does Hamid live with?
his mother ☐
his grandmother ☐

2 What do Ravi and Hamid fight about?
money ☐
food ☐

4 What do you think is growing on the tree?

....

24

The Magic Money Tree

1 Ravi lives with his mother in the city of Gulzar. Ravi's friend, Hamid, and his grandmother live there, too. There are no trees in their neighborhood. There is no park. The people of Gulzar don't have much.

2 One day, Ravi's mother looks in the kitchen cupboard. It's empty. At Hamid's house the cupboard is empty, too.

3 Ravi and Hamid are playing. There's something on the path. "Money!" Hamid shouts. "Mine!" Ravi shouts. "No, mine!" says Hamid. Hamid's grandmother hears them. "Why are you fighting?" She grabs the coin. It falls into a crack in the ground. "Now we've lost the coin!" she says.

4 The next morning, Ravi looks out of the window. He sees a tree where the coin fell. Strange. Something is growing on the tree!

Reader Read the story in your Reader on pages 5–7.

25

Warmer: How much money do I have?

Take out a few coins and count the total amount—but do not tell the children the total. Ask *How much money do I have?* Elicit answers. If they guess too low, say *More!* If they guess too high, say *Less!* Use hand gestures to make the meaning clear. Repeat, with different amounts and different children taking over your role.

Functional language

1 2.3 Listen and read. Then use the words to make new dialogue.

- Have the children look at the pictures and dialogue. Ask *What are they doing?* (*having lunch*) *What does Jason want?* (*a sandwich*)
- Play Track 2.3. The children listen and read along.
- Play Track 2.3 again, pausing for the children to repeat.
- The children practice the dialogue in pairs, substituting different foods for *sandwich*.

Before reading

2 Look at the story on page 25. What do you think about the characters? Circle and complete.

- The children look at the title and pictures. Ask *Who do you see? Are they rich or poor?*
- The children circle the correct word in each group and use the words to complete the sentences. Elicit answers.

Answers

1 friends **2** poor **3** old/small house **4** food / money

3 2.4 Listen and read. Check (✓) the correct answer.

- Play Track 2.4. The children listen and read along. Ask questions to check comprehension, e.g. *Do Hamid and Ravi's families have food?* (*no*) *Where is the coin now?* (*in a crack in the ground/lost*)
- Play Track 2.4 again for the children to check the correct options. Elicit answers.

Answers

1 his grandmother **2** money

4 What do you think is growing on the tree?

- Have the children write their prediction. Elicit ideas including reasons, but do not confirm. Say they will have to read the story to find out.

Answer

Children's own answers.

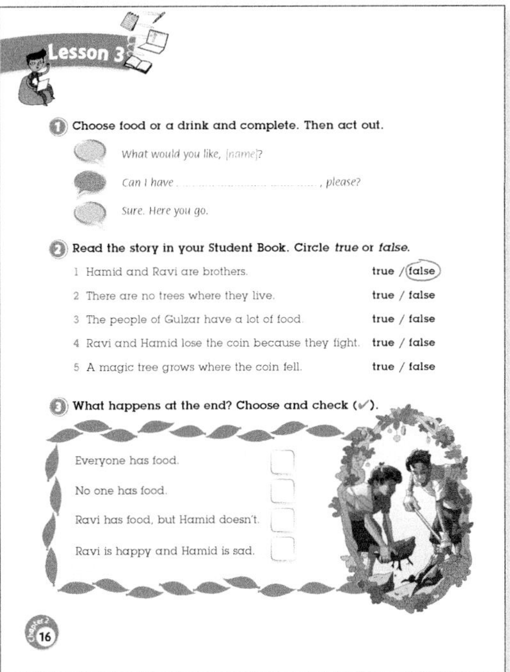

Lesson 3

1 Choose food or a drink and complete. Then act out.

What would you like, [name]?

Can I have ...., please?

Sure. Here you go.

2 Read the story in your Student Book. Circle *true* or *false*.

1	Hamid and Ravi are brothers.	true / (false)
2	There are no trees where they live.	true / false
3	The people of Gulzar have a lot of food.	true / false
4	Ravi and Hamid lose the coin because they fight.	true / false
5	A magic tree grows where the coin fell.	true / false

3 What happens at the end? Choose and check (✓).

Everyone has food. ☐

No one has food. ☐

Ravi has food, but Hamid doesn't. ☐

Ravi is happy and Hamid is sad. ☐

16

1 Choose food or a drink and complete. Then act out.

The children complete the dialogue with a food or drink of their choice. Elicit answers. Then they act out the dialogue in pairs. Have pairs act out for the class.

Answers

Children's own answers.

2 Read the story in your Student Book. Circle true or false.

The children circle *true* or *false* for each sentence. Elicit answers, including the correct versions of the false statements.

Answers

1 false **2** true **3** false **4** true **5** true

3 What happens at the end? Choose and check (✓).

The children predict the end of the story by checking one of the options. Elicit ideas.

Answers

Children's own answers.

Cooler: I am Ravi

Ask the children to imagine they are Ravi. Ask *What can you do to make life better?* Give the children two minutes to discuss with a friend. Elicit ideas and write key verbs on the board (e.g. *sell, study, play, help, plant, grow, make*).

Competency Focus

Collaborate and Communicate

The children act out an authentic dialogue together, putting into practice new functional language.

Think! Critical Thinking

The children apply reading skills (exploiting pictures and text clues) to understand the story.

Digital Resources

Student eBook • TIP Choose the audio button on the SB page to access recordings for listening activities.

Digital Activity Book • In AB Activity 3, have the children use *Pen* to draw a tally mark by each option. Ask children to count the marks to identify the most popular choice as a class.

The Magic Money Tree

1
Ravi lives with his mother in the city of Gulzar. Ravi's friend, Hamid, and his grandmother live there, too. There are no trees in their neighborhood. There is no park. The people of Gulzar don't have much.

2
One day, Ravi's mother looks in the kitchen cupboard. It's empty. At Hamid's house, the cupboard is empty, too.

3
Ravi and Hamid are playing. There's something on the path. "Money!" Hamid shouts. "Mine!" Ravi shouts. "No, mine!" says Hamid. Hamid's grandmother hears them. "Why are you fighting?" She grabs the coin. It falls into a crack in the ground. "Now we've lost the coin!" she says.

4
The next morning, Ravi looks out of the window. He sees a tree where the coin fell. Strange. Something is growing on the tree!

5
"Money!" exclaims Ravi. He runs and tells Hamid. "Look! There's a money tree." The boys pick the money off the tree.

6
Ravi and his mother buy eggs and chicken. They buy bread, potatoes, and melons. "We need chocolate and cake," says Ravi. "Yes," his mother says. "We have a lot of money now!"

7
But Hamid's grandmother puts the money in her money box. "Let's save this."

8
Every day, the boys get more money from the tree. Ravi's mother buys new dresses, and a bicycle for Ravi. But Hamid's grandmother just makes tomato soup for lunch every day, and puts more money into her money box.

9
Then, one day, the magic money tree dies.

10
The next day, Ravi's mother looks in the cupboard. No food! They go to Hamid's apartment. "We have no food, and the money tree is gone!"

11
"You can eat tomato soup with us," Hamid's grandmother says.

"Thank you," says Ravi's mother. Hamid's grandmother gets money from the money box and sends Hamid to buy bread. They all eat.

"This is good," says Ravi's mother.

"And I still have money in my money box!" says Hamid's grandmother.

Hamid has an idea. "Can I have these seeds, please?"

12
"We can still grow vegetables," says Hamid. "And we can use money from the money box to buy tools. We can build a garden for everyone."

Soon, there are a lot of vegetables. They sell the extra vegetables. Everyone has food to eat, and everyone is happy.

Lesson objectives: read and understand the modern fable *The Money Tree* in the Reader
Materials: Track 2.5; Reader

Warmer: Visualization

Have the children close their eyes and imagine they are Ravi or Hamid. Say *You're at home in your bedroom. What can you see? What can you hear? Now go outside to play. Who's there? What games do you play?* Have them open their eyes and share with a friend what they imagined.

Story Summary

Two poor boys, Ravi and Hamid, find a coin and a magic money tree grows from it. Ravi's family spends their money while Hamid's grandmother saves their money. The tree dies but Hamid's family helps Ravi's family by sharing their food. Together they grow food and help the community.

Value: Save for the future.

2.5 While reading

- Have the children look at the pictures in the Reader. Ask *What different food can you see? What are the people doing?*
- Play Track 2.5. The children listen and read along. Ask *Did they all have things to eat at the end?* (*yes*)
- Play Track 2.5 again. Ask questions to check comprehension, e.g. *Who did something clever with their coins?* (*Hamid's grandmother—she saved them*) *How do they use their money in the end?* (*to grow and sell vegetables*)

After reading: Reflect

- Ask questions to give the children the opportunity to think about the issues raised by the story, e.g. *Why does Hamid's grandmother save the money? Who do you think had the best ideas for the money? Why do we have to be careful about how we spend our money?*

Optional activity: My magic pen

Have the children imagine they find three magic coins. Ask *What would you do?* Elicit ideas, e.g. *buy something, go on a trip*, etc. Have the children draw three pictures and present them to the class.

Story Time

Distinguishing between voices

It is helpful for the children to distinguish between narration and dialogue within a story. Read aloud different phrases to the children and ask *Dialogue or narration?* This will help them better identify who is talking and what is happening in the story.

Reading Strategy

Summarizing

Summarizing is a very useful strategy for readers of all ages in every context. It helps them focus on the most important points of a story and look for the underlying message. It activates their critical reading skills and improves their memory.

For additional explanation and activities, see the Literacy Handbook on the Teacher Resource Center.

Cooler: Creativity

Have the children think of other things they would like to find growing on a tree outside their house. Write suggestions on the board. Have the children discuss with a friend their favorite titles for a new story. Elicit ideas, e.g. *The Magic Cell Phone Tree! The Magic Puppy Tree!*

Digital Resources

Reader eBook • Ask the children to recall their predictions for what is growing on the tree. Minimize the story. Ask *What's growing on the tree?* Show Picture 5. The children raise their hand as soon as they know the answer.

- Point to Pictures 6 and 7. Elicit what is happening in both. Ask *How does Ravi feel? How does Hamid feel? Why? Who do you agree with?* to elicit the different attitudes towards the money.

Reading Comprehension and Critical Literacy

Lesson objectives: focus on the use of speech marks for showing direct speech; reflect on the story theme and relate it to personal behavior
Materials: Track 2.5; Reader

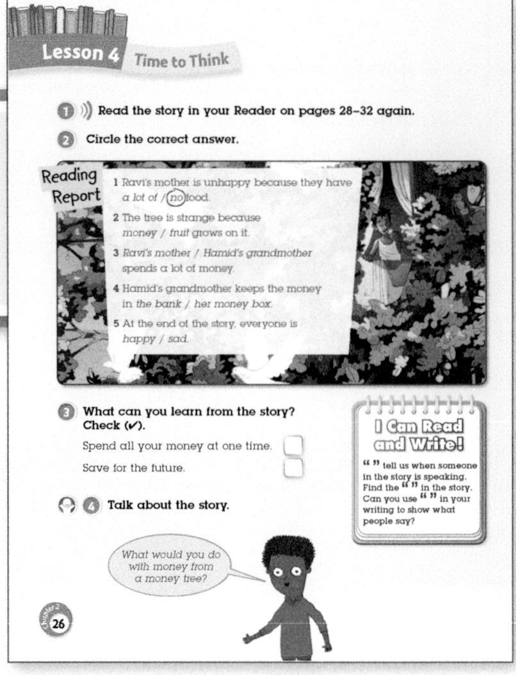

Lesson 4 Time to Think

1 Read the story in your Reader on pages 28–32 again.

2 Circle the correct answer.

Reading Report

1 Ravi's mother is unhappy because they have a lot of / no food.
2 The tree is strange because money / fruit grows on it.
3 Ravi's mother / Hamid's grandmother spends a lot of money.
4 Hamid's grandmother keeps the money in the bank / her money box.
5 At the end of the story, everyone is happy / sad.

3 What can you learn from the story? Check (✓).

Spend all your money at one time.
Save for the future.

4 Talk about the story.

I Can Read and Write!

" " tell us when someone in the story is speaking. Find the " " in the story. Can you use " " in your writing to show what people say?

Note: Please ensure that your class has read the Reader story before you do this lesson.

Warmer: Story extract review

Divide the class into small groups. Write *Ravi* and *Hamid* on the board. Give them three minutes to remember everything they can about the two characters. Elicit statements about them. Challenge the class to come up with seven or more facts between them.

1 2.5 Read the story in your Reader.

- Have the children read the story. (Alternatively, play Track 2.5 and have them read along.) Ask whether they were correct in their predictions in Lesson 3 Activity 4.
- Check comprehension by asking *What did Ravi's mother buy with the money? (a lot of food, dresses, a bicycle) Is everyone happy at the end of the story? (yes) Why? (Everyone has food to eat.)*

2 Circle the correct answer.

- Read out the example. Have the children circle the correct answer, referring to the story in their Reader as necessary. Alternatively, challenge them to remember the story without opening their Reader.
- Have them compare answers in pairs. Elicit answers.

Answers

1 no **2** money **3** Ravi's mother **4** her money box **5** happy

3 What can you learn from the story? Check (✓).

- Have the children read and choose one of the options. Elicit answers, including reasons why each idea is good or bad. Use the story to elicit suggestions.
- Ask *Do you save money? Where do you put it? How much do you save every week?*

Answer

Save for the future.

4 Talk about the story. 

- Have a child read out Jason's question. Ask *What would you do with money from a money tree?* Have the children discuss their ideas in small groups.
- Elicit answers and write them on the board. Find out the most common answer in class.

I Can Read!

Point out that speech marks are used when a character is talking in the story. Have the children take turns reading out text in speech marks from the story and identifying who says it.

Optional activity: Speech or story?

Have the children look back at the first story in the Reader (*You Have to Listen!*). Divide the class into pairs and have each child choose a short phrase to read to their friend. Their friend decides if it uses speech marks or not. They check in their Reader.

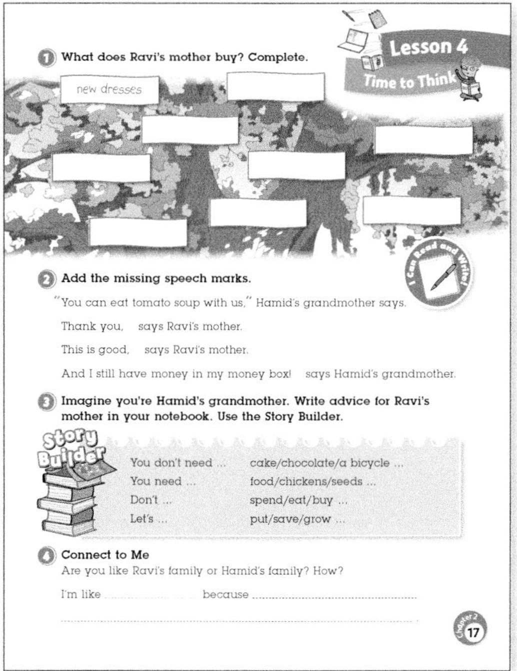
Lesson 4
Time to Think

1 What does Ravi's mother buy? Complete.

new dresses

2 Add the missing speech marks.

"You can eat tomato soup with us," Hamid's grandmother says.

Thank you, says Ravi's mother.

This is good, says Ravi's mother.

And I still have money in my money box! says Hamid's grandmother.

3 Imagine you're Hamid's grandmother. Write advice for Ravi's mother in your notebook. Use the Story Builder.

Story Builder

You don't need ...	cake/chocolate/a bicycle ...
You need ...	food/chickens/seeds ...
Don't ...	spend/eat/buy ...
Let's ...	put/save/grow ...

4 Connect to Me

Are you like Ravi's family or Hamid's family? How?

I'm like .... because ....

17

1 What does Ravi's mother buy? Complete.

The children write the items on the money tree, referring to their Reader as necessary. Elicit answers.

Answers

new dresses, eggs, chicken, bread, potatoes, melons, chocolate, cake, a bicycle

2 Add the missing speech marks.

The children practice the **I Can Read and Write!** feature by writing in the speech marks. Elicit answers, writing them on the board in the form *"You …* and *us."*

Answers

"You can eat tomato soup with us," Hamid's grandmother says.
"Thank you," says Ravi's mother.
"This is good," says Ravi's mother.
"And I still have money in my money box!" says Hamid's grandmother.

3 Imagine you're Hamid's grandmother. Write advice for Ravi's mother in your notebook. Use the Story Builder.

Use the **Story Builder** prompts to elicit ideas. The children write the advice in their notebook, then swap with a friend to check. Have children read out their advice for the class.

Answers

Children's own answers.

4 Connect to Me

Elicit ideas on how the children feel their family resembles Ravi's family or Hamid's family. The children write their own response, then compare with a friend. Elicit responses.

Answers

Children's own answers.

Cooler: Spot the mistakes

Read out the story to the children, but change some key words for a funny alternative, e.g. *Ravi lives with his dinosaur in the city of …* Have the children shout *Stop!* and tell you what the correct word should be.

Competency Focus

Me: Critical Literacy

The children use critical literacy skills to reflect on the story theme and discuss what they have learned about spending or saving money.

Digital Resources

Reader eBook • Display the Reader. Show one picture of the story at a time. Use this for a guided retelling of the story.

Student eBook, Digital Activity Book • TIP You can move the answer key pop-up window around the screen to have the activity and the answers side by side.

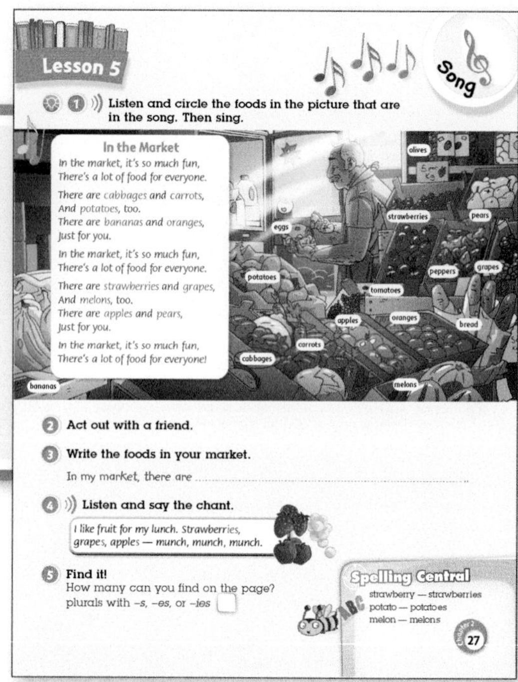

Lesson 5

Song

1 Listen and circle the foods in the picture that are in the song. Then sing.

In the Market

In the market, it's so much fun,
There's a lot of food for everyone.
There are cabbages and carrots,
And potatoes, too.
There are bananas and oranges,
Just for you.
In the market, it's so much fun,
There's a lot of food for everyone.
There are strawberries and grapes,
And melons, too.
There are apples and pears,
Just for you.
In the market, it's so much fun,
There's a lot of food for everyone!

2 Act out with a friend.

3 Write the foods in your market.

In my market, there are ……

4 Listen and say the chant.

I like fruit for my lunch. Strawberries, grapes, apples — munch, munch, munch.

5 Find it!
How many can you find on the page?
plurals with *–s, –es,* or *–ies* ☐

Spelling Central
strawberry — strawberries
potato — potatoes
melon — melons

Chapter 2 27

Vocabulary, Song, and Spelling

Lesson objectives: identify and talk about fruits and vegetables; practice spelling plural endings

Key vocabulary: *apples, bananas, cabbages, carrots, grapes, melons, oranges, pears, potatoes, strawberries*

Secondary language: *In my market, there's/there are …*

Materials: Tracks 2.6 and 2.7; pictures for Key vocabulary (Warmer ; Phonics Worksheet 2 [TRC] (optional)

Warmer: Pre-teach vocabulary

Pre-teach the vocabulary using pictures of the fruits and vegetables or draw pictures on the board. Show the pictures twice and have the children repeat. Then play a prediction game by showing the pictures in the same order to elicit what comes next.

1 2.6 Listen and circle the foods in the picture that are in the song. Then sing.

- Ask *What can you see in the picture? Where is this?* (*a market*) Play Track 2.6. Have the children listen and circle the foods in the picture. Elicit answers and check with the class.
- Play Track 2.6 again for the children to sing along.

Answers

cabbages, carrots, potatoes, bananas, oranges, strawberries, grapes, melons, apples, pears

2 Act out with a friend.

- Have two children read out the example in Activity 2. Ask *Who's speaking?* (*market vendor/customer*) Elicit some more questions and answers. (The children can invent prices.)
- The children ask and answer in pairs.

3 Write the foods in your market.

- Have the children write a list of the foods that they would like to sell in their market. You can make it more challenging by asking the children to add two more foods that are not on the page, or by asking them to write them in alphabetical order, which increases their attention to the written form.

Answer

Children's own answers.

Optional activity: Go shopping

Write on the board *cabbages, oranges, pears, potatoes.* Each child chooses one and writes it on a piece of paper. Choose four "shoppers." They mingle, asking the other children questions to find all the foods on the list, e.g. *Do you have cabbages?* If they find a child with the food, they take their paper. The winner is the first person to "buy" all the items on the list. Repeat using different shoppers and a different list.

Spelling Central

Plural endings

Write on the board *tomato, orange, cherry.* Write the plural endings *–ies, –es, –s* and elicit which to add for each word. Invite children to add them on the board. Elicit the spelling rules: *–y changes to –ies, –es is added after –o, and –s is added after –e.*

4 2.7 **Listen and say the chant.**

- Have the children look at the picture. Ask *What can you see?*
- Play Track 2.7. The children listen and read along. Elicit the plural words, monitoring pronunciation.
- Play Track 2.7 again, pausing for the children to repeat.

5 Find it!

- Set a time limit for the children to find words with different plural forms. Elicit answers.

Answers

12—foods, cabbages, carrots, bananas, oranges, grapes, melons, apples, pears; potatoes, tomatoes; strawberries

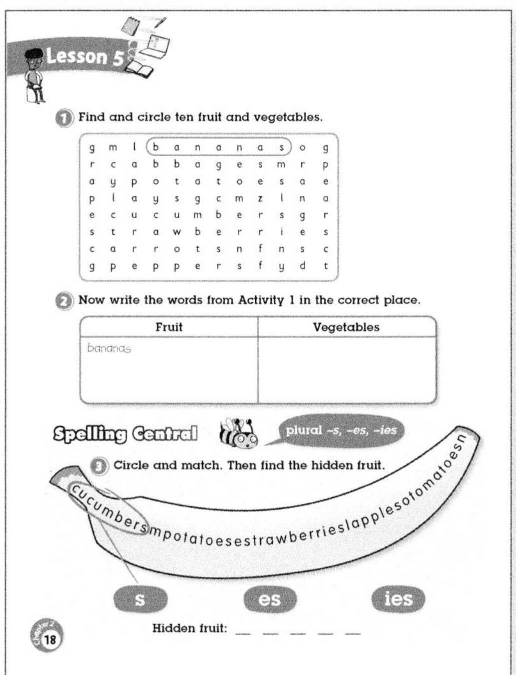

Lesson 5

1 Find and circle ten fruit and vegetables.

g	m	l	b	a	n	a	n	a	s	o	g
r	c	a	b	b	a	g	e	s	m	r	p
a	y	p	o	t	a	t	o	e	s	a	e
p	l	a	y	s	g	c	m	z	l	n	a
e	c	u	c	u	m	b	e	r	s	g	r
s	t	r	a	w	b	e	r	r	i	e	s
c	a	r	r	o	t	s	n	f	n	s	c
g	p	e	p	p	e	r	s	f	y	d	t

2 Now write the words from Activity 1 in the correct place.

Fruit	Vegetables
bananas	

Spelling Central — plural -s, -es, -ies

3 Circle and match. Then find the hidden fruit.

cucumbersmpotatoesestrawberrieslapplesotomatoesn

s es ies

Hidden fruit: _ _ _ _ _

18

1 Find and circle ten fruit and vegetables.

The children find and circle the fruit and vegetables, then compare with a friend.

Answers

Horizontal: bananas, cabbages, potatoes, cucumbers, strawberries, carrots, peppers

Vertical: grapes, oranges, pears

2 Now write the words from Activity 1 in the correct place.

The children write the words they circled in Activity 1 in the correct column. Elicit answers.

Answers

Fruit: bananas, strawberries, grapes, oranges, pears
Vegetables: cabbages, potatoes, cucumbers, carrots, peppers

3 Circle and match. Then find the hidden fruit.

The children circle the words and match them to the plural ending. Then they find the hidden fruit (using the letters not circled). Elicit answers.

Answers

–s: cucumbers, apples
–es: potatoes, tomatoes
–ies: strawberries
Hidden fruit: melon

Cooler: Sing the song together

2.6

Play the song again for the children to sing along.

Competency Focus

Think! Critical Thinking

The children use critical thinking skills to identify food items by processing the written and spoken forms.

Digital Resources

Student eBook • After SB Activity 2, choose the karaoke version of Music Video 2.1 (2.2) and encourage the children to dance and sing along, using the lyrics on screen. Associating movements with words makes them more memorable. Pause the video for the children to continue dancing and singing.

Teacher Resource Center • For phonics practice, print out Phonics Worksheet 2.

Lesson 6

1 Listen and read. What are the children doing?

The Surprise Party

2 Look at the story.

1 There are some .... grapes.
2 There .... strawberries.
3 .... any drinks?
4 .... some fruit.
5 There .... cookies.

Grammar Central

Are there any sandwiches?
There are some sandwiches.
There aren't any cookies.
Is there any fruit?
There is some fruit.
There isn't any cake.

Grammar Booster on page 33

28

Grammar and Reading

Lesson objectives: ask and answer about food using *some/any*

Key grammar: *Are there any (sandwiches)? There are some (sandwiches). There aren't any (cookies). Is there any (fruit)? There is some (fruit). There isn't any (cake).*

Secondary language: *I have …*

Materials: Track 2.8; Grammar Worksheet 2B [TRC printout] (optional)

Warmer: Play "Food Ping-Pong"

Divide the class into two teams. Any child can call out a food as a prompt. The other team has to respond with another food. If they repeat a food or take longer than five seconds, the other team wins a point. The team with the most points wins.

1 2.8 Listen and read. What are the children doing?

- Have the children look at the story. Ask *What are the children doing?* (*They're preparing for a party.*)
- Play Track 2.8. Ask *What day is it today?* (*Jason's birthday*)
- Play Track 2.8 again. The children listen and count the different food and drinks mentioned (there are 11: *sandwiches, turkey, tomato, fruit, strawberries, grapes, melon, apple juice, orange juice, cookies, cake*)
- Say *There is/There are* statements from the story for the children to repeat.

2 Look at the story.

- Have a child read the example. Elicit why *are some* is correct. (*because* grapes *is plural and the sentence is positive*)
- Have the children continue the activity, referring to the dialogue and completing the sentences. Elicit answers.

Answers

1 There are some grapes. **2** There are some strawberries. **3** Are there any drinks? **4** There is some fruit. **5** There aren't any cookies.

Grammar Central

Are there any sandwiches? …

Have the children look at the patterns. Ask *When do we use* any? (*in questions and negative statements*) Ask *When do we use* some? (*in positive statements, when we're talking about something you can't count*)

For extra practice, try the **Grammar Booster** section in the Student Book (p. 33–35).

Answers p. 33

Activity 1: **1** some **2** any **3** any **4** some **5** any **6** are some **7** aren't any **8** any **9** are some **10** aren't any

Activity 2: **1** Isn't any **2** are some **3** isn't any **4** there aren't any **5** there are some

Activity 3: Children's own examples.

p. 34

Activity 1: **1** There isn't **2** aren't any **3** there any **4** Is there **5** are **6** They're **7** How much

Activity 2: **1** Are there any grapes? **2** There are some grapes but there aren't any oranges. **3** There isn't any cake in the house. **4** How much are the apples? **5** How much is that turkey?

p. 35

Activity 1: **1** are **2** is **3** aren't **4** isn't **5** some **6** there **7** any **8** Are **9** much **10** are **11** can't **12** have

Activity 2: Children's own answers.

Optional activity: Draw and label

Have the children draw and label a table with their favorite food for a party. They work in pairs to ask and answer questions about the food, e.g. *Is there any ice cream? Yes, there is. Are there any pizzas? No, there aren't.* Then the children write some sentences about their party table. The drawings can be made into a wall display.

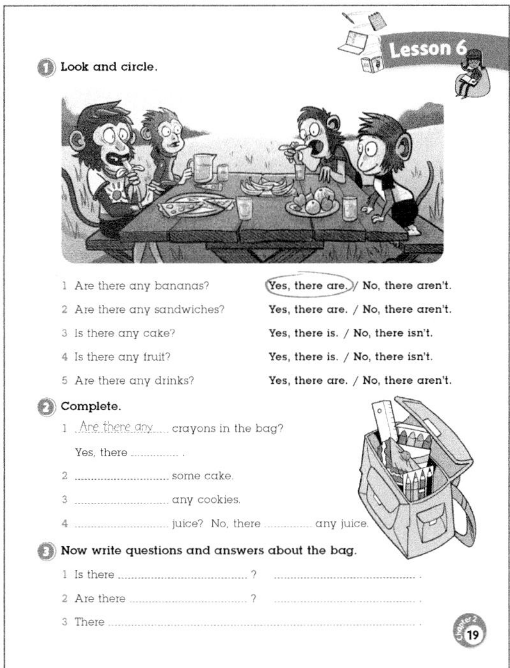

Lesson 6

1 Look and circle.

1 Are there any bananas? Yes, there are. / No, there aren't.
2 Are there any sandwiches? Yes, there are. / No, there aren't.
3 Is there any cake? Yes, there is. / No, there isn't.
4 Is there any fruit? Yes, there is. / No, there isn't.
5 Are there any drinks? Yes, there are. / No, there aren't.

2 Complete.

1 Are there any crayons in the bag? Yes, there ....
2 .... some cake.
3 .... any cookies.
4 .... juice? No, there .... any juice.

3 Now write questions and answers about the bag.

1 Is there .... ? ....
2 Are there .... ? ....
3 There ....

Chapter 2 19

1 Look and circle.

The children look at the picture and circle the correct answers. Elicit answers.

Answers

1 Yes, there are. **2** No, there aren't. **3** No, there isn't.
4 Yes, there is. **5** Yes, there are.

2 Complete.

The children complete the questions and answers, according to what they can see in the picture. Elicit answers by choosing children to read out a question and answer.

Answers

1 Are there any; are **2** There's **3** There aren't
4 Is there any; isn't

3 Now write questions and answers about the bag.

The children use the information in the picture to write more questions and answers. Elicit responses.

Answers

Children's own answers.

Cooler: Play "Ready, Set, Draw!"

Play "Ready, Set, Draw!" (see Games Bank p. 19) with food words from Chapter 2.

Ask the children to bring in any foreign coins or bills they have for the next lesson.

Competency Focus

Learn

The children demonstrate and consolidate their understanding of the new language by reading the text and completing the activity.

Digital Resources

Student eBook • Display the SB page on the board. Read through the Story Central story one picture at a time. Ask questions to check comprehension as you go.

Student eBook, Digital Activity Book • Use *Add personal note* to write yourself a reminder to tell the children to bring in foreign money for the AB It's My World! in the next lesson.

Teacher Resource Center • For extra grammar practice, print out Grammar Worksheet 2B.

CLIL: Math—At the market

Lesson objective: develop their math abilities with food prices
Materials: money from different countries (It's My World!); CLIL Graphic Organizer 2 [TRC printout] (optional)

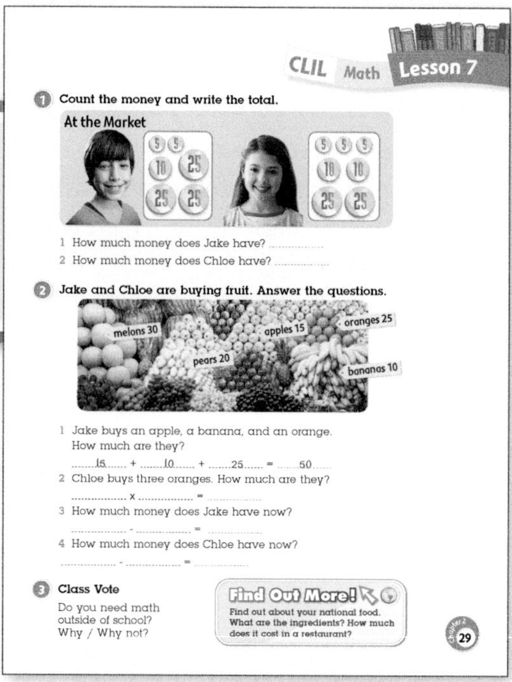
CLIL Math Lesson 7

1 Count the money and write the total.

At the Market

1 How much money does Jake have? ....
2 How much money does Chloe have? ....

2 Jake and Chloe are buying fruit. Answer the questions.

1 Jake buys an apple, a banana, and an orange. How much are they?
....15.... + ...10.... + ...25.... = ...50....
2 Chloe buys three oranges. How much are they?
.... x .... = ...
3 How much money does Jake have now?
.... - .... = ...
4 How much money does Chloe have now?
.... - .... = ...

3 Class Vote
Do you need math outside of school? Why / Why not?

Find Out More!
Find out about your national food. What are the ingredients? How much does it cost in a restaurant?

29

Warmer: Food math

Write the numbers 0 to 9 on the board and the math symbols for + (plus), – (minus), x (times), = (equals). Elicit a food name to write next to each number. Say *Now do some food math! Let's say 2 is banana, 6 is cake, and 8 is orange. What's banana plus cake? Orange!* If answers go into double figures, use two foods (so 26 is banana-cake!).

1 Count the money and write the total.

- Say *Jake and Chloe have some money to spend at the market.* Count Jake's money as a class. Use *plus* and *equals* to elicit the answer. The children write it down.
- Have the children total Chloe's money and write the answer. Elicit the answer using *plus* and *equals* again.

Answers

1 95 cents **2** 85 cents

2 Jake and Chloe are buying fruit. Answer the questions.

- Elicit the fruit in the picture and the prices, e.g. *Melons cost 30 cents.* Do the example with the class so the children can follow the math. You can use dollars as well as cents, if you want.
- Point out the math symbols in questions 2–4. The children work individually to write the numbers and answer the questions. Elicit answers.

Answers

1 50 cents **2** 75 cents **3** 45 cents **4** 10 cents

3 Class Vote

- Ask *Do you need math outside of school?* Elicit ideas, e.g. *when paying in a store, to count points when playing a game,* etc.
- Take a class vote by asking the children to move to one side of the class to vote yes, and to the other side to vote no. Count the votes and elicit children's reasons for voting the way they did. Remind the class that it is important to be able to explain the reasons for your opinions. (They might need to use L1.)

Find Out More!  

Elicit which national dish children are going to research, asking them to give reasons for their choice. Prompt as necessary. Suggest appropriate resources, e.g. Internet, recipe books, family, etc. The children will need to complete this research before doing the follow-up activity in the Activity Book. (It could be set as homework.)

Optional activity: More Math …

Use the prices from Activity 2 to set more math questions for the children, e.g. *Jake buys 2 apples, and 1 banana. How much are they? Chloe buys an orange and 2 bananas. How much are they?* The children can work together in small groups to find the answer. (They can write down their calculations.)

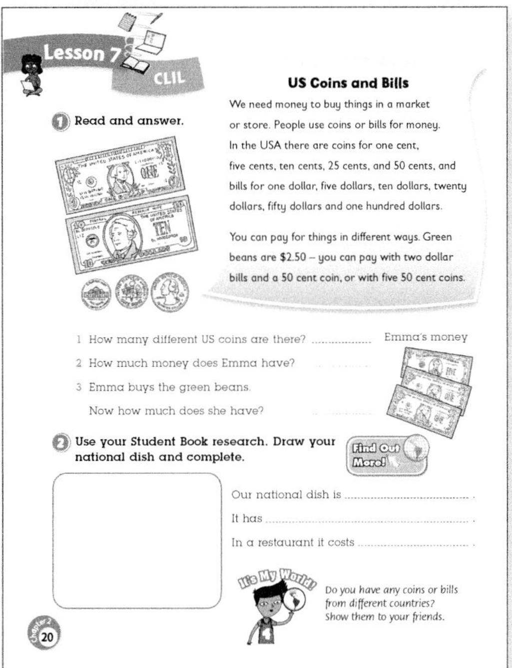
Lesson 7 CLIL

US Coins and Bills

1 Read and answer.

We need money to buy things in a market or store. People use coins or bills for money. In the USA there are coins for one cent, five cents, ten cents, 25 cents, and 50 cents, and bills for one dollar, five dollars, ten dollars, twenty dollars, fifty dollars and one hundred dollars.

You can pay for things in different ways. Green beans are \$2.50 – you can pay with two dollar bills and a 50 cent coin, or with five 50 cent coins.

1 How many different US coins are there? ....
2 How much money does Emma have? ....
3 Emma buys the green beans. Now how much does she have? ....

Emma's money

2 Use your Student Book research. Draw your national dish and complete.

Find Out More!

Our national dish is ....
It has ....
In a restaurant it costs ....

It's My World! Do you have any coins or bills from different countries? Show them to your friends.

Chapter 2 20

1 Read and answer.

The children look at the pictures of coins and bills. Ask *What numbers can you see?* Then they read the text and underline the different types of coins and bills. (*cents: 1, 5, 10, 25, 50; dollars: 1, 5, 10, 20, 100*) The children read the text again to answer the questions. Elicit answers.

Answers

1 5 **2** \$7.00 **3** \$4.50

2 Use your Student Book research. Draw your national dish and complete.

Divide the class into groups of four. Have the children pool the information learned from their research in the Student Book and the Activity Book. They draw their researched dish and complete the sentences individually. Have children show their drawings and read their sentences to the class.

Answers

Children's own answers.

It's My World!

Ask the children to show money from other countries or show them money you brought. Talk about where they are from and what they are worth in the children's own currency.

Cooler: Play "Fizz!"

Ask the children to stand up. Explain they will count around the class, with each child saying one number. But every multiple of 5 has to be replaced by the word *Fizz!* So the children will count *1, 2, 3, 4, Fizz!, 6, 7, 8, 9, Fizz!,* etc. Anyone who makes a mistake sits down. Repeat with different Fizz numbers, e.g. multiples of 3 or 4.

Competency Focus

Act

The children carry out research to find out about their national dishes. They relate what they learn to their world, both inside and outside the classroom.

Digital Resources

Student eBook • Use *Pen* to practice counting. Call out amounts using 5, 10, and 25 for children to write and calculate, e.g. *10 + 10 + 25 = (45).*

- TIP Set a time limit using *Timer* to make any activity more competitive and fun. Use it here for SB Activity 2.

Teacher Resource Center • Print out CLIL Graphic Organizer 2 for the children to use in collating their Find Out More! research.

CLIL eBook • The children can use the CLIL eBook to expand their knowledge of the lesson topic.

Project

Lesson objectives: review language from Chapter 2; make a money box; act out the story from the Reader

Materials: a snack container with plastic lid, scissors, tape, colored tissue, and other things to decorate; shoebox (alternative craft); two game pieces and a coin for each pair

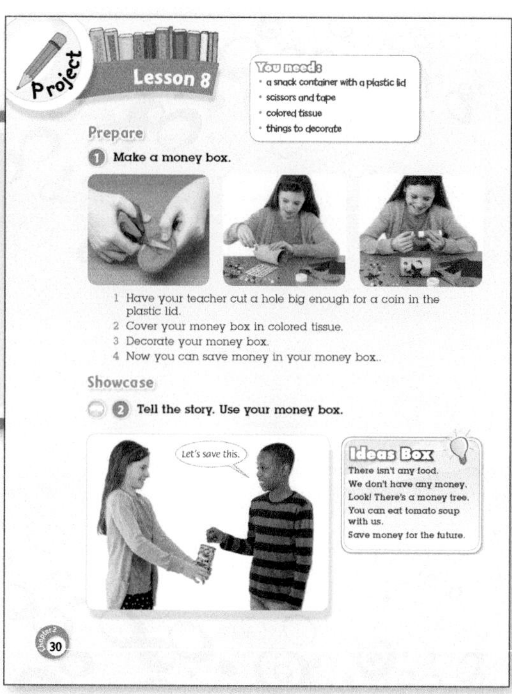
Project
Lesson 8

You need:
- a snack container with a plastic lid
- scissors and tape
- colored tissue
- things to decorate

Prepare

1 Make a money box.

1 Have your teacher cut a hole big enough for a coin in the plastic lid.
2 Cover your money box in colored tissue.
3 Decorate your money box.
4 Now you can save money in your money box..

Showcase

2 Tell the story. Use your money box.

Ideas Box
There isn't any food.
We don't have any money.
Look! There's a money tree.
You can eat tomato soup with us.
Save money for the future.

Chapter 2 30

Warmer: Play "Tic-Tac-Toe"

Play the game with *pepper, turkey, oranges, strawberries, sandwiches, juice, cookies, cabbage, cucumber* as oral prompts (see Games Bank p. 19). The children spell the word correctly to win the square.

Prepare

1 Make a money box.

- Distribute the materials. Read through the instructions together and ensure the children are clear on what to do.
- Have the children follow the instructions to make their money box. You will need to cut the coin hole for them. Give support as necessary.

Alternative craft activity

An easier project is to make a big vocabulary box for "saving" words. Give the children a shoebox (or similar container) to decorate. Then they write the vocabulary they can remember on separate slips of paper, and post the papers in the box. You can return to this box on a regular basis and use the words to remember the stories, or for spelling/drawing/mime games, etc.

Showcase 

2 Tell the story. Use your money box.

- Divide the class into groups of five: Ravi, Hamid, mother, grandmother, narrator. If the class does not divide exactly, extra children can share narration.
- Give the children five minutes to find the parts of the story in the Reader featuring the money box and practice, using the **Ideas Box** for support. If they made a money box in the craft activity, they can use this as a prop. Give support as necessary.
- Invite groups to perform their version for the class.

Optional activity: Saving for a purpose

Discuss with the class the concept of giving money to charity. (You might need to use L1.) Have the class make a class money box so that you can collect for a charity—agree with the class which charity they would like to support. You could then organize a dress-up day for charity, where the children dress up as their favorite story character and bring a small donation to put in the money box.

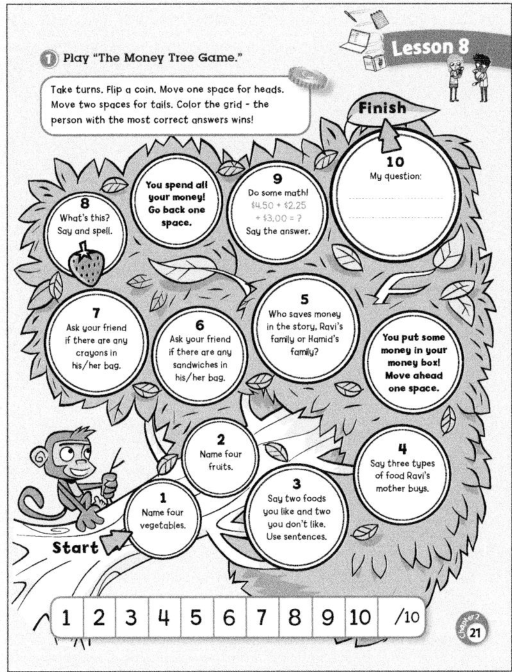

1 Play "The Money Tree Game."

See p. 43 for instructions on how to play the game.

Answers

1 potatoes, cabbages, cucumbers, peppers, etc. **2** bananas, grapes, pears, strawberries, etc. **3** I like + *2 foods*. I don't like + *2 foods*. **4** eggs, chicken, bread, etc. **5** Hamid's family **6** Are there any sandwiches in your schoolbag? **7** Are there any crayons in your schoolbag? **8** strawberry **9** $9.75 **10** Children's own answers.

Cooler: Play "Monkey!"

Divide the class into two teams (A and B), who stand up facing each other. Have the first child in Team A begin reading the story. When you shout *Monkey!*, the reading switches over to the first child on Team B. Continue in this way, shouting M*onkey!* at random points for the reading to switch.

Competency Focus

Collaborate and Communicate

By acting out the story, the children consolidate their understanding in a fun and engaging way. They also demonstrate their ability to work with friends and use interpersonal skills.

Digital Resources

Student eBook • Use *Timer* to give the children one minute to study the Ideas Box. Minimze the page. Elicit the sentences one at a time, asking different children to say the next word. Get class agreement before uncovering the line to confirm.

- TIP Show the pictures, stage by stage, as you talk the class through the activity process.

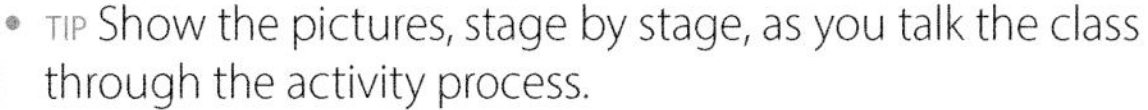

Language Review

Lesson objective: review language from Chapter 2
Materials: Tracks 2.9, AB 2.1 and AB 2.2

Review

1 Listen and complete the prices. Then write the total cost.

$2.00

Total

2 Complete with *some* or *any* and the correct form of the verb *to be*.

1 Come and buy! There is some .... healthy fruit.
2 .... there .... bananas?
3 No, sorry. There .... bananas.
4 There .... nice green apples.
5 .... there .... cheese?
6 No, sorry. There .... cheese — only fruit, vegetables, and bread.

3 Think about Chapter 2. Color and complete for you.

I'm not sure. OK! Got it!

My favorite page in Chapter 2 is ....

Treasure Hunt!

Look back at pages 4 and 5.

How much are the strawberries?

31

Warmer: Who said that?

Read out two phrases spoken by people in the chapter to elicit who said it (these can be from the story, from the dialogues in Lessons 3 and 6, Jason's questions, etc.). Then have the children continue the task in pairs, taking turns prompting and responding.

1 2.9 Listen and complete the prices. Then write the total cost.

- Have the children look at the picture in Activity 1 and say what they can see.
- Play Track 2.9 twice. The children listen and write the prices and total cost. Elicit answers.

Audioscript

Boy: *Come and buy! Healthy food. Carrots only $2.00. Freshly-baked bread. A lot of delicious fruit. Delicious apples – only $2.50!*
Woman: *How much are the strawberries, please?*
Boy: *They're $3.50.*
Woman: *OK. I need some strawberries. And how much are the melons?*
Boy: *They're $1.00 each.*
Woman: *OK. Two melons, please.*
Boy: *And how about vegetables? There are some nice onions—only $1.75, and some healthy cabbages—$1.25.*
Woman: *No, thank you, but I would like some bread. How much is the bread?*
Boy: *It's only $1.50.*
Woman: *OK, add that to my strawberries and melons, please. So, how much is it for the bread, the strawberries, and the two melons?*

Answers

carrots: $2.00, apples: $2.50, strawberries: $3.50, melons: $1.00, onions: $1.75, cabbages: $1.25, bread: $1.50, Total: $7.00

2 Complete with *some* or *any* and the correct form of the verb *to be*.

- The children complete the sentences.

Answers

1 is some **2** Are/any **3** aren't any **4** are some **5** Is/any **6** isn't any

3 Think about Chapter 2. Color and complete for you.

- Have the children look back at Chapter 2. Elicit their favorite parts. The children then color the circle which represents how they feel about their own progress (self-evaluation).
- Have the children complete the sentence.

Treasure Hunt!

Have the children look at pp. 4–5 to find out how much the strawberries cost. Elicit the answer. (*$1.00*)

Cooler: Play "Sentence Builders"

Play the game with four key sentences from the chapter (see Games Bank p. 19).

Competency Focus

Me: Self-evaluation

The children reflect on the chapter and express their opinions about their own progress.

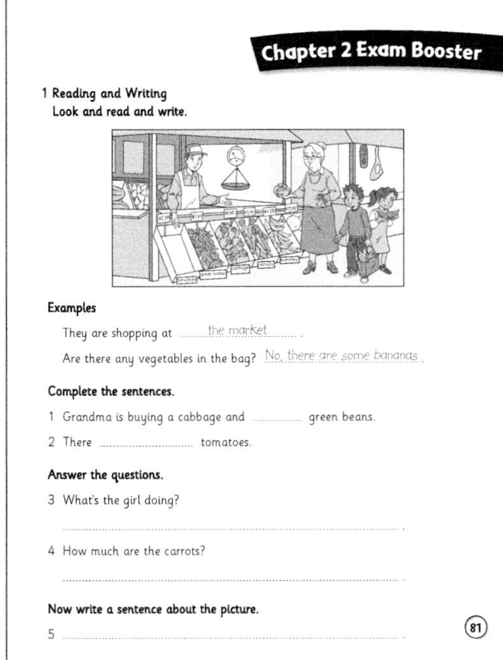

Chapter 2 Exam Booster

1 Reading and Writing
Look and read and write.

Examples

They are shopping at the market.

Are there any vegetables in the bag? No, there are some bananas.

Complete the sentences.

1 Grandma is buying a cabbage and .... green beans.

2 There .... tomatoes.

Answer the questions.

3 What's the girl doing?

4 How much are the carrots?

Now write a sentence about the picture.

5 ....

81

2 Listening
Listen and Write. There is one example.

Party

When is it? tomorrow

1 Number of people:

2 Kind of cake:

3 Price of cheese:

4 Fruit:

5 Total cost of shopping:

82

3 Listening
Listen and write. There is one example.

Banana Surprise

Number of people: eight

1 Recipe from: Mrs. ....

2 Fruit we need to buy:

3 The store is next to:

4 You have to wait for: .... minutes

5 How much is it:

Exam Tip
Don't panic if you miss a question. Follow the dialogue carefully when you hear it again.

83

1 Reading and Writing. Look and read and write.

The children use the picture to complete sentences and answer questions.

Answers

1 some **2** aren't any **3** She's eating watermelon. **4** $1.75, **5** Children's own answers

2))) AB 2.1 Listening. Listen and write. There is one example.

The children read the notice. Play Track AB 2.1 twice. They listen and write a single-word answer for each prompt. Check answers.

Answers (Audioscript on p. 222)

1 fifteen **2** apple **3** $1.25 **4** strawberries **5** $5.50

3))) AB 2.2 Listening. Listen and write. There is one example.

The children read the notice. Play Track AB 2.2 twice. They listen and write an answer for each prompt. Check answers.

Answers (Audioscript on p. 222)

1 Robinson **2** strawberries **3** the park **4** 30 **5** $4.50

Digital Resources

Student eBook • Display the SB page. Open the Welcome page to give feedback on Treasure Hunt. Ask a child to find and circle the price of the strawberries using *Pen*.

Teacher Resource Center • Print out Test Chapter 2 to use at the end of this lesson. The Test Generator also allows you to create customized tests.

• Print out Festival Worksheet: Halloween to expand the children's knowledge of celebrations throughout the world.

Chapter 3

Make Believe

Overview

The children will:

- use critical thinking skills to identify adjectives for feelings.
- describe people's feelings in the past using *was/weren't.*
- read, understand, and act out a story.
- talk about different types of performers.
- ask and answer questions about the past using *was/were.*
- find out about the history of the theater.
- make a string puppet.

Reading Skills

Story: *Coppelia*
Genre: traditional story based on a ballet

Literacy Development

- predict story content from title and pictures
- reflect on the theme of the story and compare it to similar stories
- focus on the use of *because* to explain detail in a story

Key Vocabulary

Adjectives of feeling:
angry, excited, happy, sad, scared, surprised, tired, worried
Entertainment and performers:
acrobat, actor, dancer, musician, puppet, singer

Functional Language

- I'm going to tell you a story.
- What's it about?
- It's about …

Key Grammar

- She was (tired).
- I wasn't (at home).
- They were (worried).
- My friends weren't (angry).
- When was the (show)?
- It was (last week).
- Who were the (singers)?
- Was he (good)? Yes, he was. / No, he wasn't.

Spelling

Endings for jobs *–or, –er*

CLIL: Performing Arts—The history of the theater

The children find out about the theater in Ancient Greece.

Competency Focus

The children will:

use critical thinking skills to identify adjectives of feeling. (Lesson 1) predict the content of a story. (Lesson 3) identify and talk about types of performers. (Lesson 5)	apply new grammar to previously learned vocabulary. (Lesson 2) ask and answer about past events. (Lesson 6)	work in threes to act out a dialogue. (Lesson 3) work in groups to act out the story. (Lesson 8)	use critical skills to reflect on the story and how it is similar to others they know. (Lesson 4) evaluate their own progress in the chapter. (Review)	develop cultural understanding by finding out about shadow plays. (Lesson 7)

Digital Overview

Teacher Presentation

Student eBook and Digital Activity Book

- Oral Storytelling Video 3.1: *Coppelia*
- Interactive versions of AB activities
- Integrated audio and answer key for all activities

Teacher resources for planning, lesson delivery, and homework

Teacher Resource Center

- Class Planner Chapter 3
- Worksheets to print out (including notes and answers):
  - Grammar Worksheet 3A: She was.... I wasn't.../They were/ weren't...
  - Grammar Worksheet 3B: When was ...? It was ...
  - Oral Storytelling Video Worksheet 3: *Coppelia*
  - Phonics Worksheet 3
  - CLIL Graphic Organizer 3
  - Festival Worksheet: Christmas
  - Test Chapter 3
- Test Generator
- Speaking Assessment: Cambridge English Young Learners Exams

Watch the Oral Storytelling Video

- Literacy Handbook

Children's resources for learning and practicing at home

Student eBook and Reader eBook

- Oral Storytelling Video 3.1: *Coppelia*

The Inks Student's App

Vocabulary games: Adjectives of feeling and entertainment and performers

Chapter 3

Make Believe

Lesson 1

Vocabulary

Lesson objective: identify and use adjectives for feelings
Key vocabulary: *angry, excited, happy, sad, scared, surprised, tired, worried*
Materials: Track 3.1

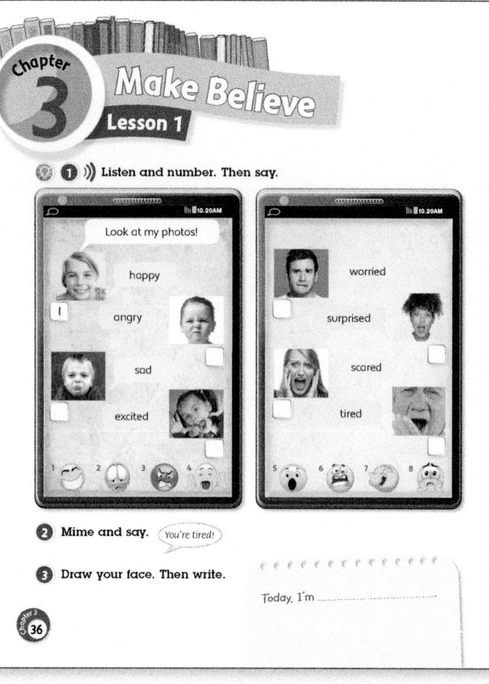

Warmer: Talk about photos

Tell the children about the last photo that you took. Say where it was and why, and how you felt. Repeat with the last photo that someone took of you. Have the children talk about the same topics in pairs.

1 3.1 Listen and number. Then say. 

- Have the children look at the pictures. Ask *What are they?* (*cell phones*) *What are the people sending?* (*photos*)
- Play Track 3.1. The children listen and find each emotion. They number the emotions using the emoticons pictured.
- Play Track 3.1 again, pausing after each emotion for the children to point and repeat.

Audioscript

Girl: *Look at my photos. This is me in the first photo. I'm happy. I'm playing computer games!*
Boy: *Cool. Use the happy face. Look at my photo. This is my little sister. She's really angry. Mom is telling her to go to bed.*
Girl: *OK, so use the angry face then. Look, my baby brother is sad right now. He's crying.*
Boy: *Oh, no! Use the sad face. But look at this picture of my friend. She's excited about the school trip. I'm going to use the excited face!*
Girl: *And look at my big brother. I think he's worried about his tests.*
Boy: *Hey, look at my mom at her birthday party. She was really surprised.*
Girl: *And look at my grandma. She's scared of Tom!*
Boy: *And my grandpa is very tired. Look, he's yawning.*

Answers

happy 1, angry 3, sad 2, excited 4, worried 8, surprised 5, scared 6, tired 7

2 Mime and say.

- Pass your hands in front of your face (top to bottom and/or bottom to top) and change expression while your hands cover your face. Ask the children to call out the emotion you mime each time.
- Have the children continue this game in pairs.

3 Draw your face. Then write.

- Draw a happy and a tired emoticon on the board and elicit *happy* and *tired.* Write *Today, I'm … and …*
- Have the children describe their own emotions by drawing and writing about two emoticons in their notebook. Have them show and talk about their drawings in small groups. Encourage careful listening by having the class respond *Me, too!* or *Not me!*

Answers

Children's own answers.

Optional activity: Show your emotions!

Have one child make a series of emotion expressions quickly, one after the other, while their friend tries to copy them. Both children call out the emotion. The first one to laugh loses!

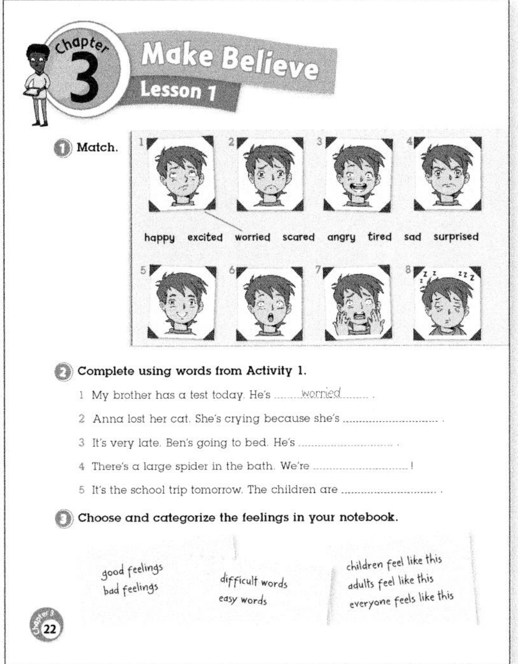
Chapter 3 Make Believe
Lesson 1

1 Match.

happy excited worried scared angry tired sad surprised

2 Complete using words from Activity 1.

1 My brother has a test today. He's ......worried...... .
2 Anna lost her cat. She's crying because she's ....
3 It's very late. Ben's going to bed. He's ....
4 There's a large spider in the bath. We're .... !
5 It's the school trip tomorrow. The children are ....

3 Choose and categorize the feelings in your notebook.

good feelings
bad feelings

difficult words
easy words

children feel like this
adults feel like this
everyone feels like this

22

1 Match.

The children match the pictures to the words. Elicit answers.

Answers

1 happy **2** sad **3** excited **4** angry **5** worried **6** surprised **7** scared **8** tired

2 Complete using words from Activity 1.

The children complete the sentences with words from Activity 1. Elicit answers.

Answers

1 worried **2** sad **3** tired **4** scared **5** excited

3 Choose and categorize the feelings in your notebook.

Elicit an example for each category listed. Ask *Which categories would you choose?* Elicit ideas, prompting children to give a reason for their choice. The children choose a pair of categories and list the words in their notebook, then compare with a friend.

Answers

Children's own answers.

Cooler: How do you feel?

Divide the class into pairs. The children take turns drawing an emoticon in their notebook and identifying the emotion expressed.

Ask the children to bring photos of their family to talk about in the next lesson.

Competency Focus

Think! Critical Thinking

The children use critical thinking skills to identify adjectives for feelings by using visual clues and processing the written and spoken forms.

Digital Resources

Digital Activity Book • Ask children to do the AB interactive digital activities or set them for homework.

Grammar

Lesson objective: talk about the past using *was/were*
Key grammar: *She was (tired). I wasn't (at home). They were (worried). My friends weren't (angry).*
Secondary language: *on stage, school play*
Materials: Track 3.2; pictures of your family and the children's families (Student Book Activity 3); Grammar Worksheet 3A [TRC printout] (optional)

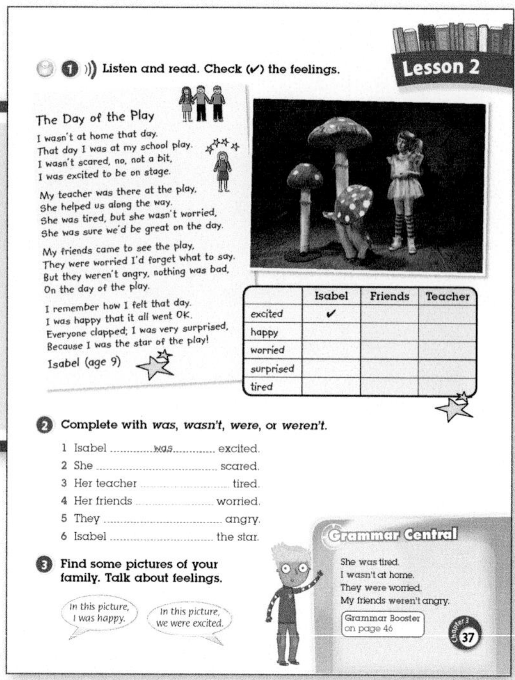

Lesson 2

1 Listen and read. Check (✔) the feelings.

The Day of the Play

I wasn't at home that day.
That day I was at my school play.
I wasn't scared, no, not a bit,
I was excited to be on stage.

My teacher was there at the play,
She helped us along the way.
She was tired, but she wasn't worried,
She was sure we'd be great on the day.

My friends came to see the play,
They were worried I'd forget what to say.
But they weren't angry, nothing was bad,
On the day of the play.

I remember how I felt that day.
I was happy that it all went OK.
Everyone clapped; I was very surprised,
Because I was the star of the play!

Isabel (age 9)

	Isabel	Friends	Teacher
excited	✔		
happy			
worried			
surprised			
tired			

2 Complete with *was, wasn't, were,* or *weren't.*

1 Isabel ......was...... excited.
2 She .... scared.
3 Her teacher .... tired.
4 Her friends .... worried.
5 They .... angry.
6 Isabel .... the star.

3 Find some pictures of your family. Talk about feelings.

Grammar Central

She was tired.
I wasn't at home.
They were worried.
My friends weren't angry.

Grammar Booster on page 46

Chapter 3 37

Warmer: Scrambled words

Write scrambled versions of the emotion words from Lesson 1 on the board. As soon as a child knows an answer, have them write it on the board. Ask different children to draw faces or emoticons next to the words.

1 3.2 Listen and read. Check (✔) the feelings.

- Have the children look at the picture and ask *Where is the girl? What's happening?* Elicit that the text is a poem.
- Read through the names and the feelings in the table. Play Track 3.2 twice. Have the children read along and check the correct boxes in the table. They compare answers in pairs. Elicit answers.

Answers

Isabel: excited, happy, surprised
Friends: worried
Teacher: tired

2 Complete with was, wasn't, were, or weren't.

- Have a child read the example out loud. The children refer to the poem and complete the sentences with *was/wasn't* and *were/weren't.*
- Nominate children to read out sentences.

Answers

1 was **2** wasn't **3** was **4** were **5** weren't **6** was

Grammar Central

She was tired. …

Have the children look at the patterns. Ask *Do these sentences talk about the present or the past?* (*past*) Elicit the equivalent of *was/wasn't* and *were/weren't* in the present. (*is/isn't* and *are/aren't*) Read the sentences aloud and have the children repeat. Pay particular attention to the weaker sound of *was/wasn't* and *were/weren't.*

For extra practice, try the **Grammar Booster** section in the Student Book (p. 46).

Answers p. 46

Activity 1: **1** was **2** wasn't **3** were **4** weren't **5** was **6** wasn't **7** were **8** weren't

Activity 2: **1** weren't **2** were **3** were **4** wasn't **5** was **6** were **7** wasn't **8** was

Activity 3: Children's own answers.

3 Find some pictures of your family. Talk about feelings.

- Have the children show the family photos they brought.
- Show a photo of yours and ask *How does this person feel?* Confirm and give a reason, e.g. *Yes, in this picture I was happy. It was my birthday!* Have the children talk about their photos in pairs/groups. Monitor and help as necessary.

Optional activity: Remember emotions

Ask the children to remember a time when they felt *happy/ surprised/angry/worried*, etc. Have them draw a picture of the occasion and label it with a sentence or two, e.g. *I was at the zoo. I was scared!* These can be used to make an Emotions wall display.

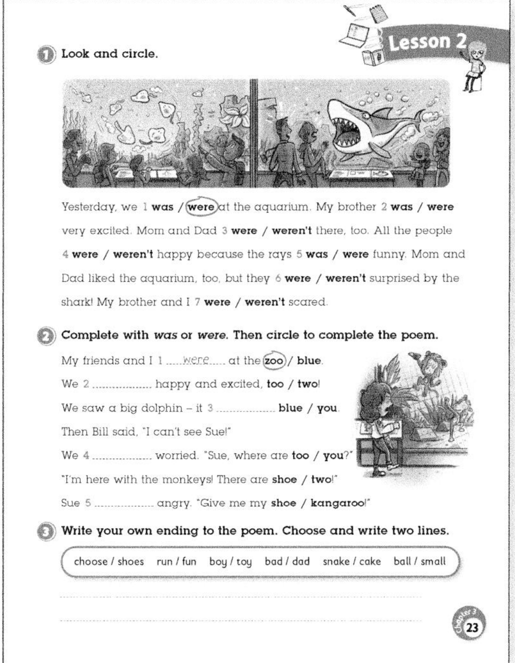

Lesson 2

1 Look and circle.

Yesterday, we 1 **was** / **were** at the aquarium. My brother 2 **was** / **were** very excited. Mom and Dad 3 **were** / **weren't** there, too. All the people 4 **were** / **weren't** happy because the rays 5 **was** / **were** funny. Mom and Dad liked the aquarium, too, but they 6 **were** / **weren't** surprised by the shark! My brother and I 7 **were** / **weren't** scared.

2 Complete with *was* or *were*. Then circle to complete the poem.

My friends and I 1 ......were...... at the **zoo** / **blue**.
We 2 .... happy and excited, **too** / **two**!
We saw a big dolphin – it 3 .... **blue** / **you**.
Then Bill said, "I can't see Sue!"
We 4 .... worried. "Sue, where are **too** / **you**?"
"I'm here with the monkeys! There are **shoe** / **two**!"
Sue 5 .... angry. "Give me my **shoe** / **kangaroo**!"

3 Write your own ending to the poem. Choose and write two lines.

choose / shoes run / fun boy / toy bad / dad snake / cake ball / small

Chapter 3 23

1 Look and circle.

The children look at the picture and complete the text by circling the correct option in each pair. Elicit answers.

Answers

1 were **2** was **3** were **4** were **5** were **6** were **7** weren't

2 Complete with was or were. Then circle to complete the poem.

The children fill in the blanks with *was* or *were*. Then they circle the correct words to complete the poem.
Elicit answers.

Answers

1 were **2** were **3** was **4** were **5** was
Circled words: zoo, too, blue, you, two, shoe

3 Write your own ending to the poem. Choose and write two lines.

The children work in pairs to write an ending to the poem. Monitor and help as necessary. Elicit responses.

Answers (suggested)

Run, little monkey, run, run, run! / Monkeys have a lot of fun!
Next to Sue there was a boy. / The monkey's friend took his toy!.

Cooler: Read aloud chain

Have the children read out the poem from Student Book Activity 1—one line each around the class. The first time it is difficult to make it sound natural, but with a little practice they can make it sound more fluent!

Competency Focus

Learn

The children use previously acquired vocabulary in a different context with new grammatical structures.

Digital Resources

Student eBook • Use *Pen* for the Warmer activity.

Teacher Resource Center • For extra grammar practice, print out Grammar Worksheet 3A.

Reading: Story Extract

Lesson objectives: offer to tell a story and ask what it's about; predict story content from title and pictures; read the extract from *Coppelia* (beginning)
Functional language: *I'm going to tell you a story. What's it about? It's about …*
Secondary language: *alive, pretend*
Materials: Tracks 3.3 and 3.4

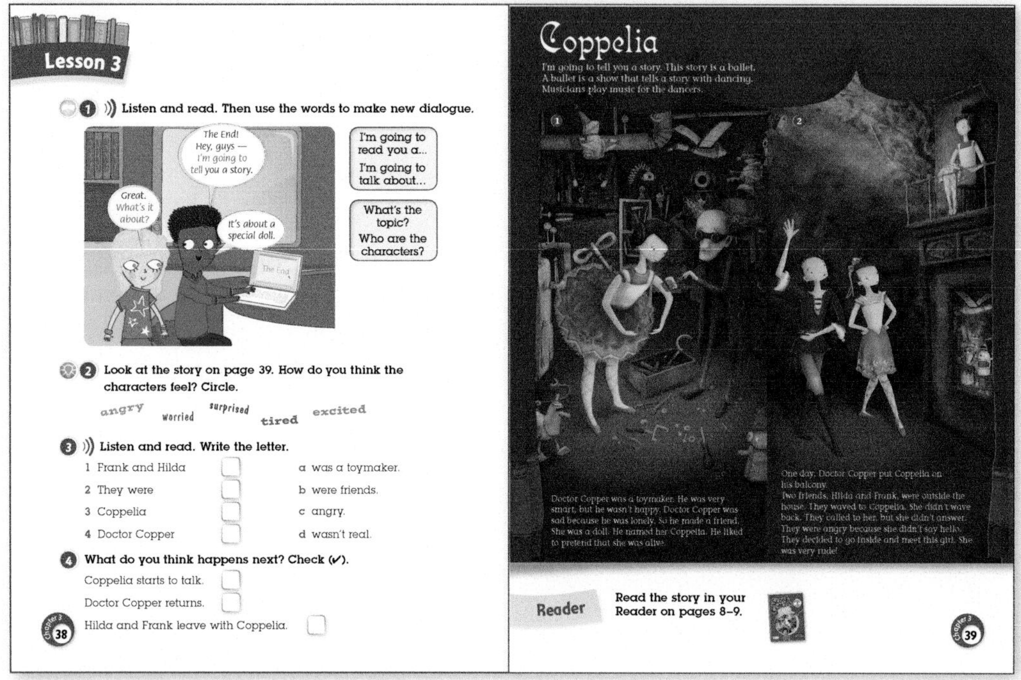

Lesson 3

1 Listen and read. Then use the words to make new dialogue.

2 Look at the story on page 39. How do you think the characters feel? Circle.

angry worried surprised tired excited

3 Listen and read. Write the letter.

1 Frank and Hilda ☐ a was a toymaker.
2 They were ☐ b were friends.
3 Coppelia ☐ c angry.
4 Doctor Copper ☐ d wasn't real.

4 What do you think happens next? Check (✓).

Coppelia starts to talk. ☐
Doctor Copper returns. ☐
Hilda and Frank leave with Coppelia. ☐

Chapter 3 38

Coppelia

I'm going to tell you a story. This story is a ballet. A ballet is a show that tells a story with dancing. Musicians play music for the dancers.

1 Doctor Copper was a toymaker. He was very smart, but he wasn't happy. Doctor Copper was sad because he was lonely. So he made a friend. She was a doll. He named her Coppelia. He liked to pretend that she was alive.

2 One day, Doctor Copper put Coppelia on his balcony. Two friends, Hilda and Frank, were outside the house. They waved to Coppelia. She didn't wave back. They called to her, but she didn't answer. They were angry because she didn't say hello. They decided to go inside and meet this girl. She was very rude!

Reader Read the story in your Reader on pages 8–9.

Chapter 3 39

Warmer: Ballet dancing

Ask the children if they have been to see a ballet or watched one on TV. Ask *What do we call the women and girls who dance?* (*ballerinas*) *What kind of stories do ballets tell?* (*all different kinds*) Ask *Would you like to be a dancer? Why?/Why not?* Elicit opinions.

1 3.3 Listen and read. Then use the words to make new dialogue.

- Have the children look at the pictures and ask *Who's using a computer?* (*Jason*) *What's he going to do?* (*tell them a story*)
- Play Track 3.3. The children listen and read along.
- Play Track 3.3 again, pausing for the children to repeat.
- The children practice the dialogue in threes, substituting different story topics and opinions. (e.g. *fantastic/boring*).

Before reading

2 Look at the story on page 39. How do you think the characters feel? Circle.

- Have the children look at the title and pictures and circle the adjectives describing how the characters feel. Elicit answers with reasons. (They might need to use L1.)

3 3.4 Listen and read. Write the letter.

- Play Track 3.4. The children listen and read along. Then they write the letter of the correct ending for each sentence opening. Elicit answers.
- Ask questions to check comprehension: *How do you know Coppelia is important in the story?* (*Coppelia is the story title.*) *Is Coppelia a real girl?* (*No, she's a doll.*) *Do the children know she's a doll?* (*No. They think she's a rude girl.*)

Answers

1 b **2** c **3** d **4** a

4 What do you think happens next? Check (✔).

- Have the children check their prediction. Elicit ideas including reasons, but do not confirm. Say they will have to read the story to find out.

Answers

Children's own answers.

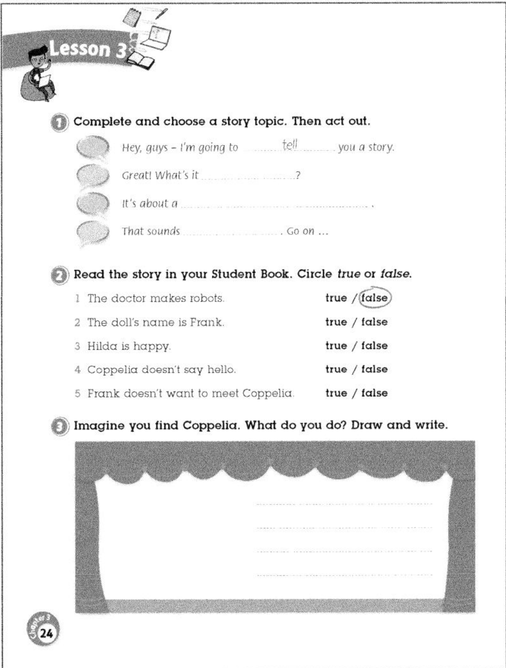

Lesson 3

1 Complete and choose a story topic. Then act out.

Hey, guys – I'm going to tell you a story.

Great! What's it ______ ?

It's about a ______ .

That sounds ______ . Go on …

2 Read the story in your Student Book. Circle *true* or *false*.

1	The doctor makes robots.	true / (false)
2	The doll's name is Frank.	true / false
3	Hilda is happy.	true / false
4	Coppelia doesn't say hello.	true / false
5	Frank doesn't want to meet Coppelia.	true / false

3 Imagine you find Coppelia. What do you do? Draw and write.

Chapter 3 24

1 Complete and choose a story topic. Then act out.

The children complete the dialogue, adding their own story ideas. They practice their dialogues in pairs. Have pairs act out for the class.

Answers

1 tell **2** about **3** children's own answer **4** good/great

2 Read the story in your Student Book. Circle true or false.

Read the example and elicit why the answer is false. (*He makes toys/dolls.*) The children read the Student Book story extract again, then circle *true* or *false* for each sentence. Elicit answers, including the correct versions of the false statements.

Answers

1 false **2** false **3** false **4** true **5** false

3 Imagine you find Coppelia. What do you do? Draw and write.

Elicit ideas on what they do when they find Coppelia. (They may need L1 to explain their ideas at this point. You can give some useful vocabulary on the board.) The children then draw a scene and write about it. Have them show each other in pairs or small groups.

Answers

Children's own answers.

Cooler: Don't be rude!

Pick up on one of the topics of the story: being rude. Write *Don't be rude!* on the board. Elicit words/phrases in English that are very polite, e.g. *Thank you. …, please. Excuse me. I'm sorry. May I (go to the bathroom)? Could I borrow your …?*, etc. Say for the children to repeat. Encourage them to use these expressions as often as possible.

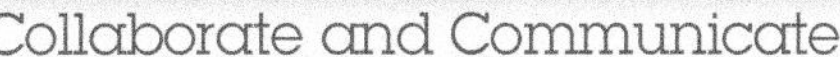

Competency Focus

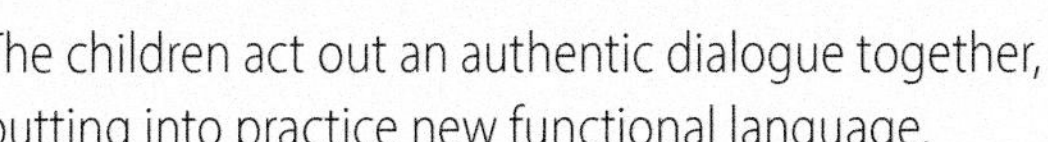

Collaborate and Communicate

The children act out an authentic dialogue together, putting into practice new functional language.

Think! Critical Thinking

The children apply reading skills (exploiting pictures and text clues) to understand the story characters.

Digital Resources

Student eBook, Digital Activity Book, Reader eBook • Do not be afraid to turn off the screen! Children benefit from variety of pace and focus and sometimes you will want to work just with books or without prompts. Work the digital materials into your teaching in the way that suits you best.

Student eBook • Show Picture 1 in the SB story extract. Ask *What can you see?* Encourage the children to use the detail in the picture to figure out the context of the story.

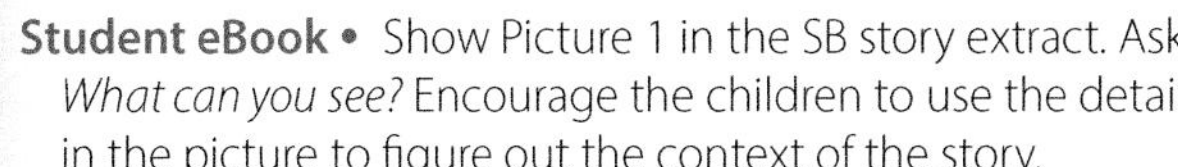

Coppelia

1
I'm going to tell you a story. This story is a ballet. A ballet is a show that tells a story with dancing. Musicians play music for the dancers.

Doctor Copper was a toymaker. He was very smart, but he wasn't happy. Doctor Copper was sad because he was lonely. So he made a friend. She was a doll. He named her Coppelia. He liked to pretend that she was alive.

2
One day, Doctor Copper put Coppelia on his balcony. Two friends, Hilda and Frank, were outside the house. They waved to Coppelia. She didn't wave back. They called to her, but she didn't answer. They were angry because she didn't say hello. They decided to go inside and meet this girl. She was very rude!

3
Inside the workshop, Hilda and Frank saw Coppelia. Why was she so still? Hilda touched Coppelia. She was very surprised because Coppelia wasn't real. She was a doll.

4
Then, Frank and Hilda heard a noise. Someone was coming. They were worried. They looked for a place to hide. Frank stepped into a box, but there was no room for Hilda. She had an idea. She moved Coppelia, and sat in the doll's chair.

5
Doctor Copper came into the workshop. He turned on a special box. It was a magical machine. Doctor Copper was excited. He wanted the machine to bring Coppelia to life. The machine started working but Frank was inside!

6
Doctor Copper was very excited about his doll. He pressed the button on his machine. Now, he could bring his doll to life. Hilda saw what Doctor Copper was doing. She pretended to be the doll. She danced for Doctor Copper. Doctor Copper was very happy because he thought his doll was alive.

7
Hilda danced over to the machine and opened it. Frank was confused. Was Hilda the doll? No, she wasn't. The doll was on the floor, but Hilda was pretending to be the doll. Frank quickly got out of the machine.

8
Hilda and Frank ran away from the workshop. Doctor Copper chased them down the street, but they escaped.

Lesson objectives: read and understand the traditional story based on a ballet *Coppelia* in the Reader
Materials: Track 3.5; Reader; Oral Storytelling Video Worksheet 3 [TRC printout] (optional)

Warmer: Dance activities

Point out to the children that in a ballet, the actions are done in dance. Call out some activities for the children to "dance." Say e.g. *Cook like a dancer!* and mime cooking with the children, along with dancing movements. The children suggest other actions for the class to do in this way.

Story Summary

Doctor Copper, a lonely toymaker, makes a dancing doll, Coppelia. He pretends that she is alive. Two children, Hilda and Frank, want to meet Coppelia. Frank hides in a machine used to bring Coppelia to life and Hilda pretends to be Coppelia. Doctor Copper is angry and the children escape.

Value: Friends are important. 

3.5 While reading

- Have the children look at the pictures in the Reader. Ask *What activities can you see? How do the people feel?*
- Play Track 3.5. The children listen and read along. Ask *Does Coppelia really come to life?* (*no*)
- Play Track 3.5 again. Ask questions to check comprehension, e.g. *How did Hilda find out Coppelia was a doll?* (*She touched her.*) *Why did Hilda pretend she was Coppelia?* (*because she was afraid of Doctor Copper*) *Why was Frank confused?* (*because Hilda looked like the doll*)

After reading: Reflect

- Ask questions to give the children the opportunity to think about the issues raised by the story, e.g. *Why did Doctor Copper make Coppelia? Were Hilda and Frank trying to be nice to Coppelia? How did Doctor Copper feel at the end?*

Optional activity: Reading aloud

- This story is ideal for the children to practice reading aloud. Have the children read it out, one sentence each, around the class. Help with pronunciation as necessary.

Story Time

Exploiting the visuals

A story like this one with little or no dialogue is ideal for telling the children in a circle or group around you on the floor. When there is no dialogue, you can ask a lot of questions without interrupting the story. Ask questions about the pictures: names, activities, colors, feelings, what happens next, etc. The children will feel more involved with the story.

Reading Strategy

Story Map

Using a story map helps the children identify the characters of a story and the parts of the plot, and the setting, problem, and solution. A basic story map focuses on the main parts of the story (beginning, middle, and end).

For additional explanation and activities, see the Literacy Handbook on the Teacher Resource Center.

Cooler: A happy ending?

Ask the children if they think the story has a happy ending for everyone. (*No. Doctor Copper seems sad and/or angry.*) Ask the children for ideas for a happier ending, so that everyone is happy.

Digital Resources

Reader eBook • Before the children read the story, show Reader Picture 6. *Ask, What's happening? Who's dancing? What's on the floor? Where's Frank?*

• Oral Storytelling Video 3.1 gives the story with a different ending. Watch it together at the end of the lesson, then discuss the differences.

Teacher Resource Center • Print out Oral Storytelling Video Worksheet 3 to get the most out of the video.

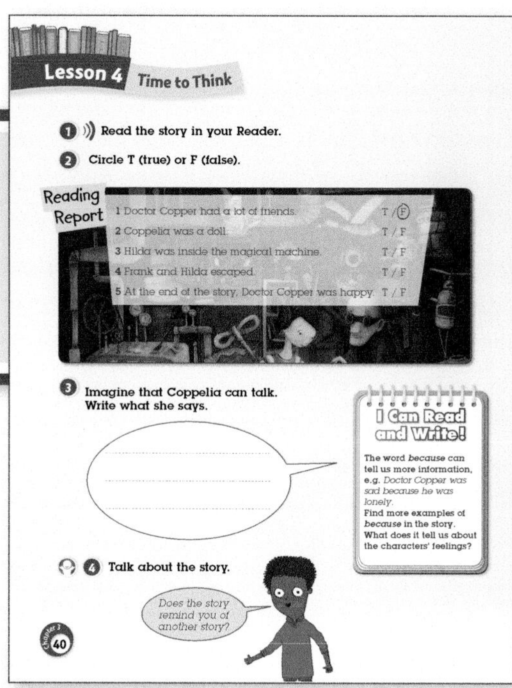

Lesson 4 Time to Think

1 Read the story in your Reader.

2 Circle T (true) or F (false).

Reading Report

1 Doctor Copper had a lot of friends. T / (F)
2 Coppelia was a doll. T / F
3 Hilda was inside the magical machine. T / F
4 Frank and Hilda escaped. T / F
5 At the end of the story, Doctor Copper was happy. T / F

3 Imagine that Coppelia can talk. Write what she says.

I Can Read and Write!

The word *because* can tell us more information, e.g. *Doctor Copper was sad because he was lonely.*
Find more examples of *because* in the story. What does it tell us about the characters' feelings?

4 Talk about the story.

Does the story remind you of another story?

Chapter 3 40

Reading Comprehension and Critical Literacy

Lesson objectives: focus on the use of the word *because* to explain detail in a story; reflect on the story theme and compare it to other similar stories
Materials: Track 3.5; Reader; Oral Storytelling Video Worksheet 3 [TRC printout] (optional)

Note: Please ensure that your class has read the Reader story before you do this lesson.

Warmer: Character review

Write *Doctor Copper, Frank, Hilda,* and *Coppelia* on the board. Give the children two minutes in pairs to brainstorm three words for each one.

1 3.5 Read the story in your Reader.

- Have the children read the story. (Alternatively, play Track 3.5 and have them read along). Elicit whether they were correct in their predictions in Lesson 3 Activity 4.
- Check comprehension by asking *What did Hilda do? (She danced and pretended to be Coppelia.) What did Hilda and Frank do at the end? (They ran away.)*

2 Circle T (true) or F (false).

- Read sentence 1 and elicit why it is false. (*because the story says he was lonely*)
- The children circle T (true) or F (false) for each sentence.
- Elicit answers, including the correct versions of false sentences.

Answers

1 F **2** T **3** F **4** T **5** F

3 Imagine that Coppelia can talk. Write what she says.

- Give the children some help in getting started by writing on the board some beginnings of phrases that Coppelia might say: *Hello, … / I'm a … / Please … / I can …,* etc. Elicit some ideas.
- The children complete the speech bubble. Monitor and help as necessary. Have them compare in pairs. Elicit answers and check with the class.

Answers

Children's own answers.

4 Talk about the story. 

- Have one child read out Jason's question: *Does the story remind you of another story?* to elicit ideas. (L1 may be necessary to help explain the similarities.) *Pinocchio* may be familiar to some children (a puppet that comes to life and dances). *Frankenstein* is scarier, but is also about a creation that is brought to life.

I Can Read and Write!

Point out that because gives more information about people's opinions, feelings, or actions. Have the children look for more examples of because in the story and see what extra information they learn.

Optional activity: Who is it?

Describe the characters in the story at different points to elicit the character name, e.g. *He was lonely.* (*Doctor Copper*) *They were angry.* (*Frank and Hilda*) *She wasn't a real girl.* (*Coppelia*) *She was surprised.* (*Hilda*) *They were worried.* (*Hilda and Frank*) *He was excited.* (*Doctor Copper*) *He was confused.* (*Frank*) *He was very happy.* (*Doctor Copper*)

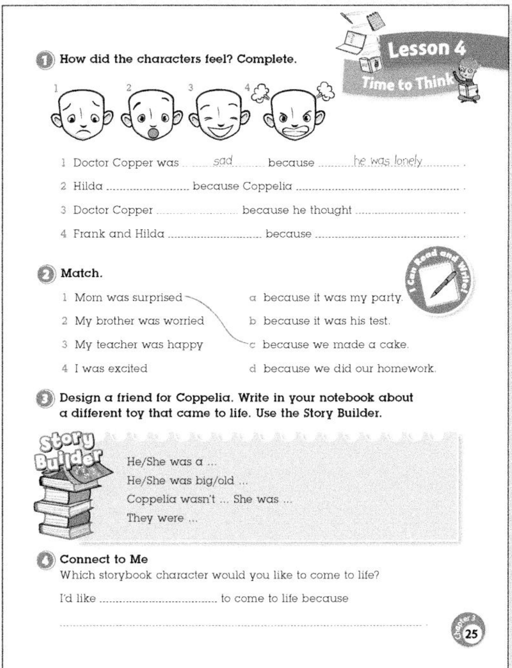

Lesson 4
Time to Think

1 How did the characters feel? Complete.

1 Doctor Copper was ..... sad ..... because ..... he was lonely ..... .
2 Hilda ..... because Coppelia ..... .
3 Doctor Copper ..... because he thought ..... .
4 Frank and Hilda ..... because ..... .

2 Match.

I Can Read and Write!

1 Mom was surprised — a because it was my party.
2 My brother was worried — b because it was his test.
3 My teacher was happy — c because we made a cake.
4 I was excited — d because we did our homework.

3 Design a friend for Coppelia. Write in your notebook about a different toy that came to life. Use the Story Builder.

Story Builder
He/She was a ...
He/She was big/old ...
Coppelia wasn't ... She was ...
They were ...

4 Connect to Me
Which storybook character would you like to come to life?
I'd like ..... to come to life because
.....

Chapter 3 25

1 How did the characters feel? Complete.

The children complete the sentences with information from the story, then compare with a friend. Elicit answers.

Answers

1 sad/he was lonely **2** was surprised/was a doll/wasn't real **3** was excited/Coppelia was real **4** were angry/Coppelia didn't wave back

2 Match.

The children practice the **I Can Read and Write!** feature by matching the sentence halves to make logical sentences. Elicit answers.

Answers

1 c **2** b **3** d **4** a

3 Design a friend for Coppelia. Write in your notebook about a different toy that came to life. Use the Story Builder.

Use the **Story Builder** prompts to elicit ideas. The children write about a friend for Coppelia in their notebook, then swap with a friend to check. Have children read out their description for the class.

Answers

Children's own answers.

4 Connect to Me

Elicit ideas for storybook characters who could come to life. The children write their own response, then compare with a friend. Elicit responses.

Answers

Children's own answers.

Cooler: Play "Sentence Builders"

Play the game with five sentences from the story (see Games Bank p. 19).

Competency Focus

Me: Critical Literacy

The children use critical literacy skills to reflect on the story theme and identify similar stories.

Digital Resources

Digital Activity Book • Use the AB page to give feedback on activities, using the answer key or the interactive digital activities.

Student eBook, Digital Activity Book • TIP Give children the opportunity to be your assistant! Ask a child to be responsible for choosing the relevant buttons.

Student eBook, Reader eBook • If you haven't already, show Oral Storytelling Video 3.1.

Teacher Resource Center • If you haven't already, print out Oral Storytelling Video Worksheet 3 to do the support activities.

Lesson 5

1 Listen and circle the correct answer. Then sing.

Song

I'm a Performer

I'm an (actor) / a puppet,
In a play.
I'm a musician / dancer,
I dance in the ballet!
I'm a puppet / dancer,
In a TV show.
I'm an actor / acrobat,
In a circus, you know!
I'm a dancer / musician,
I play the guitar.
I'm a singer / actor,
And I'm a big pop star!

2 Think of your favorite performer. Tell a friend.

Justin is my favorite singer.

3 Write riddles for your friend.

I play the guitar. What am I?

A musician.

4 Listen and say the chant.

The actor and the dancer are singing with the teacher.

5 Find it!
How many can you find on the page?
words ending in –er and –or

Spelling Central

–or and –er have the same sound at the end of the word. There are more job words ending in –er than –or.

Chapter 3 41

Vocabulary, Song, and Spelling

Lesson objectives: identify and talk about types of performers; practice spelling words ending *–or/–er*
Key vocabulary: *acrobat, actor, dancer, musician, puppet, singer*
Secondary language: *I'm a/an ..., I play ...*
Materials: Tracks 3.6 and 3.7; pictures for Key vocabulary (Warmer) ; Phonics Worksheet 3 [TRC] (optional)

Warmer: Pre-teach vocabulary

Pre-teach the vocabulary using pictures of the performers or using mimes. Have the children mime each one with you, then mime and repeat, and then mime and say the vocabulary on their own. Change the pictures faster and faster and see if they can keep up!

1 3.6 Listen and circle the correct answer. Then sing.

- Play Track 3.6 and have the children stand up whenever they hear a type of performer mentioned.
- Play Track 3.6 again. Have the children read the song, and circle the correct option in each pair.
- Play Track 3.6 again for the children to sing along. Stop before the word choices and have the children sing the correct word.

Answers

actor, dancer, puppet, acrobat, musician, singer

2 Think of your favorite performer. Tell a friend.

- Tell the children about a favorite performer of yours to model the activity, e.g. *Madonna is my favorite singer.* Divide the class into pairs and have the children tell each other above their favorite performers.
- To extend the activity, the children can also use true or false sentences, e.g. *Brad Pitt is my favorite actor. True or false?*

3 Write riddles for your friend.

- Write on the board an example riddle: *I'm in a movie and I dance. Who am I?* Elicit guesses. (*Pinocchio*)
- Have the children write similar riddles in their notebook. Monitor and support with vocabulary, but encourage them to use what they know as far as possible.
- Have the children read their riddles to friends around them in class. Elicit riddles and answers.

Answers

Children's own answers.

Spelling Central

Words ending –or, –er

Say *Teacher. Actor.* Ask *Is the pronunciation of the* –or *and* –er *different?* (*no*) Encourage them to say other job words with *–er* or *–or*, e.g. *doctor,* (*soccer*) *player, cleaner, writer, firefighter,* etc.

4 3.7 Listen and say the chant.

- Have the children look at the picture. Ask *What can you see?*
- Play Track 3.7. The children listen and read along. Elicit the words with *–er/–or* endings.
- Play Track 3.7 again, pausing for the children to repeat.

5 Find it!

- Set a time limit for the children to find words ending in *–er* and *–or* on the page. Elicit answers.

Answers

5—actor, dancer, singer, performer, teacher

Optional activity: Dictation

Have the children dictate simple sentences about professions to each other, e.g. *My father is a doctor. Miguel is a teacher.* After each pair of sentences, the children can check each other's spelling and then continue.

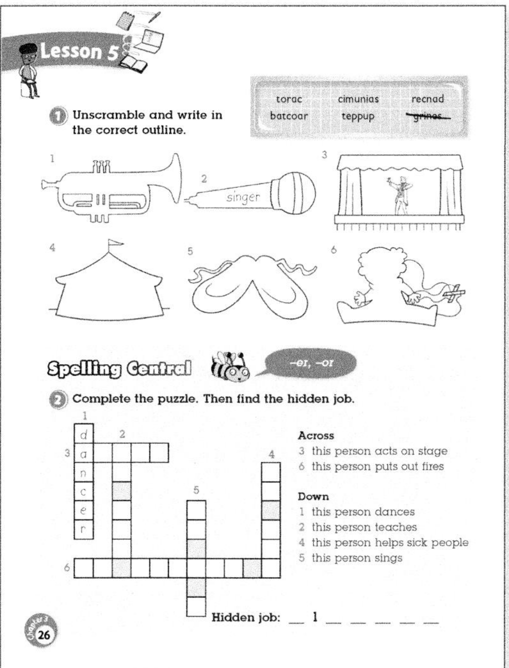

Lesson 5

1 Unscramble and write in the correct outline.

torac cimunias recnad
batcoar teppup ~~grines~~

Spelling Central –er, –or

2 Complete the puzzle. Then find the hidden job.

Across
3 this person acts on stage
6 this person puts out fires

Down
1 this person dances
2 this person teaches
4 this person helps sick people
5 this person sings

Hidden job: __ l __ __ __ __ __

26

1 Unscramble and write in the correct outline.

The children unscramble the words and write them in the corresponding outline. Elicit answers.

Answers

1 musician **2** singer **3** actor **4** acrobat **5** dancer **6** puppet

2 Complete the puzzle. Then find the hidden job.

The children complete the puzzle and find the hidden job. They can do this in pairs as a class race. Elicit answers.

Answers

Across: **3** actor **6** firefighter
Down: **1** dancer **2** teacher **4** doctor **5** singer
Hidden job: cleaner

Cooler: Sing and mime

 **3.6**

Play the song again for the children to sing along and mime.

Competency Focus

Think! Critical Thinking

The children use critical thinking skills to identify different types of performers by processing the written and spoken forms.

Digital Resources

Student eBook • Use *Add personal note* to store links to key vocabulary pictures to use in the Warmer.

- TIP Display the SB page for "heads-up" singing. This will enable you to check the children are participating and identify any who are struggling.

Student's App • Encourage the children to play the games on their smartphone/tablet. Ask them to record their scores to compare in the next lesson. (*The Inks* Apps are free and available on the App Store and Google Play.)

Teacher Resource Center • For phonics practice, print out Phonics Worksheet 3.

Grammar and Reading

Lesson objectives: ask and answer about the past using *was/were*

Key grammar: *When was the (show)? It was (last week). Who were the (singers)? Was he (good)? Yes, he was. / No, he wasn't.*

Secondary language: *terrible*

Materials: Track 3.8; pieces of paper with sentences (Cooler); Grammar Worksheet 3B [TRC printout] (optional)

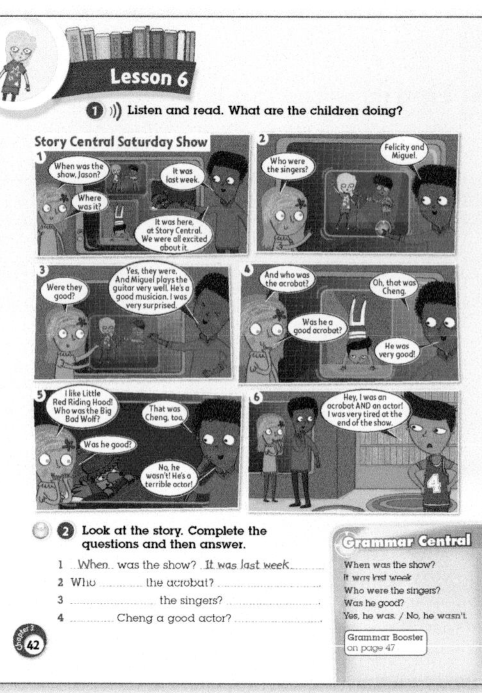

Lesson 6

1 Listen and read. What are the children doing?

2 Look at the story. Complete the questions and then answer.

1 When was the show? It was last week.
2 Who .... the acrobat? ....
3 .... the singers? ....
4 .... Cheng a good actor? ....

Grammar Central

When was the show?
It was last week.
Who were the singers?
Was he good?
Yes, he was. / No, he wasn't.

Grammar Booster on page 47

Chapter 3 42

Warmer: Play "Simon Says"

Play the game (see Games Bank p. 19) with different jobs, e.g. (*Simon says*) *be a teacher!*

1 3.8 Listen and read. What are the children doing?

- Have the children look at the story. Ask *What are the children talking about?* (*a show*)
- Play Track 3.8 and ask *What can you see?* Elicit answers. (*singer, musician, acrobat, actor,* etc.)
- Play Track 3.8 again, and have the children repeat some key phrases from the audio—especially ones featuring questions with *was/were*.

2 Look at the story. Complete the questions and then answer.

- Have a child read the example out loud.
- The children look at the story and complete the questions and answers.
- Invite children to read out a question and answer.
- Have the children practice saying the questions and answers in pairs. Monitor and correct pronunciation as necessary.

Answers

1 When—It was last week **2** was—Cheng
3 Who—Felicity and Miguel **4** Was—No, he wasn't.

Grammar Central

When was the show? …

Have the children look at the patterns. Ask *Are we asking about the present or the past?* (*past*) Elicit the verb used for one (*was*) and for more than one (*were*). Read the questions and answers for the children to repeat after you.

For extra practice, try the **Grammar Booster** section in the Student Book (p. 47–49).

Answers p. 47

Activity 1: **1** When was **2** was **3** Who were **4** was **5** Was **6** wasn't **7** were **8** Were they **9** weren't

Activity 2: **1** Was Jenny sad?; Yes, she was. **2** Was Jack surprised? ; No, he wasn't. **3** Were the children at home? ; No, they weren't. **4** Were the actors happy? ; Yes, they were.

Activity 3: Children's own answers.

p. 48

Activity 1: **1** were **2** Who **3** were **4** weren't **5** Was **6** was

Activity 2: **1** Yes, they were. **2** Mr. Mago was the star of the show. **3** The ballet shoes were in the red bag. **4** No, they weren't. **5** Yes it was.

Activity 3: Children's own answers.

p. 49

Activity 1: **1** were **2** were **3** are **4** Is **5** weren't **6** were **7** aren't **8** were **9** was **10** wasn't **11** was

Activity 2: **1** were the animals in circuses happy? **2** Who was Grimaldi?

Optional activity: Imagine a show

Ask the children to imagine a show in their school with their friends as singers, acrobats, musicians, and actors. Elicit and practice questions, e.g. *Where was the show? Who were the singers? Were they good?*, then divide the class into pairs to continue the dialogue.

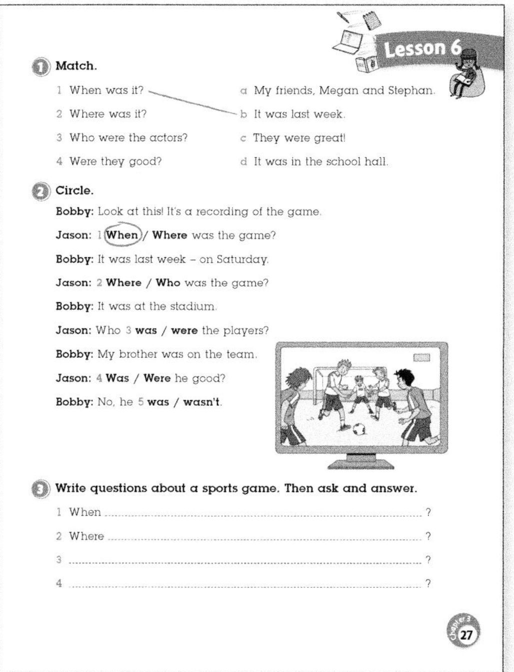
Lesson 6

1 Match.

1 When was it? a My friends, Megan and Stephan.
2 Where was it? b It was last week.
3 Who were the actors? c They were great!
4 Were they good? d It was in the school hall.

2 Circle.

Bobby: Look at this! It's a recording of the game.
Jason: 1 **When** / **Where** was the game?
Bobby: It was last week – on Saturday.
Jason: 2 **Where** / **Who** was the game?
Bobby: It was at the stadium.
Jason: Who 3 **was** / **were** the players?
Bobby: My brother was on the team.
Jason: 4 **Was** / **Were** he good?
Bobby: No, he 5 **was** / **wasn't**.

3 Write questions about a sports game. Then ask and answer.

1 When ....?
2 Where ....?
3 ....?
4 ....?

27

1 Match.

The children draw lines to match the questions and answers. Elicit answers.

Answers

1 b **2** d **3** a **4** c

2 Circle.

The children circle the words to complete the dialogue. Elicit answers.

Answers

1 When **2** Where **3** were **4** Was **5** wasn't

3 Write questions about a sports game. Then ask and answer.

The children write three questions with *was/were*. Then they ask and answer in pairs.

Answers

Children's own answers.

Cooler: Running dictation

Write the sentences from Student Book Activity 2 on separate pieces of paper, and stick them on the wall around the classroom (or outside). Divide the class into pairs. One child runs to read the sentence and dictates it to their friend. Pairs swap to check each other's work.

Competency Focus

Learn

The children demonstrate and consolidate their understanding of the new language by completing the activity.

Digital Resources

Student eBook • Show the Grammar Central box. Have children use *Highlighter* to identify the past tense questions and answers in the SB Activity 1 text.

Digital Activity Book • Have children use *Pen* to circle the answers in AB Activity 2 before you use the answer key to confirm. Alternatively, do the interactive digital activity as a class.

Teacher Resource Center • For extra grammar practice, print out Grammar Worksheet 3B.

CLIL: Performing Arts—The history of the theater

Lesson objective: find out about the theater in Ancient Greece
Materials: CLIL Graphic Organizer 3 [TRC printout] (optional)

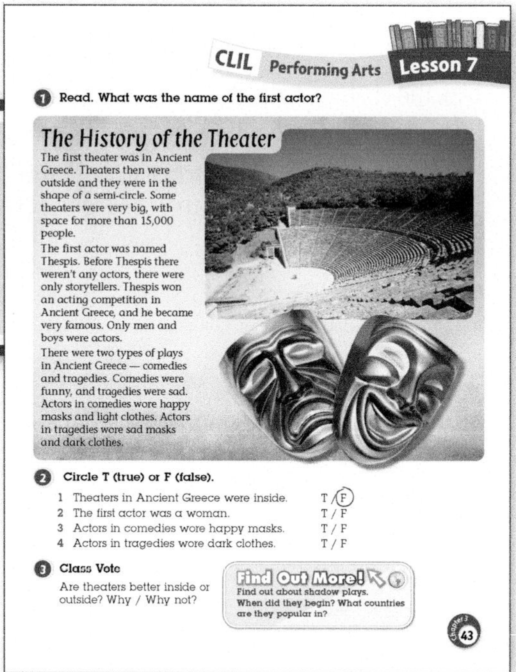
CLIL Performing Arts Lesson 7

1 Read. What was the name of the first actor?

The History of the Theater

The first theater was in Ancient Greece. Theaters then were outside and they were in the shape of a semi-circle. Some theaters were very big, with space for more than 15,000 people.

The first actor was named Thespis. Before Thespis there weren't any actors, there were only storytellers. Thespis won an acting competition in Ancient Greece, and he became very famous. Only men and boys were actors.

There were two types of plays in Ancient Greece — comedies and tragedies. Comedies were funny, and tragedies were sad. Actors in comedies wore happy masks and light clothes. Actors in tragedies wore sad masks and dark clothes.

2 Circle T (true) or F (false).

1 Theaters in Ancient Greece were inside. T / F
2 The first actor was a woman. T / F
3 Actors in comedies wore happy masks. T / F
4 Actors in tragedies wore dark clothes. T / F

3 Class Vote

Are theaters better inside or outside? Why / Why not?

Find Out More!
Find out about shadow plays.
When did they begin? What countries are they popular in?

Chapter 3 43

Warmer: Theater and the movies

Write *Theater* and *The Movies* on the board. Have a class discussion about similarities and differences between the theater and the movies. (You might need to use L1.) Have a class vote about which is more fun.

1 Read. What was the name of the first actor?

- Have the children skim the article quickly to find the name of the first actor. (*Thespis*)
- They then read the text carefully. Ask them to tell you about comedy and tragedy.
- Ask *What is a storyteller?* (*someone who tells stories*) *Are there storytellers today?* (*Yes! parents/grandparents/teachers*, etc.)

2 Circle T (true) or F (false).

- Read the example and elicit why the answer is true. (*Theaters then were outside …*)
- The children read the sentences and circle true or false for each sentence. They compare answers in pairs. Elicit answers, including the correct versions of the false statements.

Answers

1 F **2** F **3** T **4** T

Optional activity: Sad mask or happy mask?

Have the children look back at the three stories they have read so far in their Reader. Say *Imagine these stories are in Ancient Greek theater.* Point to the characters and each time elicit which mask they would have: *Sad mask or happy mask?*

3 Class Vote

- Ask *Are theaters better inside or outside?* Elicit possible advantages and disadvantages, e.g. *weather, noise, space, comfort.* (They might need to use L1.)
- Then take a class vote. Have the children write *Inside* or *Outside* on a piece of paper. Ask two children to collect the pieces of paper and count the votes. Then write the tally on the board.

Find Out More!  

Ask the children to find out more about shadow plays. Suggest appropriate resources, e.g. Internet, library books, etc. The children will need to complete this research before doing the follow-up activity in the Activity Book. (It could be set as homework.)

Lesson 7 CLIL

1 Read and complete.

Shadow Puppet Theater

In India and China around 400 B.C., there was a very different kind of theater. There weren't any actors – the characters were puppets. The puppets were cut from paper or animal skin. There was a light behind a white screen and people watched the shadow puppets move and dance. There was also music, including songs and chants. Shadow puppets are still very popular today.

This theater is different from Ancient Greek theater because it has ...

a actors ☐ b puppets ☐ c people ☐

2 Use your Student Book research. Write a Shadow Play.

- Imagine two characters.
- Write a dialogue between the characters. Write three questions and three answers.

Find Out More!

It's My World! Do you go to the theater with your family? What do you like to see? Tell your friends.

Chapter 3 28

1 Read and complete.

Ask *Where is the shadow puppet theater from?*
The children read the text to find out. (*India and China*)
They read the text once more to find the difference from the Ancient Greek theater. Elicit the answer.

Answer

b

2 Use your Student Book research. Write a Shadow Play.

Divide the class into groups of four. The children pool the information learned from their research in the Student Book and the Activity Book. Then they create two characters and a short dialogue in pairs.

Answers

Children's own answers.

It's My World!

Have the children discuss in groups whether they go to the theater and what they like to see. Elicit responses.

Cooler: Act out a shadow play

Invite pairs to present their characters from Activity Book Activity 2 and act out their dialogue.

Competency Focus

Act

The children carry out research to find out about a different type of theater. They relate what they learn to their world, both inside and outside the classroom.

Digital Resources

Student eBook, Digital Activity Book • TIP When using the board for "heads-up" teaching, give the children plenty of opportunity to participate.

Student eBook • TIP Use *Add personal note* to log the results of the class vote. Involve the children in tallying the results and writing the scores on the board.

Teacher Resource Center • Print out CLIL Graphic Organizer 3 for the children to collate their Find Out More! research.

CLIL eBook • The children can use the CLIL eBook to expand their knowledge of the lesson topic.

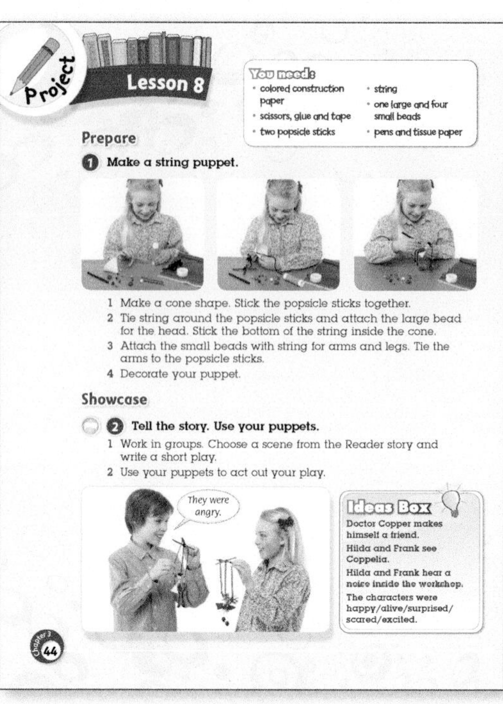

Project

Lesson 8

You need:

- colored construction paper
- scissors, glue and tape
- two popsicle sticks
- string
- one large and four small beads
- pens and tissue paper

Prepare

1 Make a string puppet.

1 Make a cone shape. Stick the popsicle sticks together.
2 Tie string around the popsicle sticks and attach the large bead for the head. Stick the bottom of the string inside the cone.
3 Attach the small beads with string for arms and legs. Tie the arms to the popsicle sticks.
4 Decorate your puppet.

Showcase

2 Tell the story. Use your puppets.

1 Work in groups. Choose a scene from the Reader story and write a short play.
2 Use your puppets to act out your play.

Ideas Box

Doctor Copper makes himself a friend.
Hilda and Frank see Coppelia.
Hilda and Frank hear a noise inside the workshop.
The characters were happy/alive/surprised/scared/excited.

Chapter 3 44

Project

Lesson objectives: review language from Chapter 3; complete a craft project—make a string puppet; act out the story from the Reader

Materials: colored construction paper, scissors, glue, tape, two popsicle sticks, string, one large and four small beads, pens, tissue paper; shadow puppet templates from the Internet (alternative craft project); two game pieces and a coin for each pair

Warmer: Play "The Shark Game"

Play the game with vocabulary from Lesson 7 (see Games Bank p. 19). Suggested words: *theater, Greece, comedy, tragedy, shadow, puppet.*

Prepare

1 Make a string puppet.

- Distribute the materials. Read through the instructions together and ensure the children are clear on what to do.
- Help the children follow the instructions to make their puppet. Give support as necessary.

Alternative craft activity

An easier project is to make paper puppets. An Internet search for "paper doll templates" provides a lot of shapes which are easy to cut out. The children can color these to act out their scene, or use them to make shadows on the board with a projector.

Showcase 

2 Tell the story. Use your puppets.

- Divide the class into groups of four (so each group has Hilda, Frank, Doctor Copper, and a narrator).
- Give the children a few minutes to look at their Reader and choose a scene to act out with their puppets, using the **Ideas Box** for support. Tell them they can add some dialogue if they want to.
- Have the children practice their version of the story. Give support as necessary.
- Invite groups to perform their version for the class.

Optional activity: Write lines of dialogue

Ask the children to imagine something that one of the characters in the story might say (it can be a question/positive or negative sentence/exclamation) and write it on a piece of paper. Collect these, shuffle them, and hand them out again. The children identify where they think the text is from in the story and use their puppets to act it out.

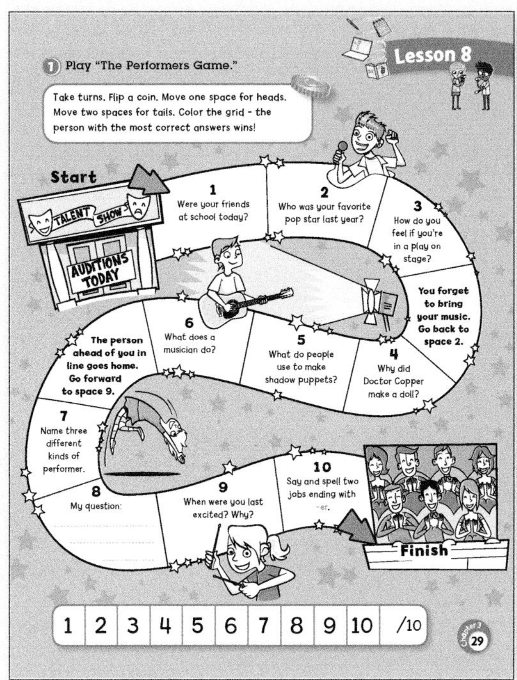

1 Play "The Performers Game."

See p. 43 for instructions on how to play the game.

Answers

1 Yes, they were. / No, they weren't. **2** Children's own answers. **3** scared, excited, etc. **4** because he was lonely **5** paper or animal skins **6** They play a musical instrument. **7** actors, pop stars, singers, etc. **8** Children's own questions. **9** Children's own answer. **10** dancer, singer, etc.

Cooler: Play "Ready, Set, Draw!"

Play the game with words/phrases from Chapter 3 (see Games Bank p. 19).

Competency Focus

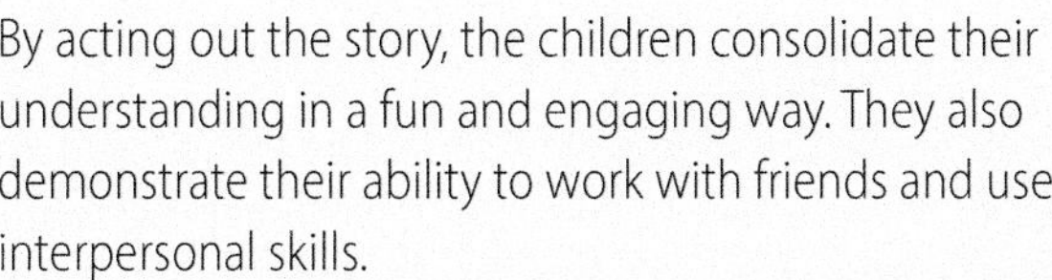

Collaborate and communicate

By acting out the story, the children consolidate their understanding in a fun and engaging way. They also demonstrate their ability to work with friends and use interpersonal skills.

Digital Resources

Student eBook • Show the pictures, stage by stage, as you talk the class through the activity process.

- Choose from vocabulary from Chapters 1–3 to review a vocabulary topic. Have the children raise their hands to vote to select a topic. Then use *Timer* and give the class one minute to recall all the words in the topic. Repeat with a different topic if you have time.

Language Review

Lesson objective: review language from Chapter 3

Materials: Tracks 3.9, AB 3.1, AB 3.2, and AB 3.3; cards for "Board Pelmanism" (Warmer)

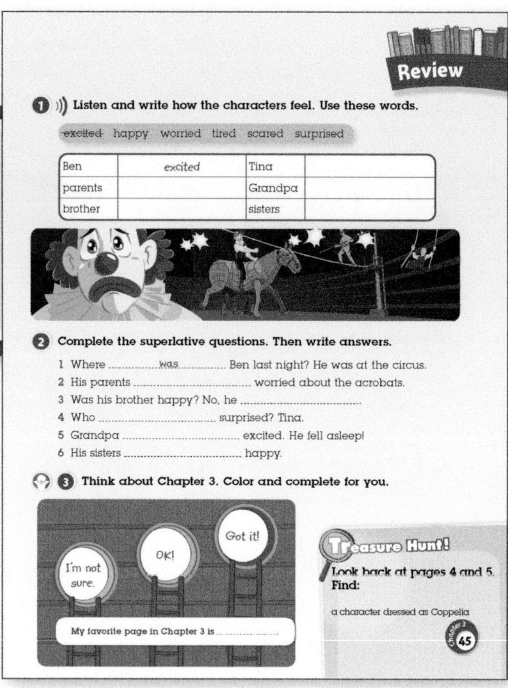

Review

1 Listen and write how the characters feel. Use these words.

~~excited~~ happy worried tired scared surprised

Ben	excited	Tina	
parents		Grandpa	
brother		sisters	

2 Complete the superlative questions. Then write answers.

1 Where ......was...... Ben last night? He was at the circus.
2 His parents .... worried about the acrobats.
3 Was his brother happy? No, he ....
4 Who .... surprised? Tina.
5 Grandpa .... excited. He fell asleep!
6 His sisters .... happy.

3 Think about Chapter 3. Color and complete for you.

My favorite page in Chapter 3 is ....

Treasure Hunt!

Look back at pages 4 and 5. Find:

a character dressed as Coppelia

Chapter 3 45

Warmer: Play "Board Pelmanism"

Prepare cards using key Chapter 3 vocabulary (two for each word). Play the game (see Games Bank p. 19).

1 3.9 Listen and write how the characters feel. Use these words.

- Have the children look at the picture. Ask *What can you see?*
- Play Track 3.9 twice. Have the children complete the table with an adjective for each person.
- Nominate children to read out answers, e.g. *I think Ben is excited.* Ask for class agreement.

Audioscript

Tina: *Hello, Ben. Where were you last night?*
Ben: *Well, Tina, last night I wasn't at home—I was at the circus with my family.*
Tina: *Wow! Were you excited?*
Ben: *Yes, I was ... but my parents were worried.*
Tina: *Why were they worried?*
Ben: *They were worried about the acrobats. They were very high on the swings!*
Tina: *Was your little brother happy?*
Ben: *No, he wasn't. He was scared of the clown. He doesn't like clowns.*
Tina: *I'm surprised! Clowns are funny.*
Ben: *This clown wasn't. He was a sad clown.*
Tina: *Was the show good?*
Ben: *Yes, but it was very long. My grandpa was tired. He fell asleep! But my sisters were happy—they loved the dancers on horses.*
Tina: *Were the horses real?*
Ben: *No! They weren't. They were incredible puppets!*

Answers

Ben—excited, parents—worried, brother—scared, Tina—surprised, Grandpa—tired, sisters—happy

2 Complete the sentences. Use *was, were, wasn't* or *weren't*.

- The children complete the sentences with *was, were, wasn't* or *weren't.*

Answers

1 was **2** were **3** wasn't **4** was **5** wasn't **6** were

3 Think about Chapter 3. Color and complete for you.

- Children color the circle which represents how they feel about their own progress (self-evaluation).
- Have the children complete the sentence.

Treasure Hunt!

Have the children look at pp. 4–5 to find a character dressed as Coppelia.

Cooler: Play "Back to the Board"

Choose ten key words from Chapter 3. Divide the class into two teams. One child from each team sits at the front. Write a word on the board—they cannot look! Teammates explain the word for the children to guess.

Competency Focus

Me: Self-evaluation

The children reflect on the chapter and express their opinions about their own progress.

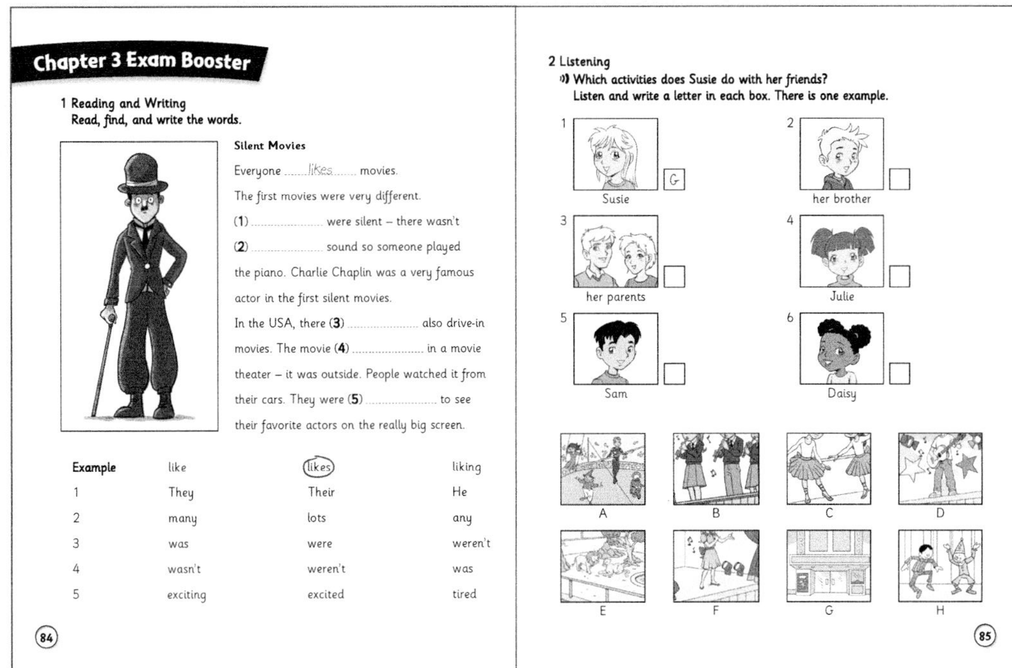

Chapter 3 Exam Booster

1 Reading and Writing
Read, find, and write the words.

Silent Movies

Everyone ......likes...... movies.
The first movies were very different.
(1) .... were silent – there wasn't
(2) .... sound so someone played
the piano. Charlie Chaplin was a very famous
actor in the first silent movies.
In the USA, there (3) .... also drive-in
movies. The movie (4) .... in a movie
theater – it was outside. People watched it from
their cars. They were (5) .... to see
their favorite actors on the really big screen.

Example	like	(likes)	liking
1	They	Their	He
2	many	lots	any
3	was	were	weren't
4	wasn't	weren't	was
5	exciting	excited	tired

84

2 Listening
Which activities does Susie do with her friends?
Listen and write a letter in each box. There is one example.

1 Susie G
2 her brother
3 her parents
4 Julie
5 Sam
6 Daisy

A B C D
E F G H

85

3 Speaking
1 Look at the pictures and listen to the examples.

There is a ... / There isn't a ...
There are some ... / There aren't any ...

2 Find four more differences. Tell your friend.

3 Now listen and compare.

Exam Tip
Study the pictures well before you start to speak.

86

1 Reading and Writing. Read, find, and write the words.

The children complete the text.

Answers

1 They **2** any **3** were **4** wasn't **5** excited

2))) AB3.1 Listening. Which activities does Susie do with her friends? Listen and write a letter in each box. There is one example.

Play Track AB 3.1 twice. The children listen and match.

Answers (Audioscript on p. 222)

2 B **3** E **4** A **5** H **6** C

3.1))) AB3.2 Speaking. Look at the pictures and listen to the examples.

The children look and listen to prepare for activity 2.
(Audioscript on p. 222)

3.2 Speaking. Find four more differences. Tell your friend.

Ask the children to find four more differences and tell their friend. Children use the examples from 3.1.

3.3))) AB3.3 Speaking. Now listen and compare.

Ask the children to listen and compare their answers.
(Audioscript on p. 222)

Digital Resources

Teacher Resource Center • Print out Test Chapter 3 to use at the end of this lesson. The Test Generator also allows you to create customized tests.

- Print out Festival Worksheet: Christmas to expand the children's knowledge of celebrations throughout the world.

At Home
Overview

Reading Skills
Story: *Cinderella Goes to the Party*
Genre: modern fairy tale

The children will:
- use critical thinking skills to identify household appliances.
- talk about the past using *there was/there were*.
- read, understand, and act out a story.
- talk about household chores.
- talk about how often they do things or how often things happen.
- find out about how to save energy in the home.
- make an eco-display.

Literacy Development
- predict story content from title and pictures
- reflect on and personalize the theme of the story
- appreciate how likeable and unlikeable story characters are

Key Vocabulary
Household appliances: broom, candle, dishwasher, kettle, lamp, microwave, vacuum cleaner, washing machine
Household chores: clean your room, do the dishes, pick up your clothes, put the kettle on, sweep the floor, turn off the lamp

Functional Language
- Come and see this.
- Wow! Isn't that . . .?
- It sure is!

Spelling
Words with *ee* and *ea*

Key Grammar
- There was a (fire).
- There were (candles).
- There wasn't (electricity).
- There weren't (dishwashers).
- How often do you (sweep the floor)?
- I sometimes (sweep the floor).
- I often (pick up books).
- There's never a (power outage).
- Jason always (writes a story).

CLIL: Social sciences—Saving energy
The children find out how to save energy at home.

Competency Focus

The children will:

use critical thinking skills to identify household appliances. (Lesson 1) predict the content of a story. (Lesson 3) identify and talk about household chores. (Lesson 5)	apply new grammar to previously learned vocabulary. (Lesson 2) talk about how often they do things or how often things happen. (Lesson 6)	work in threes to act out a dialogue. (Lesson 3) work in groups to act out a story. (Lesson 8)	reflect on the story and which version of it they prefer. (Lesson 4) evaluate their own progress in the chapter. (Review)	develop a wider understanding of ways to save energy at school. (Lesson 7)

Digital Overview

Teacher Presentation

Student eBook and Digital Activity Book

- Music Video 4.1 (4.2): *Our Chores*
- Interactive versions of AB activities
- Integrated audio and answer key for all activities

Teacher resources for planning, lesson delivery, and homework

Teacher Resource Center

- Class Planner Chapter 4
- Worksheets to print out (including notes and answers):
  - Grammar Worksheet 4A: There was/were … There were/weren't…
  - Grammar Worksheet 4B: How often …? I sometimes/often …
  - Phonics Worksheet 4
  - CLIL Graphic Organizer 4
  - Test Chapter 4
- Test Generator
- Literacy Handbook

Watch the Music Video

Children's resources for learning and practicing at home

Student eBook

- Music Video 4.1 (4.2): *Our Chores*

The Inks Student's App

Vocabulary games: Household appliances and household chores

Chapter 4 At Home

Lesson 1

Chapter 4 At Home
Lesson 1
1 Listen and number. Then say.
2 Compare the items you have at home with a friend.
We have a lamp.
We don't have a kettle.
3 Write the items in size order from small to big.
1 candle
2
For Sale
dishwasher 1
vacuum cleaner
broom
lamp
washing machine
kettle
microwave
candle
50

Vocabulary

Lesson objective: identify and talk about household appliances
Key vocabulary: *broom, candle, dishwasher, kettle, lamp, microwave, vacuum cleaner, washing machine*
Materials: Track 4.1

Warmer: What's in your house?

Put the class into pairs to talk about the picture in Student Book Activity 1. They can talk about the colors, what people are wearing, and which things pictured they have at home. Alternatively, do this as a class discussion.

1 4.1 Listen and number. Then say. 

- Have the children look at the pictures. Ask *Where are the people?* (*in a yard / outside a house*) Elicit the names of any items they know.
- Play Track 4.1. The children listen and find each appliance. They write the picture number of each appliance by the word.
- Play Track 4.1 again, pausing after each appliance for the children to point and repeat.

Audioscript

Woman: *Hi there, what are you selling?*
Man: *Well, I have a dishwasher. It washes the dishes very well. Do you need a dishwasher?*
Woman: *Yes, I do want a dishwasher. And I really like the green color.*
Man: *Do you need a washing machine? This one's old, but it works fine. It's very big, too.*
Woman: *Hm … it is big. I don't need a washing machine.*
Man: *How about the vacuum cleaner?*
Woman: *The one next to you? No. We don't have any rugs to clean, so we don't need a vacuum cleaner.*
Man: *The brooms are new. There are two.*
Woman: *I have a broom, thanks. And the lamp is just twelve dollars?*
Man: *That's right.*
Woman: *Robbie, please stop playing with that candle! Does the microwave work?*
Man: *Yes.*
Woman: *But it's very small isn't it? Robbie, stop kicking that old kettle!*

Answers

dishwasher 1, vacuum cleaner 3, broom 4, lamp 5, washing machine 2, kettle 8, microwave 7, candle 6

2 Compare the items you have at home with a friend.

- Say *At home, I have a lamp. I don't have a kettle.* Elicit similar sentences from a confident child. Have the children do the same in pairs.

3 Write the items in size order from small to big.

- Say *The candle is small. It is first.* Make sure the children understand the concept of ordering from small to big. Write *candle* on the board. Ask *What's next?* prompting as necessary to elicit the next biggest item. (*kettle*)
- Have the children write the list in size order in their notebook. Elicit answers.

Answers (suggested)

candle, kettle, lamp, broom, microwave, vacuum cleaner, dishwasher/washing machine

Optional activity: You need a …

Prompt with different situations to elicit the item you need, using *You need a …!* Suggestions: *My clothes are dirty.* (*washing machine*) *The floor is dirty.* (*broom or vacuum cleaner*) *I want to make some tea.* (*kettle*), etc.

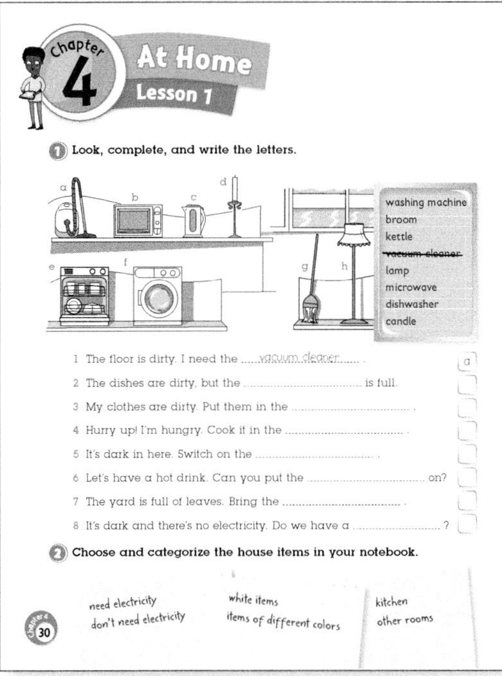

Chapter 4 At Home Lesson 1

1 Look, complete, and write the letters.

washing machine
broom
kettle
~~vacuum cleaner~~
lamp
microwave
dishwasher
candle

1 The floor is dirty. I need the ......vacuum cleaner...... . a
2 The dishes are dirty, but the .... is full.
3 My clothes are dirty. Put them in the ....
4 Hurry up! I'm hungry. Cook it in the ....
5 It's dark in here. Switch on the ....
6 Let's have a hot drink. Can you put the .... on?
7 The yard is full of leaves. Bring the ....
8 It's dark and there's no electricity. Do we have a .... ?

2 Choose and categorize the house items in your notebook.

need electricity
don't need electricity

white items
items of different colors

kitchen
other rooms

Chapter 4 30

1 Look, complete, and write the letters.

The children complete the sentences using the words supplied. Then they write the picture letter by each sentence. Elicit answers.

Answers

1 vacuum cleaner a **2** dishwasher e **3** washing machine f **4** microwave b **5** lamp h **6** kettle c **7** broom g **8** candle d

2 Choose and categorize the house items in your notebook.

Elicit an example for each category listed. Ask *Which categories would you choose?* Elicit ideas, prompting children to give a reason for their choice. The children choose a pair of categories and list the words in their notebook, then compare with a friend.

Answers

Children's own answers.

Cooler: Mime time

Mime using a dishwasher (loading it then closing the door and pressing a button). Ask *What am I using?* to elicit *dishwasher*. Have the children continue the mime activity in pairs.

Competency Focus

Think! Critical Thinking

The children use critical thinking skills to identify different household appliances by using visual clues and processing the written and spoken forms.

Digital Resources

Student eBook, Digital Activity Book • TIP For audio that does not appear on the SB page, show the audioscript.

Grammar

Lesson objective: talk about situations in the past using *there was/there were*

Key grammar: *There was a (fire). There were (candles). There wasn't (electricity). There weren't (dishwashers).*

Secondary language: *electricity, fire, gas, stove*

Materials: Track 4.2; Grammar Worksheet 4A [TRC printout] (optional)

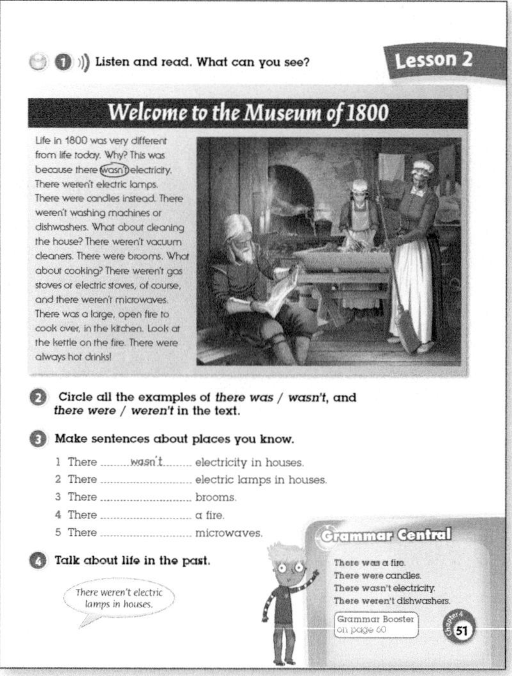

1 Listen and read. What can you see?

Lesson 2

Welcome to the Museum of 1800

Life in 1800 was very different from life today. Why? This was because there wasn't electricity. There weren't electric lamps. There were candles instead. There weren't washing machines or dishwashers. What about cleaning the house? There weren't vacuum cleaners. There were brooms. What about cooking? There weren't gas stoves or electric stoves, of course, and there weren't microwaves. There was a large, open fire to cook over, in the kitchen. Look at the kettle on the fire. There were always hot drinks!

2 Circle all the examples of *there was / wasn't*, and *there were / weren't* in the text.

3 Make sentences about places you know.

1 There ....wasn't.......... electricity in houses.
2 There .... electric lamps in houses.
3 There .... brooms.
4 There .... a fire.
5 There .... microwaves.

4 Talk about life in the past.

Grammar Central

There was a fire.
There were candles.
There wasn't electricity.
There weren't dishwashers.

Grammar Booster on page 60

Chapter 4 51

Warmer: Imagine a museum

Have a class discussion on museums. Ask *Do you go to museums? Which is your favorite? What can you see there? What museum would you like to visit?* Elicit answers. (They might need to use L1.)

1 4.2 Listen and read. What can you see?

- Have the children look at the picture. Ask *What can you see?* Explain that the text is from a museum brochure.
- Play Track 4.2. The children listen and read along. Have them underline the words for things they can see in the picture. Elicit answers. (*candles, brooms, open fire, kettle*)
- Play Track 4.2 again. Ask *Can you see a washing machine or dishwasher in the picture?* (*no*) *Why not?* (*because there was no electricity*)

2 Circle all the examples of *there was / wasn't* and *there were / weren't* in the text.

- Have the children circle the examples in the text. Elicit answers. (*there was x 2, there were/weren't x 8—see text*)

Grammar Central

There was a fire. …

Have the children look at the patterns. Ask *Which forms are for one thing?* (*there was/wasn't*) *Which forms are for more than one?* (*there were/weren't*) Elicit that they refer to the past. Read out the sentences for the children to repeat. Pay particular attention to the weak pronunciation of *was/were*.

For extra practice, try the **Grammar Booster** section in the Student Book (p. 60).

Answers p. 60

Activity 1: **1** There was **2** There wasn't **3** There was **4** There wasn't **5** There were **6** There weren't

Activity 2: **1** there weren't **2** There were **3** there wasn't **4** There wasn't

Activity 3: **1** There wasn't **2** there wasn't **3** There weren't **4** there weren't **5** There was **6** There were

3 Complete the sentences.

- Have a child read the example. Elicit why *wasn't* is correct. (*singular and negative because they didn't have electricity*)
- The children complete the sentences. Elicit answers and check with the class.

Answers

1 wasn't **2** weren't **3** were **4** was **5** weren't

4 Talk about life in the past.

- Have two children read out the examples. Elicit other ideas. Encourage the children to use *was, wasn't, were, weren't.*
- The children talk about life in the past in pairs. Monitor and help as necessary.

Optional activity: 1900s interview

The children imagine they travel back in time to the 1900s. In groups, they write four questions to ask the people they meet there, e.g. *How do you wash your clothes? How do you go to work?* Ask children to be people from the 1900s. The class interviews them with their questions.

Lesson 2

1 Circle *true* or *false*.

1 In 1800, there wasn't electricity in houses. true / false
2 In 1800, there were washing machines. true / false
3 In 1800, there weren't microwaves. true / false
4 In 1800, there weren't vacuum cleaners. true / false
5 In 1800, there were dishwashers. true / false

2 Look and complete with *was, wasn't, were,* or *weren't.*

In Australia in 1800, there 1 ...weren't... big houses. In the kitchen, there 2 .... a fire for cooking. Of course, there 3 .... electricity in houses.

Transportation was difficult. There 4 .... cars or buses, but there 5 .... horses and there 6 .... bicycles, too!

3 Imagine your life now is in a museum of the future. Choose and write the museum brochure.

houses
transportation
house items
schools

WELCOME TO THE MUSEUM OF 20........

In my country in .... there were

31

1 Circle *true* or *false*.

The children circle *true* or *false* for each sentence. Elicit answers, including the correct version of each false statement.

Answers

1 true **2** false **3** true **4** true **5** false

2 Look and complete with was, wasn't, were, or weren't.

The children look at the pictures and complete the sentences with the correct verb form. Elicit answers.

Answers

1 weren't **2** was **3** wasn't **4** weren't **5** were **6** were

3 Imagine your life now is in a museum of the future. Choose and write the museum brochure.

Elicit ideas for the museum of the future in each of the categories. The children write their museum brochure, then compare ideas in pairs. Have children read out their responses.

Answers

Children's own answers.

Cooler: Play "The Shark Game"

 **4.2** Divide the class into two teams. Give one child from each team a board pen. Play Track 4.2 (Activity 1), pausing after key vocabulary. (Alternatively, read the text aloud.) The children run to the board and write the last word. Continue in this way, with a different child responding each time.

Competency Focus

Learn

The children use previously acquired vocabulary in a different context with new grammatical structures.

Digital Resources

Digital Activity Book • Have children write answers to AB Activity 2 on the board using *Pen*, before you use the answer key. Alternatively, do the interactive digital activity as a class.

Student eBook, Digital Activity Book • TIP You can move the answer key pop-up window around the screen to have the activity and the answers side by side.

Teacher Resource Center • For extra grammar practice, print out Grammar Worksheet 4A.

Reading: Story Extract

Lesson objectives: give a positive reaction when someone shows something; predict story content from title and pictures; read the extract from *Cinderella Goes to the Party* (middle)

Functional language: *Come and see this. Wow! Isn't that …? It sure is!*

Secondary language: *pick up, stepmother, stepsister*

Materials: Tracks 4.3 and 4.4

Lesson 3

1 Listen and read. Then use the words to make new dialogs.

Isn't that fun?
Isn't that cool?
Isn't that interesting?

I love it!
It's great!
It's wonderful!

2 Look at the story on page 53. Which characters would you like to meet?

3 Listen and read. Who says these words?

1 *"Put the kettle on."*
2 *"Bring my shoes!"*
3 *"I always clean the bedroom."*

4 What do you think happens next? Check (✓).

Cinderella makes the beds.
Cinderella leaves the house.
Cinderella asks for help.

52

Cinderella Goes to the Party

3 Every day, it was always the same.
Cinderella, put the kettle on.
Cinderella! Bring my shoes!
Cinderella! Where's my hat?
Yes, Stepmother. Here, Sister. Yes, Sister.
4 One day, there was a knock at the door. It was an official from the castle. There was an invitation in his hand.
A party at the castle!
Isn't that awesome?
Oh, it sure is!
the Prince,
is pleased to invite you
to his party at The Palace on
Saturday night.
5 And it was fun for everyone. Everyone except Cinderella.
Cinderella, where's my dress?
Cinderella, pick up my clothes.
Cinderella, my bedroom's a mess!
6
I always clean the bedroom, and I always pick up the clothes. They never do it. Well, not any more …

Reader — Read the story in your Reader on pages 10–13.

53

Warmer: Visualization

Have the children close their eyes and imagine they are in a kitchen in 1900. Ask *What can you see/hear/smell? Is it hot or cold? What are the people doing? Do they look happy?* Have them open their eyes and share with a friend what they imagined.

Functional language

1 4.3 Listen and read. Then use the words to make new dialogs.

- Have the children look at the pictures. Ask *What are they looking at?* (*a typewriter*)
- Play Track 4.3. The children listen and read along.
- Play Track 4.3 again, pausing for the children to repeat.
- Divide the class into threes and have them practice the dialogue, substituting different adjectives for *awesome*, e.g. *exciting, brilliant, fantastic*.

Before reading

2 Look at the story on page 53. Which characters would you like to meet?

- Ask the children to look at the title and pictures. Elicit the characters' names. (*Cinderella, Stepmother, Stepsister*)
- They write the names of the characters they would like to meet. Elicit answers and reasons. Take a class vote on the character the children would most like to meet.

3 4.4 Listen and read. Who says these words?

- Give the children time to read the sentences. Play Track 4.4 twice. The children listen, read along, and write the character names. Elicit answers and check with the class.

Answers

1 Stepmother **2** Stepsister **3** Cinderella

4 What do you think happens next? Check (✔).

- Have the children check their prediction. Elicit ideas including reasons, but do not confirm. Say they will have to read the story to find out.

Answers

Children's own answers.

Lesson 3

1 Unscramble and write. Then act out.

this. / and / Come / see ....

A / Wow! / ......typewriter! ....

that / awesome? / Isn't ....

sure / is! / It ....

2 Read the story in your Student Book. Write answers.

1 Does Cinderella have to do a lot of work in the house?

2 Does she have fun?

3 Does Cinderella like her stepmother and stepsisters? Why/Why not?

4 How does Cinderella look in the last picture?

3 Imagine you are Cinderella. Write what you want to say to your stepsisters and stepmother.

32

1 Unscramble and write. Then act out.

The children unscramble and write the sentences. Elicit answers. Then they act out the dialogue in pairs. Have pairs act out for the class.

Answers

Come and see this. / Wow! A typewriter! / Isn't that awesome? / It sure is!

2 Read the story in your Student Book. Write answers.

The children read the Student Book story extract again, then write answers to the questions. Elicit answers.

Answers

1 Yes, she does. **2** No, she doesn't. **3** No, because they're horrible/they don't do any work. **4** She looks angry/sad.

3 Imagine you are Cinderella. Write what you want to say to your sisters and stepmother.

The children discuss in pairs what Cinderella wants to say to her sisters and stepmother. Then they write their response individually. Elicit ideas. Have the class choose the best one.

Answers

Children's own answers.

Cooler: Play "Change the Text"

Play the game with Cinderella's thought bubble from the last picture of the story extract (see Games Bank on p. 19).

Competency Focus

Collaborate and Communicate

The children act out an authentic dialogue together, putting into practice new functional language.

Think! Critical Thinking

The children apply reading skills (exploiting pictures and text clues) to understand the story characters.

Digital Resources

Student eBook • Display the SB story extract. To develop visual literacy, use *Timer* to give the class one minute to look at the pictures. Minimize the story. Elicit the detail. Repeat with different details.

Digital Activity Book • Ask the children to do the AB interactive digital activities, or set them for homework.

Cinderella Goes to the Party

1
Cinderella was in the kitchen. Her stepmother was a horrible woman. Her two stepsisters were horrible, too!

Stepmother: Cinderella, make the beds!

Stepsister 2: Cinderella, sweep the floor!

2
Cinderella was very sad.

Cinderella: *I always make the beds. They never do it. I always sweep the floor. They never do it. It's not fair!*

3
Every day, it was always the same.

Stepmother: Cinderella, put the kettle on.

Stepsister 1: Cinderella! Bring my shoes!

Stepsister 2: Cinderella! Where's my hat?

Cinderella: Yes, Stepmother. Here, Sister. Yes, Sister.

4
One day, there was a knock at the door. It was an official from the castle. There was an invitation in his hand.

His Royal Highness the Prince is pleased to invite you to his party at the Palace on Saturday night.

Stepmother: A party at the castle!

Stepsister 1: Isn't that awesome!

Stepsister 2: Oh, it sure is!

5
And it was fun for everyone. Everyone except Cinderella.

Stepmother: Cinderella, where's my dress?

Stepsister 1: Cinderella, pick up my clothes.

Stepsister 2: Cinderella, my bedroom's a mess!

6
Cinderella: *I always clean the bedroom, and I always pick up the clothes. They never do it. Well, not any more …*

7
Suddenly, Cinderella was angry.

Cinderella: You find your dress. You pick up your clothes. And you clean your bedroom.

8
Cinderella: Is that Fairy Godmother? I need help! Please come now.

Fairy Godmother: Here I am!

9
Fairy Godmother: Why are you so angry?

Cinderella: I'm angry because I always do the work. They never help. And there's a party at the castle. Everyone is going except me! Can you help?

10
Her fairy godmother was a big help.

Fairy Godmother: Cinderella can't do everything. Do your *own* hair.

Stepsister 2: This is fun.

Fairy Godmother: You can help, too.

Stepsister 1: I can help you with your boots.

Cinderella: Thank you.

11
Cinderella: Wow, isn't this awesome?

Stepsister 1: It sure is!

Stepsister 2: My hair looks cool, and I did it myself.

Fairy Godmother: That's right. You can help Cinderella with her hair, too.

12
The party was really fun and Cinderella was very happy.

Prince: Wow! I like your style!

Stepmother: I hope they get married!

Stepsister 2: I can do Cinderella's hair for the wedding.

Stepsister 1: And I can make the cake!

13
Stepmother: Weddings are hard work!

Stepsister 1: But fun …

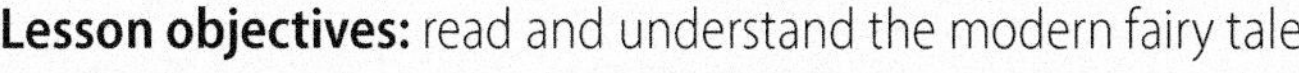

Lesson objectives: read and understand the modern fairy tale *Cinderella Goes to the Party* in the Reader
Materials: Track 4.5; Reader

Warmer: Story extract review

Elicit what happened in the story extract in Lesson 3. Help them remember all the things Cinderella does.

Story Summary

Cinderella is angry about doing all the household chores so she uses a smartphone app to find a fairy godmother. Fairy Godmother gets her stepsisters to help Cinderella prepare for the party. They enjoy helping. At the ball, Cinderella dances with the prince. She later marries him.

Value: We are all the same! 

4.5 While reading

- Have the children look at the pictures in the Reader. Ask *What other housework chores does Cinderella do? How does she feel?*
- Play Track 4.5. The children listen and read along. Ask *Why is Cinderella angry?* (*She always does the work.*)
- Play Track 4.5 again. Ask questions to check comprehension, e.g. *Why did Cinderella call Fairy Godmother?* (*to help her go to the party*) *How does she call her?* (*on her cell phone*) *How does Fairy Godmother help her?* (*She persuades the stepsisters to do things on their own and to help Cinderella.*) *Do Cinderella and her sisters have fun at the party?* (*Yes!*)

After reading: Reflect

- Ask questions to give the children the opportunity to think about the issues raised by the story, e.g. *How do the characters feel at the beginning and the end of the story? Do they change? Why?/Why not? What do they learn?*

Optional activity: I'm Fairy Godmother!

- Say characters' statements from the story for the children to repeat. Encourage them to mimic the emotion and intonation (see **Story Time**).

Story Time

Mimic the emotions

When the children are repeating phrases from the story, encourage them to mimic the emotion and intonation of the speakers, not just repeat the words. It will help them understand the emotions of the story better and engage with the characters more effectively.

Reading Strategy

Sentence Combining

The Sentence Combining strategy helps the children improve their writing skills by combining short sentences into a longer, more effective sentence. They need to develop this skill step by step and with structured guidance so that they can apply it in the future when writing longer texts.

For additional explanation and activities, see the Literacy Handbook on the Teacher Resource Center.

Cooler: Play "Ready, Set, Draw!"

Choose key words/phrases from the audioscript of the story and play the game (see Games Bank p. 19). Suggestions: *sweep the floor / make the bed / bring my shoes / pick up my clothes / clean your bedroom / make a cake.*

Digital Resources

Reader eBook • Minimize the Reader story. Reveal random details and elicit predictions on what will happen.

- Children find Cinderella in all the pictures, saying how she feels each time. Tell the children each to secretly choose their favorite picture of her. Children mime Cinderella for the class to guess and circle the correct picture using *Pen*.

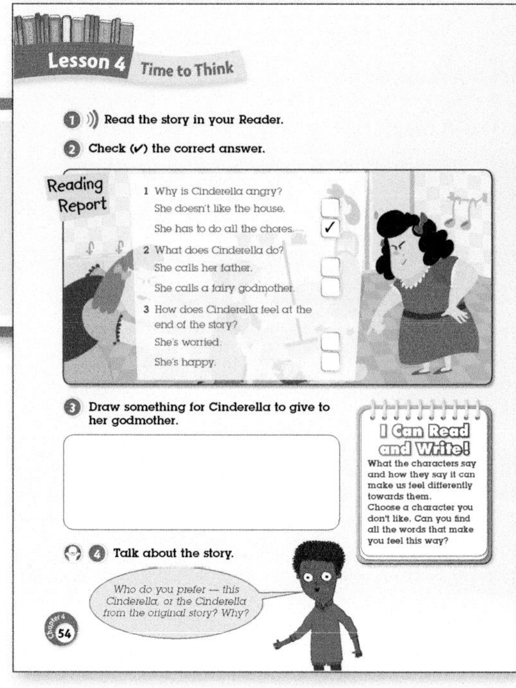

Lesson 4 Time to Think

1 Read the story in your Reader.

2 Check (✓) the correct answer.

Reading Report

1 Why is Cinderella angry?
She doesn't like the house.
She has to do all the chores. ✓

2 What does Cinderella do?
She calls her father.
She calls a fairy godmother.

3 How does Cinderella feel at the end of the story?
She's worried.
She's happy.

3 Draw something for Cinderella to give to her godmother.

I Can Read and Write!
What the characters say and how they say it can make us feel differently towards them.
Choose a character you don't like. Can you find all the words that make you feel this way?

4 Talk about the story.

54

Reading Comprehension and Critical Literacy

Lesson objectives: reflect on the story theme and think about how to behave; appreciate how likeable and unlikeable story characters are

Materials: Track 4.5; Reader

Note: Please ensure that your class has read the Reader story before you do this lesson.

Warmer: Who's speaking?

Call out two lines of the dialogue from different characters in the story to elicit who is speaking. Then invite children to read out more lines for their friends to guess.

1 4.5 Read the story in your Reader.

- Have the children read the story. (Alternatively, play Track 4.5 and have them read along). Elicit whether they were correct in their predictions in Lesson 3 Activity 4.
- Check comprehension by asking *How did Cinderella feel at the beginning of the story? (sad) Why? (She had to do all the work on her own.) Who helped Cinderella do all the work for her wedding? (her stepsisters)*

2 Check (✓) the correct answer.

- Read the example and elicit why it is correct. (*She did all the cleaning, and she wasn't happy about it.*)
- The children answer the questions, then compare in pairs. Elicit answers, including details of the corresponding part from the story.

Answers

1 She has to do all the chores. **2** She calls a fairy godmother. **3** She is happy.

3 Draw something for Cinderella to give to her godmother.

- Have the children draw something for Cinderella to give her godmother as a thank-you in the box provided. When finished, the children can label it.

4 Talk about the story. 

- Have a child read out Jason's questions. Elicit how this version of the story is different from the original, e.g. *the stepsisters don't help Cinderella in the original story, Cinderella doesn't use a cell phone*, etc.
- Have the children discuss in small groups which version of the Cinderella character they prefer. Elicit ideas.

I Can Read and Write!

Point out that we learn a lot about the characters from what they say and how they say it. For example, Cinderella's stepsisters and stepmother do not use *Can you …?* or *please* at the beginning of the story. Find other examples with the class.

Optional activity: Up-to-date fairy tales

Ask *Do you know other fairy tales like Cinderella?* Elicit ideas, e.g. *Snow White/Jack and the Beanstalk.* Choose one and brainstorm ways in which you could change it to make it more modern.

Lesson 4
Time to Think

1 Check (✓) for nice or cross (✗) for not nice.

1 Bring my shoes! ✗
2 I can help you with your boots. ....
3 I can make the cake for the party. ....
4 Cinderella, my bedroom is a mess. ....
5 Pick up my clothes. ....

I Can Read and Write!

2 Complete.

happy everyone helps her angry Fairy Godmother she has to do all the work ~~sad~~

Problem: At the beginning, Cinderella feels ...sad... because ....

Action: So she tells her .... about her problem. She feels ....

Solution: At the end, ... and she feels ....

3 Write about a character who isn't nice in your notebook. Use the Story Builder.

Story Builder

My character is ... / He/She isn't nice because ... / This makes me feel ... because ...
The fairy helps me. / Then ... is different. / He/She helps ... / Now I feel ... because ...

4 Connect to Me

What makes you feel better when someone isn't nice to you?

Talking to ... my parents ☐ my friend ☐ my teacher ☐

Chapter 4 33

Cooler: That's awesome!

Show the children some simple possessions you have with you, for example your bag or your pen. Say *Hey, look! This is my bag/pen!* to elicit (e.g.) *Wow! That's awesome!* Have the children continue the activity in pairs, showing possessions and giving positive opinions.

1 Check (✓) for nice or cross (✗) for not nice.

The children decide whether each sentence is nice/polite or not. Elicit answers.

Answers

1 ✗ 2 ✓ 3 ✓ 4 ✗ 5 ✗

2 Complete.

The children practice the **I Can Read and Write!** feature by completing sentences about the story using the words supplied. Elicit answers.

Answers

1 sad, she has to do all the work **2** Fairy Godmother, angry **3** everyone helps her, happy

3 Write about a character who isn't nice in your notebook. Use the Story Builder.

Use the **Story Builder** prompts to elicit ideas. The children write a story in their notebook, then swap with a friend. Have children read out their story for the class.

Answers

Children's own answers.

4 Connect to Me

Elicit ideas on what makes the children feel better when someone is not nice to them. The children write their own response, then compare with a friend. Elicit responses.

Answers

Children's own answers.

Competency Focus

Me: Critical Literacy

The children use critical literacy skills to reflect on the story theme and think about which version of it they prefer and why.

Digital Resources

Reader eBook • Display the Reader on the board. Show Picture 4. Elicit what happened before and after this. Repeat with Pictures 7 and 12.

Student eBook, Digital Activity Book • You can move the answer key pop-up window around the screen to have the activity and the answers side by side.

Vocabulary, Song, and Spelling

Lesson objectives: identify and talk about household chores; practice spelling words with *ee* and *ea*

Key vocabulary: *clean your room, do the dishes, pick up your clothes, put the kettle on, sweep the floor, turn off the lamp*

Secondary language: *chores, a mess*

Materials: Tracks 4.6 and 4.7; cards with the housework verbs written on them (optional); red and green pens/pencils Phonics Worksheet 4 [TRC] (optional)

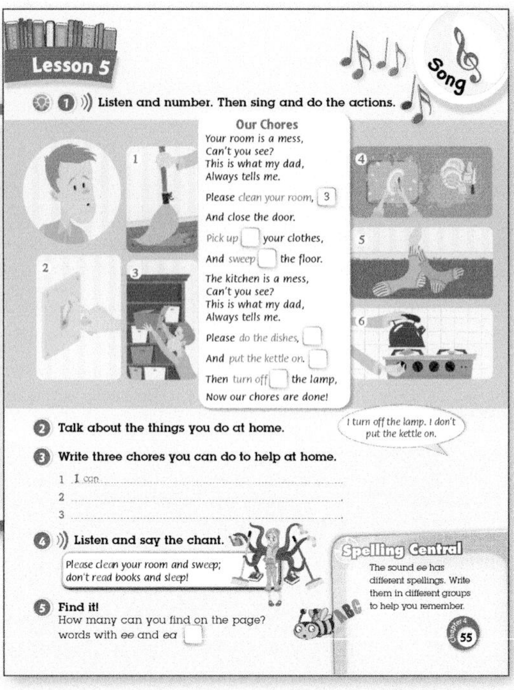

Lesson 5

Song

1 Listen and number. Then sing and do the actions.

Our Chores

Your room is a mess,
Can't you see?
This is what my dad,
Always tells me.
Please clean your room, 3
And close the door.
Pick up ☐ your clothes,
And sweep ☐ the floor.
The kitchen is a mess,
Can't you see?
This is what my dad,
Always tells me.
Please do the dishes, ☐
And put the kettle on. ☐
Then turn off ☐ the lamp,
Now our chores are done!

2 Talk about the things you do at home.

3 Write three chores you can do to help at home.

1 I can ……
2 ……
3 ……

4 Listen and say the chant.

Please clean your room and sweep;
don't read books and sleep!

5 Find it!
How many can you find on the page?
words with *ee* and *ea* ☐

Spelling Central
The sound *ee* has different spellings. Write them in different groups to help you remember.

Chapter 4 55

Warmer: Pre-teach vocabulary

Pre-teach the vocabulary by saying what chores you do, e.g. *Every day I do my chores. I …* and miming the activities as you say them. Then say the words for the children to mime.

1 4.6 Listen and number. Then sing and do the actions.

- Play Track 4.6. Have the children raise a hand whenever they hear the chores from the Warmer. They write the correct numbers on the pictures.
- Play Track 4.6 again for the children to sing along and do the actions.

Answers

1 sweep **2** turn off **3** clean your room **4** do the dishes
5 pick up **6** put the kettle on

2 Talk about the things you do at home.

- Write on the board *Me, too!* and *I don't!* Tell the children some things you do at home, and encourage them to respond with one of the phrases on the board.
- The children continue the same interaction in pairs.

3 Write three chores you can do to help at home.

- Elicit suggestions for things they can do at home to help. Provide new verbs or phrases as necessary.
- Have them write three sentences and compare with a friend.

Answers

Children's own answers.

Spelling Central

Words with ee and ea

Write *see* and *sea* on the board. Say them with the children and point out that the long *ee* sound can be written *ee* or *ea*. Repeat with *eat* and *tree*.

4 4.7 Listen and say the chant.

- Have the children look at the picture. Ask *What can you see?*
- Play Track 4.7. The children listen and read along. Elicit the words with *ee* and *ea*.
- Play Track 4.7 again, pausing for the children to repeat.

5 Find it!

- Set a time limit for the children to find words with *ea* and *ee* on the page. Elicit answers.

Answers

6—please, clean, read; see, sweep, sleep

Optional activity: Mime time

Choose seven children to come to the front of the class. Give each a verb card with a household chore on it. They mime their chore for 20 seconds, then when you say *Stop!*, they have to freeze in position. The other children identify what each one is doing, e.g. *Manuel is picking up clothes. Carmo is sweeping the floor.* Repeat with different children.

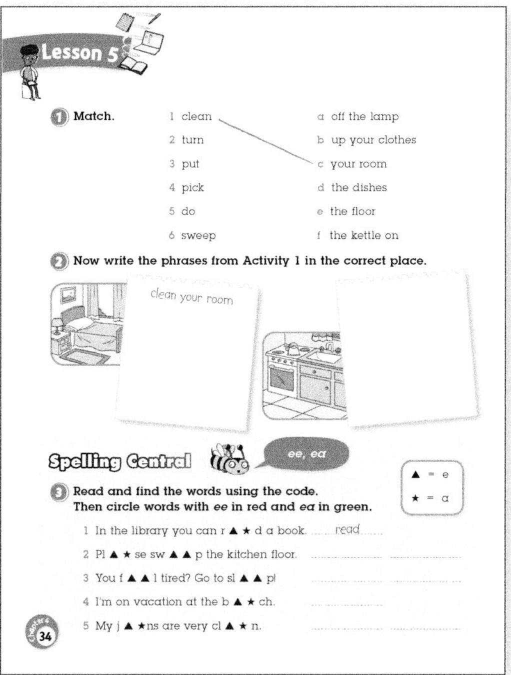

Lesson 5

1 Match.

1 clean	a off the lamp
2 turn	b up your clothes
3 put	c your room
4 pick	d the dishes
5 do	e the floor
6 sweep	f the kettle on

2 Now write the phrases from Activity 1 in the correct place.

clean your room

Spelling Central

ee, ea

▲ = e

★ = a

3 Read and find the words using the code. Then circle words with *ee* in red and *ea* in green.

1 In the library you can r ▲ ★ d a book. read

2 Pl ▲ ★ se sw ▲ ▲ p the kitchen floor.

3 You f ▲ ▲ l tired? Go to sl ▲ ▲ p!

4 I'm on vacation at the b ▲ ★ ch.

5 My j ▲ ★ns are very cl ▲ ★ n.

34

1 Match.

The children match to make phrases. Elicit answers.

Answers

1 c **2** a **3** f **4** b **5** d **6** e

2 Now write the phrases from Activity 1 in the correct place.

The children write the phrases in the correct place (bedroom or kitchen), then compare with a friend. Elicit answers.

Answers

By bedroom picture: clean your room, turn off the lamp, pick up your clothes

By kitchen picture: put the kettle on, do the dishes, sweep the floor

3 Read and find the words using the code. Then circle words with ee in red and ea in green.

The children complete and write the words using the code. Then they circle *ee* words in red and *ea* words in green. Elicit answers.

Answers

1 read **2** please, sweep **3** feel, sleep **4** beach
5 jeans, clean

Circled red: sweep, feel, sleep

Circled green: read, please, beach, jeans, clean

Cooler: Sing the song again

 4.6

Play the song, pausing after every second line for the children to sing the next one. Continue playing so that they can check.

Competency Focus

Think! Critical Thinking

The children use critical thinking skills to identify different household chores by processing the written and spoken forms.

Digital Resources

Student eBook • For SB Activity 1, choose the karaoke version of Music Video 4.1 (4.2) and encourage the children to dance and sing along, using the lyrics on screen. Pause the video for the children to continue dancing and singing.

Digital Activity Book • Use the AB page for feedback on activities using the answer key or the interactive digital activities.

Teacher Resource Center • For phonics practice, print out Phonics Worksheet 4.

Grammar and Reading

Lesson objectives: ask and answer about how often children do things at home or how often things happen
Key grammar: *How often do you (sweep the floor)? I sometimes (sweep the floor). I often (pick up books). There's never a (power outage). Jason always (writes a story).*
Secondary language: *(almost) every day, once a month*
Materials: Track 4.8; frequency cards (Cooler); Grammar Worksheet 4B [TRC printout] (optional)

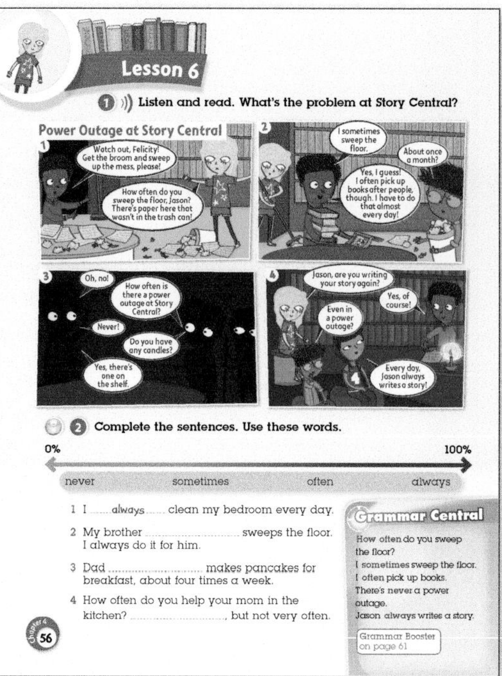

Warmer: Play "Disappearing Words"

Play the game with 12 words elicited from *Cinderella Goes to the Party* (see Games Bank p. 19).

1 4.8 Listen and read. What's the problem at Story Central?

- Have the children look at the story. Ask *What are the children doing?* (*They're cleaning.*)
- Play Track 4.8. The children listen. Ask *What's the problem?* (*There's a power outage.*)
- Play Track 4.8 again, pausing for the children to repeat some key phrases—especially ones featuring questions with *how often* and answer with frequency adverbs. (Alternatively, read the phrases out for the class to repeat.)

2 Write the words in the correct place. Then complete the sentences.

- Elicit answers to the diagram. Have the children repeat the adverbs after you.
- Elicit why the answer to number 1 is *always*. (*because it says every day*) Encourage the children to read carefully to find the information which will help them choose the correct word. Have the children complete the sentences and check with the class.

Answers

In diagram: never, sometimes, often, always
1 always **2** never **3** often **4** Sometimes

Grammar Central

How often do you sweep the floor? …

Have the children look at the patterns. Ask *What comes first—sometimes/often or sweep/pick up?* (*sometimes/often*) *What comes first—never or there's?* (*there's*) Point out that the verb *to be* always comes before words like *sometimes, often, never, always*. Ask more *How often do you …?* questions, e.g. *go to the movies, make your bed, have ice cream after dinner,* etc.

For extra practice, try the **Grammar Booster** section in the Student Book (p. 61–63).

Answers p. 61

Activity 1: **1** How often **2** How often **3** often **4** always **5** never **6** sometimes

Activity 2: **1** always **2** often **3** sometimes **4** never

Activity 3: Children's own answers.

p. 62

Activity 1: **1** often **2** always **3** There **4** was **5** wasn't **6** never

Activity 2: **1** There were books on the floor. **2** There was a shoe on the bed. **3** There were papers on the floor.

Activity 3: Children's own answers.

p. 63

Activity 1: **1** was **2** Can I **3** weren't **4** was **5** there **6** often **7** there wasn't **8** always **9** there was **10** there

Activity 2: Children's own answers.

Optional activity: Make it true for you

Have the children change the sentences in Activity 2 so they are true for each child. Give an example for yourself, e.g. *Dad never makes pancakes for breakfast!/Dad sometimes makes toast for breakfast.* Have the children write the sentences in their notebook, then compare with a friend. Elicit examples.

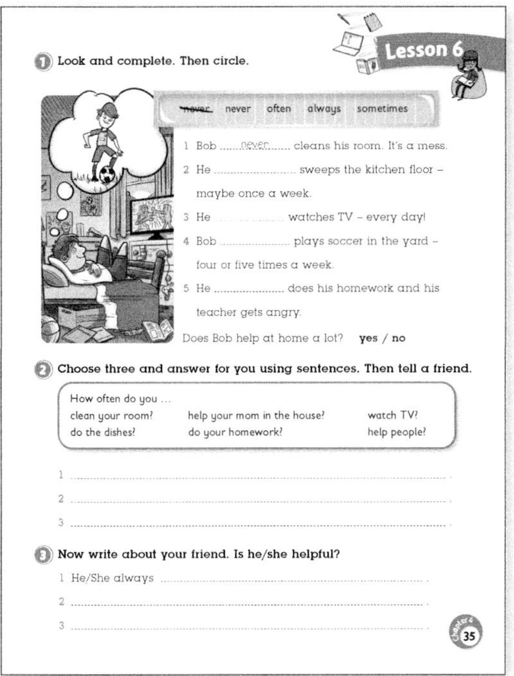

Lesson 6

1 Look and complete. Then circle.

~~never~~ never often always sometimes

1 Bob ......never...... cleans his room. It's a mess.
2 He .... sweeps the kitchen floor – maybe once a week.
3 He .... watches TV – every day!
4 Bob .... plays soccer in the yard – four or five times a week.
5 He .... does his homework and his teacher gets angry.

Does Bob help at home a lot? **yes / no**

2 Choose three and answer for you using sentences. Then tell a friend.

How often do you ...
clean your room? help your mom in the house? watch TV?
do the dishes? do your homework? help people?

1 ....
2 ....
3 ....

3 Now write about your friend. Is he/she helpful?

1 He/She always ....
2 ....
3 ....

Chapter 4 35

1 Look and complete. Then circle.

The children look at the picture and complete the sentences using the words supplied. Then they answer the question. Elicit answers.

Answers

1 never **2** sometimes **3** always **4** often **5** never; no

2 Choose three and answer for you using sentences. Then tell a friend.

The children choose three questions and write answers. Then they ask and answer with a friend. Ask pairs to tell the class.

Answers

Children's own answers.

3 Now write about your friend. Is he/she helpful?

The children write sentences about their friend based on the information from Activity 2. Elicit responses.

Answers

Children's own answers.

Cooler: Frequency practice

Prepare four cards with *never, sometimes, often, always* written on them (big enough to see on the walls). Stick them on the four walls of the classroom. Call out sentences about activities and have the children point to the word that is true for them. Elicit a complete sentence for each one. Write more phrases on the board and invite children to call out one for the class: *I clean my room. / I sweep the floor. / I make my breakfast. / I do my homework in the morning.*, etc.

Competency Focus

Learn

The children demonstrate and consolidate their understanding of the new language by completing the activity.

Digital Resources

Student eBook • Display the SB page. Use *Highlighter* to show the grammar structures in the story.

Teacher Resource Center • For extra grammar practice, print out Grammar Worksheet 4B.

CLIL: Social Sciences—Saving energy

Lesson objective: find out about how to save energy at home

Materials: CLIL Graphic Organizer 4 [TRC printout] (optional)

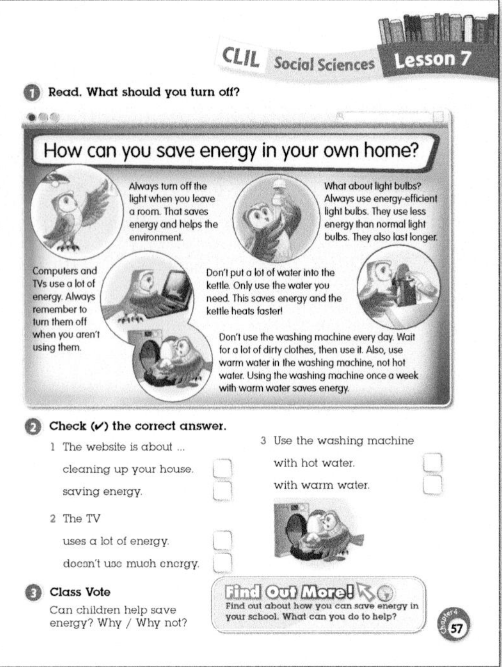

CLIL Social Sciences Lesson 7

1 Read. What should you turn off?

How can you save energy in your own home?

Always turn off the light when you leave a room. That saves energy and helps the environment.

What about light bulbs? Always use energy-efficient light bulbs. They use less energy than normal light bulbs. They also last longer.

Computers and TVs use a lot of energy. Always remember to turn them off when you aren't using them.

Don't put a lot of water into the kettle. Only use the water you need. This saves energy and the kettle heats faster!

Don't use the washing machine every day. Wait for a lot of dirty clothes, then use it. Also, use warm water in the washing machine, not hot water. Using the washing machine once a week with warm water saves energy.

2 Check (✔) the correct answer.

1 The website is about ...
cleaning up your house.
saving energy.

2 The TV
uses a lot of energy.
doesn't use much energy.

3 Use the washing machine
with hot water.
with warm water.

3 Class Vote
Can children help save energy? Why / Why not?

Find Out More!
Find out about how you can save energy in your school. What can you do to help?

57

Warmer: Using energy

Write *Energy* on the board. Say *We need energy to use a computer.* Divide the class into groups. Give them two minutes to list as many things as possible that need energy, e.g. *lights, video games, washing machine, dishwasher, hairdryer.* (They might need to use L1.) Elicit ideas.

1 Read. What should you turn off?

- Have the children look at the pictures and say what they can see. Ask *Do you have these things in your home?*
- Have the children read the text and underline the answers. Ask *What should you turn off at home to save energy?* (*light, computers, and TVs*) Elicit answers and check with the class. If necessary, explain *light bulb* with a drawing on the board.

2 Check (✔) the correct answer.

- Have the children check the correct option in each pair—remind them to scan for the right section and then read carefully for the answer.
- Elicit answers, including the corresponding part in the text.

Answers

1 saving energy **2** uses a lot of energy **3** with warm water

3 Class Vote

- Ask *Can children help save energy? Why/Why not?* Elicit that everyone can do something to help save energy—it is not just the responsibility of adults. Use the examples of saving energy in the text as prompts. Elicit other ideas, e.g. *walk to school instead of going by car, make sure the refrigerator is closed properly,* etc.
- Have a class vote by asking the children to stand up if their answer is yes and remain seated if it is no. Ask the children standing up how they will save energy at home from now on.

Find Out More!  

Have the children think of ideas in small groups. They can also ask their school teachers, cleaners, principal, etc. These people know the school well and can help give ideas. The children will need to complete this research before doing the follow-up activity in the Activity Book. (It could be set as homework.)

Optional activity: Making energy-saving decisions

Divide the class into pairs. Have the children look at the text in Activity 1 again and put the energy-saving ideas in order of how much energy they would save (the one saving most energy first). Elicit ideas.

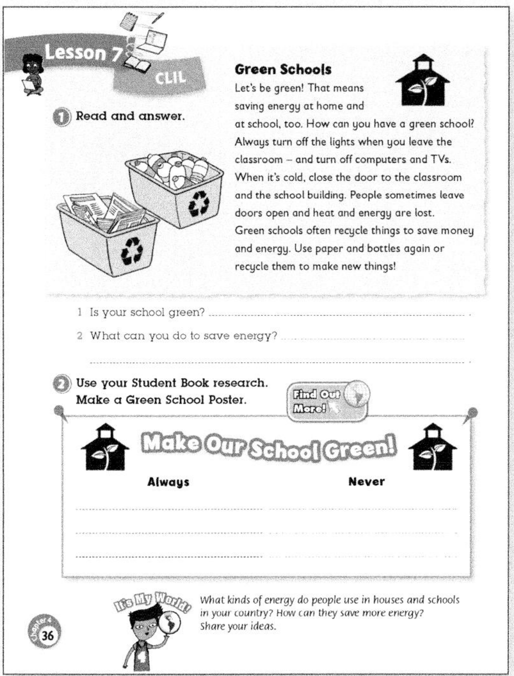
Lesson 7 CLIL

Green Schools

Let's be green! That means saving energy at home and at school, too. How can you have a green school? Always turn off the lights when you leave the classroom – and turn off computers and TVs. When it's cold, close the door to the classroom and the school building. People sometimes leave doors open and heat and energy are lost. Green schools often recycle things to save money and energy. Use paper and bottles again or recycle them to make new things!

1 Read and answer.

1 Is your school green? ....

2 What can you do to save energy? ....

2 Use your Student Book research. Make a Green School Poster.

Find Out More!

Make Our School Green!

Always	Never

It's My World! *What kinds of energy do people use in houses and schools in your country? How can they save more energy? Share your ideas.*

Chapter 4 36

1 Read and answer.

The children read the text. Ask *How can students have green schools?* Then they answer the two questions about their school. Elicit answers.

Answers

1 Children's own answers **2** You can turn off machines, close doors, turn off lights, and recycle things to save energy.

2 Use your Student Book research. Make a Green School Poster.

Divide the class into groups of four. Have the children pool the information learned from their research in the Student Book and the Activity Book. Then they complete the poster individually.

It's My World!

Have a class discussion to elicit ideas on what energy is used in the children's country and what can be done to save more energy.

Cooler: Browse the posters

Have the children leave their Activity Book open, then walk around the classroom to browse the Green School posters. Elicit ideas they read. Take a class vote on the best idea.

Competency Focus

Act

The children carry out research to find out about ways of saving energy. They relate what they learn to their world, both inside and outside the classroom.

Digital Resources

Student eBook • Display the SB page for a "heads-up" introduction to the topic.

• Children use *Highlighter* to find the relevant parts in the text to answer the SB Activity 1 question.

Digital Activity Book • Elicit ideas from the class for AB Activity 2 and use *Pen* to create a model answer.

Teacher Resource Center • Print out CLIL Graphic Organizer 4 for the children to use in collating their Find Out More! research.

CLIL eBook • The children can use the CLIL eBook to expand their knowledge of the lesson topic.

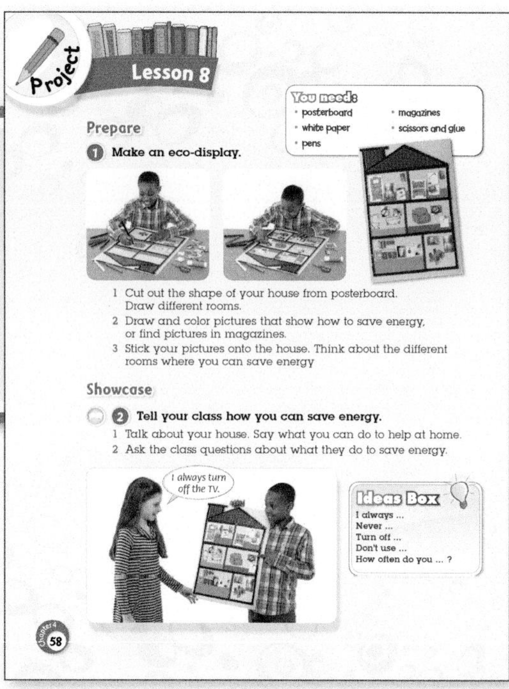

Project

Lesson 8

You need:
- posterboard
- white paper
- pens
- magazines
- scissors and glue

Prepare

1 Make an eco-display.

1 Cut out the shape of your house from posterboard. Draw different rooms.
2 Draw and color pictures that show how to save energy, or find pictures in magazines.
3 Stick your pictures onto the house. Think about the different rooms where you can save energy

Showcase

2 Tell your class how you can save energy.

1 Talk about your house. Say what you can do to help at home.
2 Ask the class questions about what they do to save energy.

Ideas Box
I always ...
Never ...
Turn off ...
Don't use ...
How often do you ... ?

58

Project

Lesson objectives: review language from Chapter 4; make an eco-display; share ideas on how to save energy

Materials: posterboard, white paper, pens, magazines, scissors, glue; slips of colored paper and sticky tape (alternative craft activity); two game pieces and a coin for each pair

Warmer: Did you save energy?

Have the children stand up. Ask them to think of one thing they did to save energy at home since the last lesson. Call out some energy-saving ideas from Lesson 7. If they did it, they sit down. Leave *turn off the lights* to last—they probably all did that! If you use all the phrases and there are still children standing, ask what they did.

Prepare

1 Make an eco-display.

- Distribute the materials. Read through the instructions together and ensure the children are clear on what to do.
- Have the children follow the instructions to make their eco-display. Give support as necessary.

Alternative craft activity

An easier project is to make individual labels to put on items in the classroom that can be controlled/managed to help protect the environment. Elicit appropriate items and write them on the board, e.g. *doors, windows, lamps, light switches, computer, heaters/air conditioners, CD player, projector.* Have the children choose one each and write and illustrate a label giving advice, e.g. *Remember to turn off lights!* Then they stick their eco-labels in the appropriate place with tape.

Showcase 

2 Tell your class how you can save energy.

- Divide the class into groups of five. Give them a few minutes to plan and practice what they will say about saving energy, using the **Ideas Box** for support.
- Have each child present their ideas to their group, using their eco-display if you did the main craft activity.
- Have each group choose one child to present their ideas to the class and ask them questions about how they save energy. The class ask questions for the other group members to answer.

Optional activity: True or false?

Say some true and some false statements about saving energy. The children stand up for the false statements. Elicit why they are false, e.g. *Fill up the kettle.* (*only put in what you need*) *Use hot water in the washing machine.* (*use warm water*), etc.

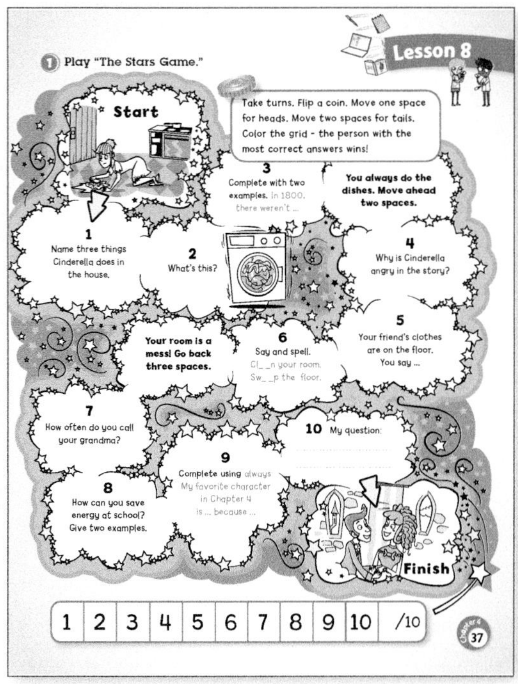

Lesson 8
1 Play "The Stars Game."
Start
Take turns. Flip a coin. Move one space for heads. Move two spaces for tails. Color the grid - the person with the most correct answers wins!
1 Name three things Cinderella does in the house.
2 What's this?
3 Complete with two examples. In 1800, there weren't ...
You always do the dishes. Move ahead two spaces.
4 Why is Cinderella angry in the story?
5 Your friend's clothes are on the floor. You say ...
6 Say and spell. Cl_ _n your room. Sw_ _p the floor.
Your room is a mess! Go back three spaces.
7 How often do you call your grandma?
8 How can you save energy at school? Give two examples.
9 Complete using always: My favorite character in Chapter 4 is ... because ...
10 My question:
Finish
1 2 3 4 5 6 7 8 9 10 /10
Chapter 4
37

1 Play "The Stars Game."

See p. 43 for instructions on how to play the game.

Answers

1 She sweeps the floor, picks up the clothes, cleans the bedroom, etc. **2** a washing machine **3** lamps, dishwashers, microwaves, etc. **4** She has to do all the work. **5** Pick up your clothes! **6** clean, sweep **7** Children's own answers. **8** You can turn off the lights/computers, etc. **9–10** Children's own answers.

Cooler: Play "Simon Says"

Use energy-saving actions to play the game (see Games Bank p. 19). Suggestions: *turn off the light, turn off the TV, close the door, close the window, change the light bulbs, turn down the heater, put a little water in the kettle.*

Competency Focus

Collaborate and Communicate

By presenting their ideas, the children consolidate their understanding of the language in a fun and engaging way. They also demonstrate their ability to work with friends and use interpersonal skills.

Digital Resources

Student eBook • Show the finished eco-display. Ask the children to identify the rooms in the house and elicit ideas for saving energy in each one.

- Show the pictures, stage by stage, as you talk the class through the activity process.
- Children use *Highlighter* to identify frequency words in the Ideas Box. Elicit other frequency words/phrases from the class (e.g. *sometimes, every day.*), asking children to write them in *Add personal note* using *Pen*.

Language Review

Lesson objective: review language from Chapter 4
Materials: Tracks 4.9 and AB 4.1; cards for "Board Pelmanism" (Warmer)

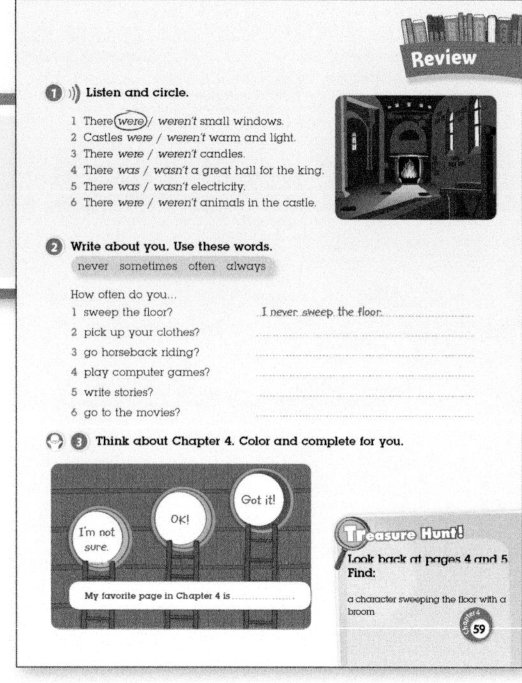
Review

1 Listen and circle.

1 There (were) / weren't small windows.
2 Castles were / weren't warm and light.
3 There were / weren't candles.
4 There was / wasn't a great hall for the king.
5 There was / wasn't electricity.
6 There were / weren't animals in the castle.

2 Write about you. Use these words.

never sometimes often always

How often do you ...
1 sweep the floor? I never sweep the floor.
2 pick up your clothes?
3 go horseback riding?
4 play computer games?
5 write stories?
6 go to the movies?

3 Think about Chapter 4. Color and complete for you.

My favorite page in Chapter 4 is ...

Treasure Hunt!
Look back at pages 4 and 5. Find:
a character sweeping the floor with a broom

59

Warmer: Play "Board Pelmanism"

Prepare cards using key vocabulary from Chapter 4 (*washing/machine, vacuum/cleaner, tea/kettle, clean/your room, pick up/your clothes, sweep/the floor, do/the dishes, turn off/the lamp*). Play the game (see Games Bank p. 19).

1 4.9 Listen and circle.

- Have the children look at the picture and say what they can see.
- Play Track 4.9 twice. The children listen and circle the correct word in each sentence.
- Elicit answers and check with the class.

Audioscript

Now listen, class ... It's time for history. Today we're going to learn about castles. Look at the picture. There were very small windows, so castles were cold and dark. There weren't lamps, but there were candles. Inside there was a great hall—a big room for the king and his people. There wasn't electricity, of course, so there was a large, open fire. There weren't any gas or electric stoves, but there was a kettle to heat water. There were cats and dogs in the castle, too—to eat all the rats!

Answers

1 were **2** weren't **3** were **4** was **5** wasn't **6** were

2 Write about you. Use these words.

- Have a child read the example sentence. Ask if that information is also true for them.
- The children complete the sentences, then compare with a friend. Elicit responses.

Answers

Children's own answers.

3 Think about Chapter 4. Color and complete for you.

- Have the children look back at Chapter 4. Elicit their favorite parts. The children then color the circle which represents how they feel about their own progress (self-evaluation).
- Have the children complete the sentence about their favorite page. Elicit responses.

Treasure Hunt!

Have the children look at pp. 4–5 to find a character sweeping the floor with a broom. They hold up their Student Book and point to the right place on the page.

Cooler: Play "The Chain Game"

Play the game with household chores (see Games Bank p. 19). Start the chain with *Every day, I pick up my clothes.* Each time you start a new chain, use a different frequency phrase.

Competency Focus

Me: Self-evaluation

The children reflect on the chapter and express their opinions about their own progress. This encourages them to evaluate and make decisions about how they learn and what they need to revisit.

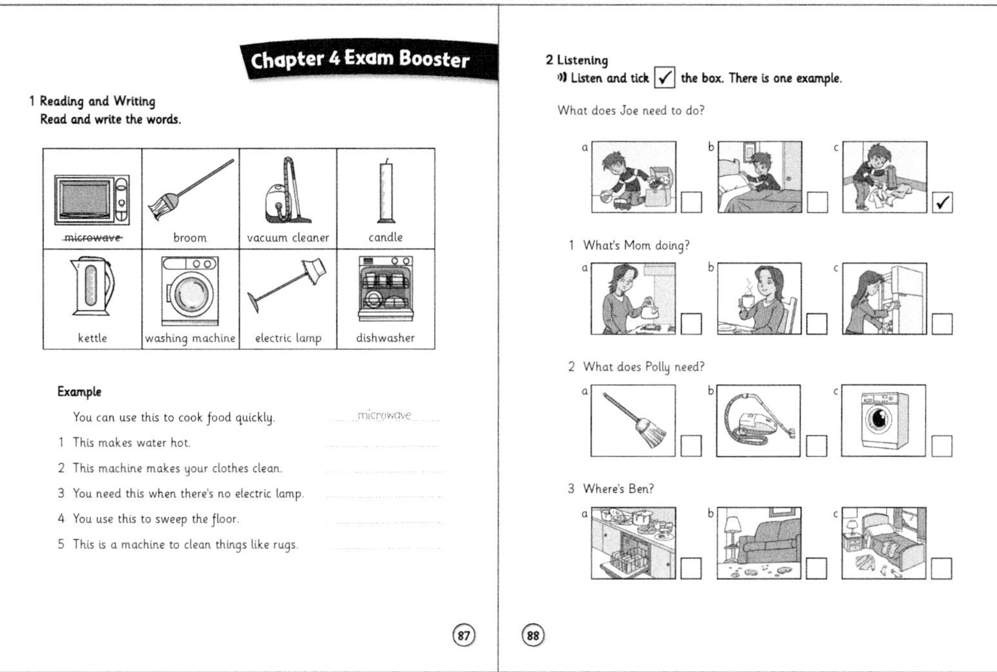

Chapter 4 Exam Booster

1 Reading and Writing
Read and write the words.

~~microwave~~	broom	vacuum cleaner	candle
kettle	washing machine	electric lamp	dishwasher

Example

You can use this to cook food quickly. microwave

1 This makes water hot.
2 This machine makes your clothes clean.
3 You need this when there's no electric lamp.
4 You use this to sweep the floor.
5 This is a machine to clean things like rugs.

87

2 Listening
Listen and tick ✓ the box. There is one example.

What does Joe need to do?

1 What's Mom doing?

2 What does Polly need?

3 Where's Ben?

88

3 Reading and Writing
Look and read. Choose the correct words and write them on the lines. There is one example.

dishwasher	washing machine	vacuum cleaner	Acrobat
actor	cucumber	pepper	~~sandwich~~

Example

To make this, you put cheese or meat between two pieces of bread. sandwich

Questions

1 This person performs in a play.
2 This machine helps you do the dishes.
3 This person often performs in a circus.
4 You can use this long green vegetable to make a salad.
5 You clean the floor or carpet with this electric machine.

Exam Tip
Remember to check the spelling after you write your answers!

89

1 Reading and Writing. Read and write the words.

The children write the items described, choosing from the options supplied. Check answers.

Answers

1 kettle **2** washing machine **3** candle **4** broom
5 vacuum cleaner

2 AB 4.1 Listening. Listen and tick (✓) the box. There is one example.

The children read the questions. Play Track AB 4.1 twice. Then they listen and check the correct picture in each section. Check answers.

Answers (Audioscript on p. 222)

1 a **2** b **3** b

3 Reading and Writing. Look and read. Choose the correct words and write them on the lines. There is one example.

The children write the items described, choosing from the options supplied. Check answers.

Answers

1 actor **2** dishwasher **3** Acrobat **4** cucumber
5 vacuum cleaner

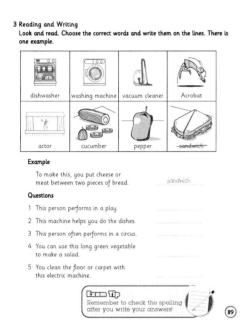

Digital Resources

Teacher Resource Center • Print out Test Chapter 4 to use at the end of this lesson. The Test Generator also allows you to create customized tests.

Student's App • Encourage the children to play the games on their smartphone/tablet. Have a class vote on which of the three games they played is their favorite. (*The Inks* Apps are free and available on the App Store and Google Play.)

Chapter 5 Egypt Overview

The children will:

- use critical thinking skills to identify verbs for everyday life.
- talk about life in the past.
- read, understand, and act out a story.
- use a range of verbs to talk about life in their country.
- talk about what people did/didn't do in the past.
- find out about Tutankhamun's tomb.
- make a pyramid display.

Key Vocabulary

Verbs for everyday life 1: believe, celebrate, fish, hunt, live, paint, prepare, use
Verbs for everyday life 2: build, drink, grow, keep, paint, sell, speak, write

Key Grammar

- They prepared (their food in ovens).
- They hunted (crocodiles).
- He built (his house).
- He didn't speak (English).

Reading Skills

Story: *Journey into the Past*
Genre: time travel adventure

Literacy Development

- predict story content from title and pictures
- reflect on and personalize the theme of the story
- focus on the use of past verbs

Functional Language

- What do you know about …?
- I know that …
- Let's find out more about …

Spelling

Words ending in *–ll*

CLIL: History—Tutankhamun's tomb

The children find out about the excavation of Tutankhamun's tomb.

Competency Focus

The children will:

use critical thinking skills to identify verbs for everyday life. (Lesson 1) predict the content of a story. (Lesson 3) identify and use verbs for everyday life. (Lesson 5)	apply new grammar to previously learned vocabulary. (Lesson 2) talk about things people did/didn't do. (Lesson 6)	work in pairs to act out a dialogue. (Lesson 3) work in groups to act out the story. (Lesson 8)	personalize the story by imagining a journey they make into the past. (Lesson 4) evaluate their own progress in the chapter. (Review)	develop a historical understanding by finding out more about hieroglyphics. (Lesson 7)

Digital Overview

Teacher Presentation

Student eBook and Digital Activity Book

- Oral Storytelling Video 5.1: *Journey into the Past*
- Interactive versions of AB activities
- Integrated audio and answer key for all activities

Teacher resources for planning, lesson delivery, and homework

Teacher Resource Center

- Class Planner Chapter 5
- Worksheets to print out (including notes and answers):
  - Grammar Worksheet 5A: They prepared/hunted ...
  - Grammar Worksheet 5B: He built/didn't speak ...
  - Oral Storytelling Video Worksheet 5: *Journey into the Past*
  - Phonics Worksheet 5
  - CLIL Graphic Organizer 5
- Test Chapter 5 and Mid-year Test
- Test Generator
- Literacy Handbook

Watch the Oral Storytelling Video

Children's resources for learning and practicing at home

Reader eBook and Student eBook

- Oral Storytelling Video 5.1: *Journey into the Past*

The Inks Student's App

Vocabulary games: Verbs for everyday life

Egypt

Lesson 1

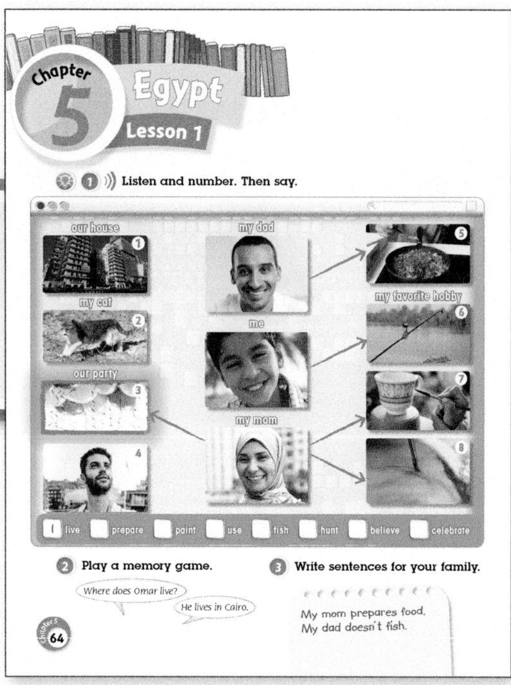

Vocabulary

Lesson objective: identify and use verbs for everyday life

Key vocabulary: *believe, celebrate, fish, hunt, live, paint, prepare, use*

Materials: Track 5.1

Warmer: Play "The Shark Game"

Play the game with *mother, factory, country* (see Games Bank p. 19).

1 5.1 Listen and number. Then say.

- Have the children look at the pictures. Ask *What's a blog? What activities can you see?*
- Play Track 5.1. The children listen and find each activity. They write each picture number by the correct word.
- Play Track 5.1 again, pausing after each verb for the children to point and repeat.

Audioscript

My name's Omar. I live with my mom and dad in an apartment in Cairo. My dad is a chef. He prepares food in a big restaurant. My mom owns her own shop. She makes and sells plates and dishes. She uses special gold paint. My favorite hobby is fishing. I fish in the Nile River. My dad doesn't like fishing. My cat likes hunting. He hunts birds. Today is March 21st. That is Mother's Day in Egypt. Egyptians believe mothers are very important. We are having a party at home to celebrate Mother's Day this afternoon.

Answers

live 1, prepare 5, paint 7, use 8, fish 6, hunt 2, believe 4, celebrate 3

2 Play a memory game.

- Have two children read out the example. Elicit two more questions.
- The children close their books and take turns asking and answering in pairs.

3 Write sentences for your family.

- Give examples about your own family first. Say and write on the board, e.g. *I always celebrate birthdays with my family. My mom and dad live in a house in*
- Have the children write sentences about their family in their notebook. Set a time limit, not a number of sentences, so they can achieve as much as possible at their own pace. Elicit answers and have other children say *same* or *different* compared to their own family.

Answers

Children's own answers.

Optional activity: Listen and mime

5.1

Attaching a physical action to verbs helps many children remember them better. Play Track 5.1 from Activity 1 again, and have the children mime everything they can. (Some things like *That is Mother's Day in Egypt* may be difficult to mime—encourage them to be inventive!)

Chapter 5 Egypt Lesson 1

1 Write. Then complete.

~~live~~ paint use prepare fish celebrate hunt believe

Amina's Blog All About Me!

1 live 2 3

4 5 6

Hi, I'm Amina. I a live in Cairo with my family. On weekends, we b .... our car to go to the lake to c .... and have fun. In my family, we d .... birthdays are important. We always e .... with a family party. We f .... delicious food.

2 Choose and categorize the verbs in your notebook.

easy words / difficult words

outside / inside / both

my family does this / my family doesn't do this

38

Competency Focus

The children use critical thinking skills to identify verbs for everyday life by using visual clues and processing the written and spoken forms.

1 Write. Then complete.

The children label the pictures using the words supplied. Then they complete the sentences using the appropriate verbs. Elicit answers.

Answers

1 live **2** prepare **3** fish, hunt **4** paint, use **5** believe **6** celebrate

a live **b** use **c** fish **d** believe **e** celebrate **f** prepare

2 Choose and categorize the verbs in your notebook.

Elicit an example for each category listed. Ask *Which categories would you choose?* Elicit ideas, prompting children to give a reason for their choice. The children choose a pair of categories and list the words in their notebook, then compare with a friend.

Answers

Children's own answers.

Cooler: Play "Tic-Tac-Toe"

Play the game with key vocabulary from the lesson and *like* (see Games Bank p. 19). To win a square, a child says a sentence with the verb.

Digital Resources

Student eBook • Play "Kim's Game" with the new vocabulary. Display the SB page. Have the class read the verbs aloud. Use *Timer* to give them one minute to memorize the pictures, then one minute to recall them. Repeat.

Digital Activity Book • Ask the children to do the AB interactive digital activities, or set them for homework.

Grammar

Lesson objective: talk about life in the past
Key grammar: *They prepared (their food in ovens). They hunted (crocodiles).*
Secondary language: *ancient, hieroglyphics, makeup, tomb*
Materials: Track 5.2; map of Egypt (Warmer); Grammar Worksheet 5A [TRC printout] (optional)

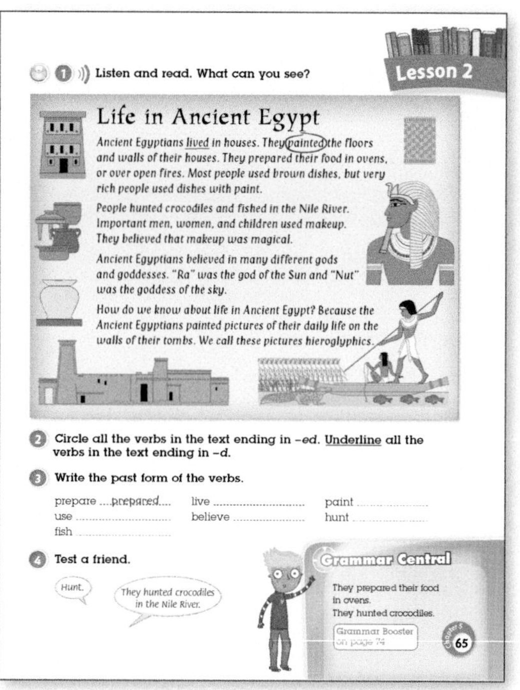

Warmer: Brainstorm

Ask *What do you know about Egypt?* If possible, show them where it is on a map. Elicit ideas and build a mind-map on the board. Prompt as necessary with questions about monuments, weather, history, food, etc.

1 5.2 Listen and read. What can you see? 

- Have the children look at the pictures. Read the title and explain that the text is on a history blog.
- Play Track 5.2 twice. The children listen and read along. Elicit what each picture shows. (Egyptian house, painted floor, dishes, hunt crocodiles, daily life, god)

2 Circle all the verbs in the text ending in *-ed*. Underline all the verbs in the text ending in *-d*.

- Have the children find the first example of words ending in *–ed* or *–d*. (*lived—line 1, painted—line 1*) The children then find the rest of the verbs on their own. Elicit answers. Make sure the children are pronouncing the verbs correctly.

Answers

–ed: painted, hunted, fished

–d: lived, prepared, used, believed

Grammar Central

They prepared their food in ovens. …

Have the children look at the patterns. Ask *Are we talking about the present or the past?* (*the past*) Elicit how the past is formed. (*Add* –ed *or just* –d *if the verb ends in* –e.)

Read out the sentences for the children to repeat. Pay particular attention to the pronunciation of the *–ed* endings.

For extra practice, try the **Grammar Booster** section in the Student Book (p. 74).

Answers p. 74

Activity 1: **1** walked **2** cleaned **3** looked **4** listened **5** liked **6** believe **7** prepared

Activity 2: **1** lived **2** painted **3** played **4** hunted **5** prepared

Activity 3: Children's own answers.

3 Write the past form of the verbs.

- The children complete the verbs by writing *–d/–ed* as appropriate. Elicit answers, asking children to spell the complete words for the class to check.

Answers

prepared, lived, painted, used, believed, hunted, fished

Optional activity: -ed or not?

Read out sentences featuring the key verbs from Lesson 1 in the present and past (e.g. *I prepare my lunch. He lived in New York.*) The children stand up when they hear a past tense and sit down for a present tense.

4 Test a friend.

- Read out the example with a child. Divide the class into pairs. They take turns prompting with a verb from Activity 3 and saying the corresponding sentence from Activity 1.

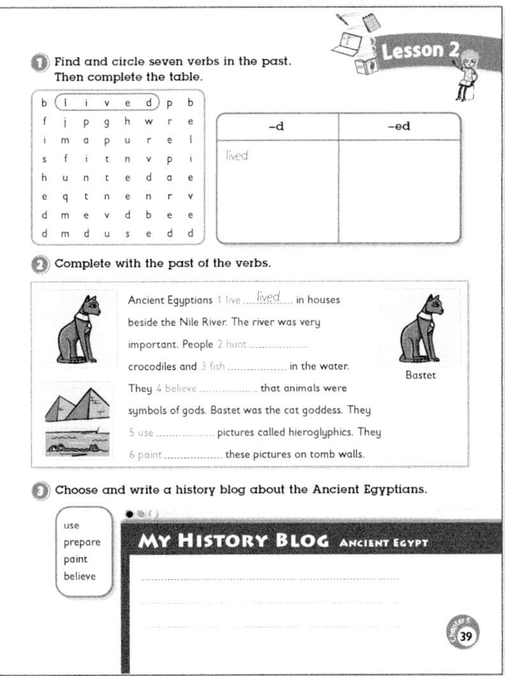

Lesson 2

1 Find and circle seven verbs in the past. Then complete the table.

b	l	i	v	e	d	p	b
f	j	p	g	h	w	r	e
i	m	a	p	u	r	e	l
s	f	i	t	n	v	p	i
h	u	n	t	e	d	a	e
e	q	t	n	e	n	r	v
d	m	e	v	d	b	e	e
d	m	d	u	s	e	d	d

-d	-ed
lived	

2 Complete with the past of the verbs.

Ancient Egyptians 1 live ...lived... in houses beside the Nile River. The river was very important. People 2 hunt .... crocodiles and 3 fish .... in the water. They 4 believe .... that animals were symbols of gods. Bastet was the cat goddess. They 5 use .... pictures called hieroglyphics. They 6 paint .... these pictures on tomb walls.

Bastet

3 Choose and write a history blog about the Ancient Egyptians.

use
prepare
paint
believe

MY HISTORY BLOG ANCIENT EGYPT

Chapter 5 39

1 Find and circle seven verbs in the past. Then complete the table.

The children find the verbs in the wordsearch, then write them in the correct column. (according to how the past is formed—*d* or *ed* added). Elicit answers, asking children to spell out the words.

Answers

Horizontal: lived, hunted, used
Vertical: fished, painted, prepared, believed
–d: lived, prepared, believed, used
–ed: fished, painted, hunted

2 Complete with the past of the verbs.

The children complete the text with the past form of the verb prompts. Elicit answers by asking children to read each sentence out loud.

Answers

1 lived **2** hunted **3** fished **4** believed **5** used **6** painted

3 Choose and write a history blog about the Ancient Egyptians.

The children write a blog post using the verbs supplied in the past tense. Have children read their texts.

Answers

Children's own answers.

Cooler: What's different?

Have the children close their books. Read out the text from Activity 1 again, but make some funny changes. Every time the children hear something different, they call out *Stop!* and tell you what the original was. Examples: *Ancient Egyptians lived in supermarkets. They painted the floors and the televisions of their houses.*

Competency Focus

Learn

The children use previously acquired vocabulary in a different context with new grammatical structures.

Digital Resources

Digital Activity Book • Use the AB page to give feedback on activities using the answer key or the interactive digital activities.

Teacher Resource Center • For extra grammar practice, print out Grammar Worksheet 5A.

Reading: Story Extract

Lesson objectives: find out what others know and react positively; predict story content from title and pictures; read the extract from *Journey into the Past* (beginning)
Functional language: *What do you know about . . . ? I know that . . . Let's find out more about . . .*
Secondary language: *find out, watch out*
Materials: Tracks 5.3 and 5.4; large pieces of paper with *True* and *False* (Cooler)

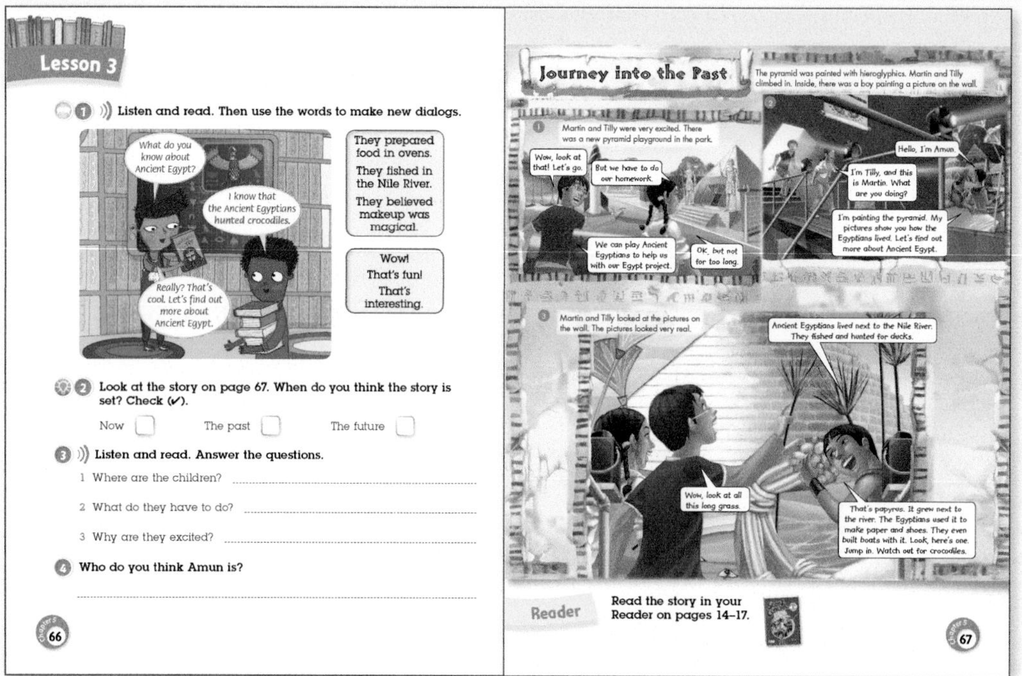

Lesson 3

1 Listen and read. Then use the words to make new dialogs.

They prepared food in ovens.
They fished in the Nile River.
They believed makeup was magical.

Wow!
That's fun!
That's interesting.

2 Look at the story on page 67. When do you think the story is set? Check (✓).

Now ☐ The past ☐ The future ☐

3 Listen and read. Answer the questions.

1 Where are the children? ....
2 What do they have to do? ....
3 Why are they excited? ....

4 Who do you think Amun is?

....

66

Journey into the Past

1 Martin and Tilly were very excited. There was a new pyramid playground in the park.

2 The pyramid was painted with hieroglyphics. Martin and Tilly climbed in. Inside, there was a boy painting a picture on the wall.

3 Martin and Tilly looked at the pictures on the wall. The pictures looked very real.

Reader Read the story in your Reader on pages 14–17.

67

Warmer: Visualization

Have the children close their eyes and imagine they are in a town in Ancient Egypt. Ask *What can you see/hear/smell? Is it hot or cold? What are the people doing? What are they wearing? Do they look happy?* Have them open their eyes and share with a friend what they imagined.

Functional language

1 5.3 Listen and read. Then use the words to make new dialogs.

- Have the children look at the pictures. Ask *What are they talking about?* (*life in Ancient Egypt*)
- Play Track 5.3. The children listen and read along.
- Play Track 5.3 again, pausing for the children to repeat.
- Elicit more facts they remember about Ancient Egypt. The children practice the dialogue in pairs, substituting different facts about life in Ancient Egypt.

Before reading

2 Look at the story on page 67. When do you think the story is set? Check (✓).

- Have the children look at the pictures and check one of the three options. Ask *When do you think the story is set?* Elicit ideas with reasons. (*It starts in the present, then moves to the past/Ancient Egypt.*)

3 5.4 Listen and read. Answer the questions.

- Give the children time to read the questions. Play Track 5.4 twice. The children listen and read along.
- The children write answers to the questions. Elicit answers and check with the class.

Answers

1 They are in the park. **2** They have to do their homework. **3** because there's a new pyramid playground in the park

4 Who do you think Amun is?

- Have the children write their prediction. Elicit ideas including reasons, but do not confirm. Say they will have to read the story to find out.

Answers

Children's own answers.

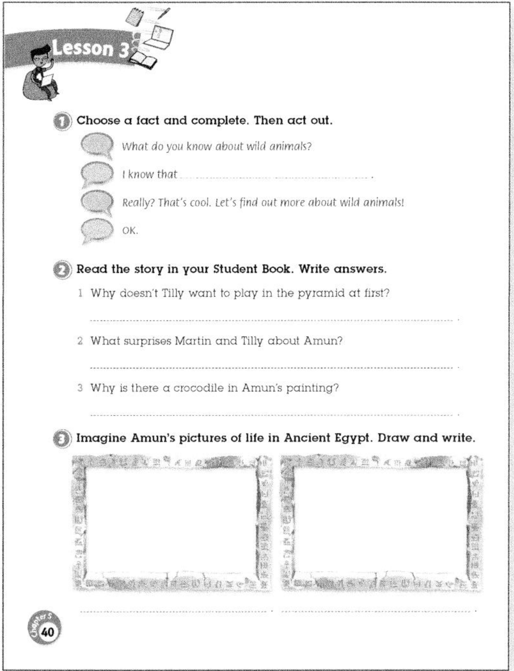
Lesson 3

1 Choose a fact and complete. Then act out.

What do you know about wild animals?

I know that ....

Really? That's cool. Let's find out more about wild animals!

OK.

2 Read the story in your Student Book. Write answers.

1 Why doesn't Tilly want to play in the pyramid at first?

....

2 What surprises Martin and Tilly about Amun?

....

3 Why is there a crocodile in Amun's painting?

....

3 Imagine Amun's pictures of life in Ancient Egypt. Draw and write.

....

40

1 Choose a fact and complete. Then act out.

The children come up with a fact about a wild animal and complete the dialogue. They act out their dialogues in pairs. Have pairs act out for the class.

Answers

Children's own answers.

2 Read the story in your Student Book. Write answers.

The children read the Student Book story extract again and write answers to the questions. Elicit answers.

Answers

1 They have to do their homework. **2** He's painting a picture on a pyramid wall that looked very real. **3** There are crocodiles in the Nile River.

3 Imagine Amun's pictures of life in Ancient Egypt. Draw and write.

The children imagine and draw pictures that Amun might have drawn. Then they write a fact about Ancient Egypt under each picture. Monitor and remind them to use past verbs.

Answers

Children's own answers.

Cooler: True or False?

Stick a large sign on each side of the classroom: one reading *True*, the other *False*. Say true/false statements based on the lesson. Have the children call out *True!* or *False!* and point to the right side of the classroom. Elicit the correct version of false sentences.

Competency Focus

Collaborate and Communicate

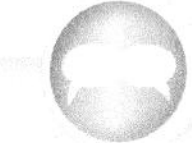

The children act out an authentic dialogue together, putting into practice new functional language. This helps motivate and engage them in the act of reading.

Think! Critical Thinking

The children apply reading skills (exploiting pictures and text clues) to understand the story context.

Digital Resources

Digital Activity Book • Display AB page for Activity 3 feedback. Have children use *Pen* to draw what they imagine Amun's picture of life in Ancient Egypt looks like. Elicit who in the class had the same details in their picture.

Student eBook, Digital Activity Book • TIP With the answer key, you can show the answers all at once or one by one to customize feedback.

Journey into the Past

1
Martin and Tilly were very excited. There was a new pyramid playground in the park.

Martin: Wow, look at that! Let's go.

Tilly: But we have to do our homework.

Martin: We can play Ancient Egyptians to help us with our Egypt project.

Tilly: OK, but not for too long.

2
The pyramid was painted with hieroglyphics. Martin and Tilly climbed in. Inside, there was a boy painting a picture on the wall.

Amun: Hello, I'm Amun.

Tilly: I'm Tilly, and this is Martin. What are you doing?

Amun: I'm painting the pyramid. My pictures show you how the Egyptians lived. Let's find out more about Ancient Egypt.

3
Martin and Tilly looked at the pictures on the wall. The pictures looked very real.

Amun: Ancient Egyptians lived next to the Nile River. They fished and hunted for ducks.

Martin: Wow, look at all this long grass.

Amun: That's papyrus. It grew next to the river. The Egyptians used it to make paper and shoes. They even built boats with it. Look, here's one. Jump in. Watch out for crocodiles.

4
Martin and Tilly climbed into the boat with Amun. The boat floated down the river. Up ahead, there was a big building.

Tilly: What's that?

Amun: That's a temple. The Egyptians believed in a lot of gods and goddesses. They built temples and painted them. They painted pictures and wrote stories about the gods on the walls.

5
Martin: Like the pictures you painted?

Amun: That's right. I'm learning to be a scribe. Scribes wrote stories and kept records.

Tilly: That's how we know about Ancient Egypt.

Amun gave Tilly a roll of papyrus.

6
The boat stopped beside a pyramid.

Tilly: I want to write down this story so I can remember it!

7
There was a noise in the long grass.

Tilly: Look out! Crocodile! Run!

8
Martin and Tilly ran into the pyramid. Suddenly, they were back at the playground.

Martin: Wow! That was cool.

Tilly: That crocodile almost got me!

Martin: It's lucky that Amun escaped in the boat.

9
Tilly: Let's go home and finish our project.

10
Martin and Tilly wrote about their adventure and built a small pyramid. They were very excited to show their project.

Teacher: So, Martin and Tilly, what do you know about Ancient Egypt?

Martin: Ancient Egyptians built pyramids and temples.

Tilly: They were very good at drawing. They used pictures for their alphabet.

11
Teacher: Great project! But what happened to this papyrus?

Tilly: You won't believe us if we tell you!

Lesson objective: read and understand the Chinese folk tale *Chen's Magic Pen* in the Reader
Materials: Track 5.5; Reader; Oral Storytelling Video Worksheet 5 [TRC printout] (optional)

Warmer: Predictions

Ask the children to remember where Martin and Tilly were at the end of the story extract. (*in a boat with Amun in Ancient Egypt*) Brainstorm with the children things they think Martin and Tilly will see and do. Make two lists on the board. You can compare these lists with the story after reading.

Story Summary

Martin and Tilly, two schoolchildren, enter a playground pyramid, which transports them to Ancient Egypt with Amun, a boy who teaches them about Ancient Egyptian culture. After escaping from a crocodile, they return to school and present a project about Ancient Egypt to their class.

Value: It's important to study. 

5.5 While reading

- Have the children look at the pictures in the Reader. Ask *What places can you see in the pictures? What activities are the children doing?*
- Play Track 5.5. The children listen and read along. Ask *What does Amun want to be?* (*a scribe*)
- Play Track 5.5 again. Ask questions to check comprehension, e.g. *Why do the children need to be careful near the river?* (*There are crocodiles.*) *Why are the children in the playground in picture 8?* (*They traveled back in time and they're in the present again.*)

After reading: Reflect

- Ask questions to give the children the opportunity to think about the issues raised by the story, e.g. *What did Martin and Tilly learn about Ancient Egypt? Where did they use what they learned? Why do Martin and Tilly think their teacher won't believe their story?*

Optional activity: This is my town

Ask the children to imagine a visit from Amun to their town. Ask *What do you think is strange for Amun in your town?* Have them discuss with a friend. Elicit ideas.

Story Time

Using cultural context

Interesting artwork like the examples in this story provide more opportunity for discussion and enhancing understanding in the context of the children's own culture. Point to some of the pictures and ask, e.g. *Do you have temples in your country? Do they have a different name?*

Reading Strategy

Audio-assisted Reading

Audio-assisted Reading is a strategy where the children read the story aloud as they listen to it. This strategy helps them improve their reading skills, pronunciation, and intonation.

For additional explanation and activities, see the Literacy Handbook on Teacher Resource Center.

Cooler: Who's speaking?

Have the children close their Student Book. Say lines of dialogue from the story extract to elicit who is speaking: Martin, Tilly, or Amun. This can be played as a team game for points. You could invite children to read out a sentence for the other team to guess.

Digital Resources

Reader eBook • Oral Storytelling Video 5.1 gives the story with a different ending. Watch it together at the end of the lesson, then discuss the differences.

Teacher Resource Center • Print out Oral Storytelling Video Worksheet 5 to help you get the most out of the video.

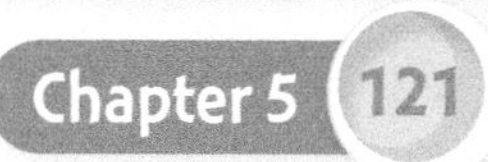

Reading Comprehension and Critical Literacy

Lesson objectives: focus on the use of the past in telling a story; reflect on the story theme and think about a similar adventure
Materials: Track 5.5; Reader; Oral Storytelling Video Worksheet 5 [TRC printout] (optional)

Lesson 4 Time to Think

1 Read the story in your Reader.

2 Complete the Reading Report. Circle T (true) or F (false).

Reading Report
1 A boy was inside the pyramid. (T) / F
2 Ancient Egyptians used papyrus to make things. T / F
3 Martin and Tilly climbed into a car. T / F
4 Martin and Tilly stayed in Ancient Egypt for a long time. T / F
5 The teacher liked their project. T / F

3 Write a postcard about life in Ancient Egypt.

Dear Martin and Tilly,
The Ancient Egyptians lived along the Nile River.
From,
Amun

I Can Read and Write!
Look at what Amun says. Why does he use verbs in the past?
Can you use verbs in the past in your writing?

4 Talk about the story.

Would you like to go on a journey into the past? Where?

68

Note: Please ensure that your class has read the Reader story before you do this lesson.

Warmer: Search the pictures

Have the children look at the story. Name four key objects, animals or actions shown in the pictures to elicit the number of the picture they appear in. Then invite children to prompt for the class.

1 5.5 Read the story in your Reader.

- Have the children read the story. (Alternatively, play Track 5.5 and have them read along). Elicit whether they were correct in their predictions in Lesson 3 Activity 4.
- Check comprehension by asking *What did Amun show Martin and Tilly? (papyrus, a temple) What happened to the papyrus? (A crocodile ate a bit of it.)*

2 Complete the Reading Report. Circle T (true) or F (false).

- Do the example and elicit why it is true. (*Inside, a boy was painting a picture.*)
- Have the children circle true or false for each sentence. Elicit answers, including the correct version of the false statements.

Answers

1 T **2** T **3** F **4** F **5** T

I Can Read and Write!

Point out that Amun uses verb forms like *grew* and *used.* Elicit why. (*To make it clear he's talking about the past, not the present.*) Encourage the children to say when they use the past in their writing.

3 Write a postcard about life in Ancient Egypt.

- Elicit ideas for the postcard, but write only the verbs in the simple past on the board.
- Have the children complete the postcard with a minimum of two sentences. Monitor and help as necessary.
- Have the children read each other's postcards. Did they write about the same things?

Answers

Children's own answers.

4 Talk about the story. 

- Have one child read out Jason's questions. Have the children discuss in pairs whether they would like to travel into the past. Elicit opinions and ask the class if they agree. (They might need to use L1.)

Optional activity: Play "Disappearing Text" 

Play the game with *The Ancient Egyptians lived next to the Nile River. They fished and hunted for ducks.* (see Games Bank p. 19).

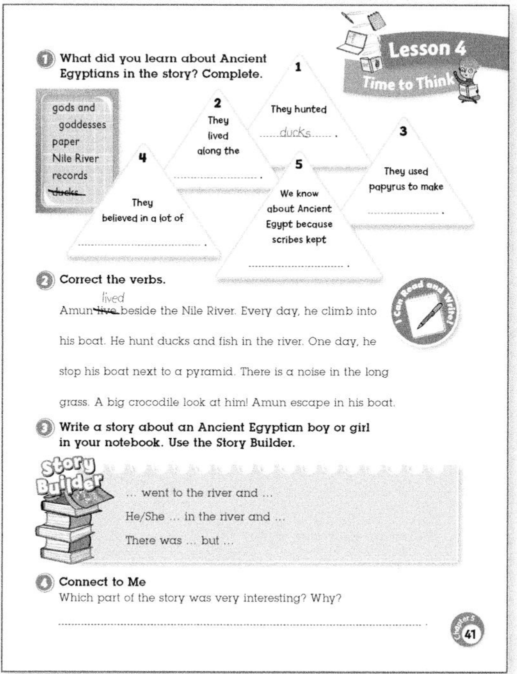

Lesson 4
Time to Think

1 What did you learn about Ancient Egyptians in the story? Complete.

gods and goddesses
paper
Nile River
records
~~ducks~~

1 They hunted ....ducks.... .
2 They lived along the ....
3 They used papyrus to make ....
4 They believed in a lot of ....
5 We know about Ancient Egypt because scribes kept ....

2 Correct the verbs.

I Can Read and Write!

Amun ~~live~~ lived beside the Nile River. Every day, he climb into his boat. He hunt ducks and fish in the river. One day, he stop his boat next to a pyramid. There is a noise in the long grass. A big crocodile look at him! Amun escape in his boat.

3 Write a story about an Ancient Egyptian boy or girl in your notebook. Use the Story Builder.

Story Builder
... went to the river and ...
He/She ... in the river and ...
There was ... but ...

4 Connect to Me
Which part of the story was very interesting? Why?
....

Chapter 5 41

1 What did you learn about Ancient Egyptians in the story? Complete.

The children complete the sentences using the words supplied. Elicit answers.

Answers

1 ducks **2** Nile River **3** paper **4** gods and goddesses **5** records

2 Correct the verbs.

The children practice the **I Can Read and Write!** feature by correcting the present tense verbs to past tense. Elicit answers.

Answers

lived, climbed, hunted, fished, stopped, was, looked, escaped

3 Write a story about an Ancient Egyptian boy or girl in your notebook. Use the Story Builder.

Use the **Story Builder** prompts to elicit ideas. The children write a story in their notebook, then swap with a friend to check. Have children read out their story for the class.

Answers

Children's own answers.

4 Connect to Me

Elicit ideas on interesting parts of the story. The children write their own response, then compare with a friend. Elicit responses.

Answers

Children's own answers.

Cooler: Play "Ready, Set, Draw!"

5.5 Play Track 5.5. The children listen to the story again with the Reader open. They raise both arms above their head and lower them quickly every time they hear and see a past verb. They need to be attentive—there are 20 verbs!

Competency Focus

Me: Critical Literacy

The children use critical literacy skills to reflect on the story and think about whether they would like to have a similar adventure.

Digital Resources

Student eBook, Reader eBook • If you haven't already, show Oral Storytelling Video 5.1.

Teacher Resource Center • If you haven't already, print out Oral Storytelling Video Worksheet 5 to do the support activities.

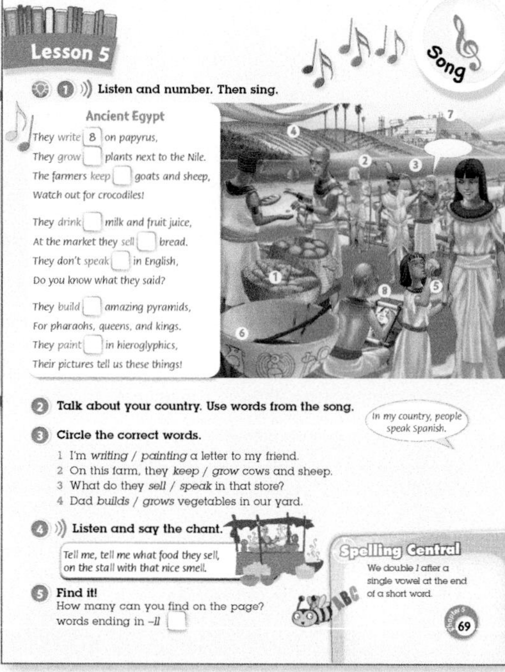

Lesson 5

Song

1 Listen and number. Then sing.

Ancient Egypt

They write 8 on papyrus,
They grow ☐ plants next to the Nile.
The farmers keep ☐ goats and sheep,
Watch out for crocodiles!

They drink ☐ milk and fruit juice,
At the market they sell ☐ bread.
They don't speak ☐ in English,
Do you know what they said?

They build ☐ amazing pyramids,
For pharaohs, queens, and kings.
They paint ☐ in hieroglyphics,
Their pictures tell us these things!

2 Talk about your country. Use words from the song.

3 Circle the correct words.

1 I'm *writing / painting* a letter to my friend.
2 On this farm, they *keep / grow* cows and sheep.
3 What do they *sell / speak* in that store?
4 Dad *builds / grows* vegetables in our yard.

4 Listen and say the chant.

Tell me, tell me what food they sell,
on the stall with that nice smell.

5 Find it!
How many can you find on the page?
words ending in *–ll* ☐

Spelling Central
We double *l* after a single vowel at the end of a short word.

69

Vocabulary, Song, and Spelling

Lesson objectives: identify and use verbs for everyday life; practice spelling words ending in *–ll*

Key vocabulary: *build, drink, grow, keep, paint, sell, speak, write*

Secondary language: *goats, pharaoh, plants, sheep, stall*

Materials: Tracks 5.6 and 5.7; Phonics Worksheet 5 [TRC] (optional)

Warmer: Pre-teach vocabulary

Have the children look at the red words in the song quickly. Mime some of the words and have the children guess them. Write the words on the board as they guess.

1 5.6 Listen and number. Then sing. 

- Play Track 5.6 with the Student Book closed. The children listen and raise their hand whenever they hear the verbs from the Warmer.
- Play Track 5.6 again with books open. The children write the number of the corresponding picture next to each verb. Elicit answers and check with the class.
- Play Track 5.6 again for the children to sing along.

Answers

write 8, grow 4, keep 2, drink 5, sell 1, speak 3, build 7, paint 6

Optional activity: Mime the song

5.6

Play the song again. Have the children listen and do actions for everything they can. Encourage them to be inventive! This also gives you a good view of how much of the incidental language the children understand. Based on this, you may need to check or teach words like *sheep, goat, pharaoh.*

2 Talk about your country. Use words from the song.

- Have a child read the example aloud. Elicit ideas about the children's own country using the verbs from the song.
- Divide the class into pairs to continue the activity. Elicit responses.

3 Circle the correct words.

- Have the children complete the sentences by circling the correct option in each pair.
- Elicit answers and check with the class.

Answers

1 writing **2** keep **3** sell **4** grows

Spelling Central

Words ending in –ll

Write *spel* on the board. Shake your head and add *l* at the end. Repeat with *tel(l)*. Say *sell* and ask a child to write it on the board. Explain that in a short word, *l* at the end is doubled to *ll*.

4 5.7 Listen and say the chant.

- Play Track 5.7. The children listen and read along. Elicit the words with *ll*.
- Play Track 5.7 again, pausing for the children to repeat.
- Have the children practice the chant in pairs. Invite pairs to perform for the class.

5 Find it!

- Set a time limit for the children to find words ending in *–ll* on the page. Elicit answers.

Answers

4—sell, tell, stall, smell

Cooler: Play "Ready, Set, Draw!"

Play the game with verb phrases from the song, e.g. *write on papyrus, grow plants, drink milk, sell bread* (see Games Bank p. 19).

Competency Focus

Think! Critical Thinking

The children use critical thinking skills to identify verbs for everyday routine by processing the written and spoken forms.

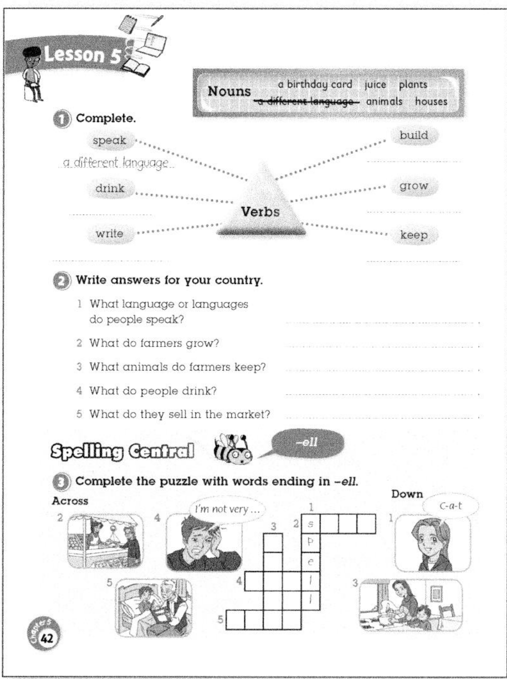

1 Complete.

The children complete the diagram using the words supplied. Elicit answers.

Answers

speak—a different language, drink—juice, write—a birthday card, build—houses, grow—plants, keep—animals

2 Write answers for your country.

The children answer the questions in pairs. Elicit answers.

Answers

Children's own answers.

3 Complete the puzzle with words ending in -ell.

The children complete the puzzle. Elicit answers.

Answers

Across: 2 sell 4 well 5 tell
Down: 1 spell 3 smell

Digital Resources

Student eBook • TIP Children use *Highlighter* to identify the words which illustrate the spelling feature on the page (here, words with *ll*).

- TIP Use *Timer* to set a time limit for SB Activity 5.

Student's App • Encourage the children to play the games on their smartphone/tablet. They could do this with a friend as a fun way to review the chapter vocabulary together. (*The Inks* Apps are free and available on the App Store and Google Play.)

Teacher Resource Center • For phonics practice, print out Phonics Worksheet 5.

Lesson 6

1 Listen and read. Who is Miguel talking about?

A Family History

1
Who's this?
My grandfather. He lived in Mexico. He was a farmer. He grew vegetables and kept chickens. He sold his food at the market.

2
That's cool. What about this picture?
This picture was when I went to Mexico with my dad. I was six. The bus trip took three hours.

3
My grandfather lived in a beautiful house in Mexico. He built the house himself.

4
Tell me more!
He was a musician, too. He played the guitar. He didn't write songs, but he sang songs to me.

5
Wow! Were the songs in English?
No. He didn't speak English. He only spoke Spanish.

6
What was your grandfather like?
He was a lot of fun.

2 Circle the correct words.

1 Miguel's grandfather *grew* / *didn't grow* food.
2 He *wrote* / *didn't write* songs.
3 He *built* / *didn't build* his house.
4 He *spoke* / *didn't speak* English
5 He *lived* / *didn't live* in the US.

Grammar Central

He built his house.
He didn't speak English

Grammar Booster on page 75

Chapter 5 70

Grammar and Reading

Lesson objective: talk about what people did/didn't *do* in the past

Key grammar: *He built (his house). He didn't speak (English).*

Secondary language: *bus trip*

Materials: Track 5.8; Grammar Worksheet 5B [TRC printout] (optional)

Warmer: Past or present?

Make statements about the past and present, e.g. *The Egyptians built pyramids. Miguel has a red backpack.* The children put both arms behind them if the verb is in the past tense and both arms up in the air for the present.

1 5.8 Listen and read. Who is Miguel talking about?

- Have the children look at the story. Ask *Where are the children?* (*in Story Central*) *What are they doing?* (*looking at pictures*)
- Play Track 5.8. The children listen. Ask *Who is Miguel talking about?* (*his grandfather*)
- Play Track 5.8 again, pausing for the children to repeat past verbs.

2 Circle the correct words. 

- Have the children read and complete the sentences by circling the correct verb forms. Check answers by saying each option and asking for a show of hands.

Answers

1 grew **2** didn't write **3** built **4** didn't speak **5** didn't live

Grammar Central

He built his house. …

Ask *Are these sentences in the present or the past?* (*the past*) Are the verbs different from the past verbs we saw in Lesson 4? (*Yes, they don't end in –ed.*) Explain that some verbs change differently in the past, e.g. *build—built*.

Point out for the past negative we use *didn't* + the unchanged verb. Elicit one more example of a past negative in the story. (*He didn't write songs.*)

For extra practice, try the **Grammar Booster** section in the Student Book (p. 75–77).

Answers p. 75

Activity 1: **1** went **2** sang **3** speak **4** wrote **5** grew **6** have **7** sell **8** took **9** built **10** didn't go **11** didn't play **12** didn't build

Activity 2: **1** built, didn't build **2** wrote, didn't write **3** went, didn't go

p. 76

Activity 1: **1** lived **2** didn't have **3** hunted **4** drank **5** didn't drink **6** climbed

Activity 2: **1** didn't live; lived **2** didn't eat; hunted **3** didn't have; had **4** didn't stay

p. 77

Activity 1: **1** was **2** lived **3** didn't have **4** was **5** loved **6** walked **7** were **8** had **9** took **10** built **11** prepared **12** listened

Activity 2: Children's own answers.

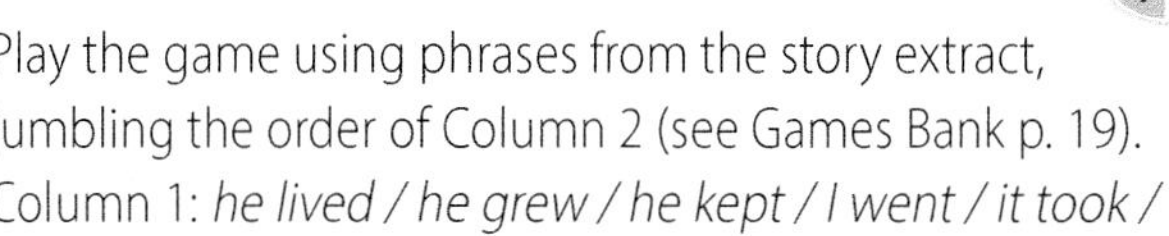

Optional activity: Play "Collocations"

Play the game using phrases from the story extract, jumbling the order of Column 2 (see Games Bank p. 19).
Column 1: *he lived / he grew / he kept / I went / it took / he built / he played / he sang.*
Column 2: *in Mexico / vegetables / chickens / to Mexico / three hours / the house / the guitar / songs*

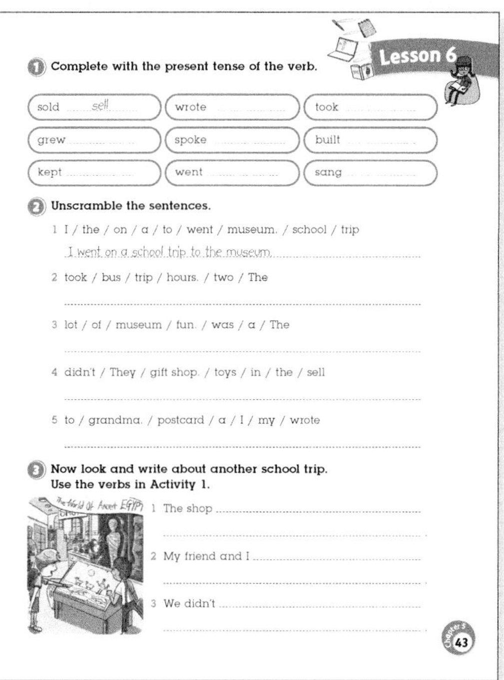

Lesson 6

1 Complete with the present tense of the verb.

sold sell	wrote	took
grew	spoke	built
kept	went	sang

2 Unscramble the sentences.

1 I / the / on / a / to / went / museum. / school / trip
I went on a school trip to the museum.
2 took / bus / trip / hours. / two / The
3 lot / of / museum / fun. / was / a / The
4 didn't / They / gift shop. / toys / in / the / sell
5 to / grandma. / postcard / a / I / my / wrote

3 Now look and write about another school trip. Use the verbs in Activity 1.

1 The shop
2 My friend and I
3 We didn't

Chapter 5 43

1 Complete with the present tense of the verb.

The children complete the present tense of the verbs. Elicit answers. Drill pronunciation as necessary.

Answers

sold—sell, grew—grow, kept—keep, wrote—write, spoke—speak, went—go, took—take, built—build, sang—sing

2 Unscramble the sentences.

The children write the sentences correctly. Elicit answers.

Answers

1 I went on a school trip to the museum. **2** The bus trip took two hours. **3** The museum was a lot of fun. **4** They didn't sell toys in the gift shop. **5** I wrote a postcard to my grandma.

3 Now look and write about another school trip. Use the verbs in Activity 1.

The children think about a different school trip and complete the sentences. They compare answers in small groups. Elicit answers.

Answers

Children's own answers.

Cooler: Play "The Chain Game"

Play the game to practice the past tense (see Games Bank p. 19). Start the chain with *My grandfather kept chickens.*

Competency Focus

Learn

The children demonstrate and consolidate their understanding of the new language by completing the activity.

Digital Resources

Digital Activity Book • Ask the children to do the AB interactive digital activities, or set them for homework.

Teacher Resource Center • For extra grammar practice, print out Grammar Worksheet 5B.

CLIL: History—Tutankhamun's tomb

Lesson objective: find out about the excavation of Tutankhamun's tomb
Materials: CLIL Graphic Organizer 5 [TRC printout] (optional)

CLIL History Lesson 7

1 Read. Who was Tutankhamun?

Tutankhamun's Tomb

What Was in the Tomb?

Tutankhamun's mummy was in the tomb. But that wasn't all. Pharaohs in Ancient Egypt built their tombs before they died. They put important things from their lives in their tombs to keep for the afterlife. There was a lot of treasure in Tutankhamun's tomb.

Who Discovered the Tomb, and When?

In 1922, an English archeologist named Howard Carter went to Egypt and discovered a small tomb in a pyramid. It was the tomb of a pharaoh named Tutankhamun. Tutankhamun was a pharaoh when he was nine. He died when he was eighteen. Carter discovered the tomb 3,000 years after Tutankhamun died.

What Was on the Walls of the Tomb?

There were paintings on the walls of the tomb. The paintings were pictures of Tutankhamun's life in this world, and in the afterlife. We know much more about life in Ancient Egypt because Howard Carter discovered Tutankhamun's tomb.

2 Answer the questions.

1 Who discovered Tutankhamun's tomb? ....
2 How many years was Tutankhamun a pharaoh? ....
3 What was in his tomb? ....
4 What was on the walls of the tomb? ....

3 Class Vote

Is history interesting?
Why / Why not?

Find Out More!
Find out more about Ancient Egypt. What were hieroglyphics? Can you write "Ancient Egypt" in hieroglyphics?

Chapter 5 71

Warmer: Play "Sentence Builders"

Write *In Ancient Egypt, …* on the board. Play the game (see Games Bank p. 19) with sentences about Egypt, e.g. *… people hunted crocodiles. / … people built big pyramids. / … people painted the floors and walls. / … people fished in the Nile River.*

1 Read. Who was Tutankhamun?

- Have the children look at the pictures. Ask *What country is this? (Egypt) Who was Tutankhamun? (Tutankhamun was a pharaoh.)* Elicit any ideas.
- Have the children read the text and underline facts about Tutankhamun. Elicit answers.

2 Answer the questions.

- Have a child read out the example and find the corresponding sentence in the text.
- The children answer the questions. Remind them to underline the right section in the text. Elicit answers and check with the class.

Answers

1 Howard Carter **2** nine years **3** Tutankhamun's mummy and a lot of treasure **4** paintings

Optional activity: Make class sentences

Explain you are going to make sentences as a class about Tutankhamun. Give the children a minute to look at the text again. Start the first sentence: *Tutankhamun …* The children take turns adding a word, e.g. *was … a … pharaoh.* When a sentence is complete, start another.

3 Class Vote

- Elicit the parts of history the class looked at in this chapter. (*Ancient Egypt, and family history—a Mexican grandfather*) Then ask *Is history interesting?*
- Take a class vote with a show of hands for yes or no. Count the votes and write them on the board. Invite children to explain why they answered yes or no (they might need help or to use L1 to explain this).

Find Out More!  

Elicit ideas on what hieroglyphics are. Suggest appropriate resources for the children to use to find out how to write *Ancient Egypt* in hieroglyphics, e.g. Internet, library books, etc. The children will need to complete this research before doing the follow-up activity in the Activity Book. (It could be set as homework.)

Lesson 7 CLIL

1 Read and find the words in the text.

The Rosetta Stone

In Tutankhamun's tomb, there were a lot of painted pictures called hieroglyphics. At first, people didn't understand hieroglyphics. But in 1799, a soldier discovered a special stone in Egypt – the Rosetta Stone. People looked at the writing on it. The writing was in three different languages: Greek, hieroglyphics, and another Egyptian language. They used the stone to translate hieroglyphic symbols. So Howard Carter could understand the pictures on the walls of Tutankhamun's tomb.

1 a picture system of writing .... hieroglyphics
2 find something new ....
3 change from one language to another ....
4 a picture to represent a letter ....

2 Use your Student Book research. Write your name in hieroglyphics. Find Out More!

It's My World! Make up your own system of ancient writing. Work with a friend and design pictures for two words.

Chapter 5 44

1 Read and find the words in the text.

The children read the text and write words next to the definitions. Elicit answers.

Answers

1 hieroglyphics **2** discover **3** translate **4** symbol

2 Use your Student Book research. Write your name in hieroglyphics.

Divide the class into groups of four. Have the children pool the information learned from their research in the Student Book and the Activity Book. Show them your name in hieroglyphics. Then they write their own name in hieroglyphics. Have children show their name to a friend.

It's My World!

The children work in pairs to create a new system of ancient writing for two words. They can choose any words they want. Elicit ideas.

Cooler: Browse the hieroglyphics

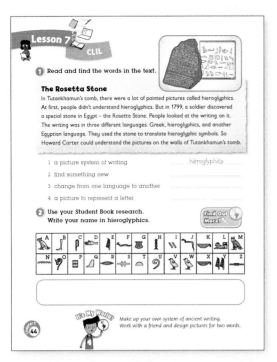

Have the children walk around the classroom to look at each other's words from **It's My World**. Can they guess the words?

Competency Focus

Act

The children carry out research to find out about hieroglyphics. They relate what they learn to their world, both inside and outside the classroom.

Digital Resources

Student eBook • To give feedback on SB Activity 2, have children use *Highlighter* to identify the section of the text which gives them the answer to each question.

• TIP Remember—you can use *Add personal note* to log the results of the class vote. Involve the children in tallying the results and writing the scores on the board.

Teacher Resource Center • Print out CLIL Graphic Organizer 5 for the children to use in collating their Find Out More! research.

CLIL eBook • The children can use the CLIL eBook to expand their knowledge of the lesson topic.

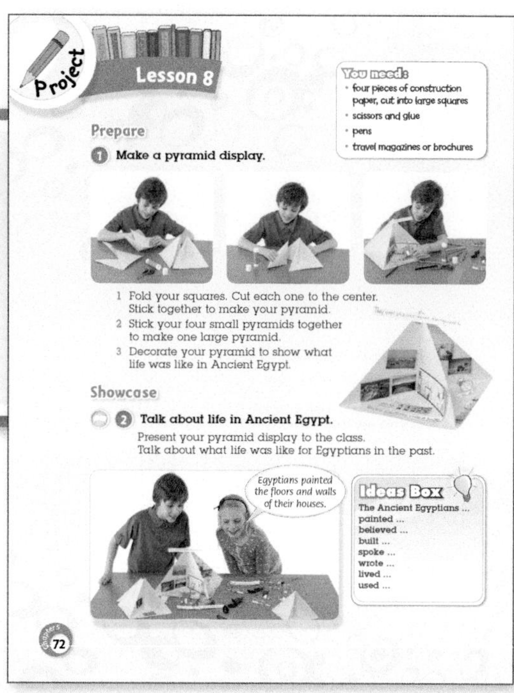

Project

Lesson 8

You need:
- four pieces of construction paper, cut into large squares
- scissors and glue
- pens
- travel magazines or brochures

Prepare

1 Make a pyramid display.

1 Fold your squares. Cut each one to the center. Stick together to make your pyramid.
2 Stick your four small pyramids together to make one large pyramid.
3 Decorate your pyramid to show what life was like in Ancient Egypt.

Showcase

2 Talk about life in Ancient Egypt.

Present your pyramid display to the class.
Talk about what life was like for Egyptians in the past.

Ideas Box
The Ancient Egyptians ...
painted ...
believed ...
built ...
spoke ...
wrote ...
lived ...
used ...

72

Project

Lesson objectives: review language from Chapter 5; make a pyramid display; talk about life in Ancient Egypt

Materials: four pieces of construction paper cut into large squares, scissors, glue, pens, travel magazines or brochures; two game pieces and a coin for each pair

Warmer: What's the question?

Write the answers to the questions in Student Book Lesson 7 Activity 2 on the board. Have the children work in pairs or small groups to recall the question that gives each answer. Set a time limit and invite children to say their questions.

Prepare

1 Make a pyramid display.

- Distribute the materials. Read through the instructions together and ensure the children are clear on what to do.
- Help the children follow the instructions to make and decorate their pyramid display. Give support as necessary.

Alternative craft activity

An easier project is to make one class display about life in Ancient Egypt. Elicit facts and write the key vocabulary on the board. Have one group of four children make the pyramid display as described above. Have the other children choose an item from the board and draw and label a picture to stick on it. The class pyramid can be placed on a table, and the labeled pictures displayed around it.

Showcase 

2 Talk about life in Ancient Egypt.

- Divide the class into groups of four. Give them time to plan and practice what they will say about life in Ancient Egypt, using the **Ideas Box** for support.
- Have each group choose a child to present to the class, showing their pyramid display if you did the main craft activity. Have the class ask questions for the other group members to answer.

Optional activity: Memory challenge

Divide the class into small groups. Give them a set time to come up with as many facts as they can about Egypt. Ask how many facts they found and have the group with the most list their facts. Get class feedback on whether they are correct. If, after checking, other groups think they have more, they take a turn. Elicit any facts that groups have missed.

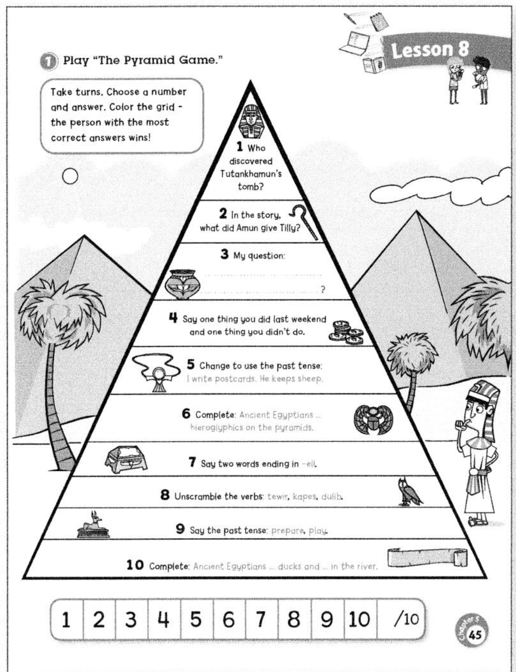
Lesson 8

1 Play "The Pyramid Game."

Take turns. Choose a number and answer. Color the grid - the person with the most correct answers wins!

1 Who discovered Tutankhamun's tomb?

2 In the story, what did Amun give Tilly?

3 My question: ...?

4 Say one thing you did last weekend and one thing you didn't do.

5 Change to use the past tense: I write postcards. He keeps sheep.

6 Complete: Ancient Egyptians ... hieroglyphics on the pyramids.

7 Say two words ending in -ell.

8 Unscramble the verbs: tewir, kapes, dulib.

9 Say the past tense: prepare, play.

10 Complete: Ancient Egyptians ... ducks and ... in the river.

1	2	3	4	5	6	7	8	9	10	/10

Chapter 5 45

1 Play "The Pyramid Game."

See p. 43 for instructions on how to play the game.

Answers

1 Howard Carter **2** a roll of papyrus **3** Children's own answer. **4** Last weekend, I ... I didn't ... **5** I wrote postcards. He kept sheep. **6** painted **7** *any two of:* sell, tell, smell, well, etc. **8** write, speak, build **9** prepared, played **10** hunted, fished

Cooler: Play "Disappearing Words"

Play the game with key vocabulary from Lessons 1 and 5 (see Games Bank p. 19).

Competency Focus

Collaborate and communicate

By presenting their ideas, the children consolidate their understanding of the story in a fun and engaging way. They also demonstrate their ability to work with friends and use interpersonal skills.

Digital Resources

Student eBook • Show the pictures, stage by stage, as you talk the class through the activity process.

Digital Activity Book • For "The Pyramid Game" in AB Activity 1, you can use *Timer*. Set a time limit. The child who has the most correct answers when the time is up wins.

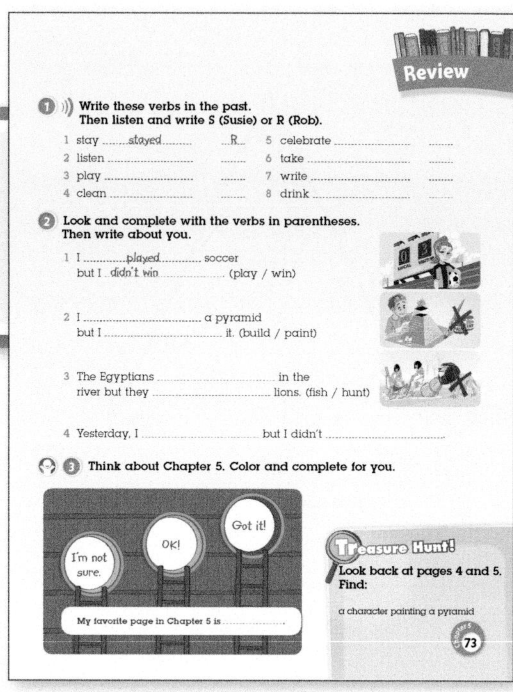

Review

1 Write these verbs in the past. Then listen and write S (Susie) or R (Rob).

1 stay ......stayed...... ...R...
2 listen ....
3 play ....
4 clean ....
5 celebrate ....
6 take ....
7 write ....
8 drink ....

2 Look and complete with the verbs in parentheses. Then write about you.

1 I ....played.......... soccer
but I ..didn't win.................. (play / win)

2 I .... a pyramid
but I .... it. (build / paint)

3 The Egyptians .... in the river but they .... lions. (fish / hunt)

4 Yesterday, I .... but I didn't ....

3 Think about Chapter 5. Color and complete for you.

Treasure Hunt!
Look back at pages 4 and 5. Find:
a character painting a pyramid

73

Language Review

Lesson objective: review language from Chapter 5
Materials: Tracks 5.9, AB 5.1, and AB 5.2; large pieces of paper with *Yes* and *No* (Cooler)

Warmer: Vocabulary recall

The children look back at the vocabulary introduced in Lessons 1 and 5. Then they close their Student Book. Give them two minutes to write down as many of the words as they can. Then they swap with another pair to check each other's work. The pair with the most correct words wins.

1 5.9 Write the past tense of the verb. Then listen and write S (Susie) or R (Rob).

- Have the children complete the past forms of the verbs. Check answers by saying the verb in the present to elicit the past form and how it is spelled.
- Play Track 5.9 twice. The children listen and write *S* or *R*, according to who did the action.
- Elicit answers.

Audioscript

Susie: *Hi, Rob, how was your day?*
Rob: *Hi, Susie. It was good, thank you. I stayed home all day today.*
Susie: *That sounds boring.*
Rob: *Well, actually I did a lot of things. This morning, I listened to some new music and I wrote an email to my friend in Canada. How about you, Susie?*
Susie: *Well, Rob, my day was great! It was my sister's birthday so we celebrated. We went to a pizza restaurant. I drank a really big milkshake and I took a lot of pictures. Oh, and we played games.*
Rob: *That sounds fun! This afternoon, I cleaned my room.*
Susie: *Well, we can do something fun tomorrow, then!*

Answers

1 stayed (R) **2** listened (R) **3** played (S) **4** cleaned (R) **5** celebrated (S) **6** took (S) **7** wrote (R) **8** drank (S)

2 Look and complete with the verbs in parentheses. Then write about you.

- The children complete the sentences.

Answers

1 played / didn't win **2** built / didn't paint **3** fished / didn't hunt **4** Children's own answers.

3 Think about Chapter 5. Color and complete for you.

- Children color the circle which represents how they feel about their own progress (self-evaluation).
- Have the children complete the sentence.

Treasure Hunt!

Have the children look at pp. 4–5 to find a character painting a pyramid.

Cooler: Yes or no?

Write *Yes* and *No* on large pieces of paper. Make statements about life in Ancient Egypt, e.g. *In Ancient Egypt, they painted their houses.* The children point to the *Yes* or *No* if the statements are true or false.

Competency Focus

Me: Self-evaluation

The children reflect on the chapter and express their opinions about their own progress.

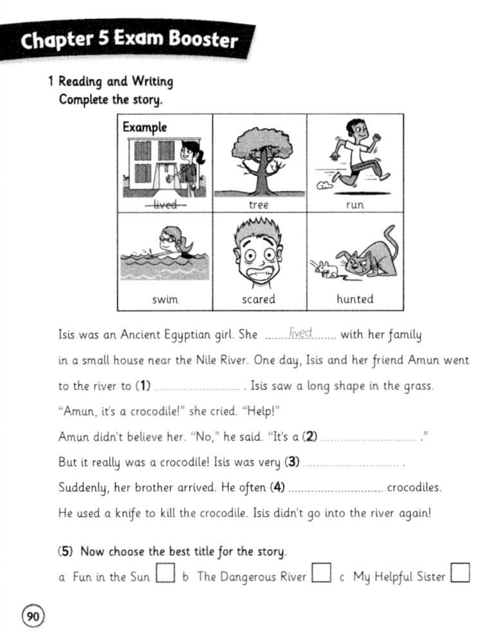

Chapter 5 Exam Booster

1 Reading and Writing
Complete the story.

Example		
~~lived~~	tree	run
swim	scared	hunted

Isis was an Ancient Egyptian girl. She ......lived...... with her family in a small house near the Nile River. One day, Isis and her friend Amun went to the river to (1) .... Isis saw a long shape in the grass.

"Amun, it's a crocodile!" she cried. "Help!"

Amun didn't believe her. "No," he said. "It's a (2) ...."

But it really was a crocodile! Isis was very (3) ....

Suddenly, her brother arrived. He often (4) .... crocodiles.

He used a knife to kill the crocodile. Isis didn't go into the river again!

(5) Now choose the best title for the story.

a Fun in the Sun ☐ b The Dangerous River ☐ c My Helpful Sister ☐

90

2 Listening
Listen and draw lines. There is one example.

91

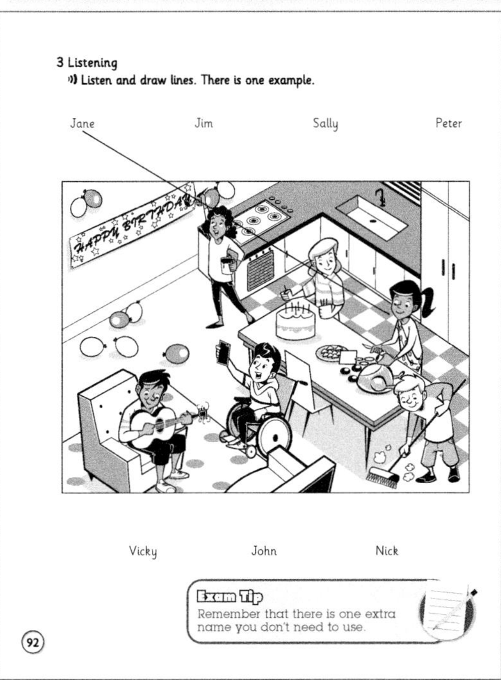

3 Listening
Listen and draw lines. There is one example.

Exam Tip
Remember that there is one extra name you don't need to use.

92

Answers (Audioscript on p. 223)

Lines between:
Mary—girl making a cake ; Vicky—girl writing poem by window; Tony—boy making model; Alex—boy wearing tiger T-shirt; Daisy—girl watching movie

3))) AB 5.2 Listening. Listen and draw lines. There is one example.

Play Track AB 5.2 twice. The children listen and match the names to the characters pictured. Check answers.

Answers (Audioscript on p. 223)

Lines between: Vicky—girl putting candles on cake; Peter—boy sweeping floor; Sally—girl painting sign; Nick—boy with cell phone; John—boy playing guitar

1 Reading and Writing. Complete the story.

The children complete the text using the words supplied and choose the best title. Check answers.

Answers

1 swim **2** tree **3** scared **4** hunted **5** b

2))) AB 5.1 Listening. Listen and draw lines. There is one example.

Play Track AB 5.1 twice. The children listen and match the names to the characters pictured. Check answers.

Digital Resources

Student eBook • Open the Welcome spread to give feedback on Treasure Hunt. Ask a child to find and circle the character painting a pyramid using *Pen*.

Teacher Resource Center • Print out Test Chapter 5 and Mid-year Test to use at the end of this lesson. The Test Generator also allows you to create customized tests.

The children will:

- use critical thinking skills to identify geographical features.
- compare geographical features.
- read, understand, and act out a story.
- talk about the weather.
- talk about extreme geographical features using the superlative.
- find out about places with extreme weather.
- make a wind vane.

Key Vocabulary

Geographical features: desert, island, lake, mountain, ocean, volcano, waterfall
Weather adjectives: bright, chilly, damp, foggy, freezing, icy, stormy, warm

Key Grammar

- Kilimanjaro is colder than (Table Mountain).
- Kilimanjaro is bigger than (Table Mountain).
- Table Mountain is sunnier than (Kilimanjaro).
- (Antarctica) is the coldest place in the world.
- (Asia) is the largest (continent) in the world.
- What is the biggest (city) in the world?
- Where is the windiest (place) in the world?

Reading Skills

Story: *Goanna and the Moon*
Genre: Australian aboriginal myth

Literacy Development

- predict story content from title and pictures
- reflect on the theme of the story and imagine alternative endings
- focus on the use of adjectives to give more information in a story

Functional Language

- This … looks good!
- No, I like this … better. It's …, too.
- OK, you win! Let's …

Spelling

Comparatives forms: –*er*, double consonant + –*er*, –*ier*

CLIL: Geography—Extreme Earth

The children find out about the hottest and coldest places in the world.

Competency Focus

The children will:

use critical thinking skills to identify geographical features. (Lesson 1) predict the content of a story. (Lesson 3) identify and talk about weather. (Lesson 5)	apply new grammar to previously learned vocabulary. (Lesson 2) talk about things that are unique in the world. (Lesson 6)	work in pairs to act out a dialogue. (Lesson 3) work in groups to act out the story. (Lesson 8)	personalize the story by talking about who tells them stories. (Lesson 4) evaluate their own progress in the chapter. (Review)	develop world understanding by finding out about weather in other parts of the world. (Lesson 7)

Digital Overview

Teacher Presentation

Student eBook and Digital Activity Book

- Music Video 6.1 (6.2): *Our World Weather*
- Interactive versions of AB activities
- Integrated audio and answer key for all activities

Teacher resources for planning, lesson delivery, and homework

Teacher Resource Center

- Class Planner Chapter 6
- Worksheets to print out (including notes and answers):
  - Grammar Worksheet 6A: Kilimanjaro is colder/bigger than …
  - Grammar Worksheet 6B: Antarctica is the coldest/largest
  - Phonics Worksheet 6
  - CLIL Graphic Organizer 6
  - Festival Worksheet: Father's Day
  - Test Chapter 6
- Test Generator
- Speaking Assessment: Cambridge English Young Learners Exams

Watch the Music Video

- Literacy Handbook

Children's resources for learning and practicing at home

Student eBook

- Music Video 6.1 (6.2): *Our World Weather*

The Inks Student's App

Vocabulary games: Geographical features and weather adjectives

Our World

Lesson 1

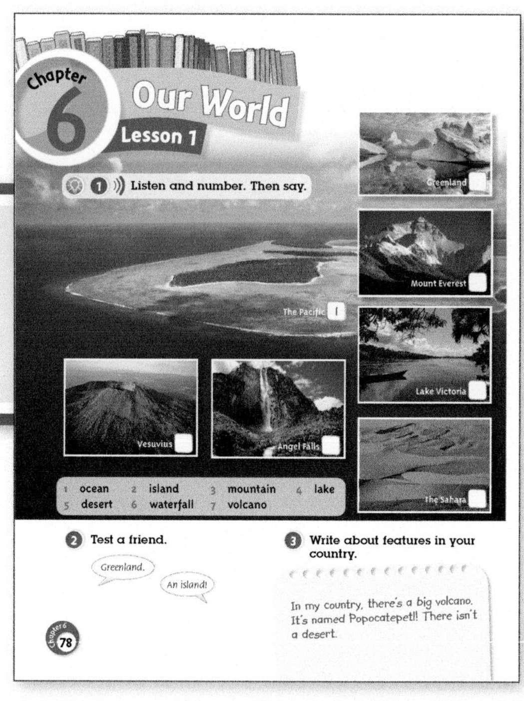

Vocabulary

Lesson objective: identify and talk about geographical features
Key vocabulary: *desert, island, lake, mountain, ocean, volcano, waterfall*
Materials: Track 6.1; cards for "Board Pelmanism" (optional)

Warmer: Board race

Divide the class into two teams and give each team a board pen. The children on each team take turns running to the board to write things you see if you go for a walk in the countryside (places, animals, etc.). Teams check each other's answers. Then elicit sentences using some of the key words.

1 6.1 Listen and number. Then say. 

- Have the children look at the pictures. Ask *What can you see?* Elicit any vocabulary the children already know.
- Play Track 6.1. The children listen and find each place. They write the picture number by the correct word.
- Play Track 6.1 again, pausing after each geography feature (ocean, island, etc.) for the children to point and repeat.

Audioscript

The Pacific is a very deep ocean. Its waters cover almost a third of the earth's surface!
Greenland is a big island. It's very cold, with ice covering most of the island. Not many people live there.
Mount Everest is a very tall mountain. It's in the Himalayas, between China and Nepal. Look at all that snow!
Lake Victoria is a big lake. It's the biggest tropical lake in the world, and it's in Africa. It provides a lot of fish.
The Sahara is a very hot desert. It's also very big. It covers most of North Africa, including Algeria, Egypt, and Morocco.
Angel Falls is a very tall waterfall. It is more than 900 meters tall. It's in Venezuela.
Vesuvius is a dangerous volcano. It's in Italy. A lot of people live near it and you can climb up to see it. Be careful, though!

Answers

The Pacific 1, Vesuvius 7, Angel Falls 6, Greenland 2, Mount Everest 3, Lake Victoria 4, The Sahara 5

2 Test a friend.

- First have the children test you. They say a place (e.g. *Angel Falls*) and you name the feature (e.g. *waterfall*). They confirm if you are correct.
- The children then test each other in pairs (with Student Book closed when answering).

3 Write about features in your country.

- Have a child read the example aloud. Then elicit details of a geographical feature in the children's country.
- Have the children write about their country in their notebook. Set a time limit, not a number of sentences, so all children can achieve as much as possible at their own pace. They compare answers in pairs before you elicit ideas.

Answers

Children's own answers.

Optional activity: Play "Board Pelmanism" 

Prepare cards using key vocabulary from the lesson (*la/ke, oc/ean, des/ert, moun/tain, vol/cano, is/land, water/fall*). Play the game (see Games Bank p. 19).

Chapter 6 Our World
Lesson 1

1 Write. 1 desert 2 3

mountain
island
volcano
lake
waterfall
~~desert~~
ocean

4 5 6 7

2 Circle *true* or *false*. Then correct the false sentences.

1 The Pacific is a big lake. true / (false) The Pacific is an ocean.
2 Mount Everest is a volcano. true / false
3 The Sahara is a hot desert. true / false
4 Greenland is an island. true / false
5 Vesuvius is a waterfall. true / false

3 Choose and categorize the words in your notebook.

land features / water features
in my country / not in my country
I'd like to visit / I wouldn't like to visit

46

1 Write.

The children label the geographical features using the words supplied. Elicit answers.

Answers

1 desert **2** volcano **3** mountain **4** lake **5** island **6** waterfall **7** ocean

2 Circle true or false. Then correct the false sentences.

The children circle *true* or *false* for each sentence. Elicit answers, including the correct versions of the false statements.

Answers

1 false—The Pacific is an ocean. **2** false—Mount Everest is a mountain. **3** true **4** true **5** false—Vesuvius is a volcano.

3 Choose and categorize the words in your notebook.

Elicit an example for each category listed. Ask *Which categories would you choose?* Elicit ideas, prompting children to give a reason for their choice. The children choose a pair of categories and list the words in their notebook, then compare with a friend.

Answers

Children's own answers.

Cooler: Play "Sentence Builders"

Play the game with the opening sentences in the Student Book Activity 1 audioscript, e.g. *The Pacific is a very deep ocean. The Sahara is a very hot desert.* (see Games Bank p. 19)

Competency Focus

Think! Critical Thinking

The children use critical thinking skills to identify geographical features by using visual clues and processing the written and spoken forms.

Digital Resources

Digital Activity Book • Use the AB page to give feedback on activities, using the answer key or the interactive digital activities.

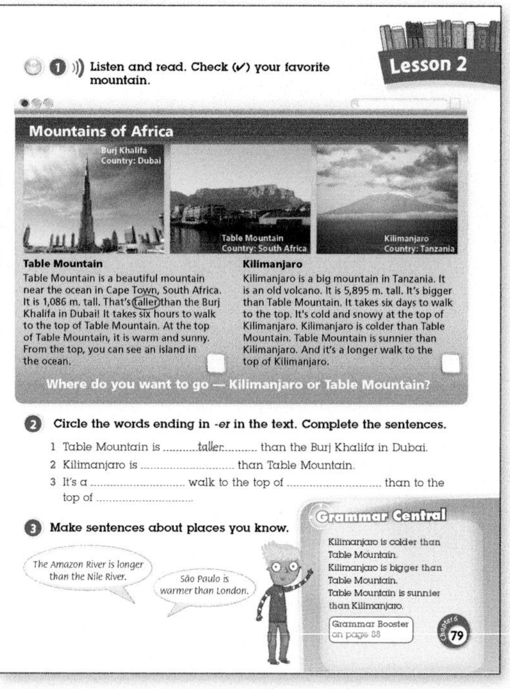

Lesson 2

1 Listen and read. Check (✓) your favorite mountain.

Mountains of Africa

Burj Khalifa
Country: Dubai

Table Mountain
Country: South Africa

Kilimanjaro
Country: Tanzania

Table Mountain

Table Mountain is a beautiful mountain near the ocean in Cape Town, South Africa. It is 1,086 m. tall. That's taller than the Burj Khalifa in Dubai! It takes six hours to walk to the top of Table Mountain. At the top of Table Mountain, it is warm and sunny. From the top, you can see an island in the ocean.

Kilimanjaro

Kilimanjaro is a big mountain in Tanzania. It is an old volcano. It is 5,895 m. tall. It's bigger than Table Mountain. It takes six days to walk to the top. It's cold and snowy at the top of Kilimanjaro. Kilimanjaro is colder than Table Mountain. Table Mountain is sunnier than Kilimanjaro. And it's a longer walk to the top of Kilimanjaro.

Where do you want to go — Kilimanjaro or Table Mountain?

2 Circle the words ending in *-er* in the text. Complete the sentences.

1 Table Mountain is ....taller.......... than the Burj Khalifa in Dubai.
2 Kilimanjaro is .... than Table Mountain.
3 It's a .... walk to the top of .... than to the top of ....

3 Make sentences about places you know.

Grammar Central

Kilimanjaro is colder than Table Mountain.
Kilimanjaro is bigger than Table Mountain.
Table Mountain is sunnier than Kilimanjaro.

Grammar Booster on page 88

Chapter 6 79

Grammar

Lesson objective: compare geographical features using the comparative form of short adjectives

Key grammar: *Kilimanjaro is colder than (Table Mountain). Kilimanjaro is bigger than (Table Mountain). Table Mountain is sunnier than (Kilimanjaro).*

Secondary language: *snowy, sunny*

Materials: Tracks 6.1 and 6.2; large pieces of paper with *True* and *False* (Cooler); Grammar Worksheet 6A [TRC printout] (optional)

Warmer: What was the last word?

6.1

Divide the class into two teams. Give one child from each team a board pen. Play Track 6.1 (Student Book Lesson 1 Activity 1), pausing after key vocabulary. (Alternatively, read the text aloud.) The children run to the board and write the last word. Continue in this way, with a different child responding each time.

1 6.2 Listen and read. Check (✓) your favorite mountain.

- Have the children look at the pictures and ask *What can you see? Would you like to go here?* Elicit that this is a website.
- Play Track 6.2 twice. The children listen and read along, raising their hand for every number.
- Take a vote on the class's favorite mountain by a show of hands. Elicit reasons for choices.

2 Circle the words ending in -er in the text. Complete the sentences.

- Have the children find the *–er* words. Elicit answers.
- Read the example aloud. The children complete the sentences using the words they circled. Elicit answers.

Answers

–er words: taller, bigger, colder, sunnier, longer

1 taller **2** bigger **3** longer, Kilimanjaro, Table Mountain

Grammar Central

Kilimanjaro is colder than Table Mountain. …

Have the children look at the patterns. On the board write *Kilimanjaro—5ºC and Table Mountain—?* Elicit ideas on the temperature there. Accept any temperature higher than 5ºC. Say *Kilimanjaro is colder than Table Mountain.*

Ask *How do we change cold to compare two things?* (*Add –er.*) *What word do we use after colder?* (*than*) Write on the board *Table Mountain is … … Kilimanjaro.* and elicit the missing words. (*hotter than*)

For extra practice, try the **Grammar Booster** section in the Student Book (p. 88).

Answers p. 88

Activity 1: **1** slower **2** wider **3** sunny **4** heavier **5** hot **6** bigger

Activity 2: **1** warmer than **2** taller than **3** longer than **4** smaller than **5** bigger than

3 Make sentences about places you know.

- Have two children read out the example. Elicit another example.
- The children take turns in pairs saying facts from the text in Activity 1. Elicit answers.

Optional activity: Play "Tic-Tac-Toe"

Play the game, prompting with *tall, sunny, big, snowy, hot, windy, long, warm, cool* to elicit the comparatives (see Games Bank p. 19).

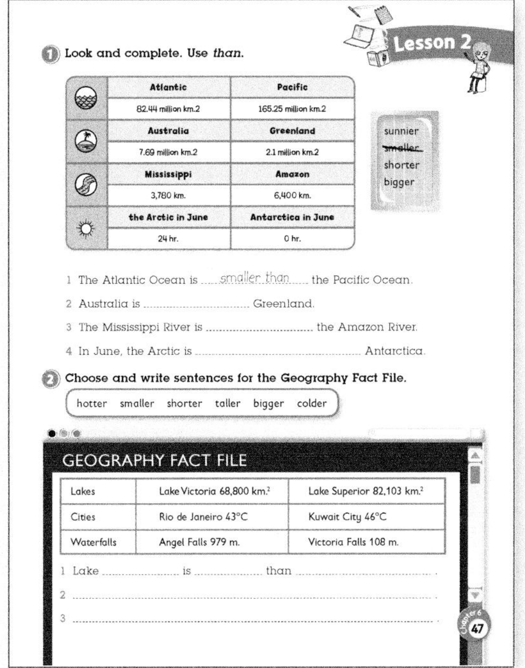
Lesson 2

1 Look and complete. Use *than*.

Atlantic	Pacific
82.44 million km.2	165.25 million km.2
Australia	**Greenland**
7.69 million km.2	2.1 million km.2
Mississippi	**Amazon**
3,780 km.	6,400 km.
the Arctic in June	**Antarctica in June**
24 hr.	0 hr.

sunnier
~~smaller~~
shorter
bigger

1 The Atlantic Ocean is ......smaller than...... the Pacific Ocean.
2 Australia is .... Greenland.
3 The Mississippi River is .... the Amazon River.
4 In June, the Arctic is .... Antarctica.

2 Choose and write sentences for the Geography Fact File.

hotter smaller shorter taller bigger colder

GEOGRAPHY FACT FILE

Lakes	Lake Victoria 68,800 km.²	Lake Superior 82,103 km.²
Cities	Rio de Janeiro 43°C	Kuwait City 46°C
Waterfalls	Angel Falls 979 m.	Victoria Falls 108 m.

1 Lake .... is .... than ....
2 ....
3 ....

Chapter 6 47

1 Look and complete. Use *than*.

The children use the information in the picture to complete the sentences with the adjectives supplied and *than*. Elicit answers.

Answers

1 smaller than **2** bigger than **3** shorter than
4 sunnier than

2 Choose and write sentences for the Geography Fact File.

The children use the information supplied to complete the Fact File. Elicit sentences and have the class check.

Answers

1 Lake Superior is bigger than Lake Victoria. / Lake Victoria is smaller than Lake Superior.
2 Kuwait City is hotter than Rio de Janeiro. / Rio de Janeiro is colder than Kuwait City.
3 Angel Falls is taller than Victoria Falls. / Victoria Falls is shorter than Angel Falls.

Cooler: True or false?

Stick a large sign on each side of the classroom: one reading *True*, the other *False*. Say true/false statements based on the lesson. Have the children call out *True!* or *False!* and point to the right side of the classroom. Elicit the correct version of false sentences.

Competency Focus

Learn

The children use previously acquired vocabulary in a different context with new grammatical structures.

Digital Resources

Student eBook • Show the SB Grammar Central box. Use *Highlighter* to focus on key grammar structures in SB Activity 1.

Student eBook, Digital Activity Book • TIP In the answer key, choose to show the answers all at once or one by one.

Teacher Resource Center • For extra grammar practice, print out Grammar Worksheet 6A.

Reading: Story Extract

Lesson objectives: exchange opinions and come to a decision; predict story content from title and pictures; read the extract from *Goanna and the Moon* (end)
Functional language: *This … looks good. No, I like this … better. It's …, too. OK, you win! Let's …*
Secondary language: *ant hill, check out, crawl, nest*
Materials: Tracks 6.3 and 6.4; picture of lizard (Warmer)

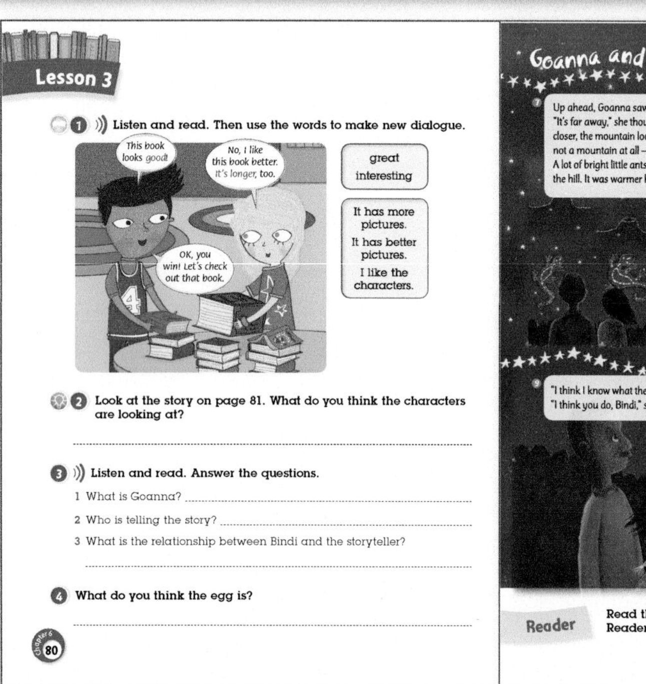

Lesson 3

1 Listen and read. Then use the words to make new dialogue.

2 Look at the story on page 81. What do you think the characters are looking at?

3 Listen and read. Answer the questions.

1 What is Goanna?
2 Who is telling the story?
3 What is the relationship between Bindi and the storyteller?

4 What do you think the egg is?

80

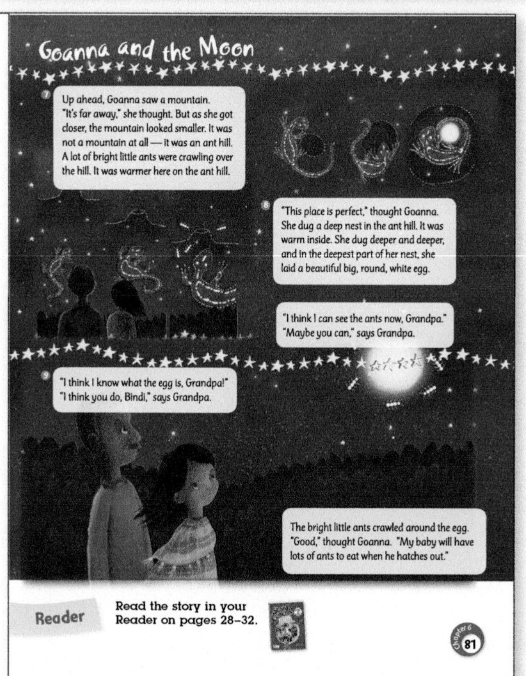

Goanna and the Moon

Up ahead, Goanna saw a mountain. "It's far away," she thought. But as she got closer, the mountain looked smaller. It was not a mountain at all — it was an ant hill. A lot of bright little ants were crawling over the hill. It was warmer here on the ant hill.

"This place is perfect," thought Goanna. She dug a deep nest in the ant hill. It was warm inside. She dug deeper and deeper, and in the deepest part of her nest, she laid a beautiful big, round, white egg.

"I think I can see the ants now, Grandpa." "Maybe you can," says Grandpa.

"I think I know what the egg is, Grandpa!" "I think you do, Bindi," says Grandpa.

The bright little ants crawled around the egg. "Good," thought Goanna. "My baby will have lots of ants to eat when he hatches out."

Reader Read the story in your Reader on pages 28–32.

81

Warmer: Lizards

Show the picture of the lizard. Ask questions to elicit what the children know, e.g. *What type of animal is it? Can you have a lizard as a pet? What do lizards eat? Do they like hot or cold weather?*

Functional language

1 6.3 Listen and read. Then use the words to make new dialogue.

- Have the children look at the pictures. Ask *What are they talking about? (which book to choose)*
- Play Track 6.3. The children listen and read along. Say *check out* means *borrow a book from a library.*
- Play Track 6.3 again, pausing for the children to repeat.
- Elicit more things they could say about a book: *It's bigger. / It has more pictures.* Have the children act out the dialogue in pairs, substituting new opinions.

Before reading

2 Look at the story on page 81. What do you think the characters are looking at?

- Ask the children to look at the title and pictures. Ask *What do you think the characters are looking at?* Have them share ideas in pairs. Elicit suggestions.

3 6.4 Listen and read. Answer the questions.

- Invite children to read out a question. Play Track 6.4. The children listen and read along.
- Play Track 6.4 again. The children discuss their answers in pairs and then write answers individually. Invite pairs to read out a question and answer.

Answers

1 Goanna is a lizard. **2** Bindi's grandpa. **3** They are grandfather and granddaughter.

4 What do you think the egg is?

- Have the children write their prediction. Elicit ideas including reasons, but do not confirm. Say they will have to read the story to find out.

Answers

Children's own answers.

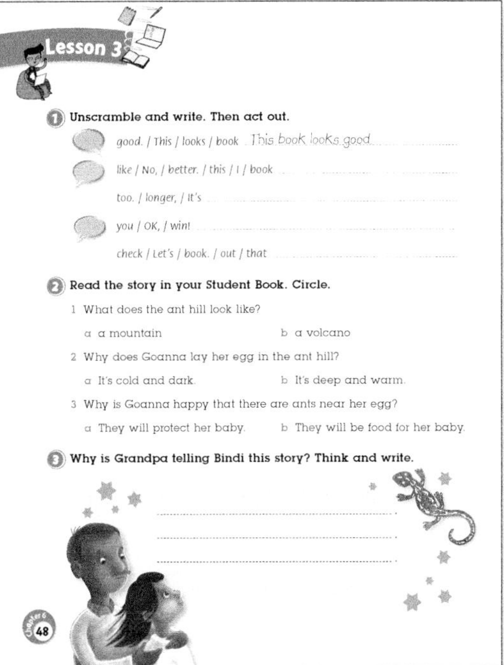
Lesson 3

1 Unscramble and write. Then act out.

good. / This / looks / book This book looks good.

like / No, / better. / this / I / book

too. / longer, / It's

you / OK, / win!

check / Let's / book. / out / that

2 Read the story in your Student Book. Circle.

1 What does the ant hill look like?

a a mountain b a volcano

2 Why does Goanna lay her egg in the ant hill?

a It's cold and dark. b It's deep and warm.

3 Why is Goanna happy that there are ants near her egg?

a They will protect her baby. b They will be food for her baby.

3 Why is Grandpa telling Bindi this story? Think and write.

48

1 Unscramble and write. Then act out.

The children write the sentences in order. Elicit answers. Then they act out the dialogue in pairs. Ask pairs to act out for the class.

Answers

This book looks good.
No, I like this book better. It's longer, too.
OK, you win! Let's check out that book.

2 Read the story in your Student Book. Circle.

The children read the Student Book story extract again. They answer the questions by circling the correct option in each pair. Elicit answers.

Answers

1 a **2** b **3** b

3 Why is Grandpa telling Bindi this story? Think and write.

The children discuss in pairs or small groups what preceded the story extract. Then they write answers individually. Elicit suggestions.

Answers

Children's own answers.

Cooler: Play "Disappearing Words"

Elicit words from the story extract and write them on the board to play the game (see Games Bank p. 19).

Competency Focus

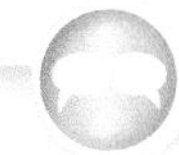

Collaborate and Communicate

The children act out an authentic dialogue together, putting into practice new functional language.

Think! Critical Thinking

The children apply reading skills (exploiting pictures and text clues) to understand the story.

Digital Resources

Student eBook • Use *Add personal note* to store one or more links to pictures of lizards for the Warmer.

- Have children write their answer for SB Activity 4 using *Pen*. Elicit class agreement. Ask how they figured out their answer.

Goanna and the Moon

1
Bindi and her grandpa are next to the lake.

"I like looking at the stars," says Bindi. "They're very bright."

"Yes, they are bright," says Grandpa. "And the moon is even brighter."

"How did the moon get there, Grandpa?"

2
Grandpa wrapped a blanket around Bindi to keep her warm.

"Are you warm now?"

"Yes, Grandpa, much warmer."

"Then I will tell you a story," says Grandpa. "A story from the Dreamtime."

3
Once upon a time, there was a lizard named Goanna. Every day, Goanna's big belly was getting bigger because soon she would lay her egg. She needed to find a warm place for it because it was chilly at night, like it is now.

4
Goanna saw a volcano. Maybe she could lay her egg inside. It looked warm. She climbed up.

"But it will be too hot in the volcano," says Bindi.

"That's right. As she climbed, it got hotter and hotter," says Grandpa.

"This is too hot," thought Goanna. "I can't lay my egg here."

5
So Goanna set off for the ocean.

The ocean was very wet.

"I can't lay my egg here," thought Goanna. "It will get damp."

6
That night, Goanna set off across the desert. The desert is freezing at night. But she was looking for a place that was warm. "It is colder here," thought Goanna. "My egg will freeze."

7
Up ahead, Goanna saw a mountain. "It's far away," she thought. But as she got closer, the mountain looked smaller. It was not a mountain at all—it was an ant hill. A lot of bright little ants were crawling over the hill. It was warmer here on the ant hill.

"I think I can see the ants now, Grandpa."

"Maybe you can," says Grandpa.

8
"This place is perfect," thought Goanna. She dug a deep nest in the ant hill. It was warm inside. She dug deeper and deeper, and in the deepest part of her nest, she laid a beautiful big, round, white egg.

9
"I think I know what the egg is, Grandpa!"

"I think you do, Bindi," says Grandpa.

The bright little ants crawled around the egg.

"Good," thought Goanna. "My baby will have a lot of ants to eat when he hatches out."

Lesson objectives: read and understand the Australian aboriginal myth *Goanna and the Moon* in the Reader
Materials: Track 6.5; Reader

Warmer: Play "Collocations"

Play the game using phrases from the story extract (see Games Bank p. 19). Column 1: *far / ant / maybe / she dug / she laid / a lot of / she got* Column 2: *an egg / you can / closer / hill / a nest / ants / an egg*

Story Summary

Bindi's grandpa, an indigenous Australian, tells her a Dreamtime story about how the moon came into existence. Goanna, a lizard, searches for somewhere to lay her egg. She chooses an ant hill. The egg represents the moon and the ants around it represent the Milky Way.

Value: Value the elderly. 

6.5 While reading

- Have the children look at the pictures in the Reader. Ask *What places and animals can you see in the pictures?*
- Play Track 6.5. The children listen and read along. Pause to elicit predictions (see **Story Time**). Ask *Where does Goanna lay her egg in the end?* (*inside an ant hill*)
- Play Track 6.5 again. Ask questions to check comprehension, e.g. *How many different places did Goanna visit? Why didn't she stay there?* (*volcano—too hot, ocean—too wet/damp, desert—too cold at night*)

After reading: Reflect

- Ask questions to give the children the opportunity to think about the issues raised by the story, e.g. *Does Bindi understand the story? Why does her grandfather tell her this story? Do you know any stories about the moon or the stars?*

Optional activity: Moon quiz

Ask true/false questions about the moon, e.g. *The moon has a dark side.* (*true*) *Earth goes around the moon.* (*false*) *There are trees on the moon.* (*false*) *The moon looks like a different shape every night.* (*true*) Encourage the children to come up with their own true/false statements for the class.

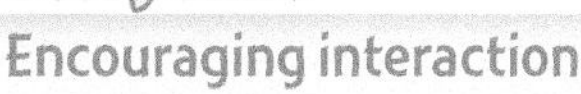

Story Time

Encouraging interaction

Tell an episodic story like this part by part, eliciting predictions, e.g. *Do you think this is a good place to lay her egg? Where do you think she will go now?*
This engages the children before they read/listen to the complete story.

Reading Strategy

Think-Pair-Share

Think–Pair–Share is a strategy that can be used before, while, and after reading. The children work individually, then in pairs or in groups of three, and then as a class. Ask questions related to the story which the children think about on their own, then discuss in pairs before sharing their ideas with the class.

For additional explanation and activities, see the Literacy Handbook on the Teacher Resource Center.

Cooler: Story settings

Divide the classroom into volcano, desert, ocean, ant hill. Elicit what each is like. (*hot/cold/wet/warm*) Agree on a mime for each. The children wander around the classroom. When you say *Stop!*, they say where they are (e.g. *I'm in the volcano!*) and do the appropriate mime.

Digital Resources

Reader eBook • Run through the story as a class. As you elicit each place that Goanna considers, have a child use *Pen* to circle the depiction of the place in the story pictures. Have a different child use *Highlighter* to identify the corresponding word in the text. Elicit why Goanna rejects/accepts each place.

- TIP Give the children the opportunity to be your assistant! Choose a child to be responsible for choosing the relevant buttons (e.g. the answer key).

Reading Comprehension and Critical Literacy

Lesson objectives: focus on the use of adjectives to give more information; reflect on the story theme and think of variations for the ending
Materials: Track 6.5; Reader

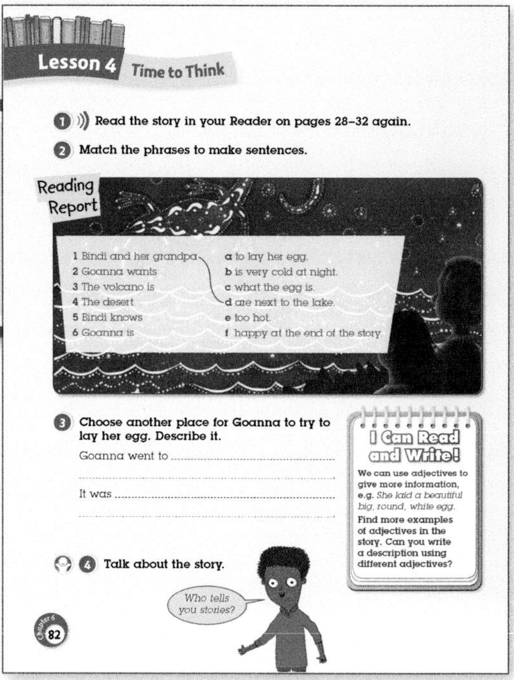
Lesson 4 Time to Think

1))) Read the story in your Reader on pages 28–32 again.

2 Match the phrases to make sentences.

Reading Report

1 Bindi and her grandpa — a to lay her egg.
2 Goanna wants — b is very cold at night.
3 The volcano is — c what the egg is.
4 The desert — d are next to the lake.
5 Bindi knows — e too hot.
6 Goanna is — f happy at the end of the story.

3 Choose another place for Goanna to try to lay her egg. Describe it.

Goanna went to ....

It was ....

I Can Read and Write!
We can use adjectives to give more information, e.g. *She laid a beautiful big, round, white egg.*
Find more examples of adjectives in the story. Can you write a description using different adjectives?

4 Talk about the story.

82

Note: Please ensure that your class has read the Reader story before you do this lesson.

Warmer: Recap the story

Write on the board *stars, lizard, volcano, ocean, desert, mountain.* Ask the children *What do you remember about the story?* Give them a little time to discuss in pairs, then elicit suggestions.

1))) 6.5 Read the story in your Reader.

- Have the children read the story. (Alternatively, play Track 6.5 and have them read along.) Elicit whether they were correct in their predictions in Lesson 3 Activity 4.
- Check comprehension by asking *What did Goanna need to find? (a warm place to lay her egg) What does the egg represent in the story? (the moon)*

2 Match the phrases to make sentences.

- Read the example. Have the children match the phrases individually. Remind them they can look at the story to confirm as necessary.
- Elicit answers in the form of complete sentences.

Answers

1 d **2** a **3** e **4** b **5** c **6** f

I Can Read and Write!

Point out that adjectives make a description more interesting by giving more information. Elicit more examples of adjectives in the story, e.g. *bright, warm, chilly, hot, wet, little,* etc. Have the children write a description of something using adjectives, e.g. their jacket, the weather today.

3 Choose another place for Goanna to try to lay her egg. Describe it.

- Elicit some ideas about possible places for Goanna to lay her egg. Ask them to say what the conditions are like, e.g. *hot, wet, cold, windy, snowy,* etc.
- Have the children complete the short text using adjectives. Elicit answers.

Answers

Children's own answers.

4 Talk about the story.

- Have a child read out Jason's question. Elicit whether Bindi's grandfather is good at telling stories and why/why not. Elicit who tells them stories.

Optional activity: What am I describing?

Call out some adjectives that are used in the story to describe places or characters to elicit what or who is being described. Suggestions: *bright* (*stars/ants*), *bigger* (*Goanna's belly*), *chilly* (*night*), *hot* (*volcano*), *warm* (*Bindi/ant hill*), *wet* (*ocean*), *freezing* (*desert*), *deep* (*nest*), *beautiful* (*egg*)

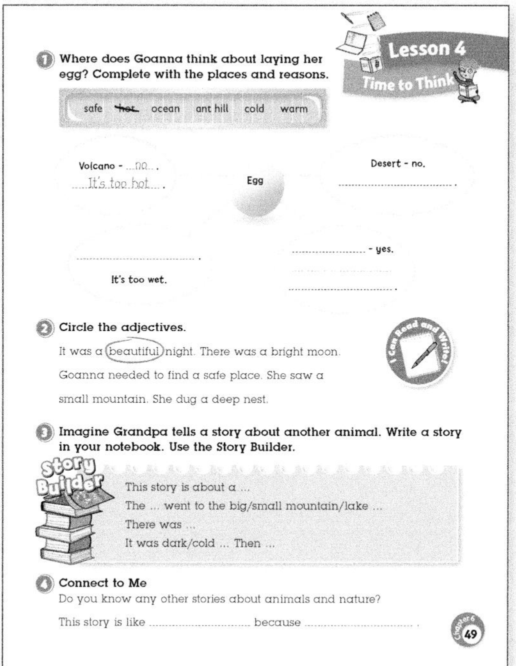

1 Where does Goanna think about laying her egg? Complete with the places and reasons.

The children complete the diagram using the words supplied. Elicit answers.

Answers

Volcano—no. It's too hot. Ocean—no. It's too wet. Desert—no. It's too cold. Ant hill—yes. It's warm and safe.

2 Circle the adjectives.

The children practice the **I Can Read and Write!** feature by circling the correct adjectives. Elicit answers.

Answers

beautiful, bright, safe, small, deep

3 Imagine Grandpa tells a story about another animal. Write a story in your notebook. Use the Story Builder.

Use the **Story Builder** prompts to elicit ideas. The children write a story in their notebook, then swap with a friend. Have children read out their story for the class.

Answers

Children's own answers.

4 Connect to Me

Elicit ideas on stories about animals and nature. The children write their own response, then compare with a friend. Elicit responses.

Answers

Children's own answers.

Cooler: Play "Ready, Set, Draw!"

6.5

Play the story. The children stand up and sit down very quickly every time they hear an adjective (or raise both arms above their head and lower them quickly instead!).

Competency Focus

Me: Critical Literacy

The children use critical literacy skills to reflect on the story and think of storytellers in their own life.

Digital Resources

Student eBook • Have children use *Highlighter* to identify the adjectives in the story for the SB I Can Read and Write! task.

Reader eBook • TIP Use *Timer* to make activities more fun and challenging. For the I Can Read and Write! task, have the children work in teams to see how many adjectives they can highlight in one minute.

Student eBook, Digital Activity Book • TIP You can move the answer key pop-up window to show the answers by the activity.

Vocabulary, Song, and Spelling

Lesson objectives: identify and talk about weather; practice comparative forms *–er* and *–ier*

Key vocabulary: *bright, chilly, damp, foggy, freezing, icy, stormy, warm*

Secondary language: *it gets, up in the, down in the*

Materials: Tracks 6.6 and 6.7; pictures for Key vocabulary (Warmer) ; Phonics Worksheet 6 [TRC] (optional)

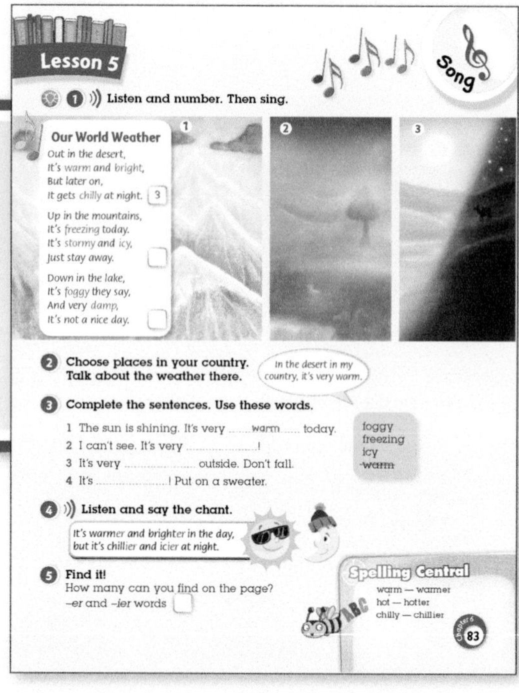

Lesson 5

Song

1 Listen and number. Then sing.

Our World Weather

Out in the desert,
It's warm and bright,
But later on,
It gets chilly at night. 3

Up in the mountains,
It's freezing today.
It's stormy and icy,
Just stay away.

Down in the lake,
It's foggy they say,
And very damp,
It's not a nice day.

1 2 3

2 Choose places in your country. Talk about the weather there.

In the desert in my country, it's very warm.

3 Complete the sentences. Use these words.

1 The sun is shining. It's very ......warm...... today.
2 I can't see. It's very ....!
3 It's very .... outside. Don't fall.
4 It's ....! Put on a sweater.

foggy
freezing
icy
~~warm~~

4 Listen and say the chant.

It's warmer and brighter in the day, but it's chillier and icier at night.

5 Find it!
How many can you find on the page?
–er and *–ier* words

Spelling Central
warm — warmer
hot — hotter
chilly — chillier

Chapter 6 83

Warmer: Pre-teach vocabulary

Pre-teach the vocabulary using weather pictures or draw symbols on the board. Have the children mime each one with you, then mime and repeat, and then mime and say the vocabulary on their own. Change the pictures faster and faster and see if they can keep up!

1 6.6 Listen and number. Then sing. 

- Have the children look at the picture. Ask *What can you see?*
- Play Track 6.6. The children listen and write the number of the appropriate picture for each verse. Elicit answers and check with the class.
- Play Track 6.6 again for the children to sing along.

Answers

3, 1, 2

2 Choose places in your country. Talk about the weather there.

- Elicit places in the children's country where the weather is different and write them on the board. Give one or two model sentences, but include a deliberate error that the children can correct: *In the desert, it's very foggy.* (*sunny/hot*)
- The children talk in pairs about the different places in their country. Elicit ideas and check with the class.

3 Complete the sentences. Use these words.

- Look at the example. The children complete the sentence, using the words supplied.
- Elicit answers and check with the class.

Answers

1 warm **2** foggy **3** icy **4** freezing

Spelling Central

Comparative endings –er and –ier

Ask *How do we compare two things using* hot*? (add –er)* Write *hoter* on the board, then score it out and write *hotter.* Explain that if the adjective is one syllable, the consonant is doubled. Repeat with *chilly/chillyer/chillier.*

4 6.7 Listen and say the chant.

- Play Track 6.7. The children listen and read along. Elicit the words with *–er.*
- Play Track 6.7 again, pausing for the children to repeat.
- The children practice, then perform the chant in pairs.

5 Find it!

- Set a time limit for the children to find words ending in *–er* and *–ier* on the page. Elicit answers.

Answers

5—warmer, brighter, hotter; chillier, icier

Optional activity: Vocabulary race

Have the children close their Student Book. Divide the class into pairs to recall the eight weather words from the song. Elicit answers.

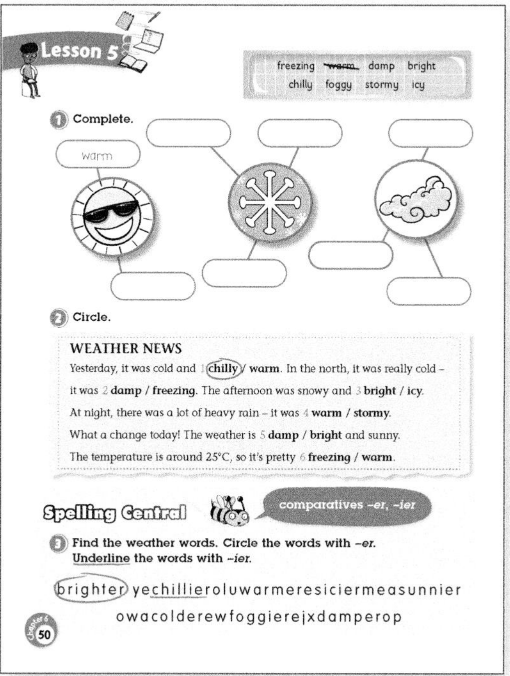

Lesson 5

freezing ~~warm~~ damp bright
chilly foggy stormy icy

1 Complete.

warm

2 Circle.

WEATHER NEWS

Yesterday, it was cold and 1 **chilly / warm**. In the north, it was really cold – it was 2 **damp / freezing**. The afternoon was snowy and 3 **bright / icy**.
At night, there was a lot of heavy rain – it was 4 **warm / stormy**.
What a change today! The weather is 5 **damp / bright** and sunny.
The temperature is around 25°C, so it's pretty 6 **freezing / warm**.

Spelling Central — comparatives *-er*, *-ier*

3 Find the weather words. Circle the words with *-er*. Underline the words with *-ier*.

brighteryechillieroluwarmeresiciermeasunnier
owacolderewfoggierejxdamperop

50

1 Complete.

The children complete the weather diagram using the words supplied. Elicit answers.

Answers

sun—warm, bright
snow—freezing, chilly, icy
cloud—damp, foggy, stormy

2 Circle.

The children read the text and circle the correct words. They compare answers in pairs. Elicit answers.

Answers

1 chilly **2** freezing **3** icy **4** stormy **5** bright **6** warm

3 Find the weather words. Circle the words with -er. Underline the words with -ier.

The children find and circle the *–er* words and underline the *–ier* words. Have them come to the board to write the words they found in two columns: *–er* and *–ier.*

Answers

circle: brighter, warmer, colder, damper
underline: chillier, icier, sunnier, foggier

Cooler: Play "Spelling Bee"

6 1 5 2 4 3

Track 6.6

Play the song again for the children to sing along.

Competency Focus

Think! Critical Thinking

The children use critical thinking skills to identify weather adjectives by processing the written and spoken forms.

Digital Resources

Student eBook • Use *Add personal note* to store links to key vocabulary pictures to use in the Warmer.

- Choose the karaoke version of Music Video 6.1 (6.2) and encourage the children to dance and sing along, using the lyrics on screen. Pause the video for the children to continue dancing and singing.

Teacher Resource Center • For phonics practice, print out Phonics Worksheet 6.

Grammar and Reading

Lesson objective: make comparisons between groups of things using the superlative form of short adjectives
Key grammar: *(Antarctica) is the coldest place in the world. (Asia) is the largest (continent) in the world. What is the biggest (city) in the world? Where is the windiest (place) in the world?*
Secondary language: *I'm not very good at …, look it up*
Materials: Track 6.8; Grammar Worksheet 6B [TRC printout] (optional)

Lesson 6

1 Listen and read. What are the children doing?

Quiz Week
1
I'm not very good at geography. What's the largest continent in the world?
Asia.
Yes!
2
Antarctica?
That's right.
Where is the coldest place in the world?
3
What is the biggest city in the world?
No. Tokyo is the biggest city in the world.
Mexico City?
4
Where is the windiest place in the world?
I don't know.
Then let's look it up on the Internet. That's what computers are for!
5
QUIZ WEEK
Are there any questions about sports? I know a lot about sports!
Oh, Cheng!

2 Complete the sentences.

1 The Amazon River is a long river. It's one of the ……longest…… rivers in the world.
2 The Arctic Ocean is a small ocean. It's one of the …………………… oceans in the world.
3 Mt. Everest is a tall mountain. It's one of the …………………… mountains in the world.
4 Lake Victoria is a big lake. It's one of the …………………… lakes in the world.

Grammar Central

Antarctica is the coldest place in the world.
Asia is the largest continent in the world.
What is the biggest city in the world?
Where is the windiest place in the world?

Grammar Booster on page 89

Chapter 6 84

Warmer: Favorite places

Tell the children about one of your favorite places, giving reasons why you like it. Include superlative adjectives if possible. Give the children some thinking time, then have them do the same in pairs. Elicit ideas and ask the class if they also know the place.

1 6.8 Listen and read. What are the children doing?

- Have the children look at the story. Ask *What place names can you see?* (*Antarctica, Tokyo, Mexico City*)
- Play Track 6.8. The children listen and read along. Ask *What are the children doing?* (*They're taking a quiz.*)
- Play Track 6.8 again, pausing for the children to repeat key language, especially superlative adjectives, e.g. *What's the largest continent?* (Alternatively, read the sentences aloud for the children to repeat.)

2 Complete the sentences. 

- Elicit why *longest* is correct in the example. (*because there's no other river longer than the Amazon River*)
- The children complete the other sentences, then compare with a friend. Elicit answers in the form of complete sentences and check with the class.

Answers

1 longest **2** smallest **3** tallest **4** biggest

Grammar Central

Antarctica is the coldest place in the world. …

Ask *Are these sentences about two different places, or one place which is "number 1"?* (*one place—number 1*)

Elicit how cold/large/big/windy are changed to talk about something that's "number 1." (*Add* –est *at the end.*) Point out the use of *the* in the sentences. Pay particular attention to the weak pronunciation of *–est*. Point out the spelling patterns.

For extra practice, try the **Grammar Booster** section in the Student Book (p. 89–91).

Answers p. 89

Activity 1: **1** fastest **2** largest **3** sunniest **4** heavy **5** hottest **6** heavy

Activity 2: **1** hottest **2** longest **3** smallest **4** biggest **5** oldest

Activity 3: Children's own answers.

p. 90

Activity 1: **1** the fastest **2** slower than **3** bigger **4** stronger **5** bigger than

Activity 2: **1** the biggest **2** slower than **3** the tallest **4** are the fastest **5** Children's own answers.

p. 91

Activity 1: **1** the biggest **2** wider than **3** fast **4** the brightest **5** bigger than **6** believed **7** there were **8** the coldest **9** the smallest **10** close **11** the fastest

Activity 2: Children's own answers.

Optional activity: Play "The Chain Game"

Play the game to practice comparatives and superlatives (see Games Bank p. 19). Start the chain with *Big.* to prompt *Big—bigger.*, then *Big—bigger—biggest.* The next child repeats and adds a new adjective, e.g. *windy.*

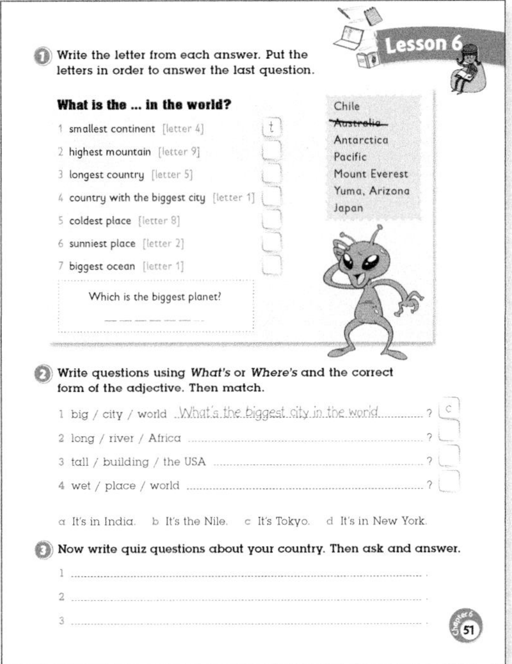

Lesson 6

1 Write the letter from each answer. Put the letters in order to answer the last question.

What is the ... in the world?

1 smallest continent [letter 4] t
2 highest mountain [letter 9]
3 longest country [letter 5]
4 country with the biggest city [letter 1]
5 coldest place [letter 8]
6 sunniest place [letter 2]
7 biggest ocean [letter 1]

Chile
~~Australia~~
Antarctica
Pacific
Mount Everest
Yuma, Arizona
Japan

Which is the biggest planet?

2 Write questions using *What's* or *Where's* and the correct form of the adjective. Then match.

1 big / city / world What's the biggest city in the world? c
2 long / river / Africa ?
3 tall / building / the USA ?
4 wet / place / world ?

a It's in India. b It's the Nile. c It's Tokyo. d It's in New York.

3 Now write quiz questions about your country. Then ask and answer.

1
2
3

Chapter 6 51

1 Write the letter from each answer. Put the letters in order to answer the last question.

The children read the questions and match the answers supplied. Elicit answers.

Answers

Australia, Mount Everest, Chile, Japan, Antarctica, Yuma, Pacific
Biggest planet: Jupiter

2 Write questions using What's or Where's and the correct form of the adjective. Then match.

The children write the questions with *What's/Where's* + the correct form of the adjective and match them to the answers. Elicit answers.

Answers

1 What's the biggest city in the world? c **2** What's the longest river in Africa? b **3** Where's the tallest building in the USA? d **4** What's the wettest place in the world? a

3 Now write quiz questions about your country. Then ask and answer.

The children write three quiz questions about their country in pairs. They exchange their book with another pair and work on the answers. Elicit questions and answers.

Answers

Children's own answers.

Cooler: Play "Sentence Builders"

Play the game with *What's the longest river in the world? Tokyo is the biggest city in the world. Australia is the smallest continent. Antarctica is the coldest place in the world. What's the foggiest place in your country?* (see Games Bank p. 19).

Competency Focus

Learn

The children demonstrate and consolidate their understanding of the new language by completing the activity.

Digital Resources

Digital Activity Book • Ask the children to do the AB interactive digital activities, or set them for homework.

Teacher Resource Center • For extra grammar practice, print out Grammar Worksheet 6B.

CLIL: Geography—Extreme Earth

Lesson objective: find out about the hottest and coldest places in the world

Materials: CLIL Graphic Organizer 6 [TRC printout] (optional)

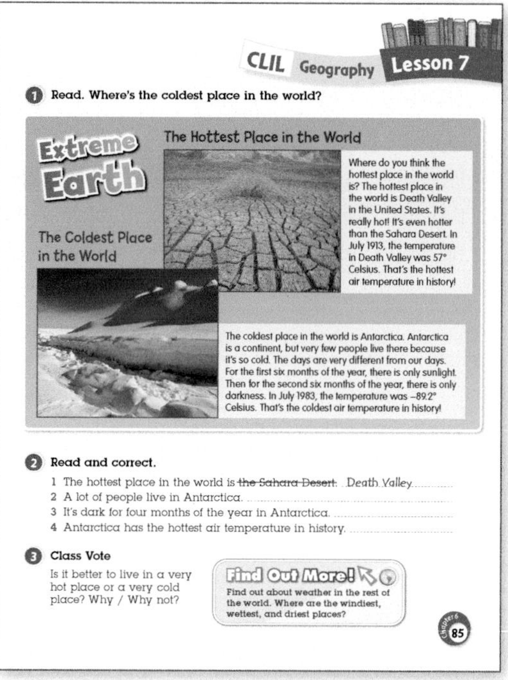

CLIL Geography Lesson 7

1 Read. Where's the coldest place in the world?

Extreme Earth

The Hottest Place in the World

Where do you think the hottest place in the world is? The hottest place in the world is Death Valley in the United States. It's really hot! It's even hotter than the Sahara Desert. In July 1913, the temperature in Death Valley was 57° Celsius. That's the hottest air temperature in history!

The Coldest Place in the World

The coldest place in the world is Antarctica. Antarctica is a continent, but very few people live there because it's so cold. The days are very different from our days. For the first six months of the year, there is only sunlight. Then for the second six months of the year, there is only darkness. In July 1983, the temperature was –89.2° Celsius. That's the coldest air temperature in history!

2 Read and correct.

1 The hottest place in the world is ~~the Sahara Desert.~~ *Death Valley*
2 A lot of people live in Antarctica.
3 It's dark for four months of the year in Antarctica.
4 Antarctica has the hottest air temperature in history.

3 Class Vote

Is it better to live in a very hot place or a very cold place? Why / Why not?

Find Out More!
Find out about weather in the rest of the world. Where are the windiest, wettest, and driest places?

Chapter 6 85

Warmer: Talk about your country

Write on the board *the coldest, the hottest, the highest, the wettest.* Ask *Which places in your country match these descriptions?* Have the children talk in pairs and then elicit some suggestions. (If you are from another country, you can add examples from your own country.)

1 Read. Where's the coldest place in the world?

- Have the children look at the pictures and say what they can see. Ask *Where do you think the places are?*
- Ask *Where's the coldest place in the world?* Have the children read the text to find the answer. (*Antarctica*)
- Encourage the children to say which of the two places they would like to visit and why. (They might need to use L1.)

2 Read and correct.

- Read the example. Have the children find the corresponding sentence in the text.
- The children correct the factual errors in the sentences. Remind them to underline the correct information in the text for each question. Elicit answers and check with the class.

Answers

1 Death Valley **2** very few people **3** six months **4** the coldest

Optional activity: School superlatives

Ask the children to discuss in pairs where the hottest, coldest, sunniest, windiest, dampest, and darkest places in their school are! Ask also which room is the biggest, smallest, and tallest in the school. Write the superlative adjectives on the board as a memory aid. Allow the children a few minutes to discuss, then elicit answers.

3 Class Vote

- Ask *Is it better to live in a very hot place or a very cold place?* Take a class vote by asking the children to write *hot* or *cold* on the board. Draw a dividing line down the board and write the headings *Cold place—better* and *Hot place—better.* Invite the children to write under their chosen heading. Count the votes and announce the result. Invite children to say why they voted hot or cold. (They might need to use L1 for this.)

Find Out More!  

Elicit appropriate resources for finding out about extreme weather, e.g. Internet, library books, etc. The children will need to complete this research before doing the follow-up activity in the Activity Book. (It could be set as homework.)

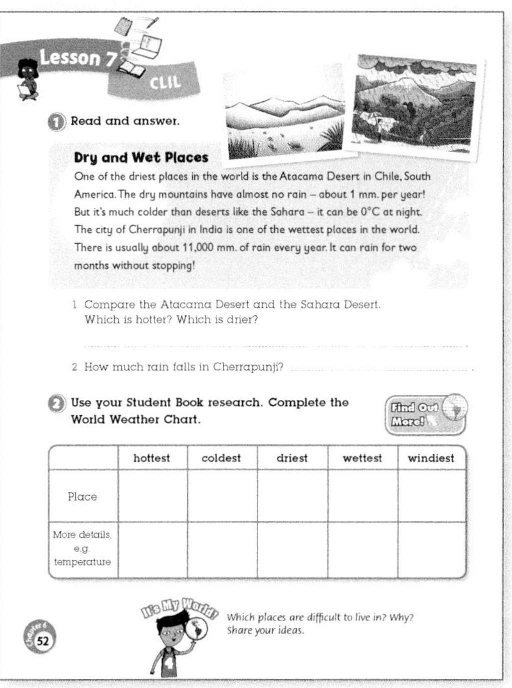

1 Read and answer.

The children write their answers to the questions. Elicit answers.

Answers

1 The Sahara is hotter but the Atacama is drier.
2 11,000 mm a year.

2 Use your Student Book research. Complete the World Weather Chart.

Divide the class into groups of four. Have the children pool the information learned from their research in the Student Book and the Activity Book. They complete the chart individually, then compare answers with a friend. Elicit answers.

Answers

Children's own answers.

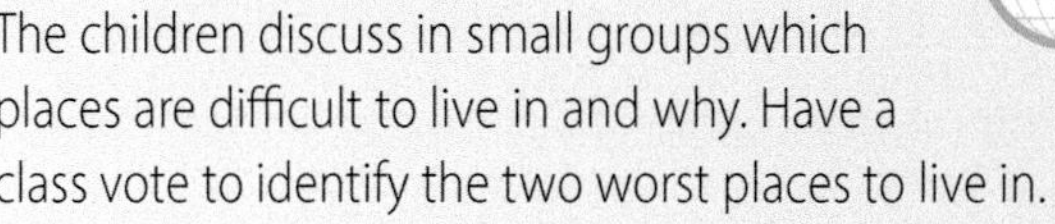

It's My World!

The children discuss in small groups which places are difficult to live in and why. Have a class vote to identify the two worst places to live in.

Cooler: Play "Simon Says"

Have the children play the game with words from the lesson (see Games Bank p. 19).

Competency Focus

Act

The children carry out research to find out other reasons why trees are important. This helps them expand their learning and relate it to their world, both inside and outside the classroom.

Digital Resources

Student eBook, Digital Activity Book, Reader eBook, CLIL eBook • Remember—do not be afraid to turn off the screen! Children benefit from variety of pace and focus—sometimes you will want to work just with books or without prompts.

Teacher Resource Center • Print out CLIL Graphic Organizer 6 for the children to collate their Find Out More! research.

CLIL eBook • The children can use the CLIL eBook to expand their knowledge of the lesson topic.

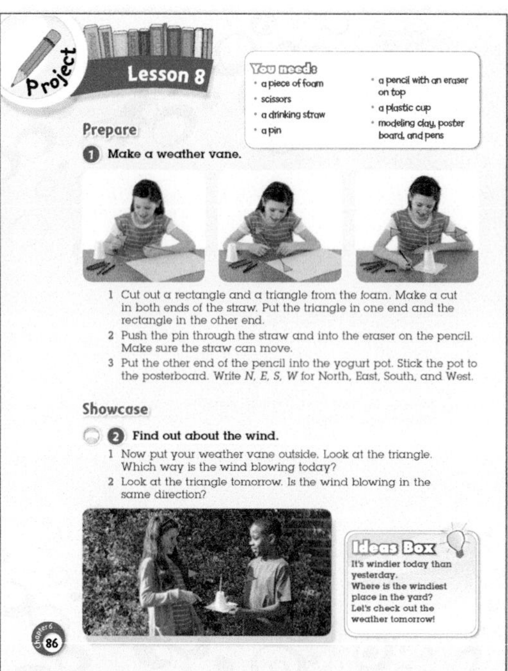
Project Lesson 8

You need:
- a piece of foam
- scissors
- a drinking straw
- a pin
- a pencil with an eraser on top
- a plastic cup
- modeling clay, poster board, and pens

Prepare

1 Make a weather vane.

1 Cut out a rectangle and a triangle from the foam. Make a cut in both ends of the straw. Put the triangle in one end and the rectangle in the other end.
2 Push the pin through the straw and into the eraser on the pencil. Make sure the straw can move.
3 Put the other end of the pencil into the yogurt pot. Stick the pot to the posterboard. Write *N, E, S, W* for North, East, South, and West.

Showcase

2 Find out about the wind.

1 Now put your weather vane outside. Look at the triangle. Which way is the wind blowing today?
2 Look at the triangle tomorrow. Is the wind blowing in the same direction?

Ideas Box
It's windier today than yesterday.
Where is the windiest place in the yard?
Let's check out the weather tomorrow!

Chapter 6 86

Project

Lesson objectives: review language from Chapter 6; make a wind vane; use their vane to check the wind

Materials: picture of a wind vane (Warmer); a piece of foam, scissors, a drinking straw, a pin, a pencil with an eraser on top, a yogurt pot, modelling clay, posterboard, pens; posterboard, 12 index cards, colored pens, tape (alternative craft); a completed wind vane (see Showcase); two game pieces and a coin for each pair; papers with weather prompts (Cooler)

Warmer: A wind vane

Show the class the picture of a wind vane you brought to class. Ask *Where do you usually see this?* (*on a roof, on the top of a building*) *Why do we use it?* (*to see which direction the wind is blowing*) *What do the letters N, S, E, W represent?* (*north, south, east, and west*)

Prepare

1 Make a wind vane.

- Distribute the materials. Read through the instructions together and ensure the children are clear on what to do.
- Have the children follow the instructions to make their wind vane. Give support as necessary.

Alternative craft activity

An easier project is to make a weather chart. Choose four children to draw a chart on the posterboard with the heading: *Today the weather is …* The rest of the class draws, colors, and labels weather symbols on the index cards: *hot, cold, warm, chilly, freezing, rainy, windy, stormy, foggy, sunny, bright, cloudy.* (It does not matter if you have more than one of each.) Fix the chart to the wall and ask *What's the weather like today?* Invite children to stick the appropriate weather symbols on the chart.

Showcase 

2 Find out about the wind.

- If your class has not done the main craft activity, make a single wind vane ahead of time that can be used to collect information for the Showcase task.
- Have the children monitor the wind in different places around the school, e.g. the playground, the entrance, etc., and make comparisons, using the **Ideas Box** for support.

Optional activity: Weather around the world

Pretend to be weather reporters. Say *Today we're in the Sahara Desert!* Elicit ideas on what the weather is like in that place. If you made the weather chart in the Alternative craft activity, have a child stick the correct symbols on the chart. Repeat with different children and places (the children can also suggest different places).

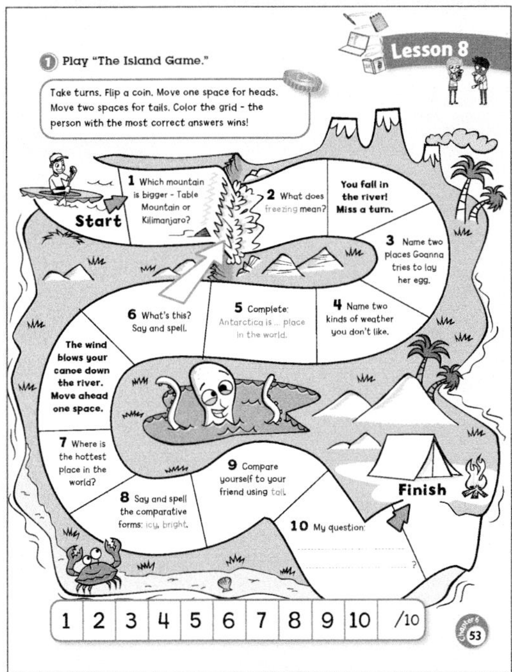

1 Play "The Island Game."

See p. 43 for instructions on how to play the game.

Answers

1 Kilimanjaro is bigger than Table Mountain. **2** very cold **3** *any two of:* a volcano, an ocean, a desert, an ant hill **4** I don't like + *two kinds of weather* **5** the coldest **6** waterfall **7** Death Valley **8** icier, brighter **9** I'm taller/ shorter than you. **10** Children's own answers.

Cooler: Mime time

Prepare pieces of paper with a weather adjective on each. Invite six children to come to the front and take a piece of paper. When you say *Go!*, they have 10 seconds to mime being in that type of weather. When you say *Stop!*, they freeze in that position. The class guess the weather for each child: *Maria's in a hot place! Ricardo's in a foggy place!* Repeat with different children.

Competency Focus

Collaborate and communicate

By making and using a wind vane, the children consolidate their understanding of the weather in a challenging and engaging way. They also demonstrate their ability to work with friends and use interpersonal skills.

Digital Resources

Student eBook • Show the pictures, stage by stage, as you talk the class through the activity process.

Language Review

Lesson objective: review language from Chapter 6
Materials: Tracks 6.9, AB 6.1, AB 6.2, and AB 6.3

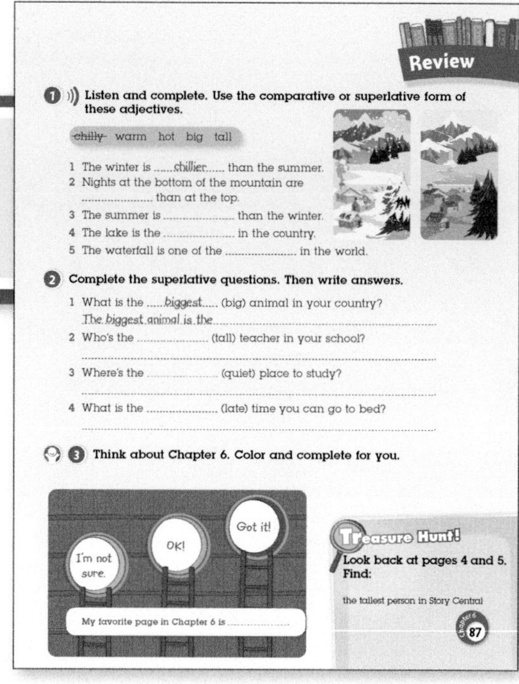

Review

1 Listen and complete. Use the comparative or superlative form of these adjectives.

~~chilly~~ warm hot big tall

1 The winter is ......chillier...... than the summer.
2 Nights at the bottom of the mountain are .... than at the top.
3 The summer is .... than the winter.
4 The lake is the .... in the country.
5 The waterfall is one of the .... in the world.

2 Complete the superlative questions. Then write answers.

1 What is the .....biggest..... (big) animal in your country?
The biggest animal is the ....
2 Who's the .... (tall) teacher in your school?
....
3 Where's the .... (quiet) place to study?
....
4 What is the .... (late) time you can go to bed?
....

3 Think about Chapter 6. Color and complete for you.

Treasure Hunt!
Look back at pages 4 and 5. Find:
the tallest person in Story Central

Chapter 6 87

Warmer: Play "Ready, Set, Draw"

Play the game with weather adjectives from Chapter 6 (see Games Bank p. 19).

1 6.9 Listen and complete. Use the comparative or superlative form of these adjectives.

- Have the children look at the example. Ask *Why is* chillier *correct?* (*because we are talking about two different things, not one "number 1"*)
- Play Track 6.9 twice, pausing as necessary. The children listen and complete the sentences.
- Elicit answers, including spelling.

Audioscript

Let's think about the seasons and compare them. Look at the pictures. In the winter, it's much chillier than in the summer. You can see the mountain is white—there's a lot of ice and snow. At night, it's warmer at the bottom of the mountain than at the top—it's much cooler at the top because it's higher.
In the summer, it's hotter and it's very sunny. The water goes down from the mountain into the lake. It's the biggest lake in the country. Look at the waterfall—it's very tall—one of the tallest in the world.

Answers

1 chillier **2** warmer **3** hotter **4** biggest **5** tallest

2 Complete the superlative questions. Then write answers.

- The children complete the sentences using the superlative form of the adjectives supplied. They then write answers.
- Elicit responses.

Answers

1 biggest **2** tallest **3** quietest **4** latest + children's own answers

3 Think about Chapter 6. Color and complete for you.

- Have the children look back at Chapter 6. Elicit their favorite parts. The children then color the circle which represents how they feel about their own progress (self-evaluation).
- Have the children complete the sentence about their favorite page. Elicit responses.

Treasure Hunt!

Have the children look at pp. 4–5 to find the tallest person in Story Central. They hold up their Student Book and point to the right place on the page.

Cooler: Play "Monkey!"

Divide the class into two teams (A and B), who stand up facing each other. Have the first child in Team A begin reading the story. When you shout *Monkey!*, the reading switches over to the first child on Team B. Continue in this way, shouting *Monkey!* at random points for the reading to switch.

Competency Focus

Me: Self-evaluation

The children reflect on the chapter and express their opinions about their own progress.

Chapter 6 Exam Booster

1 Reading and Writing

Look and read. Choose the correct words and write them on the lines. There is one example.

Example island	desert	volcano	sunny
foggy	stormy	freezing	lake

Example

This is a place in the ocean. There is water around it. island

Questions

1 This is a tall mountain. It's dangerous – be careful if you climb it! ....

2 This is a very dry place. There isn't much rain here. ....

3 When the weather is like this, you can't see very well. ....

4 This weather is very rainy. There are black clouds and the wind blows. ....

5 When the weather is like this, it's colder than cold! ....

93

2 Listening

Listen and write. There is one example.

Completing a project for ....English.... class

1 Kind of place visited: ....

2 Favorite thing: ....

3 Weather on vacation: ....

4 When he went: ....

5 Name of place he stayed: ....

94

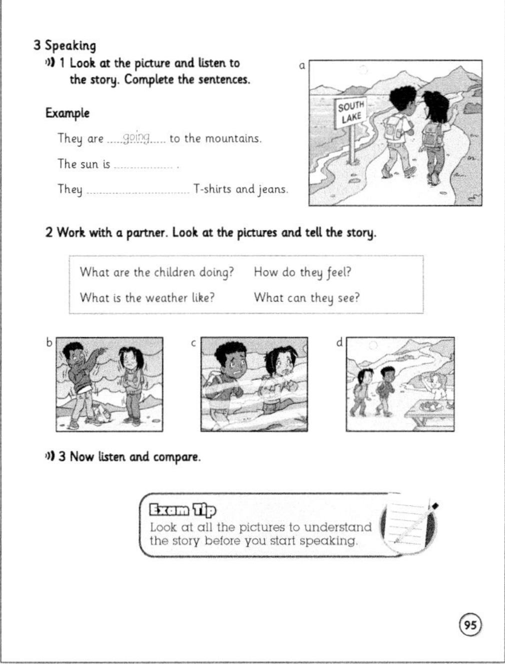

3 Speaking

1 Look at the picture and listen to the story. Complete the sentences.

Example

They are ....going.... to the mountains.

The sun is ....

They .... T-shirts and jeans.

2 Work with a partner. Look at the pictures and tell the story.

What are the children doing? How do they feel?

What is the weather like? What can they see?

3 Now listen and compare.

Exam Tip

Look at all the pictures to understand the story before you start speaking.

95

1 Reading and Writing. Look and read. Choose the correct words and write them on the lines. There is one example.

The children write the items described. Check answers.

Answers

1 volcano **2** desert **3** foggy **4** stormy **5** freezing

2 AB 6.1 Listening. Listen and write. There is one example.

Play Track AB 6.1 twice. Children listen and answer.

Answers (Audioscript on p. 223)

1 an island **2** waterfalls **3** rain **4** August **5** Bear Farm

3.1 AB 6.2 Speaking. Look at the picture and listen to the story. Complete the sentences.

The children look at the picture and listen to the story to complete the sentences.

Answers (Audioscript on p. 223)

shining, are wearing

3.2 Speaking. Work with a partner. Look at the pictures and tell the story.

Ask the children to look at the pictures and tell the story to their partner. Children use the examples from 6.1.

3.3 AB 6.3 Speaking. Now listen and compare.

Ask the children to listen and compare their answers. **(Audioscript on p. 223)**

Digital Resources

Teacher Resource Center • Print out Test Chapter 6 to use at the end of this lesson. The Test Generator also allows you to create customized tests.

• Print out Festival Worksheet: Father's Day to expand the children's knowledge of celebrations throughout the world.

Student's App • Encourage the children to play the games on their smartphone/tablet. Ask them to record their scores to compare in the next lesson. (*The Inks* Apps are free and available on the App Store and Google Play.)

Chapter 7 Champions Overview

The children will:

- use critical thinking skills to identify sports.
- ask and answer questions about past actions.
- read, understand, and act out a story.
- refer specifically to times in the past.
- ask for and give information about a person's life.
- find out about the history of the Olympic Games.
- do a presentation on a famous athlete.

Reading Skills

Story: *The Champion*
Genre: Ancient Greek legend

Key Vocabulary

Sports: boxing, discus, diving, high jump, javelin, rowing, weightlifting, wrestling
Time phrases: last month, last year, last weekend, yesterday

Literacy Development

- predict story content from title and pictures
- reflect on the theme of the story and analyze the main character
- focus on the use of questions to create interest in a story

Key Grammar

- Did you go (to Sports Day)? Yes, I did.
- Did Bella win (the race)? No, she didn't.
- When did Jesse Owens live?
- What did he do? He went (to the Olympic Games).

Functional Language

- Good luck! You can do it!
- Thanks. I hope so!

Spelling

The long *a* sound

CLIL: History—History of the Olympic Games

The children find out about the origins of the Olympic Games.

Competency Focus

The children will:

use critical thinking skills to identify sports. (Lesson 1) predict the content of a story. (Lesson 3) identify and use time phrases to talk about the past. (Lesson 5)	apply new grammar to previously learned vocabulary. (Lesson 2) ask and answer about a historical figure. (Lesson 6)	work in pairs to act out a dialogue. (Lesson 3) work in groups to act out the story. (Lesson 8)	reflect on the story and think about how it relates to the present situation. (Lesson 4) evaluate their own progress in the chapter. (Review)	develop historical understanding by finding out about the Olympic performance of their own country. (Lesson 7)

Digital Overview

Teacher Presentation

Student eBook and Digital Activity Book

- Oral Storytelling Video 7.1: *The Champion*
- Interactive versions of AB activities
- Integrated audio and answer key for all activities

Teacher resources for planning, lesson delivery, and homework

Teacher Resource Center

- Class Planner Chapter 7
- Worksheets to print out (including notes and answers):
  - Grammar Worksheet 7A: Did you go …? Yes, I did.
  - Grammar Worksheet 7B: When did Jesse Owens live?
  - Oral Storytelling Video Worksheet 7: *The Champion*
  - Phonics Worksheet 7
  - CLIL Graphic Organizer 7
  - Test Chapter 7
- Test Generator
- Literacy Handbook

Watch the Oral Storytelling Video

Children's resources for learning and practicing at home

Student eBook and Reader eBook

- Oral Storytelling Video 7.1: *The Champion*

The Inks Student's App

Vocabulary games: Sports and time phrases

Chapter 7 Champions

Lesson 1

Vocabulary

Lesson objective: identify and talk about Olympic sports
Key vocabulary: *boxing, discus, diving, high jump, javelin, rowing, weightlifting, wrestling*
Materials: Track 7.1

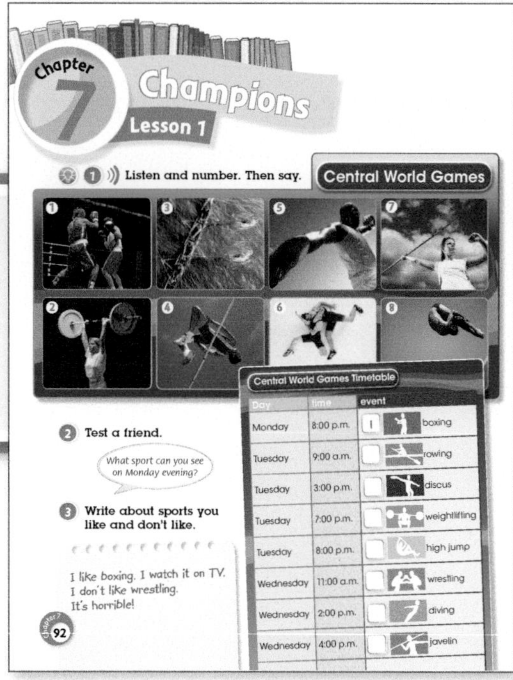
Chapter 7 Champions
Lesson 1
1 Listen and number. Then say.
Central World Games

Central World Games Timetable

Day	time	event
Monday	8:00 p.m.	1 boxing
Tuesday	9:00 a.m.	rowing
Tuesday	3:00 p.m.	discus
Tuesday	7:00 p.m.	weightlifting
Tuesday	8:00 p.m.	high jump
Wednesday	11:00 a.m.	wrestling
Wednesday	2:00 p.m.	diving
Wednesday	4:00 p.m.	javelin

2 Test a friend.
What sport can you see on Monday evening?
3 Write about sports you like and don't like.
I like boxing. I watch it on TV.
I don't like wrestling.
It's horrible!
92

Warmer: Board Race

Divide the class into two teams. Give each team a board pen. The children take turns running to the board to write a sport. The teams check each other's answers.

1 7.1 Listen and number. Then say. 

- Have the children look at the pictures. Ask *What sports can you see? Which sport would you like to try?*
- Play Track 7.1. The children listen and write the picture number by the correct word in the schedule.
- Play Track 7.1 again, pausing after each sport for the children to point and repeat.

Audioscript

On Monday, we have boxing live from the Games Center at 8:00 p.m. On Tuesday, there's rowing in the Olympic Canal at 9 o'clock in the morning. This sport wasn't in the Ancient Olympics but is now very popular! The discus competition starts at 3 o'clock in the afternoon in the Olympic Stadium on Tuesday, too. Tuesday evening we have weightlifting at the Games Center at 7:00 p.m., followed by the high jump in the Olympic Stadium at 8:00 p.m. On Wednesday, there's wrestling in the Games Center at 11:00 a.m., and then we go to the Green Park Pool for the first of the diving events at 2:00 p.m. Then, at 4:00 p.m. on Wednesday, the javelin event starts, back in the Olympic Stadium.

Answers

boxing 1, rowing 3, discus 5, weightlifting 2, high jump 4, wrestling 6, diving 8, javelin 7

2 Ask and answer.

- Ask *What sport can you see on Monday evening?* (*boxing*)
- Have children ask you the question, changing the day.
- The children ask and answer about different days in pairs. You can make it more challenging by having the child answering close their Student Book.
- Have pairs ask and answer for the class.

3 Write about sports you like and don't like.

- Have two children read the examples. Elicit whether they agree or disagree with the opinions.
- Have the children write sentences in their notebook about their likes and dislikes. Encourage them to add details as in the example. Set a time limit, not a number of sentences, so all children can achieve as much as possible at their own pace. Have them compare with a friend, then elicit answers.

Answers

Children's own answers

Optional activity: Mime time

Ask *What's this sport?* and mime doing one of the sports from the list. When a child guesses the right answer, ask *Do you like this sport?* and elicit an answer similar to the ones they gave in Activity 3. Divide the class into pairs and have them continue the game, taking turns miming and guessing. Encourage them to use the question and give an opinion each time.

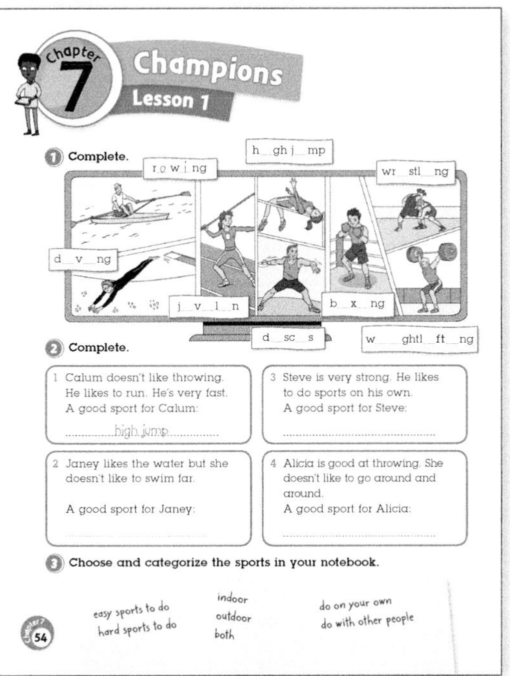
Chapter 7 Champions
Lesson 1

1 Complete.

h_gh j_mp | r o w i ng | wr_stl_ng | d_v_ng | j_v_l_n | b_x_ng | d_sc_s | w_ghtl_ft_ng

2 Complete.

1 Calum doesn't like throwing. He likes to run. He's very fast. A good sport for Calum: high jump

2 Janey likes the water but she doesn't like to swim far. A good sport for Janey:

3 Steve is very strong. He likes to do sports on his own. A good sport for Steve:

4 Alicia is good at throwing. She doesn't like to go around and around. A good sport for Alicia:

3 Choose and categorize the sports in your notebook.

easy sports to do / hard sports to do
indoor / outdoor / both
do on your own / do with other people

54

Cooler: Play "Simon Says"

Play the game with (*Simon says*) *go rowing/throw the javelin/do high jump*, etc. (see Games Bank p. 19).

Competency Focus

Think! Critical Thinking

The children use critical thinking skills to identify different Olympic sports by using visual clues and processing the written and spoken forms.

1 Complete.

The children complete the sports by writing the vowels. Elicit answers, asking children to spell the words.

Answers

1 rowing **2** high jump **3** wrestling **4** diving **5** javelin **6** discus **7** boxing **8** weightlifting

2 Complete.

The children read the information and write an appropriate sport for each person. Elicit answers.

Answers

1 high jump **2** diving **3** weightlifting **4** javelin

3 Choose and categorize the sports in your notebook.

Elicit an example for each category listed. Ask *Which categories would you choose?* Elicit ideas, prompting children to give a reason for their choice. The children choose a pair of categories and list the words in their notebook, then compare with a friend.

Answers

Children's own answers.

Digital Resources

Student eBook • Play "Kim's Game" with the new vocabulary. Focus on the labeled pictures in SB Activity 1. Use *Timer* to give the class one minute to memorize the pictures, then one minute to recall them. Repeat several times.

Grammar

Lesson objectives: ask and answer about past actions using yes/no questions and short answers
Key grammar: *Did you go (to Sports Day)? Yes, I did. Did Bella win (the race)? No, she didn't.*
Secondary language: *get a prize, sick, Sports Day*
Materials: Track 7.2; Grammar Worksheet 7A [TRC printout] (optional)

Lesson 2

1 Listen and read. Check (✓) the things Bella did.

Did you go to Sports Day yesterday, Bella?
Yes, I did. Did you go?
No, I didn't. I was sick.
Oh, too bad.
Did you run in any races?
Yes, I did. I was in one race and I was in the discus event, too.
Did you win the race?
No, I didn't.

throw the javelin ☐ do the high jump ☐ run ☐ do boxing ☐ throw the discus ☐

2 Listen again and circle the correct answers.

1 Did Bella run a race? Yes, she did. / No, she didn't.
2 Did she win the race? Yes, she did. / No, she didn't.
3 Did she throw the discus? Yes, she did. / No, she didn't.
4 Did she throw a javelin? Yes, she did. / No, she didn't.

3 Imagine you were at Sports Day. Choose two events you competed in.

4 Find out what events your friends competed in.

Did you throw the javelin?
No, I didn't.

Grammar Central
Did you go to Sports Day?
Yes, I did.
Did Bella win the race?
No, she didn't.

Grammar Booster on page 102

Chapter 7 93

Warmer: Do you watch …?

Write scrambled versions of the sports from Lesson 1 on the board. Give the children two minutes to write them correctly. Then ask a child *Do you watch boxing?* to elicit *Yes, I do.* or *No, I don't.* That child then asks another the same question, changing the sport. Continue around the class with the other sports.

1 7.2 Listen and read. Check (✓) the things Bella did.

- Ask *What are Bella and her friend doing?* (*texting*) *Do you text a lot with your friends?*
- Play Track 7.2 twice. The children listen and read along. They check the things that Bella did.
- Elicit answers.

Answers

throw the javelin ✗ do the high jump ✗ run ✓ do boxing ✗ throw the discus ✓

2 Track 7.2 Listen again and circle the correct answers.

- Play Track 7.2 again for the children to circle the correct answer.
- Ask pairs to read out questions and answers.

Answers

1 Yes, she did. **2** No, she didn't. **3** Yes, she did. **4** No, she didn't.

Grammar Central

Did you go to Sports Day? …

Have the children look at the patterns. Ask *Are these questions and answers about the present or the past?* (*the past*) Explain that as with negative sentences with *didn't*, in questions with *did* the verb does not change. Elicit answers to questions like this. (*Yes, I did. / No, I didn't.*)

For extra practice, try the **Grammar Booster** section in the Student Book (p. 102).

Answers p. 102

Activity 1: **1** Did **2** did **3** didn't **4** Did **5** did **6** didn't **7** Did **8** Yes **9** No

Activity 2: **1** Did, did **2** Did, didn't **3** Did, did **4** Did, did **5** Did, didn't

Activity 3: Children's own answers.

3 Imagine you were at Sports Day. Choose two events you competed in.

- Give an example, e.g. *I ran a race, and I was in the boxing event!* The children write two events they competed in at Sports Day in preparation for the speaking activity which follows. Make sure they know their answers do not have to be true.

Answers

Children's own answers.

4 Find out what events your friends competed in.

- Ask *What events did you compete in?* Elicit answers from a range of children.
- Have two children read out the example. The children then mingle and ask each other *Did you* + [sport]? until they find someone who has the same two events as them. Find out the most popular event.

Optional activity: Knock-out events

Have the children secretly write two sports from Lesson 1 on a piece of paper. Ask the class to stand. Then ask the first child *Did you do boxing?* If *boxing* is on their paper, they sit down. Continue around the class until only a few children are left standing.

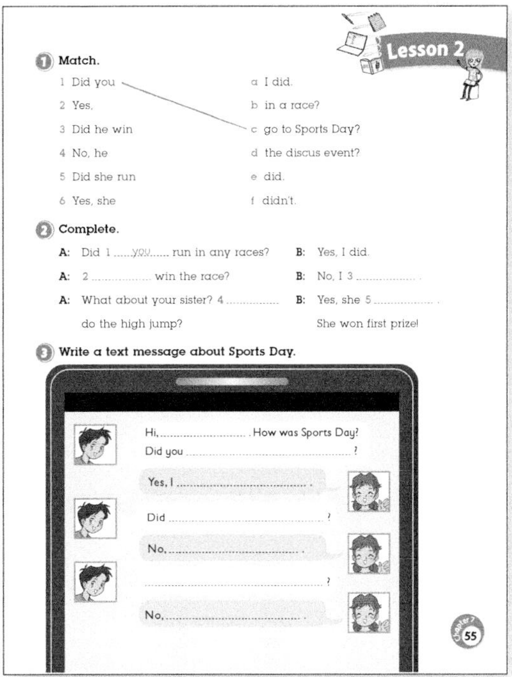
Lesson 2

1 Match.

1 Did you — a I did.
2 Yes, — b in a race?
3 Did he win — c go to Sports Day?
4 No, he — d the discus event?
5 Did she run — e did.
6 Yes, she — f didn't.

2 Complete.

A: Did 1 ......you...... run in any races? B: Yes, I did.
A: 2 .... win the race? B: No, I 3 ....
A: What about your sister? 4 .... do the high jump? B: Yes, she 5 .... She won first prize!

3 Write a text message about Sports Day.

Hi, ... How was Sports Day?
Did you .... ?
Yes, I ....
Did .... ?
No, ...
.... ?
No, ...

55

1 Match.

The children match the halves to make questions and answers. Elicit answers.

Answers

1 c **2** a **3** d **4** f **5** b **6** e

2 Complete.

The children complete the dialogue, then compare in pairs. Elicit answers.

Answers

1 you **2** Did you **3** didn't **4** Did she **5** did

3 Write a text message about Sports Day.

Elicit questions and answers to complete the conversation. The children write their text message, then compare with a friend. Have children read their texts for the class.

Answers

Children's own answers.

Cooler: Let's chant!

Write the chant on the board.

Did you run in a race? *Yes, I did! Yes, I did!*
Did you win first prize? *No, I didn't. No, I didn't.*
Did you jump very high? *Yes, I did! Yes, I did!*
Did you win first prize? *No, I didn't. No, I didn't.*
Did you like Sports Day? *Yes, I loved it!*

Chant it line by line for the children to repeat and do actions. Repeat twice. Then divide the class into two groups and chant: one the questions, the other the answers.

Competency Focus

Learn

The children use previously acquired vocabulary in a different context with new grammatical structures.

Digital Resources

Student eBook, Digital Activity Book • TIP As you monitor the children's progress, use *Add personal note* to keep a note of weaknesses in vocabulary, grammar, or pronunciation so you can review in later lessons.

Teacher Resource Center • For extra grammar practice, print out Grammar Worksheet 7A.

Reading: Story Extract

Lesson objectives: wish someone luck; predict story content from title and pictures; read the extract from *The Champion* (the end)
Functional language: *Good luck. You can do it! Thanks. I hope so.*
Secondary language: *champion, older, weaker*
Materials: Tracks 7.3 and 7.4; Olympic pictures (various sports, medal ceremonies) or access these on the Internet

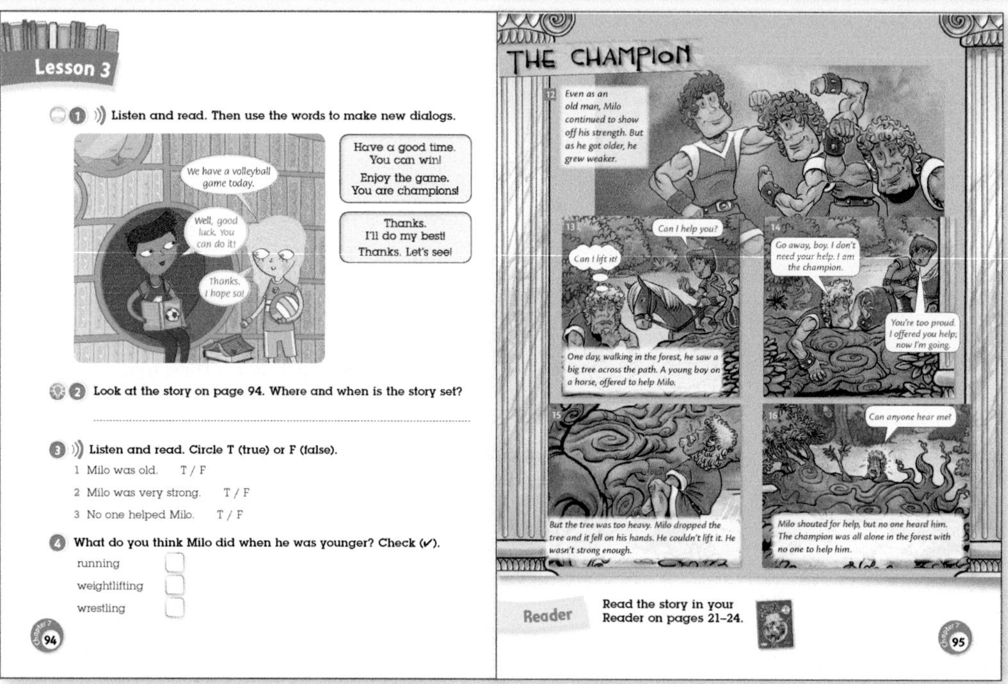

Lesson 3

1 Listen and read. Then use the words to make new dialogs.

Have a good time. You can win!
Enjoy the game. You are champions!

Thanks. I'll do my best!
Thanks. Let's see!

2 Look at the story on page 94. Where and when is the story set?

3 Listen and read. Circle T (true) or F (false).

1 Milo was old. T / F
2 Milo was very strong. T / F
3 No one helped Milo. T / F

4 What do you think Milo did when he was younger? Check (✓).

running
weightlifting
wrestling

94

THE CHAMPION

Reader Read the story in your Reader on pages 21–24.

95

Warmer: Talk about the Olympics

Show the children the Olympic pictures you brought/accessed online and ask *What's happening in these pictures? Where are they? Do you think these people are famous?* Have a discussion about the children's favorite sports. Ask, e.g. *What's your favorite sport? Is it in the Olympics? Who's your favorite athlete?*

Functional language

1 7.3 Listen and read. Then use the words to make new dialogs.

- Have the children look at the pictures and dialogue. Ask *What are they talking about? (sports)*
- Play Track 7.3. The children listen and read along.
- Play Track 7.3 again, pausing for the children to repeat.
- The children act out the dialogue in pairs, substituting different sports.

Before reading

2 Look at the story on page 95. Where and when is the story set?

- Ask the children to look at the title and pictures and discuss the questions in pairs. They write their ideas. Ask *Where is the story set? (Greece) When is it set? (a very long time ago)* Elicit ideas and check with the class.

3 7.4 Listen and read. Circle T (true) or F (false).

- Give the children time to read the sentences. Play Track 7.4 twice. The children listen and read along.
- The children circle T (true) or F (false) for each sentence.
- Elicit answers, including the correct version of the false statements.

Answers

1 T **2** F **3** T

4 What do you think Milo did when he was younger? Check (✓).

- Have the children write their prediction (they can choose more than one). Elicit ideas including reasons, but do not confirm. Say they will have to read the story to find out.

Answers

Children's own answers.

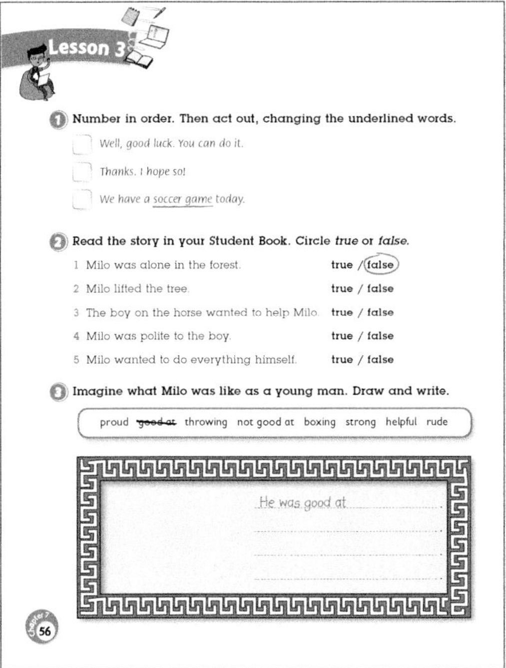

Lesson 3

1 Number in order. Then act out, changing the underlined words.

- [ ] Well, good luck. You can do it.
- [ ] Thanks. I hope so!
- [ ] We have a soccer game today.

2 Read the story in your Student Book. Circle *true* or *false*.

1	Milo was alone in the forest.	true / (false)
2	Milo lifted the tree.	true / false
3	The boy on the horse wanted to help Milo.	true / false
4	Milo was polite to the boy.	true / false
5	Milo wanted to do everything himself.	true / false

3 Imagine what Milo was like as a young man. Draw and write.

proud ~~good at~~ throwing not good at boxing strong helpful rude

He was good at

56

1 Number in order. Then act out, changing the underlined words.

The children order the dialogue by numbering the statements. Then they act out in pairs, changing the sport. Have pairs act out for the class.

Answers

1 We have a soccer game today. **2** Well, good luck. You can do it. **3** Thanks. I hope so!

2 Read the story in your Student Book. Circle true or false.

The children read the Student Book story extract again, then circle *true* or *false* for each sentence. Elicit answers, including the correct version of the false statements.

Answers

1 false **2** false **3** true **4** false **5** true

3 Imagine what Milo was like as a young man. Draw and write.

The children write about Milo when he was young, using the ideas supplied, and draw a picture of him. They swap with a friend.

Answers

Children's own answers.

Cooler: Compare the pictures

Divide the class into groups of five. Have the children show the pictures in Activity Book Activity 3. They describe Milo and say what is happening in their drawing.

Competency Focus

Collaborate and Communicate

The children act out an authentic dialogue together, putting into practice new functional language.

Think! Critical Thinking

The children apply reading skills (exploiting pictures and text clues) to understand the story context.

Digital Resources

Student eBook • Focus on Milo in each picture in the story extract. Elicit how he feels.

Student eBook, Digital Activity Book • TIP Store Internet links and other ideas in *Add personal note* for easy access during the lesson (here, links to pictures of the Olympics).

THE CHAMPION

1
Long ago, there was a boy named Milo in the city of Kroton. Like most boys in Ancient Greece, Milo liked wrestling. He was very good at wrestling.

2
When Milo was nine years old, a man visited his father.

Trainer: Milo is the best boy wrestler in Kroton. I want to train him for the Olympic Games.

Father: But he's very young.

Trainer: There are events for boys. There is wrestling, rowing, boxing, and discus. I want Milo to do the wrestling event.

Father: OK. He can do it.

3
Father: Good luck. You can do it.

Milo: Thanks, I hope so.

4
Did Milo train often? Yes, he did. He trained seven days a week. Did Milo train hard? Yes, he did. He trained all day.

5
When he competed in the Olympic Games, Milo won his first laurel crown. He was a hero in Kroton.

Crowd: Hooray! The champion! Great job!

6
Was that the end of Milo's sports career? No, it wasn't. It was only the beginning. Milo continued training, and he got better and better at wrestling.

7
Milo threw the javelin, too. He competed in the Olympic Games again and again.

8
Every time the champion competed, he won. Milo was one of the best champions of all time.

9
Milo was very strong. He was good at weightlifting. One day, an ox fell into a hole.

Ox driver: Can you help?

Milo: Yes, I can. I am the champion.

Milo lifted the ox onto his shoulders and carried it to safety.

10
Another time, a roof collapsed. Pythagoras, the famous mathematician, was in the building.

Pythagoras: Help me, please!

Milo: No problem. I am the champion.

Milo lifted the roof up, and Pythagoras escaped.

11
Milo was very famous. An artist made a bronze statue of Milo. But the statue was very big and heavy. No one could carry it. Was this a problem for Milo? No, it wasn't. The champion carried the statue himself.

Milo: I am the champion!

12
Even as an old man, Milo continued to show off his strength. But as he got older, he grew weaker.

13
One day, walking in the forest, he saw a big tree across the path. A young boy on a horse offered to help Milo.

Boy: Can I help you?

Milo: *Can I lift it?*

14
Milo: Go away, boy. I don't need your help. I am the champion.

Boy: You're too proud. I offered you help; now I'm going.

15
But the tree was too heavy. Milo dropped the tree and it fell on his hands. He couldn't lift it. He wasn't strong enough.

16
Milo: Can anyone hear me?

Milo shouted for help, but no one heard him. The champion was all alone in the forest with no one to help him.

Lesson objectives: read and understand the Ancient Greek legend *The Champion* in the Reader
Materials: Track 7.5; Reader; Oral Storytelling Video Worksheet 7 [TRC printout] (optional)

Warmer: Story extract review

Have the children explain who Milo is and what happens to him in the story extract. Ask the children to imagine they are Milo when he was young. They pose like him and mime a sport they think he did as a young man.

Story Summary

Milo, a great Olympic champion in Ancient Greece, is very strong. He lifts an ox and saves Pythagoras. Milo grows older and weaker. He is unable to lift a tree but refuses help from a boy. Milo drops the tree on his hands and is trapped.

Value: Accept help.

7.5 While reading

- Have the children look at the pictures in the Reader. Ask *What sports can you see? How are the people feeling?*
- Play Track 7.5. The children listen and read along. Ask *Why was Milo a hero in his town?* (*because he won in the Olympics Games*)
- Play Track 7.5 again. Ask questions to check comprehension, e.g. *Why did Milo leave his home and family?* (*to train for the Olympic Games*) *How did he help other people?* (*He lifted an ox and a roof.*)

After reading: Reflect

- Ask questions to give the children the opportunity to think about the issues raised by the story, e.g. *Why was Milo so proud? Do you think he was right not to accept the boy's help? Is it OK not to be the best at something? Is it normal to get weaker as we grow old?*

Optional activity: Older and younger

Divide the class into pairs and have the children make a list of things you can do when you are older that you cannot do when you are young. Prompt as necessary with *drive a car, cook food*, etc. Elicit ideas.

Story Time

Audience participation

Sometimes our opinion about a character changes. Play Track 7.5 again, and encourage the children to give their reactions to Milo at different stages, e.g. by saying *Hm …* (indifferent), *Yay!* (impressed), or *Boo!* (when they do not like something). Make a graph of the class's overall reactions on the board to show how a character can change in our estimation.

Reading Strategy

Scanning

Scanning is an essential skill used by readers to search a text quickly for specific information. By developing this strategy, the children will learn to identify the important details in a text and answer specific questions without worrying about unknown words.

For additional explanation and activities, see the Literacy Handbook on the Teacher Resource Center.

Cooler: Who's speaking?

Have the children close their Reader. Say lines of dialogue from the story to elicit who is speaking: Milo, his father, the trainer, Pythagoras, or the boy. This can be played as a team game for points.

Digital Resources

Reader eBook • For the Cooler, have children use *Pen* to write who the speaker is each time, saying the name as they do so. Record each team's scores on *Add personal note*.
• Oral Storytelling Video 7.1 gives the story with a different ending. Watch it together at the end of the lesson, then discuss the differences.

Teacher Resource Center • Print out Oral Storytelling Video Worksheet 7 to get the most out of the video.

Reading Comprehension and Critical Literacy

Lesson objectives: focus on using questions in storytelling; reflect on the story theme and analyze the main character further
Materials: Track 7.5; Reader; Oral Storytelling Video Worksheet 7 [TRC printout] (optional)

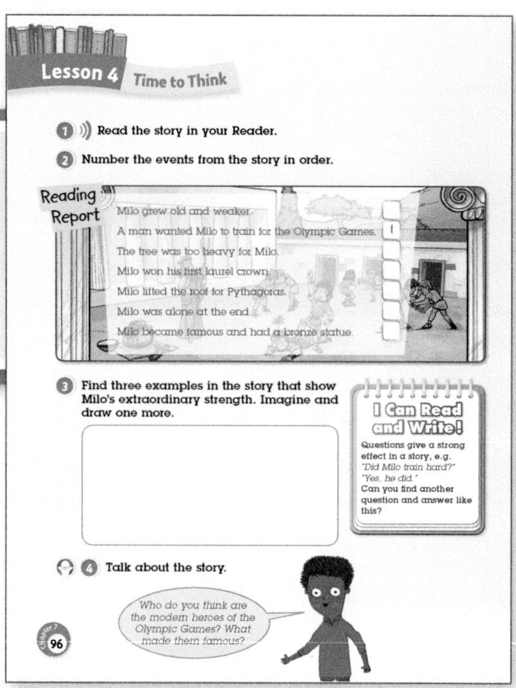
Lesson 4 Time to Think

1 Read the story in your Reader.

2 Number the events from the story in order.

Reading Report

Milo grew old and weaker.
A man wanted Milo to train for the Olympic Games. 1
The tree was too heavy for Milo.
Milo won his first laurel crown.
Milo lifted the roof for Pythagoras.
Milo was alone at the end.
Milo became famous and had a bronze statue.

3 Find three examples in the story that show Milo's extraordinary strength. Imagine and draw one more.

I Can Read and Write!
Questions give a strong effect in a story, e.g. "Did Milo train hard?" "Yes, he did." Can you find another question and answer like this?

4 Talk about the story.

Who do you think are the modern heroes of the Olympic Games? What made them famous?

96

Note: Please ensure that your class has read the Reader story before you do this lesson.

Warmer: Play "Disappearing Words"

Elicit words from *The Champion*. Write up to 20 on the board. Have the children turn away. Erase one word. Have them turn back and tell you which word is missing. Repeat until the board is empty (see Games Bank p. 19).

1 7.5 Read the story in your Reader.

- Have the children read the story. (Alternatively, play Track 7.5 and have them read along). Elicit whether they were correct in their predictions in Lesson 3 Activity 4.
- Check comprehension by asking *What was Milo famous for? (He was very strong. / He was a sports champion.) Why didn't Milo let the boy help him? (He was too proud.)*

2 Number the events from the story in order.

- Draw the children's attention to the example sentence. Have them find the information in the story. (*picture 2*) Elicit the next sentence. (*Milo won his first laurel crown.*)
- Have the children continue the activity individually. Remind them they can look at the story if they need to. Elicit answers and check with the class.

Answers

5, 1, 6, 2, 3, 7, 4

3 Find three examples in the story that show Milo's extraordinary strength. Imagine and draw one more.

- The children find examples of Milo's strength. Elicit suggestions.
- Have the children draw and label a picture of Milo showing his strength. Invite children to show and tell their pictures to the class.

Answers

Children's own answers.

I Can Read and Write!

Point out that questions can give information a stronger effect in a story. (You might need to use L1.) Ask the children to find examples of questions in the story. Have them repeat them after you in a dramatic tone!

4 Talk about the story. 

- Have a child read out Jason's questions. Discuss modern Olympic heroes and what made them famous. (The children might need to use L1.)

Optional activity: Add more questions

Ask more questions about the story in the style of the **I Can Read and Write!** questions to elicit *yes/no* answers and the picture number for where it could go. Suggestions:
Did Milo win a crown? Yes, he did! (*5*) *Was he one of the best champions? Yes, he was!* (*8*) *Did he save Pythagoras? Yes, he did!* (*10*) *Did he lift the tree? No, he didn't.* (*15*)

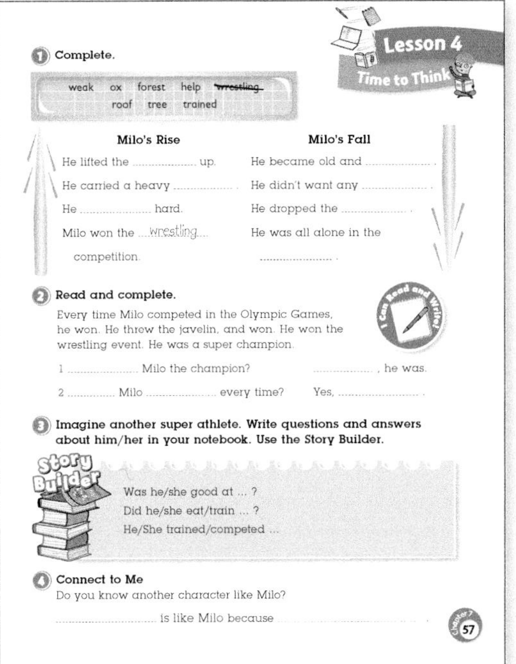

Lesson 4
Time to Think

1 Complete.

weak ox forest help ~~wrestling~~ roof tree trained

Milo's Rise	Milo's Fall
He lifted the .... up.	He became old and ....
He carried a heavy	He didn't want any ....
He .... hard.	He dropped the ....
Milo won the ...wrestling... competition.	He was all alone in the ....

2 Read and complete.

Every time Milo competed in the Olympic Games, he won. He threw the javelin, and won. He won the wrestling event. He was a super champion.

1 .... Milo the champion? .... , he was.

2 .... Milo .... every time? Yes, ...

3 Imagine another super athlete. Write questions and answers about him/her in your notebook. Use the Story Builder.

Story Builder

Was he/she good at ... ?
Did he/she eat/train ... ?
He/She trained/competed ...

4 Connect to Me

Do you know another character like Milo?

.... is like Milo because ....

57

1 Complete.

The children complete the sentences about Milo using the words supplied. Elicit answers.

Answers

Milo's Rise: (from bottom to top) wrestling, trained, ox, roof

Milo's Fall: (from top to bottom) weak, help, tree, forest

2 Read and complete.

The children practice the **I Can Read and Write!** feature by completing the questions. Elicit answers.

Answers

1 Was, Yes **2** Did, win, he did

3 Imagine another super athlete. Write questions and answers about him/her in your notebook. Use the Story Builder.

Use the **Story Builder** prompts to elicit ideas. The children write their own response, then compare with a friend. Have children read out their questions and answers for the class.

Answers

Children's own answers.

4 Connect to Me

Elicit ideas on other characters who are like Milo. The children write their own response, then compare with a friend. Elicit responses.

Answers

Children's own answers.

Cooler: Interviewing Milo

Put the class into groups of five and select one child in each group to be Milo. The other children think up questions to ask, e.g. *What do you like lifting? Where is your statue now? How old are you now?* The groups then use the questions to interview their Milo. If there is time, a different child could take the Milo role.

Competency Focus

Me: Critical Literacy

The children use critical literacy skills to reflect on the story and think of real-life people who are like the character from the story.

Digital Resources

Reader eBook • Display the Reader on the board. Show Picture 4. Elicit what happened before and after this. Repeat with Pictures 11 and 14.

Student eBook, Reader eBook • If you haven't already, show Oral Storytelling Video 7.1.

Teacher Resource Center • If you haven't already, print out Oral Storytelling Video Worksheet 7 to do the support activities.

Vocabulary, Song, and Spelling

Lesson objectives: identify and use time phrases to talk about the past; practice spelling words with the long *a* sound

Key vocabulary: *last month, last year, last weekend, yesterday*

Materials: Tracks 7.6 and 7.7; large calendar for Key vocabulary (Warmer) ; Phonics Worksheet 7 [TRC] (optional)

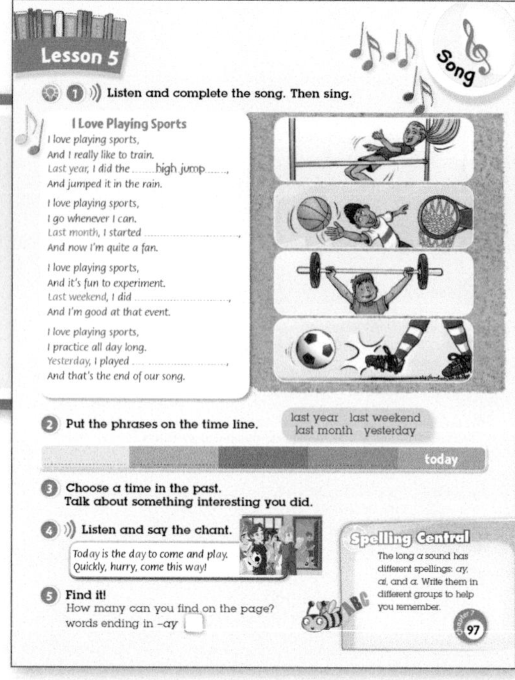

Lesson 5

Song

1 Listen and complete the song. Then sing.

I Love Playing Sports

I love playing sports,
And I really like to train.
Last year, I did the .... high jump ....,
And jumped it in the rain.

I love playing sports,
I go whenever I can.
Last month, I started ....,
And now I'm quite a fan.

I love playing sports,
And it's fun to experiment.
Last weekend, I did ....,
And I'm good at that event.

I love playing sports,
I practice all day long.
Yesterday, I played ....,
And that's the end of our song.

2 Put the phrases on the time line.

last year last weekend last month yesterday

today

3 Choose a time in the past.
Talk about something interesting you did.

4 Listen and say the chant.

Today is the day to come and play.
Quickly, hurry, come this way!

5 Find it!
How many can you find on the page?
words ending in *–ay*

Spelling Central

The long *a* sound has different spellings: *ay*, *ai*, and *a*. Write them in different groups to help you remember.

Chapter 7 97

Warmer: Pre-teach vocabulary

Pre-teach the vocabulary using a calendar. Write *last* and *yesterday* on the board. Ask *What's the day today?* and mark the day on the calendar. Point to different days/months on the calendar to pre-teach and practice *last month, last year, last weekend*, and *yesterday*.

1 7.6 Listen and complete the song. Then sing.

- Have the children look at the pictures next to the song. Ask *What activities can you see?*
- Play Track 7.6. The children listen and write the sports next to each verse. Tell them to check the spelling of the sports in Lesson 1.
- Have the children read the words in red. Ask *Are they referring to the present or past?* (past) Play Track 7.6 again for the children to sing along.

Answers

high jump, basketball, weight lifting, soccer

2 Put the phrases on the time line.

- Elicit that the line to the left goes into the past. Have the children write the phrases in order going into the past. Ask the class to all call out the phrases in order starting with *Now*.

Answers

last year, last month, last weekend, yesterday, today

3 Choose a time in the past. Talk about something interesting you did.

- Give examples for yourself, e.g. *Yesterday, I played soccer. Last weekend, I read a good book!*
- Have the children think about their past activities and then talk with a friend. Monitor, correcting any errors in past tense verbs.
- Ask children to say things they did. Encourage careful listening by having the class respond *Me, too!* or *Not me!*

Spelling Central

The long a sound

Write *day, rain*, and *father* on the board. Elicit other words with *ay, ai*, and *a*, e.g. *May, train, parent*, etc.

4 7.7 Listen and say the chant.

- Play Track 7.7. The children listen and read along. Elicit the words with *ay*. Play Track 7.7 again, pausing for the children to repeat.
- Have the children practice the chant in pairs. Invite pairs to perform for the class.

5 Find it!

- Set a time limit for the children to find words with *–ay* on the page. Elicit answers.

Answers

6—yesterday, say, today, day, play, way

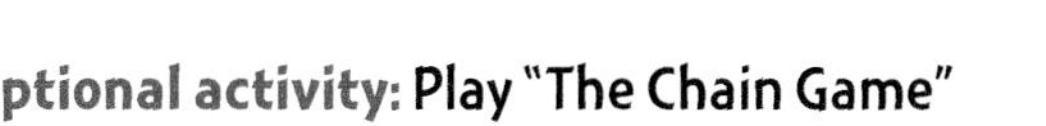

Optional activity: Play "The Chain Game"

Play the game in groups of six–eight with sentences in the past starting *Yesterday …*, *Last weekend …*, *Last month …*, or *Last year …* (see Games Bank p. 19). The children can choose which time phrase they use, so it doubles the memory challenge!

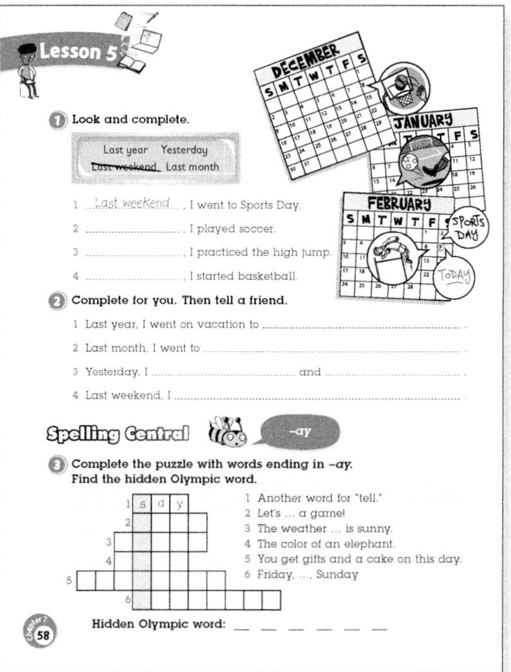

Lesson 5

1 Look and complete.

Last year Yesterday ~~Last weekend~~ Last month

1 Last weekend, I went to Sports Day.
2 ...., I played soccer.
3 ...., I practiced the high jump.
4 ...., I started basketball.

2 Complete for you. Then tell a friend.

1 Last year, I went on vacation to ....
2 Last month, I went to ....
3 Yesterday, I .... and ....
4 Last weekend, I ....

Spelling Central –ay

3 Complete the puzzle with words ending in *–ay*. Find the hidden Olympic word.

1 Another word for "tell."
2 Let's … a game!
3 The weather … is sunny.
4 The color of an elephant.
5 You get gifts and a cake on this day.
6 Friday, …, Sunday

Hidden Olympic word: _ _ _ _ _ _

Chapter 7 58

1 Look and complete.

The children complete the sentences using the phrases supplied. Elicit answers.

Answers

1 Last weekend **2** Last month **3** Yesterday **4** Last year

2 Complete for you. Then tell a friend.

The children complete the activity with their own responses, then compare with a friend. Encourage careful listening by having the class respond *Me, too!* or *Not me!*

Answers

Children's own answers.

3 Complete the puzzle with words ending in –ay. Find the hidden Olympic word.

The children complete the puzzle in pairs. Elicit answers.

Answers

1 say **2** play **3** today **4** gray **5** birthday **6** Saturday
Hidden Olympic word: sports

Cooler: Sing and mime

7.6

Play the song. The children sing and mime along.

Competency Focus

Think! Critical Thinking

The children use critical thinking skills to identify time phrases and different sports by processing the written and spoken forms.

Digital Resources

Student eBook • TIP Use *Timer* to set a time limit for SB Activity 5.

Student's App • Encourage the children to play the games on their smartphone/tablet. They could arrange to do this with a friend as a fun way to review the chapter vocabulary together. (*The Inks* Apps are free and available on the App Store and Google Play.)

Teacher Resource Center • For phonics practice, print out Phonics Worksheet 7.

Grammar and Reading

Lesson objectives: ask and answer about the past using *Wh–* questions with *did*
Key grammar: *When did Jesse Owens live? At the beginning of the twentieth century. What did he do? He went (to the Olympic Games in 1936).*
Secondary language: *competed, medals, relay*
Materials: Track 7.8; Grammar Worksheet 7B [TRC printout] (optional)

Lesson 6

1 Listen and read. Who was Jesse Owens?

A Champion at Story Central

2 Answer the quiz.

Jesse Owens Quiz

When was Jesse Owens born? He was born in 1913.
Which Olympic Games did he go to?
What events did he compete in?
How many gold medals did he win?
When did he die?

Grammar Central

When did Jesse Owens live?
What did he do?

Grammar Booster on page 103

Chapter 7 98

Warmer: Did you … yesterday?

Ask a child *Did you go to the zoo yesterday?* They respond *Yes, I did. / No, I didn't.* (Explain that their answer does not have to be true.) They then ask another child a *Did you … yesterday?* question. That child answers and asks the next child. Divide the class into groups to continue the activity.

1 7.8 Listen and read. Who was Jesse Owens?

- Have the children look at the story. Ask *What are they doing?* (*They're watching a movie.*) *What sports can you see?* (*running*)
- Play Track 7.8. The children listen and read along. Ask *Who was Jesse Owens?* (*an African-American athlete/an Olympic champion*)
- Play Track 7.8 again, pausing after the past questions (e.g. *Who was he? When did Jesse Owens live?*) and have the children repeat them. Check the meaning of *relay*.

2 Answer the quiz. 

- Have the children find the information that gives the answer to the first question. Point out they can find all the answers in the dialogue.
- The children answer the other questions.
- Ask pairs to read out the questions and answers.

Answers

He was born in 1913. He went to the Berlin Olympics in 1936. The 100m race, the 200m race, the long jump, and the relay race. He won four gold medals. He died in 1980.

Grammar Central

When did Jesse Owens live? …

Elicit the question words in each question (*when, what*) and have the children find more in the quiz. (*which, how many, who*) Ask about the word order in *Wh–* questions to elicit *1 Wh– word, 2 did, 3 subject, 4 verb.*

For extra practice, try the **Grammar Booster** section in the Student Book (p. 103–105).

Answers p. 103

Activity 1: **1** What did **2** When **3** Where **4** Who **5** Which **6** How many

Activity 2: **1** did **2** What **3** did **4** Did **5** didn't **6** Yes

Activity 3: Children's own answers.

p. 104

Activity 1: **1** run **2** didn't **3** What **4** do **5** Did **6** didn't

Activity 2: **1** Did **2** didn't **3** Did **4** didn't **5** fall **6** Yes

p. 105

Activity 1: **1** do **2** saw **3** Did **4** didn't **5** Did **6** won **7** went **8** watch **9** watched **10** went **11** were

Activity 2: **1** Did Uncle Jim win a gold medal? **2** Did the reporter see the wrestling match? **3** What other events did Tony see? **4** When did Uncle Jim's parents go to London? **5** Who did they go to see?

Optional activity: Memory test

Have the class close their Student Book. Divide the class into pairs. Read out the questions from the quiz and have the pairs decide and write the answer in their notebook. Read out the questions again and elicit answers. Ask the children how much of the information they remembered correctly.

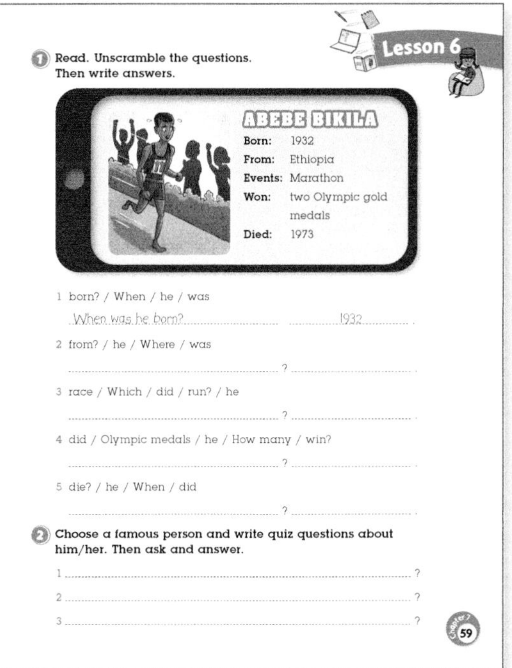

Lesson 6

1 Read. Unscramble the questions. Then write answers.

ABEBE BIKILA
Born: 1932
From: Ethiopia
Events: Marathon
Won: two Olympic gold medals
Died: 1973

1 born? / When / he / was
When was he born? 1932
2 from? / he / Where / was
........? ....
3 race / Which / did / run? / he
........? ....
4 did / Olympic medals / he / How many / win?
........? ....
5 die? / he / When / did
........? ....

2 Choose a famous person and write quiz questions about him/her. Then ask and answer.
1 ....?
2 ....?
3 ....?

59

1 Read. Unscramble the questions. Then write answers.

The children unscramble the questions and write the answers. Elicit answers and check with the class.

Answers

1 When was he born? 1932 **2** Where was he from? Ethiopia **3** Which race did he run? the Marathon **4** How many Olympic medals did he win? Two **5** When did he die? In 1973

2 Choose a famous person and write quiz questions about him/her. Then ask and answer.

Elicit famous people that the children could write about. The children choose a famous person and write their three questions. They ask and answer the questions
in pairs.

Answers

Children's own answers.

Cooler: Play "Sentence Builders"

Play the game with past questions from Lesson 6 (see Games Bank p. 19).

Competency Focus

Learn

The children demonstrate and consolidate their understanding of the new language by completing the activity.

Digital Resources

Student eBook, Digital Activity Book • TIP Children love to be involved in using digital resources. Give them as many opportunities as possible writing and drawing on the board in more open-ended tasks. Make a point of encouraging less confident children to participate, because this will help them engage.

Teacher Resource Center • For extra grammar practice, print out Grammar Worksheet 7B.

CLIL: History—History of the Olympic Games

Lesson objective: find out about the origins of the Olympic Games
Materials: CLIL Graphic Organizer 7 [TRC printout] (optional)

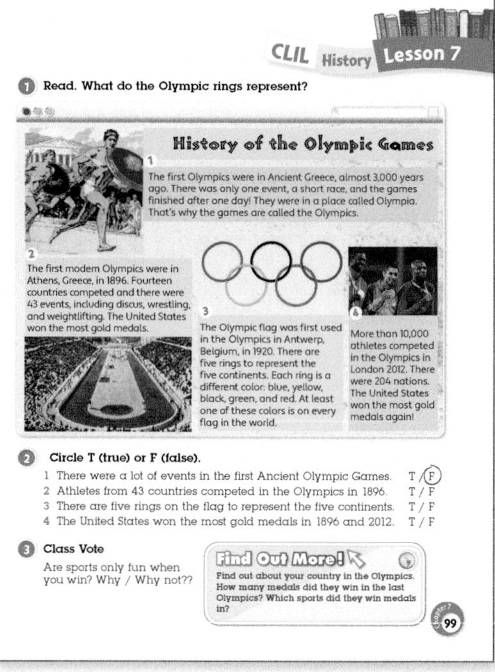
CLIL History Lesson 7

1 Read. What do the Olympic rings represent?

History of the Olympic Games

1 The first Olympics were in Ancient Greece, almost 3,000 years ago. There was only one event, a short race, and the games finished after one day! They were in a place called Olympia. That's why the games are called the Olympics.

2 The first modern Olympics were in Athens, Greece, in 1896. Fourteen countries competed and there were 43 events, including discus, wrestling, and weightlifting. The United States won the most gold medals.

3 The Olympic flag was first used in the Olympics in Antwerp, Belgium, in 1920. There are five rings to represent the five continents. Each ring is a different color: blue, yellow, black, green, and red. At least one of these colors is on every flag in the world.

4 More than 10,000 athletes competed in the Olympics in London 2012. There were 204 nations. The United States won the most gold medals again!

2 Circle T (true) or F (false).
1 There were a lot of events in the first Ancient Olympic Games. T / F
2 Athletes from 43 countries competed in the Olympics in 1896. T / F
3 There are five rings on the flag to represent the five continents. T / F
4 The United States won the most gold medals in 1896 and 2012. T / F

3 Class Vote
Are sports only fun when you win? Why / Why not??

Find Out More!
Find out about your country in the Olympics. How many medals did they win in the last Olympics? Which sports did they win medals in?

99

Warmer: Brainstorm sports

Elicit as many sports as possible and write them on the board. Ask *Which of these sports are in the Olympic Games?* Elicit ideas. Ask *Which sport do you most like to watch on TV?* Elicit answers.

1 Read. What do the Olympic rings represent?

- Have the children look at the pictures. Ask *What can you see?*
- Have the children read the text and find the answer. Ask *What do the Olympic rings represent?* (*the five continents*)
- Ask *Where were the last Olympic Games? Did you watch them?*

2 Circle T (true) or F (false).

- Read the example and elicit why the answer is false. (*There was only one event.*)
- The children circle T (true) or F (false) for each sentence.
- Elicit answers, including the correct version of the false sentences. Check with the class.

Answers

1 F **2** F **3** T **4** T

3 Class Vote

- Ask *Are sports only fun when you win?* The children discuss in pairs. Then take a vote with a show of hands for yes or no. Have a child come to the front of the class and count the votes to write them on the board. Invite children to explain why they voted how they did. (They might need to use L1.)

Ask *Where were the last Summer Olympics? Where were the last Winter Olympics? What sports did your country win medals in?* Elicit appropriate resources for research into this, e.g. Internet, family and friends, etc. The children will need to complete this research before doing the follow-up activity in the Activity Book. (It could be set as homework.)

Optional activity: Numbers Race

Divide the class into two teams. Give one child from each team a board pen. Read the text from Activity 1, stopping after each number. Have the children with the pens run to the board and write the number (in digits, not words). Pass the pen to another child and continue. This can be played as a team game for points.

Lesson 7 CLIL

1 Read and answer.

The Winter Olympics

The Summer Olympics happen every four years. There are also Winter Olympics – they happen two years after every Summer Olympics.
The sports at the Winter Olympics are very different. The bobsled is a great sport to watch because it's very fast – people race down a hill of ice! Usually teams from cold countries compete, but in 1988 Mexico and Jamaica took part. The Jamaican team came last, but they were very popular! Switzerland won the gold medal that year.

1 How often are the Winter Olympics?
a every four years b every two years
2 What countries don't usually compete in the bobsled?
a hot countries b cold countries
3 Which team did people love in 1988?
a Switzerland b Jamaica

Find Out More!

2 Use your Student Book research. In the last Olympics, how did your country do? Complete the Medals Chart.

My country:			
Summer Olympics in			
Sports			
Medals			
Winter Olympics in			
Sports			
Medals			

It's My World! *Think of a new Olympic sport. Share your ideas.*

Chapter 7 60

1 Read and answer.

The children answer the questions. Elicit answers and check with the class.

Answers

1 a **2** a **3** b

2 Use your Student Book research. In the last Olympics, how did your country do? Complete the Medals Chart.

Divide the class into groups of four. Have the children pool the information they learned from their research in the Student Book and the Activity Book. They complete the Medals Chart individually. Then they compare answers in pairs.

Answers

Children's own answers.

It's My World!

The children discuss new Olympic sports in groups. Prompt as necessary to get them started, e.g. *water ping-pong—like normal ping-pong, but the players have to swim and play in a pool!* Elicit ideas and have a class vote to identify the best new Olympic sport.

Cooler: Olympic rings

Have the children draw the Olympic rings on a piece of paper, color them, and write in each of them words for sports, names of athletes, and other sports-related words, e.g. *medal*, *win*, *gold*, etc. Elicit responses.

Competency Focus

Act

The children carry out research to find out about Olympic athletes from their country. They relate what they learn to their world, both inside and outside the classroom.

Digital Resources

Student eBook, Digital Activity Book • TIP When using the board for "heads-up" teaching, remember to give the children as much opportunity as possible to participate. Make sure you ask plenty of questions to give them the chance to engage with the text.

Teacher Resource Center • Print out CLIL Graphic Organizer 7 for the children to collate their Find Out More! research.

CLIL eBook • The children can use the CLIL eBook to expand their knowledge of the lesson topic.

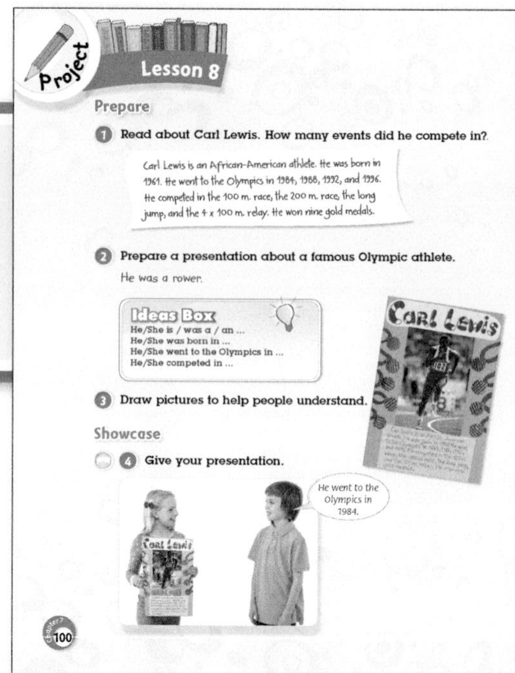
Project
Lesson 8

Prepare

1 Read about Carl Lewis. How many events did he compete in?

Carl Lewis is an African-American athlete. He was born in 1961. He went to the Olympics in 1984, 1988, 1992, and 1996. He competed in the 100 m. race, the 200 m. race, the long jump, and the 4 x 100 m. relay. He won nine gold medals.

2 Prepare a presentation about a famous Olympic athlete.

He was a rower.

Ideas Box
He/She is / was a / an ...
He/She was born in ...
He/She went to the Olympics in ...
He/She competed in ...

3 Draw pictures to help people understand.

Showcase

4 Give your presentation.

Chapter 7 100

Project

Lesson objectives: review language from Chapter 7; write and give a presentation on a famous Olympic athlete

Materials: paper and colored pens; two game pieces and a coin for each pair

Warmer: Olympic quiz

Have a class quiz on the Student Book Lesson 7 Activity 1 text. Divide the class into two teams. The team which answers the most questions correctly wins. Suggested questions: *Where were the first Olympic Games?* (*Ancient Greece*) *When were the first Olympic Games?* (*3,000 years ago*) *What was the only sport in the first Olympic Games?* (*a race*) *Where were the first Modern Olympics?* (*in Athens*)

Prepare

1 Read about Carl Lewis. How many events did he compete in?

- Have the children read the text aloud, a sentence each. Ask *How many events did Carl Lewis compete in?* (*four*)
- Ask the children to find the past verbs in the text. This will help them focus on using past verbs in their own presentations.

2 Prepare a presentation about a famous Olympic athlete.

- Divide the class into pairs. Have them decide which athlete they will present (remind them they can use athletes from previous lessons in the chapter or who they researched in Lesson 7). They write a short text, using the **Ideas Box** for support. Monitor and help as necessary.

Alternative craft activity

An easier project is to supply in note form the information the children will need for the presentation.

3 Draw pictures to help people understand.

Ask the children to imagine their presentation is in a magazine or on a website. Think about what pictures they might see next to the information. Have them draw pictures which they think help illustrate the information.

Showcase 

4 Give your presentation.

- Put the pairs into groups. Have each pair read out their presentation and show the pictures that illustrate it. Ask each group to choose one pair to present to the class.

Optional activity: Questions and answers

After each presentation, the child presenting asks the class three questions about what they said. This is a good way of encouraging the class to listen carefully to the speakers.

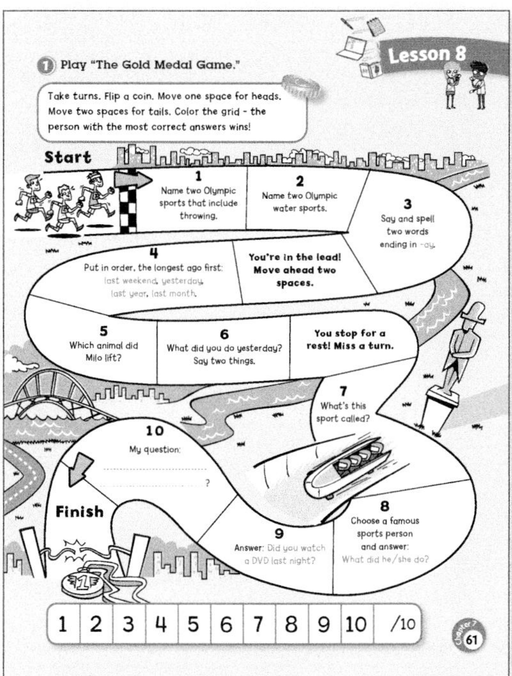

1 Play "The Gold Medal Game."

See p. 43 for instructions on how to play the game.

Answers

1 discus, javelin **2** diving, rowing **3** *any two of:* play, say, day, today, etc. **4** last year, last month, last weekend, yesterday **5** an ox **6** Children's own answers. **7** bobsled **8** Children's own answers. **9** Yes, I did. / No, I didn't. **10** Children's own answers.

Cooler: Browsing presentations

Have the children display their presentations around the classroom. Give the class time to look at them. Have a class vote to decide on the three best presentations.

Competency Focus

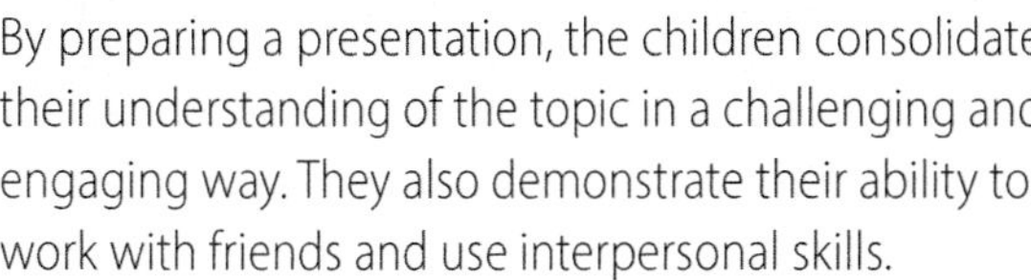

Collaborate and communicate

By preparing a presentation, the children consolidate their understanding of the topic in a challenging and engaging way. They also demonstrate their ability to work with friends and use interpersonal skills.

Digital Resources

Student eBook • Show the pictures, stage by stage, as you talk the class through the activity process.

- Choose from vocabulary from Chapters 4–7 to review a vocabulary topic. Have the children vote to select a topic and a way to review it. Then use *Timer* and give the class one minute to recall all the words in the topic. Repeat with a different topic if you have time.

Language Review

Lesson objective: review language from Chapter 7
Materials: Tracks 7.9 and AB 7.1

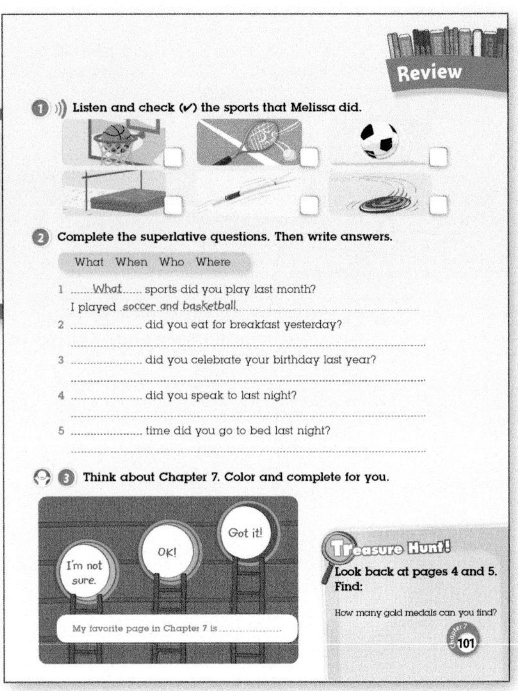
Review

1 Listen and check (✔) the sports that Melissa did.

2 Complete the superlative questions. Then write answers.

What When Who Where

1 ......What...... sports did you play last month?
I played soccer and basketball.
2 .... did you eat for breakfast yesterday?
3 .... did you celebrate your birthday last year?
4 .... did you speak to last night?
5 .... time did you go to bed last night?

3 Think about Chapter 7. Color and complete for you.

I'm not sure. OK! Got it!

My favorite page in Chapter 7 is ....

Treasure Hunt!
Look back at pages 4 and 5. Find:
How many gold medals can you find?

101

Warmer: Vocabulary recall

The children look back at the vocabulary introduced in Lessons 1 and 5. Then they close their book. Give them two minutes to write down as many of the words as they can. Then they swap with another pair to check each other's work. The pair with the most correct words wins.

1 7.9 Listen and check (✔) the sports that Melissa did.

- Have the children name the sports pictured.
- Play Track 7.9 twice. The children listen and check the sports Melissa did.
- Check answers by saying the sports to elicit *Yes* or *No*.

Audioscript

Kate: *Hi, Melissa. Did you go to the Sports Camp last weekend?*
Melissa: *Yes, I did. It was great!*
Kate: *What did you do?*
Melissa: *Well, there were a lot of sports activities.*
Kate: *Did you do the high jump?*
Melissa: *Yes, I did.*
Kate: *And, did you throw the javelin?*
Melissa: *No, I didn't. But I was good at the discus.*
Kate: *And did you play any team sports?*
Melissa: *Yes, I did. The second day we played basketball in the morning.*
Kate: *Cool! … And in the afternoon?*
Melissa: *Well … we played my favorite sport, soccer. I scored a goal and my team won!*

Answers

✔ by high jump, discus, basketball, soccer

2 Complete with these words. Then write answers for you.

- The children complete the sentences using the words supplied. Then they write answers about themselves.
- Elicit responses. Encourage careful listening by having the class respond *Me, too!* or *Not me!*

Answers

1 What **2** What **3** Where **4** Who **5** When + children's own answers

3 Think about Chapter 7. Color and complete for you.

- Have the children look back at Chapter 7. Elicit their favorite parts. The children then color the circle which represents how they feel about their own progress (self-evaluation).
- Have the children complete the sentence about their favorite page. Elicit responses.

Treasure Hunt!

Have the children look at pp. 4–5 to count the gold medals. Elicit the answer. (*seven*)

Cooler: Play "Ready, Set, Draw!"

Play the game with sports from Chapter 7 (see Games Bank p. 19).

Competency Focus

Me: Self-evaluation

The children reflect on the chapter and express their opinions about their own progress.

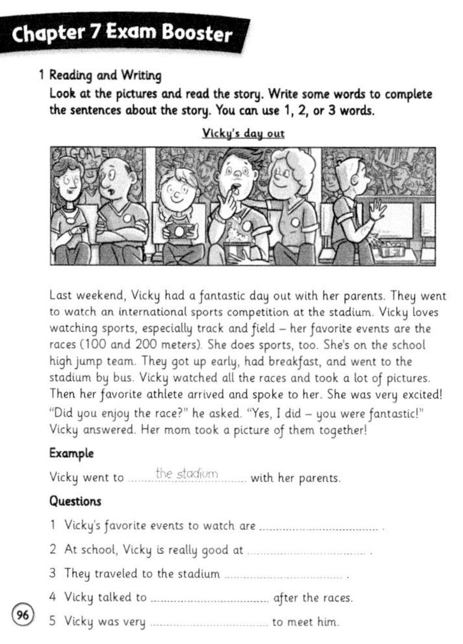

Chapter 7 Exam Booster

1 Reading and Writing

Look at the pictures and read the story. Write some words to complete the sentences about the story. You can use 1, 2, or 3 words.

Vicky's day out

Last weekend, Vicky had a fantastic day out with her parents. They went to watch an international sports competition at the stadium. Vicky loves watching sports, especially track and field – her favorite events are the races (100 and 200 meters). She does sports, too. She's on the school high jump team. They got up early, had breakfast, and went to the stadium by bus. Vicky watched all the races and took a lot of pictures. Then her favorite athlete arrived and spoke to her. She was very excited! "Did you enjoy the race?" he asked. "Yes, I did – you were fantastic!" Vicky answered. Her mom took a picture of them together!

Example

Vicky went to ......the stadium...... with her parents.

Questions

1 Vicky's favorite events to watch are ....

2 At school, Vicky is really good at ....

3 They traveled to the stadium ....

4 Vicky talked to .... after the races.

5 Vicky was very .... to meet him.

96

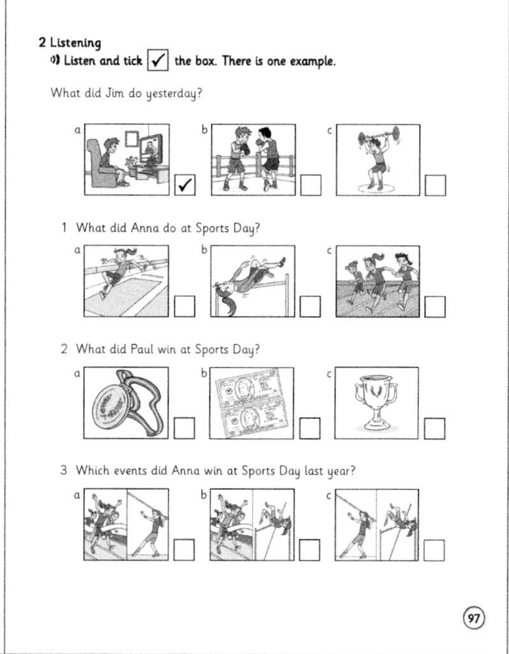

2 Listening

Listen and tick ✓ the box. There is one example.

What did Jim do yesterday?

a ✓ b c

1 What did Anna do at Sports Day?

a b c

2 What did Paul win at Sports Day?

a b c

3 Which events did Anna win at Sports Day last year?

a b c

97

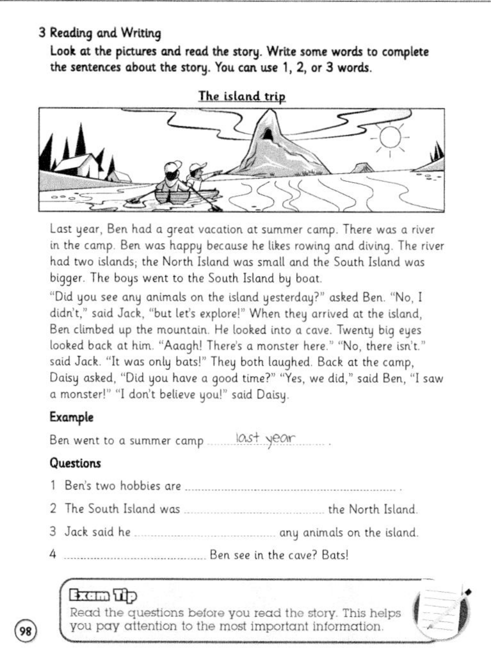

3 Reading and Writing

Look at the pictures and read the story. Write some words to complete the sentences about the story. You can use 1, 2, or 3 words.

The island trip

Last year, Ben had a great vacation at summer camp. There was a river in the camp. Ben was happy because he likes rowing and diving. The river had two islands; the North Island was small and the South Island was bigger. The boys went to the South Island by boat.

"Did you see any animals on the island yesterday?" asked Ben. "No, I didn't," said Jack, "but let's explore!" When they arrived at the island, Ben climbed up the mountain. He looked into a cave. Twenty big eyes looked back at him. "Aaagh! There's a monster here." "No, there isn't." said Jack. "It was only bats!" They both laughed. Back at the camp, Daisy asked, "Did you have a good time?" "Yes, we did," said Ben, "I saw a monster!" "I don't believe you!" said Daisy.

Example

Ben went to a summer camp ......last year...... .

Questions

1 Ben's two hobbies are ....

2 The South Island was .... the North Island.

3 Jack said he .... any animals on the island.

4 .... Ben see in the cave? Bats!

Exam Tip
Read the questions before you read the story. This helps you pay attention to the most important information.

98

1 Reading and Writing. Look at the pictures and read the story. Write some words to complete the sentences about the story. You can use 1, 2, or 3 words.

The children read the text and complete the sentences.

Answers

1 the races **2** high jump **3** by bus **4** her favorite athlete **5** happy/excited

2 AB 7.1 Listening. Listen and tick (✓) the box. There is one example.

The children read the questions. Play Track AB 7.1 twice. They listen and check the correct picture in each section.

Answers (Audioscript on p. 223)

1 b **2** a **3** b

3 Reading and Writing. Look at the pictures and read the story. Write some words to complete the sentences about the story. You can use 1, 2, or 3 words.

The children read the text and complete the sentences.

Answers

1 rowing and diving, **2** bigger than, **3** didn't see, **4** What did

Digital Resources

Student eBook • Open the Welcome page to give feedback on Treasure Hunt. Ask a child to find and circle the gold medals using *Pen*.

Teacher Resource Center • Print out Test Chapter 7 to use at the end of this lesson. The Test Generator also allows you to create customized tests.

Chapter 8

Video Games

Overview

The children will:

- use critical thinking skills to identify action verbs.
- describe different actions.
- read, understand, and act out a story.
- describe how actions are done.
- ask and answer about game playing.
- find out about "exergames."
- design a video game.

Key Vocabulary

Action verbs: collect, fly, hit, move, open, push
Adverbs: angrily, carefully, happily, loudly, quietly, well

Key Grammar

- I got (it last December).
- The spaceship moves (up).
- My mom is shouting (for me).
- Why are you shouting (so loudly)?
- It moves when you move.
- Don't fall (off the board).
- My brother fell (off the board).
- I didn't fall.

Reading Skills

Story: *Sneaky Snake*
Genre: video game story

Literacy Development

- predict story content from title and pictures
- reflect on and personalize the theme of the story
- focus on rhyme

Functional Language

- My turn!
- OK, your turn. Go for it.

Spelling

Adverb endings *–ly* and *–ily*

CLIL: Science—Exergames

The children find out about exergames—active video games.

Competency Focus

The children will:

use critical thinking skills to identify action verbs. (Lesson 1) predict the content of a story. (Lesson 3) identify and talk about how people do things. (Lesson 5)	apply new grammar to previously learned vocabulary. (Lesson 2) talk about games they are playing now or played in the past. (Lesson 6)	work in pairs to act out a dialogue. (Lesson 3) work in groups to act out the story. (Lesson 8)	personalize the story by thinking about how they might act in a similar situation. (Lesson 4) evaluate their own progress in the chapter. (Review)	develop cultural understanding by finding out more about exergames. (Lesson 7)

Digital Overview

Teacher Presentation

Student eBook and Digital Activity Book

- Music Video 8.1 (8.2): *My New Game*
- Interactive versions of AB activities
- Integrated audio and answer key for all activities

Teacher resources for planning, lesson delivery, and homework

Teacher Resource Center

- Class Planner Chapter 8
- Worksheets to print out (including notes and answers):
  - Grammar Worksheet 8A: I got it … The spaceship moves …
  - Grammar Worksheet 8B: Why are you shouting …? It moves …
  - Phonic Worksheet 8
  - CLIL Graphic Organizer 8
  - Test Chapter 8
- Test Generator
- Literacy Handbook

Watch the Music Video

Children's resources for learning and practicing at home

Student eBook

- Music Video 8.1 (8.2): *My New Game*

The Inks Student's App

Vocabulary games: Action verbs and adverbs

Chapter 8 Video Games

Lesson 1

Vocabulary

Lesson objective: identify and use verbs related to playing video games
Key vocabulary: *collect, fly, hit, move, open, push*
Materials: Track 8.1

Chapter 8 Video Games
Lesson 1
1 Listen and number. Then say.

2 Tell a friend how to play a video game.

3 Write about your favorite game.
I can fly. I collect gold coins.
106

Warmer: Verb list

Divide the class into teams, and give each team a piece of paper and a pen. They list as many verbs as they can, with the children in each team taking turns writing. Ask the team with the most answers to read them out. Elicit more verbs.

1 8.1 Listen and number. Then say. 

- Have the children look at the pictures. Ask *What can you see? Would you like to play this game?*
- The children find the actions and write the picture number by the correct word on the console. Play Track 8.1 and have the children listen and check their answers.
- Play Track 8.1 again, pausing after each verb for the children to point and repeat.

Audioscript

This is your Play Box console. See the four black arrows? Press those to move. You can move up, down, left, and right. There are a lot of stars to collect in the game. To collect the stars, you need to hit them first. To hit the stars, press the green circle and jump up. They fall to the ground. See the yellow button with a star? You press this to collect gold stars from the ground! Yes, use this button to pick the stars up. You can also push things like boxes and trucks. Just press the purple triangle. And you can open things like doors. Press the blue square to open that door. The coolest thing you can do on the Play Box is fly! To fly, press the white 'X' on the control. Look, you're flying in the sky!

Answers

push 2, collect 3, move 1, hit 5, fly 4, open 6

2 Tell a friend how to play a video game.

- Have the children repeat the example instruction after you. Ask *Is this similar to a video game you know? Which one?*
- The children think for a minute about a video game they know, then talk about it with a friend. Can their friend guess the game?
- Invite children to explain their favorite game to the class.

3 Write about your favorite game.

- Elicit two example sentences for how to play a favorite video game.
- Have the children write about their favorite game in their notebook. Monitor and give help as necessary. The children then talk about their favorite games in pairs. Elicit descriptions.

Answers

Children's own answers.

Optional activity: Mime the game

Track 8.1

Play Track 8.1 from Activity 1 again, and have the children mime the actions.

Chapter 8 Video Games
Lesson 1

1 Look, complete, and write the letters.

fly move ~~pick up~~ hit open push

1 Do you need a paintbrush? ...Pick up... the one on the floor. a
2 I'm painting the door. Don't .... it!
3 Watch out! Don't .... your head on the shelf.
4 That plane is ....ing to London.
5 The girl needs to .... the cat.
6 He's strong. He can .... the desk.

2 Choose and categorize the words in your notebook.

words with "o"
words with other vowels

easy to say
hard to say

when I play video games,
I do this
I don't do this

62

1 Look, complete, and write the letters.

The children look at the pictures and complete the sentences, using the sentences supplied. Then they write the letter of the picture detail described. Elicit answers.

Answers

1 Pick up a **2** open c **3** hit d **4** fly b **5** move f **6** push e

2 Choose and categorize the words in your notebook.

Elicit an example for each category listed. Ask *Which categories would you choose?* Elicit ideas, prompting children to give a reason for their choice. The children choose a pair of categories and list the words in their notebook, then compare with a friend.

Answers

Children's own answers.

Cooler: Imagine your own console

Ask the children to imagine the best games console they can. Give them a minute to think, then divide the class into pairs and have them discuss their ideas. Elicit ideas.

Competency Focus

Think! Critical Thinking

The children use critical thinking skills to identify action verbs by using visual clues and processing the written and spoken forms.

Digital Resources

Student eBook, Digital Activity Book • TIP As you monitor the children's progress, use *Add personal note* to keep a note of weaknesses in vocabulary, grammar, or pronunciation so you can review in later lessons.

Grammar

Lesson objective: use a range of tenses in the affirmative to describe a situation
Key grammar: *I got (it last December). The spaceship moves (up). My mom is shouting (for me).*
Secondary language: *adventure, desert, spaceship*
Materials: Track 8.2; colored pencils (red, blue, green); Grammar Worksheet 8A [TRC printout] (optional)

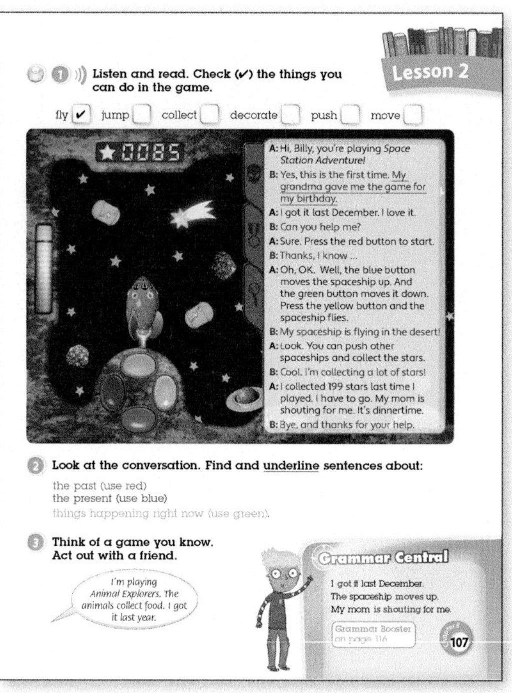

Lesson 2

1 Listen and read. Check (✔) the things you can do in the game.

fly ✔ jump ☐ collect ☐ decorate ☐ push ☐ move ☐

A: Hi, Billy, you're playing *Space Station Adventure!*
B: Yes, this is the first time. My grandma gave me the game for my birthday.
A: I got it last December. I love it.
B: Can you help me?
A: Sure. Press the red button to start.
B: Thanks, I know ...
A: Oh, OK. Well, the blue button moves the spaceship up. And the green button moves it down. Press the yellow button and the spaceship flies.
B: My spaceship is flying in the desert!
A: Look. You can push other spaceships and collect the stars.
B: Cool. I'm collecting a lot of stars!
A: I collected 199 stars last time I played. I have to go. My mom is shouting for me. It's dinnertime.
B: Bye, and thanks for your help.

2 Look at the conversation. Find and underline sentences about:

the past (use red)
the present (use blue)
things happening right now (use green).

3 Think of a game you know. Act out with a friend.

I'm playing Animal Explorers. The animals collect food. I got it last year.

Grammar Central

I got it last December.
The spaceship moves up.
My mom is shouting for me.

Grammar Booster on page 116

107

Warmer: Play "Simon Says"

Play the game with (*Simon says*) *jump up / hit the stars / collect the stars / push the box / open the door / fly / press the button* (see Games Bank p. 19).

1 8.2 Listen and read. Check (✔) the things you can do in the game.

- Have the children look at the text. Ask *Where is this conversation taking place?* (*online chatroom*) Ask *Do you chat with your friends online?*
- Have a child read out the list of actions above the picture. Ask different children *Can you do these things in computer games?*
- Play Track 8.2 twice. The children listen and read along. They check the things you can do in the game. The children read again to check their answer. Elicit answers.

Answers

fly, collect, push, move

2 Look at the conversation. Find and underline sentences about:

- The children will need a red, blue, and green pencil each. Say *You're playing Space Station Adventure—past, present, or right now?* (*right now*) Ask *What color for "right now?"* (*green*)
- The children underline, then compare in pairs. Elicit sentences in order and past, present, or right now for each one.

Answers

In the past: sentences with gave, got, collected, played
In the present: sentences with is, love, help, Press, know, moves, moves, Press/flies, push/collect, have to, It's
Happening right now: sentences with 're playing, is flying, 'm collecting, is shouting

Grammar Central

I got it last December. ...

Have the children look at the patterns. Ask *Which sentence is about the past?* (*I got it ...*) *About the present?* (*The spaceship moves ...*) *About something happening now?* (*My mom is shouting ...*) Say verbs from each tense in random order to elicit past/present/right now.

For extra practice, try the **Grammar Booster** sections in the Student Book (p. 116).

Answers p. 116

Activity 1: **1** played **2** won **3** plays **4** wins **5** playing **6** winning

Activity 2: **1** playing **2** got **3** watches **4** is doing **5** makes **6** stayed

Optional activity: Draw and label

Have the children draw a picture of someone playing their favorite video game. They label it with information about the past, present, and what is happening right now.

3 Think of a game you know. Act out with a friend.

- Give an example, e.g. *I'm playing Super Jump! I got it last weekend. You jump to catch birds! I'm jumping now!* Mime playing the game.
- Divide the class into pairs. The children take turns miming and describing what they are doing.

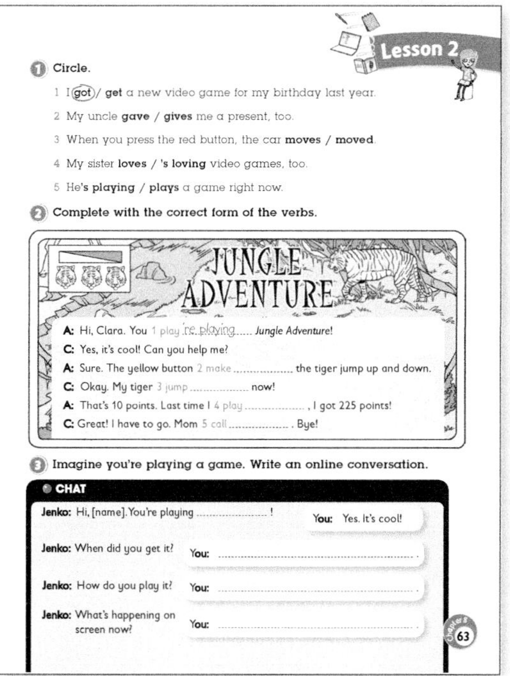

Lesson 2

1 Circle.

1 I got / **get** a new video game for my birthday last year.
2 My uncle **gave** / **gives** me a present, too.
3 When you press the red button, the car **moves** / **moved**.
4 My sister **loves** / **'s loving** video games, too.
5 He**'s playing** / **plays** a game right now.

2 Complete with the correct form of the verbs.

A: Hi, Clara. You 1 play 're playing *Jungle Adventure*!
C: Yes, it's cool! Can you help me?
A: Sure. The yellow button 2 make .... the tiger jump up and down.
C: Okay. My tiger 3 jump .... now!
A: That's 10 points. Last time I 4 play ...., I got 225 points!
C: Great! I have to go. Mom 5 call .... Bye!

3 Imagine you're playing a game. Write an online conversation.

CHAT

Jenko: Hi, [name]. You're playing ....! **You:** Yes. It's cool!
Jenko: When did you get it? **You:** ....
Jenko: How do you play it? **You:** ....
Jenko: What's happening on screen now? **You:** ....

Chapter 8 63

1 Circle.

The children complete the sentences by circling the correct options. Elicit answers and an explanation for each sentence.

Answers

1 got **2** gave **3** moves **4** loves **5** 's playing

2 Complete with the correct form of the verbs.

The children complete the conversation with the correct tense of the verbs supplied. Elicit answers and an explanation for each sentence.

Answers

1 're playing **2** makes **3** is jumping **4** played **5** is calling

3 Imagine you're playing a game. Write an online conversation.

Elicit ideas for each blank. The children write a conversation individually, then compare in pairs. Ask pairs to read out their conversation for the class.

Answers

Children's own answers.

Cooler: Play "Sentence Builders"

Play the game with *We're playing a video game with my brother. I moved the spaceship up and collected the stars.* (see Games Bank p. 19).

Competency Focus

Learn

The children use previously acquired vocabulary in a different context with new grammatical structures.

Digital Resources

Student eBook • Divide the class into teams. Give each team one minute on *Timer* to find one example of the three different tenses in the SB Activity 1 text (referring to the past, the present, and things happening right now). The other teams confirm whether answers are correct. Each correct answer wins a point. The team with the most points wins.

Teacher Resource Center • For extra grammar practice, print out Grammar Worksheet 8A.

Reading: Story Extract

Lesson objectives: take turns; predict story content from title and pictures; read the extract from *Sneaky Snake* (beginning)
Functional language: *My turn! OK, your turn. Go for it.*
Secondary language: *big mistake*
Materials: Tracks 8.3 and 8.4

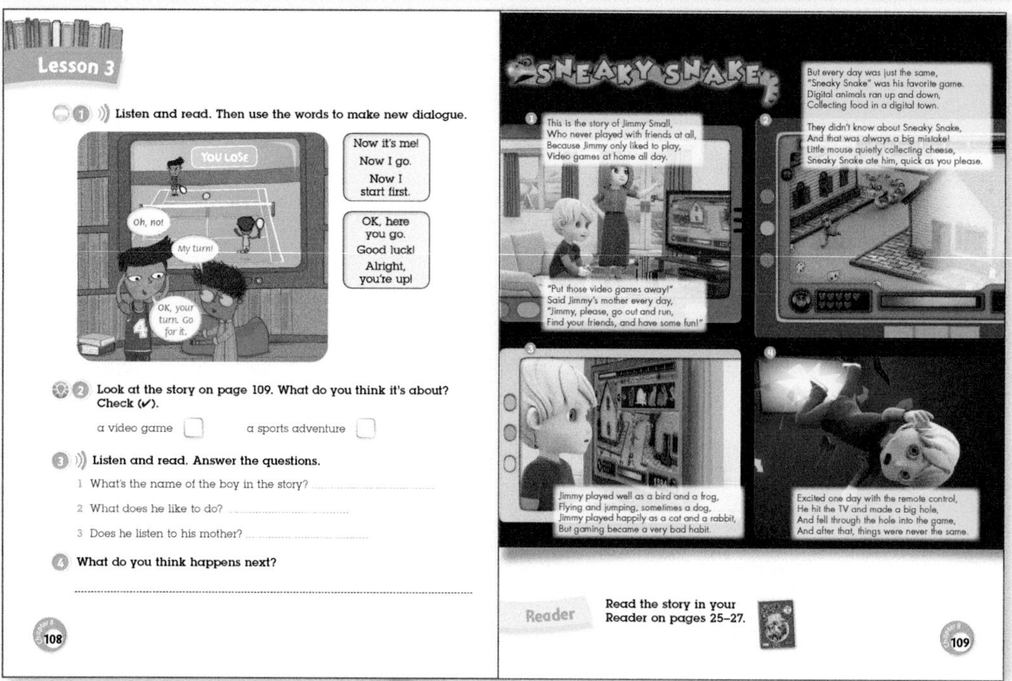

Lesson 3

1 Listen and read. Then use the words to make new dialogue.

Now it's me!
Now I go.
Now I start first.

OK, here you go.
Good luck!
Alright, you're up!

2 Look at the story on page 109. What do you think it's about? Check (✓).

a video game ☐ a sports adventure ☐

3 Listen and read. Answer the questions.

1 What's the name of the boy in the story?

2 What does he like to do?

3 Does he listen to his mother?

4 What do you think happens next?

108

SNEAKY SNAKE

1 This is the story of Jimmy Small,
Who never played with friends at all,
Because Jimmy only liked to play,
Video games at home all day.

"Put those video games away!"
Said Jimmy's mother every day,
"Jimmy, please, go out and run,
Find your friends, and have some fun!"

2 But every day was just the same,
"Sneaky Snake" was his favorite game.
Digital animals ran up and down,
Collecting food in a digital town.

They didn't know about Sneaky Snake,
And that was always a big mistake!
Little mouse quietly collecting cheese,
Sneaky Snake ate him, quick as you please.

3 Jimmy played well as a bird and a frog,
Flying and jumping, sometimes a dog,
Jimmy played happily as a cat and a rabbit,
But gaming became a very bad habit.

4 Excited one day with the remote control,
He hit the TV and made a big hole,
And fell through the hole into the game,
And after that, things were never the same.

Reader Read the story in your Reader on pages 25–27.

109

Warmer: Play "The Chain Game"

Play the game using video games actions from the chapter (see Games Bank p. 19). Start with *Yesterday, I played a video game—I collected stars.*

Functional language

1 8.3 Listen and read. Then use the words to make new dialogue.

- Have the children look at the pictures and dialogue. Ask *What are the children doing?* (*playing a video game*)
- Play Track 8.3. The children listen and read along.
- Play Track 8.3 again, pausing for the children to repeat.
- The children act out the dialogue in pairs.
- Ask *What other games do you play where you take turns?* Elicit some games with turn-taking and point out they can use these phrases when playing those games, too.

Before reading

2 Look at the story on page 109. What do you think it's about? Check (✓).

- Ask the children to look at the title and pictures and discuss in pairs, before choosing and checking one of the two options. Ask *What do you think it's about?* Elicit ideas. (*a video game*)

3 8.4 Listen and read. Answer the questions.

- Have children read out a question. Play Track 8.4 twice. The children listen and read along.
- Give the children time to write the answers. Elicit answers and check with the class.

Answers

1 Jimmy Small **2** He likes to play video games.
3 No, he doesn't.

4 What do you think happens next?

- Have the children write their prediction. Elicit ideas including reasons, but do not confirm. Say they will have to read the story to find out.

Answers

Children's own answers.

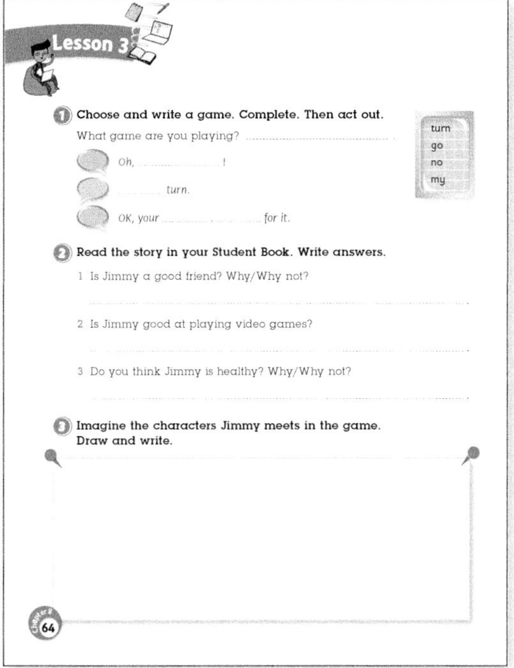

Lesson 3

1 Choose and write a game. Complete. Then act out.

What game are you playing? ....

Oh, ... !

.... turn.

OK, your .... for it.

turn / go / no / my

2 Read the story in your Student Book. Write answers.

1 Is Jimmy a good friend? Why/Why not?

....

2 Is Jimmy good at playing video games?

....

3 Do you think Jimmy is healthy? Why/Why not?

....

3 Imagine the characters Jimmy meets in the game. Draw and write.

Chapter 8 64

1 Choose and write a game. Complete. Then act out.

The children write the name of a game and then complete the dialogue. Then they act out in pairs. Have pairs act out for the class.

Answers

(children's own answer) no, My, turn, Go

2 Read the story in your Student Book. Write answers.

The children read the Student Book story extract again. They write answers to the questions. Elicit answers.

Answers

1 No, because he doesn't play with his friends.
2 Yes, he is. **3** No, because he never goes out.

3 Imagine the characters Jimmy meets in the game. Draw and write.

Elicit suggestions for game characters. The children draw and label one or two characters, then compare with a friend.

Answers

Children's own answers.

Cooler: Play "Ready, Set, Draw!"

Play the game with *video game, Sneaky Snake, little mouse, cheese, rabbit, hole* (see Games Bank, p. 19).

Competency Focus

Collaborate and Communicate

The children act out an authentic dialogue together, putting into practice new functional language.

Think! Critical Thinking

The children apply reading skills (exploiting pictures and text clues) to understand the story context.

Digital Resources

Student eBook • Before you do the book activities, display the SB page. Use *Timer* to give the children one minute to study the pictures. Then close or minimize the page and ask questions to elicit details in the pictures, e.g. *Where is Jimmy at the beginning of the story? Which animals are on the screen? What is chasing the mouse?*

SNEAKY SNAKE

1
This is the story of Jimmy Small,
Who never played with friends at all,
Because Jimmy only liked to play,
Video games at home all day.

"Put those video games away!"
Said Jimmy's mother every day.
"Jimmy, please, go out and run,
Find your friends, and have some fun!"

2
But every day was just the same,
"Sneaky Snake" was his favorite game.
Digital animals ran up and down,
Collecting food in a digital town.

They didn't know about Sneaky Snake,
And that was always a big mistake!
Little mouse quietly collecting cheese,
Sneaky Snake ate him, quick as you please.

3
Jimmy played well as a bird and a frog,
Flying and jumping, sometimes a dog,
Jimmy played happily as a cat and a rabbit,
But gaming became a very bad habit.

4
Excited one day with the remote
control,
He hit the TV and made a big hole,
And fell through the hole into the
game,
And after that, things were never the same.

5
No buttons to press, or push, or hit,
Jimmy Small had to be quick.
Sneaky Snake wanted to eat him,
So Jimmy Small had to beat him.

6
Jimmy found a place to hide,
But here came Snake, mouth open wide!
Sneaky Snake was slippery slick,
But all that practice made Jimmy quick.

7
Jimmy, of course, knew how to play,
He played "Sneaky Snake" every day,
But Sneaky Snake needed to eat,
And chased him into this small street!

So Jimmy couldn't run at all,
Jimmy's back was against the wall,
But Jimmy knew which move to make,
Jimmy must attack the snake.

8
He hit the snake—he won the game!
But broke the control, and his life changed,
Without it he couldn't stay in and play,
Video games day after day.

9
From that day, Jimmy Small,
Didn't play video games at all.
Now, he listens to his mom and goes outside,
With his friends to the park and the countryside.

Lesson objectives: read and understand the video game story *Sneaky Snake* in the Reader
Materials: Track 8.5; Reader

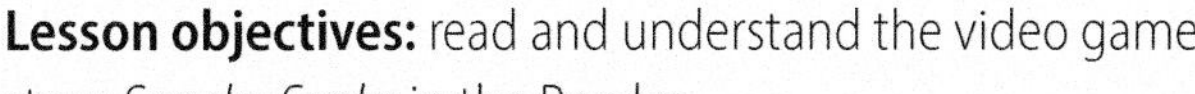

Warmer: Scrambled words

Write scrambled versions of the key words from the story extract on the board, e.g. *habit, digital, hole*. Have children write the correct version on the board. Then elicit how the word is used in the story extract.

Story Summary

Jimmy Small is a boy who loves to play video games. His favorite video game is *Sneaky Snake*. When he falls into the game, he is chased by the snake but he escapes. Jimmy stops playing video games all the time and goes to play outside with his friends.

Value: It's important to work AND play. 

8.5 While reading

- Have the children look at the pictures in the Reader. Ask *Who can you see? What games does the boy play?*
- Play Track 8.5. The children listen and read along. Ask *At the end of the story, does Jimmy still play video games all the time?* (*no*)
- Play Track 8.5 again. Ask questions to check comprehension, e.g. *How did Jimmy go into the video game?* (*through a hole in the TV*) *Why did he fight the Sneaky Snake?* (*because the snake wanted to eat him*) *Why couldn't Jimmy play video games anymore?* (*because he broke the remote control*) *Was he happy?* (*yes*)

After reading: Reflect

- Ask questions to give the children the opportunity to think about the issues raised by the story: *Did Jimmy have a good life at the beginning of the story? Do you think his life is better now? Are you like Jimmy? Do you prefer to play inside or outside? Why?*

Optional activity: Mime the story

8.5

Play the story again. The children listen and mime the actions of the story.

Story Time

Beating out the rhythm

Stories written in rhyme have a very definite rhythm, too. Have the children snap their fingers or clap quietly to the rhythm of the story. It will help them get a feel for the natural rhythm of English, as a stress-timed language.

Reading Strategy

Paired Reading

The Paired Reading strategy involves the children reading aloud to each other in pairs. Less fluent readers learn from more fluent readers, and gain confidence reading to just one person. It also benefits readers of the same ability working together.

For additional explanation and activities, see the Literacy Handbook on the Teacher Resource Center.

Cooler: Who did this?

Say actions from the story to elicit who did it, e.g. *He played video games.* (*Jimmy*) *He ate the mouse.* (*Sneaky Snake*) *He made a hole in the TV.* (*Jimmy*) *He chased Jimmy.* (*Sneaky Snake*) *He won the game.* (*Jimmy*) *They go to the park* (*Jimmy and his friends*).

Digital Resources

Reader eBook • Display the Reader. Focus on one picture at a time. Before moving on each time, elicit what is going to happen next.

- Say *run*. A child uses *Highlighter* to find *run* in the story and a word that rhymes with it. (*fun*) Repeat with different prompts and children. You could ask the class to supply the prompts.

Reading Comprehension and Critical Literacy

Lesson objectives: focus on the use of rhyme in stories; reflect on the story theme and relate it to personal behavior
Materials: Track 8.5; Reader

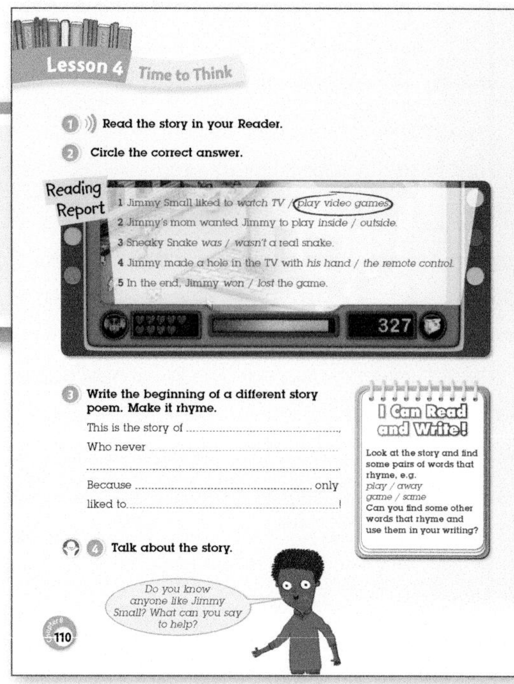

Lesson 4 Time to Think

1 Read the story in your Reader.

2 Circle the correct answer.

Reading Report

1 Jimmy Small liked to watch TV / play video games.
2 Jimmy's mom wanted Jimmy to play inside / outside.
3 Sneaky Snake was / wasn't a real snake.
4 Jimmy made a hole in the TV with his hand / the remote control.
5 In the end, Jimmy won / lost the game.

327

3 Write the beginning of a different story poem. Make it rhyme.

This is the story of ....
Who never ....
....
Because .... only
liked to ....!

I Can Read and Write!

Look at the story and find some pairs of words that rhyme, e.g.
play / away
game / same
Can you find some other words that rhyme and use them in your writing?

4 Talk about the story.

Do you know anyone like Jimmy Small? What can you say to help?

110

Note: Please ensure that your class has read the Reader story before you do this lesson.

Warmer: Imagination

Mime opening a laptop and starting to play a video game. Say *Look! I can see Sneaky Snake!* and mime giving the laptop to a child. Encourage the child to say *I can't! But I can see …* (e.g.) *stars!* and returning the laptop to you. Continue around the class, prompting children to say what they can see on the screen.

1 8.5 Read the story in your Reader.

- Have the children read the story. (Alternatively, play Track 8.5 and have them read along). Elicit whether they were correct in their predictions in Lesson 3 Activity 4.
- Check comprehension by asking *How did Jimmy beat Sneaky Snake? (He hit the snake with the remote control.) What happened after Jimmy won the game? (He didn't play video games—he played outside with his friends.)*

2 Circle the correct answer.

- Elicit the answer to question 1. Have the children continue the activity individually.
- Elicit answers and check with the class.

Answers

1 to play video games **2** outside **3** wasn't **4** the remote control **5** won

I Can Read and Write!

Explain that when words rhyme they have the same sound. Have the children look back at the story and find other pairs of rhyming words, e.g. *control—hole, game—same, frog—dog, rabbit—habit,* etc. Encourage the children to use rhyming words in Activity 3.

3 Write the beginning of a different story poem. Make it rhyme.

- Elicit an example of the first two sentences of a new poem, e.g. *This is the story of Danny Gray, Who never goes out on a rainy day.*
- Have the children work in pairs to write their poem. Monitor and give help as necessary.
- Invite pairs to read their poem to the class.

Answers

Children's own answers.

4 Talk about the story. 

- Have a child read out Jason's questions. Ask *Do you know any people who play too many video games/ don't go outside enough/spend too much time outside playing soccer?* Discuss as a class, eliciting advice for someone who spends too much time doing one thing.

Optional activity: Play "Tic-Tac-Toe"

Play the game with the children giving a rhyming word to win a square (see Games Bank p. 19)

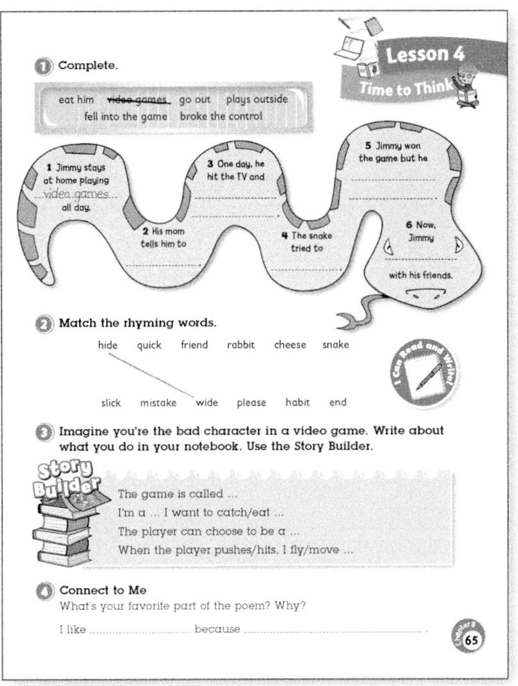
Lesson 4
Time to Think

1 Complete.

eat him ~~video games~~ go out plays outside fell into the game broke the control

1 Jimmy stays at home playing video games all day.
2 His mom tells him to ...
3 One day, he hit the TV and ...
4 The snake tried to ...
5 Jimmy won the game but he ...
6 Now, Jimmy ... with his friends.

2 Match the rhyming words.

hide quick friend rabbit cheese snake

slick mistake wide please habit end

3 Imagine you're the bad character in a video game. Write about what you do in your notebook. Use the Story Builder.

Story Builder

The game is called ...
I'm a ... I want to catch/eat ...
The player can choose to be a ...
When the player pushes/hits, I fly/move ...

4 Connect to Me
What's your favorite part of the poem? Why?

I like ... because ...

65

1 Complete.

The children complete the sentences using the words supplied. Elicit answers.

Answers

1 video games **2** go out **3** fell into the game **4** eat him **5** he broke the control **6** plays outside

2 Match the rhyming words.

The children practice the **I Can Read and Write!** feature by matching the rhyming words. Elicit answers.

Answers

hide/wide, quick/slick, friend/end, rabbit/habit, cheese/please, snake/mistake

3 Imagine you're the bad character in a video game. Write about what you do in your notebook. Use the Story Builder.

Use the **Story Builder** prompts to elicit ideas. The children write a text in their notebook, then swap with a friend to check. Have children read out their text for the class.

Answers

Children's own answers.

4 Connect to Me

Elicit ideas on favorite parts of the poem. The children write their own response, then compare with a friend. Elicit responses.

Answers

Children's own answers.

Cooler: Play "Disappearing Text"

Do this activity with the first verse of the Reader story (see Games Bank p. 19).

Competency Focus

Me: Critical Literacy

The children use critical literacy skills to reflect on the story and think of real-life people who are like the character from the story.

Digital Resources

Reader eBook • Display the Reader on the board. Have children act out one of the pictures in the story (on their own or in pairs) for the class to guess and identify.

Student eBook • Have several children use *Pen* to write their SB Activity 3 poem on the board. Have the class vote on their favorite.

Student eBook, Digital Activity Book • TIP With the answer key, you can show the answers all at once or one by one to customize feedback.

Vocabulary, Song, and Spelling

Lesson objectives: identify and talk about how people do things; practice spelling adverb endings *–ly* and *–ily*

Key vocabulary: *angrily, carefully, happily, loudly, quietly, well*

Secondary language: *laugh, read the instructions, shout*

Materials: Tracks 8.6 and 8.7; verb/adjective prompts (optional); purple, red, and blue pens/pencils ; Phonics Worksheet 8 [TRC] (optional)

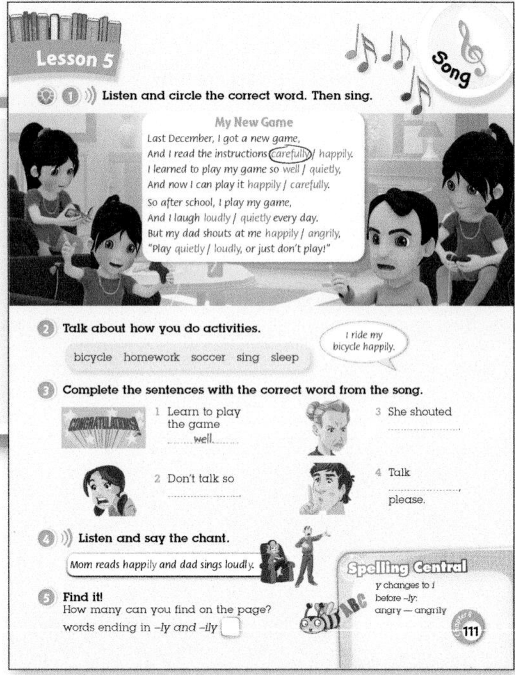

Lesson 5

Song

1 Listen and circle the correct word. Then sing.

My New Game

Last December, I got a new game,
And I read the instructions carefully / happily.
I learned to play my game so well / quietly,
And now I can play it happily / carefully.
So after school, I play my game,
And I laugh loudly / quietly every day.
But my dad shouts at me happily / angrily,
"Play quietly / loudly, or just don't play!"

2 Talk about how you do activities.

bicycle homework soccer sing sleep

I ride my bicycle happily.

3 Complete the sentences with the correct word from the song.

1 Learn to play the game well.
2 Don't talk so ....
3 She shouted ....
4 Talk ...., please.

4 Listen and say the chant.

Mom reads happily and dad sings loudly.

5 Find it!
How many can you find on the page?
words ending in *–ly and –ily*

Spelling Central
y changes to i before –ly:
angry — angrily

111

Warmer: Pre-teach vocabulary

Pre-teach the vocabulary using mimes. Have the children mime each one with you, then mime and repeat, and then mime and say the vocabulary on their own.

1 8.6 Listen and circle the correct word. Then sing.

- Have the children look at the pictures. Ask *What activities can you see?*
- Play Track 8.6. The children listen and circle the word they hear on each line.
- Read the song out loud, pausing before the circled word for the class to call out the word. Have the children repeat the word after you to check pronunciation.
- Play Track 8.6 again for the children to sing along.

Answers

carefully, well, happily, loudly, angrily, quietly

2 Talk about how you do activities.

- Give examples for yourself using the words supplied, e.g. *I sing well. I sleep loudly!*
- Have the children continue the activity in pairs. Elicit sentences.

3 Complete the sentences with the correct word from the song.

- Read the example. Have the children complete the sentences using words they circled in the song.
- Nominate children to read out the complete sentences.

Answers

1 well **2** loudly **3** angrily **4** quietly.

I Can Read!

Tell the children to look at the picture of the book cover and say what is shown. Ask the class to suggest a different picture for the book cover or add elements to the design.

Answers

The book title, the name of the author, a picture of the magic pen.

4 8.7 Listen and say the chant.

- Play Track 8.7. The children listen and read along. Elicit the words with *–ly* and *–ily.*
- Play Track 8.7 again, pausing for the children to repeat.
- Divide the class into teams. Have them say the chant loudly, quickly, slowly, etc.

5 Find it!

- Set a time limit for the children to find words ending in *–ly* and *–ily* on the page. Elicit answers.

Answers

5—carefully, quietly, loudly; happily, angrily

Optional activity: Mime time

Prepare slips of paper: six with *walk, eat, jump, dance, sing, write* and six with *loudly, quickly, slowly, happily, angrily, carefully.* Invite six children to the front of the class. Hand each a verb and an adverb paper. They mime their action in the style of their adverb (e.g. jump angrily). When you say *Stop!*, they freeze in position. The other children guess the actions and adverbs, e.g. *Eun is eating loudly! Hyo is walking angrily!*

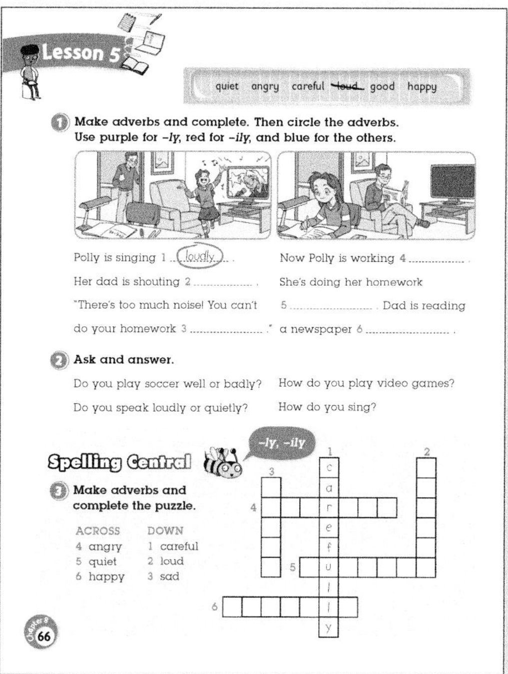

Lesson 5

quiet angry careful ~~loud~~ good happy

1 Make adverbs and complete. Then circle the adverbs. Use purple for -*ly*, red for -*ily*, and blue for the others.

Polly is singing 1 loudly.
Her dad is shouting 2 ....
"There's too much noise! You can't do your homework 3 ...."

Now Polly is working 4 ....
She's doing her homework 5 .... Dad is reading a newspaper 6 ....

2 Ask and answer.

Do you play soccer well or badly? How do you play video games?
Do you speak loudly or quietly? How do you sing?

Spelling Central

-ly, -ily

3 Make adverbs and complete the puzzle.

ACROSS
4 angry
5 quiet
6 happy

DOWN
1 careful
2 loud
3 sad

Chapter 8 66

1 Make adverbs and complete. Then circle the adverbs. Use purple for -*ly*, red for -*ily*, and blue for the others.

The children complete the sentences by looking at the pictures and using the adjectives supplied to make adverbs. Then they circle the adverbs with the correct color according to the spelling. Elicit answers.

Answers

1 loudly **2** angrily **3** well **4** quietly **5** carefully **6** happily

2 Ask and answer.

The children take turns asking and answering the questions in pairs. Have pairs ask and answer for the class.

3 Make adverbs and complete the puzzle.

The children complete the puzzle with the adverbs. Elicit answers.

Answers

Across: **4** angrily **5** quietly **6** happily
Down: **1** carefully **2** loudly **3** sadly

Cooler: Sing the song

8.6

Play the song again for the children to sing along.

Competency Focus

Think! Critical Thinking

The children use critical thinking skills to identify different adverbs by processing the written and spoken forms.

Digital Resources

Student eBook • After SB Activity 2, choose the karaoke version of Music Video 8.1 (8.2) and encourage the children to dance and sing along, using the lyrics on screen. Pause the video for the children to continue dancing and singing.

Teacher Resource Center • For phonics practice, print out Phonics Worksheet 8.

Grammar and Reading

Lesson objective: use imperatives and a range of tenses to ask and answer about game playing
Key grammar: *Why are you shouting (so loudly)? It moves when you move. Don't fall (off the board). My brother fell (off the board). I didn't fall (and) I collected (a star).*
Secondary language: *be careful, ski*
Materials: Tracks 8.8; Grammar Worksheet 8B [TRC printout] (optional)

Lesson 6

1 Listen and read. What's the game called? How do you play it?

2 Circle the correct form of the verb.

A: Why are you *shouting* / *shouted* so loudly?
B: I'm *play* / *playing* a new game.
A: How do you play?
B: You stand on this board and it *moved* / *moves*.
A: Be careful! Don't *fell* / *fall*!
C: I *play* / *played* this game last week. I *fell* / *falling* off the board so I *didn't* / *don't* collect any stars.

Chapter 8 112

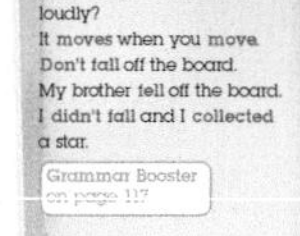
Grammar Central

Why are you shouting so loudly?
It moves when you move.
Don't fall off the board.
My brother fell off the board.
I didn't fall and I collected a star.

Grammar Booster on page 117

Warmer: Missing vowels

Write on the board *I read the instructions carefully. Now I can play it happily. I laugh loudly every day. My dad shouts at me angrily.* with all the vowels missing. When children have a full sentence, invite them to write the answers on the board.

1 8.8 Listen and read. What's the game called? How do you play it?

- Have the children look at the story. Ask *What are the children doing? (They're playing a video game.) Who can play well? (Miguel)*
- Play Track 8.8. The children listen and read along. Ask *What's the game called? (Mountain Adventure) How do you play it? (You ski down the mountain quickly.)*
- Play Track 8.8 again, pausing after the sentences that feature in the **Grammar Central** box and have the children repeat.

2 Circle the correct form of the verb. 

- Read the example and ask *When is this happening? (now)*
- Have the children complete the activity individually. Remind them they can check in the dialogue. Elicit answers in the form of sentences.

Answers

shouting, playing, moves, fall, played, fell, didn't

Grammar Central

Why are you shouting so loudly? …

Have the children look at the patterns. Ask them to find in the box: (1) a present sentence (*It moves …*) (2) a past negative (*I didn't fall …*) (3) a question about something happening now (*Why are you shouting?*) (4) a past tense (*My brother fell …*) and (5) an instruction (*Don't fall …*).

For extra practice, try the **Grammar Booster** sections in the Student Book (p. 117–119).

Answers p. 117

Activity 1: **1** Why **2** Why **3** Why **4** and **5** and **6** when **7** when

Activity 2: **1** Why **2** when **3** Why **4** when **5** and **6** and **7** Why

p. 118

Activity 1: **1** what **2** playing **3** What **4** doing **5** and **6** when **7** made

Activity 2: **1** Why **2** jumped **3** when **4** loves **5** are drinking **6** and

p. 119

Activity 1: **1** doing **2** preparing **3** making **4** do **5** play **6** and **7** played **8** do **9** went **10** got **11** buy **12** didn't

Activity 2: Children's own answers.

Optional activity: Verb jump

Ask the class to stand. Read out the dialogue in Activity 2. Every time the children hear a verb, they jump. Ask if each verb refers to the present, refers to the past, or is an instruction.

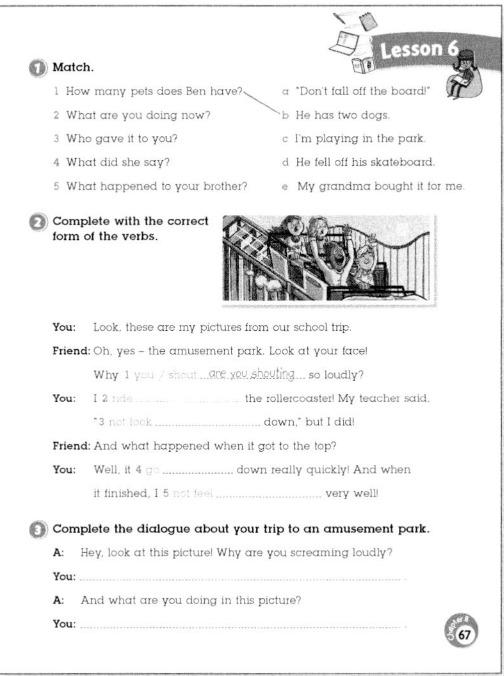

Lesson 6

1 Match.

1 How many pets does Ben have? — a "Don't fall off the board!"
2 What are you doing now? — b He has two dogs.
3 Who gave it to you? — c I'm playing in the park.
4 What did she say? — d He fell off his skateboard.
5 What happened to your brother? — e My grandma bought it for me.

2 Complete with the correct form of the verbs.

You: Look, these are my pictures from our school trip.
Friend: Oh, yes – the amusement park. Look at your face! Why 1 you / shout ...are you shouting... so loudly?
You: I 2 ride .... the rollercoaster! My teacher said, "3 not look .... down," but I did!
Friend: And what happened when it got to the top?
You: Well, it 4 go .... down really quickly! And when it finished, I 5 not feel .... very well!

3 Complete the dialogue about your trip to an amusement park.

A: Hey, look at this picture! Why are you screaming loudly?
You: ....
A: And what are you doing in this picture?
You: ....

Chapter 8 67

1 Match.

The children match the questions and answers. Elicit answers.

Answers

1 b **2** c **3** e **4** a **5** d

2 Complete with the correct form of the verbs.

The children complete the dialogue with the verbs in the correct tense. Elicit answers.

Answers

1 are you shouting **2** 'm riding **3** Don't look **4** went **5** didn't feel

3 Complete the dialogue about your trip to an amusement park.

Elicit ideas of things to do at an amusement park. The children complete the dialogue in pairs. Have pairs act out their dialogues.

Answers

Children's own answers.

Cooler: Play "Sentence Builders"

Play the game with five sentences from this lesson (see Games Bank p. 19). Include a past affirmative and negative, a present progressive, an imperative, and a simple present.

Competency Focus

Learn

The children demonstrate and consolidate their understanding of the new language by choosing the correct verb forms to complete the dialogue.

Digital Resources

Digital Activity Book • Ask the children to do the AB interactive digital activities, or set them for homework.

Teacher Resource Center • For extra grammar practice, print out Grammar Worksheet 8B.

CLIL: Science—Exergames

Lesson objective: find out about exergames—active video games
Materials: CLIL Graphic Organizer 8 [TRC printout] (optional)

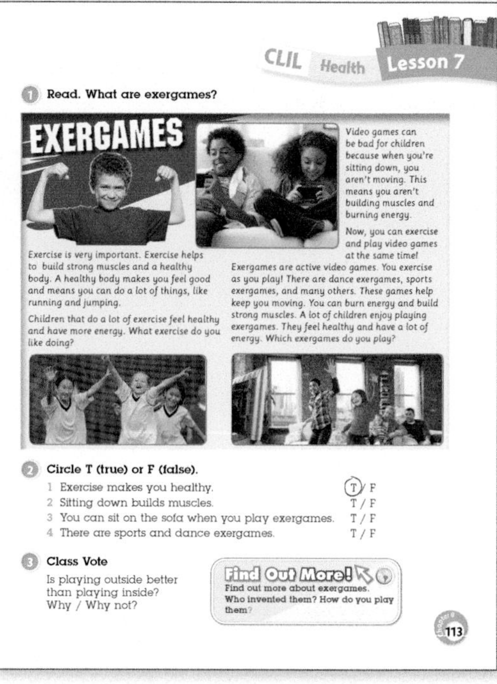

CLIL Health Lesson 7

1 Read. What are exergames?

EXERGAMES

Video games can be bad for children because when you're sitting down, you aren't moving. This means you aren't building muscles and burning energy.

Now, you can exercise and play video games at the same time!

Exercise is very important. Exercise helps to build strong muscles and a healthy body. A healthy body makes you feel good and means you can do a lot of things, like running and jumping.

Children that do a lot of exercise feel healthy and have more energy. What exercise do you like doing?

Exergames are active video games. You exercise as you play! There are dance exergames, sports exergames, and many others. These games help keep you moving. You can burn energy and build strong muscles. A lot of children enjoy playing exergames. They feel healthy and have a lot of energy. Which exergames do you play?

2 Circle T (true) or F (false).

1 Exercise makes you healthy. (T) / F
2 Sitting down builds muscles. T / F
3 You can sit on the sofa when you play exergames. T / F
4 There are sports and dance exergames. T / F

3 Class Vote

Is playing outside better than playing inside? Why / Why not?

Find Out More!
Find out more about exergames. Who invented them? How do you play them?

113

Warmer: Class discussion

Write on the board *sports, video games, housework/chores, walking*. Ask *Which activity gives you the best exercise?* Have the children discuss their answers in pairs. Elicit answers. Ask *How can video games give you exercise?* to elicit ideas.

1 Read. What are exergames?

- Have the children look at the picture. Ask *What activities can you see?*
- Ask *What are exergames?* Have the children read the text to find the answer. Elicit answers. (*Exergames are active video games.*)
- Have the children discuss in pairs if they like exergames and why. Invite children to say what they think.

2 Circle T (true) or F (false).

- Read the example and ask why it is true. (*Exercise helps build strong muscles and a healthy body.*)
- The children circle true or false for each sentence.
- Elicit answers, including the correct version of the false sentences. Check with the class.

Answers

1 T **2** F **3** F **4** T

3 Class Vote

- Ask *Is playing outside better than playing inside?* Give the children time to think. Tell the children to point to the door if they prefer playing outside or point to the ground if they prefer playing inside. Count the votes and write the results on the board. Invite children to explain why they voted that way. (They might need to use L1.)

Find Out More!

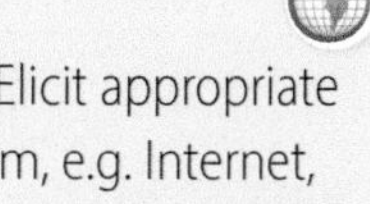

Ask *Do you know any exergames?* Elicit appropriate resources for finding out about them, e.g. Internet, friends, etc. The children will need to complete this research before doing the follow-up activity in the Activity Book. (It could be set as homework.)

Optional activity: Favorite video games

Elicit favorite video games and write them on the board. Ask the children to write a sentence about why their favorite video game is good, e.g. *I like [name of video game] because the music is nice/there are dragons.*, etc.

1 Read and answer.

The children read a text about exergames at school and answer two questions. Elicit answers.

Answers

1 tennis, dancing, baseball, skateboarding
2 children's own answer

2 Use your Student Book research. Design a poster for your own exergame.

Divide the class into groups of four. The children pool the information they learned from their research in the Student Book and the Activity Book. They design a poster for an exergame individually.

Answers

Children's own answers.

It's My World!

The children discuss in pairs the best types of exercise for staying in shape. Elicit ideas and have a class discussion.

Cooler: Browse the posters

Have the children walk around the classroom and look at each other's exergame posters. Invite children to say which was their favorite.

Competency Focus

Act

The children carry out research to find out about exergames. They relate what they learn to their world, both inside and outside the classroom.

Digital Resources

Student eBook • Display the SB page for a "heads-up" introduction to the topic in Activity 1. Children use *Highlighter* to identify adjectives in the text.

Digital Activity Book • Have several children use *Pen* to draw a poster for AB Activity 2.

Teacher Resource Center • Print out CLIL Graphic Organizer 8 for the children to use in collating their Find Out More! research.

CLIL eBook • The children can use the CLIL eBook to expand their knowledge of the lesson topic.

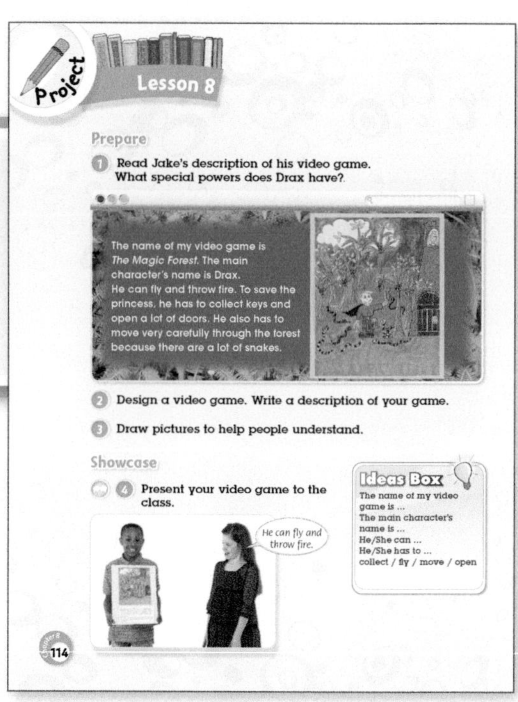
Project
Lesson 8

Prepare

1 Read Jake's description of his video game. What special powers does Drax have?

The name of my video game is *The Magic Forest*. The main character's name is Drax. He can fly and throw fire. To save the princess, he has to collect keys and open a lot of doors. He also has to move very carefully through the forest because there are a lot of snakes.

2 Design a video game. Write a description of your game.

3 Draw pictures to help people understand.

Showcase

4 Present your video game to the class.

He can fly and throw fire.

Ideas Box
The name of my video game is ...
The main character's name is ...
He/She can ...
He/She has to ...
collect / fly / move / open

114

Project

Lesson objectives: review language from Chapter 8; design a video game; present their video game to the class
Materials: paper and colored pens; two game pieces and a coin for each pair

Warmer: Exergame mime

Divide the class into small groups. Have the children mime an exergame activity for their group to guess.

Prepare

1 Read Jake's description of his video game. What special powers does Drax have?

- Have the children read the text. Ask *What special powers does Drax have?* (*He can fly and throw fire.*)
- Ask *Does this sound like a good game?*

2 Design a video game. Write a description of your game.

- Brainstorm features for the game, e.g.
  places: *forest, castle, underwater*
  powers: *fly, be invisible, make holes*
  dangers: *snakes, monsters, sharks*
  You could do this as a mind map on the board for the children to refer to for ideas.
- The children design their own video game, using Activity 1 as a model and the **Ideas Box** for support. They can work individually or in pairs.

Alternative craft activity

An easier project is to have the class choose a video game that they actually play and base their description on this.

3 Draw pictures to help people understand.

- Elicit what pictures we usually see in a magazine or a web page about a video game. (*a scene from the game, a picture of the main character, the cover of the box*) Have them draw pictures to illustrate their game.

Showcase 

4 Present your video game to the class.

- Divide the class into groups of four to five children. Have each child present their game to the group and show their pictures. Each group chooses one child to present their work to the class. Have the class ask questions for the other group members to answer.

Optional activity: Video game vote

Take a vote on the best game presented to the class.

1 Play "Jimmy's Game."

See p. 43 for instructions on how to play the game.

Answers

1 loudly **3** Push, moves **5** strong muscles/a healthy body **8** played, collected **10** Children's own answers (using present progressive). **11** happily/angrily or any other *–ily* adverb **12** carefully **14** *any four of:* snake, mouse, bird, frog, dog, cat, rabbit **16** Children's own answer (using simple past). **18** Children's own answers.

Cooler: I like video games!

Have the children say why they like video games, encouraging them to come up with as many good reasons as possible. List ideas on the board.

Competency Focus

Collaborate and communicate

By preparing a presentation, the children consolidate their understanding of the topic in a challenging and engaging way. They also demonstrate their ability to work with friends and use interpersonal skills.

Digital Resources

Student eBook • Show the pictures, stage by stage, as you talk the class through the activity process.

Language Review

Lesson objective: review language from Chapter 8
Materials: Tracks 8.9, AB 8.1, and AB 8.2

Warmer: Play "The Shark Game"

Play the game with a selection of key vocabulary from Chapter 8 (see Games Bank p. 19)

1 8.9 Listen and write the names.

- Have the children read the questions and find the activities.
- Play Track 8.9, pausing after *It's my new video game, The Sylvesters.* to elicit the answer to question 1. (*Ben*) Play Track 8.9 twice, giving the children time between questions to write the correct name.
- Ask children to read out the sentences and say the name. Ask for class agreement.

Audioscript

Lou: *Hi, Ben. Oooh, what's that?*
Ben: *Hi, Lou. It's my new video game, The Sylvesters. I got it last week.*
Lou: *Who gave it to you?*
Ben: *My dad. Look at the characters I made. Here's the mom, she's reading a book quietly.*
Lou: *And who's that?*
Ben: *That's the sister, Emma. She's playing ping-pong. And this is the dog, Teddy. He jumps and runs a lot.*
Lou: *They look great!*
Ben: *And look at this. I played it last week with Dad. Dad didn't know how to play! He pushed the wrong button and changed all of the characters.*
Lou: *Ha, ha! What a fun video game! Can I make a character?*
Ben: *Yeah. Here, press the red button to start. But, be careful!*
Lou: *OK …*

Answers

1 Ben **2** Mom **3** Emma **4** Teddy **5** Dad

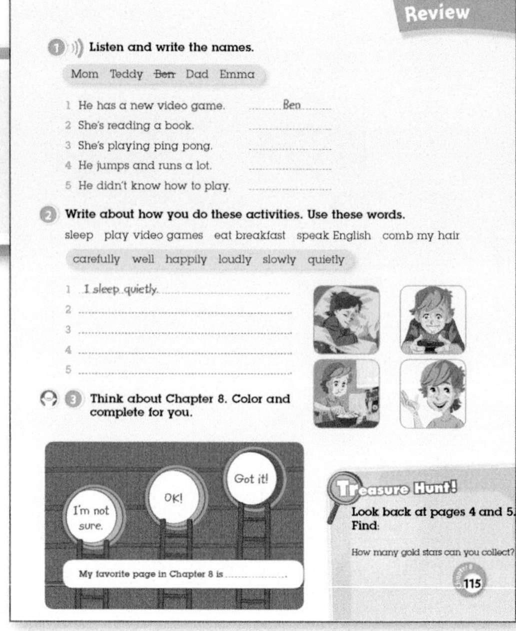
Review

1 Listen and write the names.

Mom Teddy ~~Ben~~ Dad Emma

1 He has a new video game. ....Ben........
2 She's reading a book. ....
3 She's playing ping pong. ....
4 He jumps and runs a lot. ....
5 He didn't know how to play. ....

2 Write about how you do these activities. Use these words.

sleep play video games eat breakfast speak English comb my hair

carefully well happily loudly slowly quietly

1 I sleep quietly.
2 ....
3 ....
4 ....
5 ....

3 Think about Chapter 8. Color and complete for you.

I'm not sure. OK! Got it!

My favorite page in Chapter 8 is ....

Treasure Hunt!
Look back at pages 4 and 5. Find:
How many gold stars can you collect?

115

2 Write about how you do these activities. Use these words.

- The children write sentences.
- Elicit responses. Encourage careful listening by having the class respond *Me, too!* or *Not me!*

Answers

Children's own answers.

3 Think about Chapter 8. Color and complete for you.

- Children color the circle which represents how they feel about their own progress (self-evaluation).
- Have the children complete the sentence.

Treasure Hunt!

Have the children look at pp. 4–5 to count the gold stars. Elicit the answer. (*seven*)

Cooler: Draw and label

Have the children look back through the chapter and find a moment they liked. Have them draw a picture and label it,.

Competency Focus

Me: Self-evaluation

The children reflect on the chapter and express their opinions about their own progress.

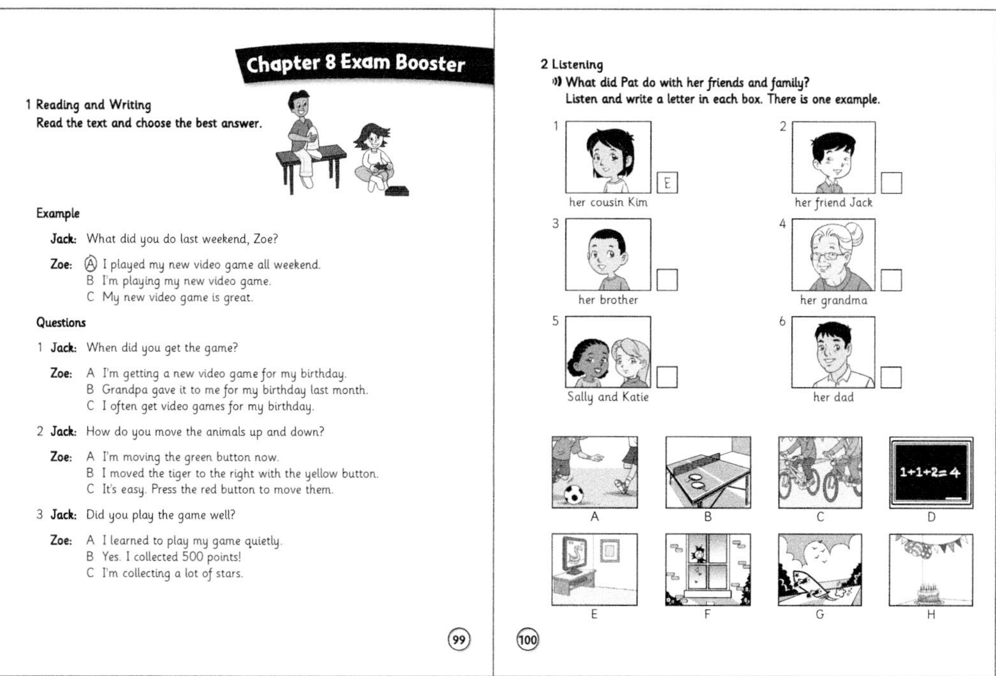

Chapter 8 Exam Booster

1 Reading and Writing
Read the text and choose the best answer.

Example

Jack: What did you do last weekend, Zoe?

Zoe: (A) I played my new video game all weekend.
B I'm playing my new video game.
C My new video game is great.

Questions

1 **Jack:** When did you get the game?

Zoe: A I'm getting a new video game for my birthday.
B Grandpa gave it to me for my birthday last month.
C I often get video games for my birthday.

2 **Jack:** How do you move the animals up and down?

Zoe: A I'm moving the green button now.
B I moved the tiger to the right with the yellow button.
C It's easy. Press the red button to move them.

3 **Jack:** Did you play the game well?

Zoe: A I learned to play my game quietly.
B Yes. I collected 500 points!
C I'm collecting a lot of stars.

99

2 Listening
What did Pat do with her friends and family?
Listen and write a letter in each box. There is one example.

1 her cousin Kim [E]
2 her friend Jack
3 her brother
4 her grandma
5 Sally and Katie
6 her dad

A B C D E F G H

100

3 Listening
Mrs. Brown is talking to Tom about the people in her family. What did each person do last weekend? Listen and write a letter in each box. There is one example.

1 her dad [D]
2 her son
3 her daughter
4 her friend Jim
5 her sister
6 her brother

A B C D E F G H

Exam Tip
Read and listen to the instructions carefully to understand the topic before you hear the conversations.

101

1 Reading and Writing. Read the text and choose the best answer.

The children read the dialogue and choose the best response from the three options each time.

Answers

1 B **2** C **3** B

2 AB 8.1 Listening. What did Pat do with her friends and family? Listen and write a letter in each box. There is one example.

Play Track AB 8.1 twice. The children listen and match.

Answers (Audioscript on p. 223)

2 D **3** A **4** F **5** C **6** H

3 AB 8.2 Listening. Mrs. Brown is talking to Tom about the people in her family. What did each person do last weekend? Listen and write a letter in each box. There is one example.

Play Track AB 8.2 twice. The children listen and match.

Answers (Audioscript on p. 224)

2 F **3** B **4** H **5** E **6** A

Digital Resources

Teacher Resource Center • Print out Test Chapter 8 to use at the end of this lesson. The Test Generator also allows you to create customized tests.

Student's App • Encourage the children to play the games on their smartphone/tablet. Ask them to record their scores to compare in the next lesson. (*The Inks* Apps are free and available on the App Store and Google Play.)

Chapter 9 Vacation Time

Overview

The children will:

- use critical thinking skills to identify summer camp activities.
- talk about things they are/aren't going to do.
- read, understand, and act out a story.
- talk about a beach vacation.
- ask and answer questions about what they are going to do.
- find out about sun safety.
- do a science experiment about wearing pale colors in the sun.

Key Vocabulary

Summer camp activities: camping, having barbecues, kayaking, mountain biking, rock climbing, snorkeling, water-skiing
Beach essentials: bathing suit, camera, sandals, suitcase, sunblock, sunglasses, towel

Key Grammar

- I'm going to (go snorkeling).
- I'm not going to (have a barbecue).
- He's going to (go water-skiing).
- He isn't going to (go rock climbing).
- Are you going to (go to the beach)?
- Yes, I am. / No, I'm not.
- What are you going to (take)?
- I'm going to (take my sunblock).

Reading Skills

Story: *Holly's Vacation*
Genre: modern story

Literacy Development

- predict story content from title and pictures
- reflect on and personalize the theme of the story
- focus on the use of time phrases in a story to provide structure

Functional Language

- I'm going to … this weekend.
- Don't forget your …!

Spelling

Words with silent *gh*

CLIL: Science—Sun safety

The children find out about the benefits/dangers of exposure to the Sun.

Competency Focus

The children will:

use critical thinking skills to identify summer camp activities. (Lesson 1) predict the content of a story. (Lesson 3) identify and name vacation items. (Lesson 5)	apply new grammar to previously learned vocabulary. (Lesson 2) talk about going to the beach. (Lesson 6)	work in pairs to act out a dialogue. (Lesson 3) work in groups to act out the story. (Lesson 8)	personalize the story by thinking about summer camps in their own country and how they feel about them. (Lesson 4) evaluate their own progress in the chapter. (Review)	develop an environmental understanding by finding out more about the Sun. (Lesson 7)

Digital Overview

Teacher Presentation

Student eBook and Digital Activity Book

- Oral Storytelling Video 9.1: *Holly's Vacation*
- Interactive versions of selected AB activities
- Integrated audio and answer key for all activities

Teacher resources for planning, lesson delivery, and homework

Teacher Resource Center

- Class Planner Chapter 9
- Worksheets to print out (including notes and answers):
  - Grammar Worksheet 9A: I'm going to go/I'm not going to go…
  - Grammar Worksheet 9B: Are you going to go to the beach?
  - Oral Storytelling Video Worksheet 9: *Holly's Vacation*
  - Phonics Worksheet 9
  - CLIL Graphic Organizer 9
  - Test Chapter 9 and End-of-year Test
- Test Generator
- Speaking Assessment: Cambridge English Young Learners Exams

Watch the Oral Storytelling Video

- Literacy Handbook

Children's resources for learning and practicing at home

Student eBook and Reader eBook

- Oral Storytelling Video 9.1: *Holly's Vacation*

The Inks Student's App

Vocabulary games: Summer camp activities and beach essentials

Vacation Time

Lesson 1

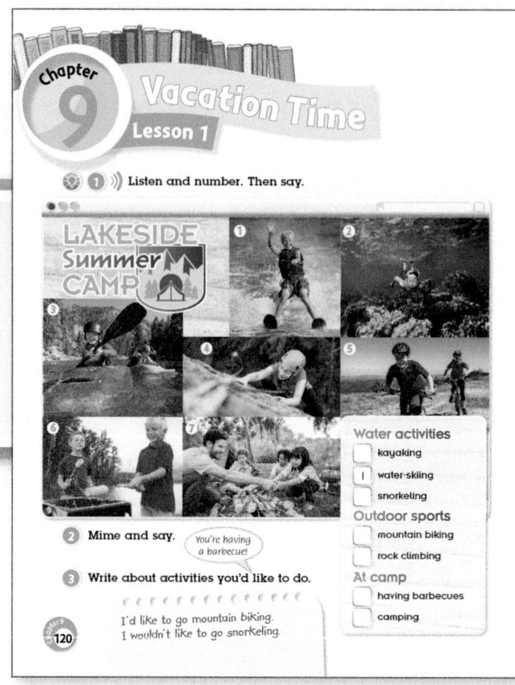

Vocabulary

Lesson objective: identify and talk about summer camp activities
Key vocabulary: *camping, having barbecues, kayaking, mountain biking, rock climbing, snorkeling, water-skiing*
Materials: Track 9.1; cards for "Board Pelmanism" (optional)

Warmer: On vacation, I like to ...

Brainstorm vacation activities and write them on the board. Take a class vote to elicit the three most popular activities. Each child can vote twice.

1 9.1 Listen and number. Then say. 

- Have the children look at the pictures. Ask *What can you see? Which activity looks fun?*
- Play Track 9.1. The children listen and find the activities. They write the activity number next to the correct word.
- Play Track 9.1 again, pausing after each activity for the children to point and repeat.

Audioscript

Come to Lakeside Summer Camp this vacation and have fun. If you're good at swimming, there are plenty of water activities you can do. Go water-skiing on the lake. The boat goes fast and it's very exciting! Try snorkeling. You can see a lot of different types of fish—yellow, black, and orange. Go kayaking on the river, but be careful—the water's cold and moves quickly! We provide you with all the safety equipment you need, though. If you prefer to stay on dry land, you can explore the beautiful countryside. In the mountains, you can go rock climbing and mountain biking. Back at camp, put up your tent and have delicious barbecues for dinner. In the evening, you can sit around the camp fire and have a fun time camping with your new friends. Come to Lakeside Summer Camp. We're waiting for you!

Answers

kayaking 3, water-skiing 1, snorkeling 2, mountain biking 5, rock climbing 4, having barbecues 6, camping 7

2 Mime and say.

- Mime doing a vacation activity for the children to guess (e.g. *You're snorkeling!*)
- Have the children play the game in pairs or small groups.
- Invite children to do a mime for the class.

3 Write about activities you'd like to do.

- Have two children read out the examples. Elicit whether the children agree with the sentences. Point out the use of *go* before the activities. Ask *Which activity doesn't use "go?"* (*having barbecues*)
- Have the children write sentences in their notebook about the activities they would/wouldn't like to do. Ask them to compare in pairs. Then elicit answers.

Answers

Children's own answers.

Optional activity: Play "Board Pelmanism"

Prepare cards using key vocabulary from the lesson (*water/skiing, snor/keling, kay/aking, rock/climbing, mountain/biking, making/barbecues, cam/ping*). Play the game (see Games Bank p. 19).

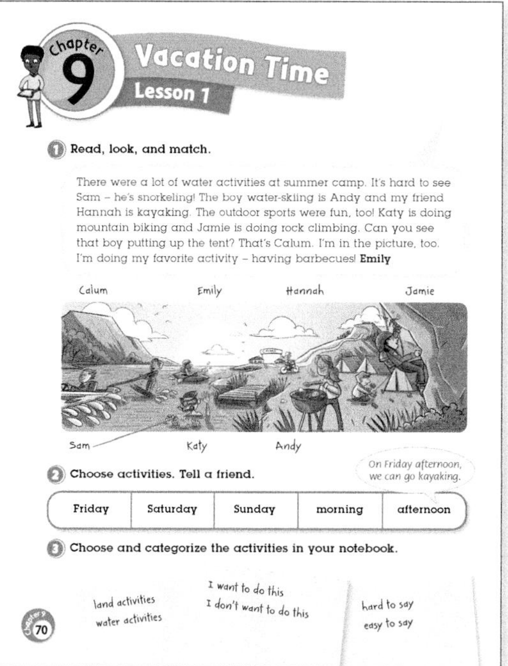

Chapter 9 Vacation Time
Lesson 1

1 Read, look, and match.

There were a lot of water activities at summer camp. It's hard to see Sam – he's snorkeling! The boy water-skiing is Andy and my friend Hannah is kayaking. The outdoor sports were fun, too! Katy is doing mountain biking and Jamie is doing rock climbing. Can you see that boy putting up the tent? That's Calum. I'm in the picture, too. I'm doing my favorite activity – having barbecues! **Emily**

2 Choose activities. Tell a friend.

On Friday afternoon, we can go kayaking.

Friday	Saturday	Sunday	morning	afternoon

3 Choose and categorize the activities in your notebook.

land activities
water activities

I want to do this
I don't want to do this

hard to say
easy to say

Chapter 9 70

1 Read, look, and match.

The children read the text and match the names to the people pictured. Elicit answers.

Answers

Lines between: Sam—boy snorkeling; Andy—boy water-skiing; Hannah—girl kayaking; Calum—boy putting up tent; Emily—girl having a barbecue; Jamie—boy rock climbing; Katy—girl mountain biking

2 Choose activities. Tell a friend.

Have a child read the example. The children choose activities and compare ideas in pairs.

3 Choose and categorize the activities in your notebook.

Elicit an example for each category listed. Ask *Which categories would you choose?* Elicit ideas, prompting children to give a reason for their choice. The children choose a pair of categories and list the words in their notebook, then compare with a friend.

Answers

Children's own answers.

Cooler: Vote for your favorite activity

 **9.1**

Play Track 9.1. Tell the children to stand up when they hear their favorite activities. They can vote for two different activities. Pause Track after each activity to count the children standing up. Ask *Which activity is our favorite?*

Competency Focus

Think! Critical Thinking

The children use critical thinking skills to identify different vacation activities by using visual clues and processing the written and spoken forms.

Digital Resources

Student eBook • Play "Kim's Game" with the new vocabulary. Show the labeled pictures in SB Activity 1. Divide the class into teams. Use *Timer* and give them one minute to memorize the pictures, then one minute to recall them in order. Repeat several times.

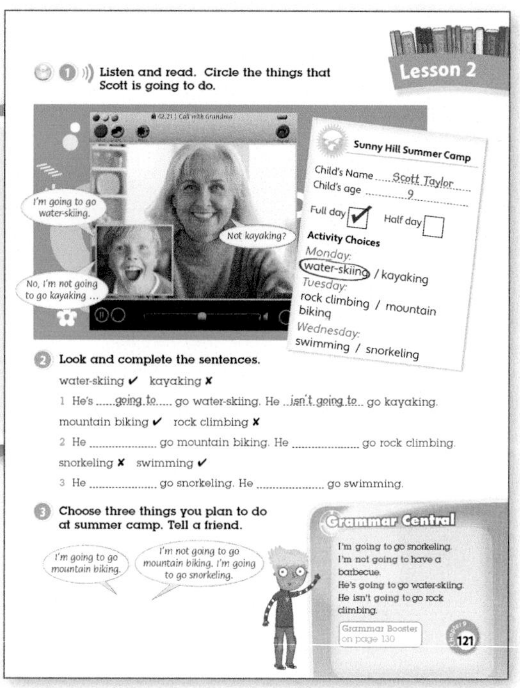

Lesson 2

1 Listen and read. Circle the things that Scott is going to do.

2 Look and complete the sentences.

water-skiing ✔ kayaking ✘

1 He's ......going to...... go water-skiing. He ..isn't going to.. go kayaking.

mountain biking ✔ rock climbing ✘

2 He .... go mountain biking. He .... go rock climbing.

snorkeling ✘ swimming ✔

3 He .... go snorkeling. He .... go swimming.

3 Choose three things you plan to do at summer camp. Tell a friend.

Grammar Central

I'm going to go snorkeling.
I'm not going to have a barbecue.
He's going to go water-skiing.
He isn't going to go rock climbing.

Grammar Booster on page 130

121

Grammar

Lesson objective: talk about future plans using *going to*
Key grammar: *I'm going to (go snorkeling). I'm not going to (have a barbecue). He's going to (go water-skiing). He isn't going to (go rock climbing).*
Secondary language: *choices*
Materials: Track 9.2; Grammar Worksheet 9A [TRC printout] (optional)

Warmer: Play "Simon Says"

Play the game with (*Simon says*) *go water-skiing/snorkeling/kayaking/rock climbing/mountain biking/camping* (see Games Bank p. 19).

1 9.2 Listen and read. Circle the things that Scott is going to do.

- Play Track 9.2 twice. The children listen and read along. They check the things Scott is going to do. Elicit answers and check with the class.

Audioscript

Grandmother: *Hello, Scott.*
Scott: *Hi, Grandma. I'm going to go to summer camp on Monday.*
Grandmother: *That's great, Scott.*
Scott: *There's water-skiing and kayaking.*
Grandmother: *Wow!*
Scott: *I'm going to go water-skiing.*
Grandmother: *Not kayaking?*
Scott: *No, I'm not going to go kayaking.*
Grandmother: *Water-skiing sounds good.*
Scott: *And there's rock climbing and mountain biking. I'm going to go mountain biking.*
Grandmother: *Nice!*
Scott: *There's swimming and snorkeling, too. I'm not going to go snorkeling though. I'm going to go swimming. I love swimming.*

Answers

Monday: water-skiing; *Tuesday:* mountain biking; *Wednesday:* swimming

2 Look and complete the sentences.

- Draw a check and ask *Going to or not going to?* (*going to*) Repeat with a cross. (*not going to*)
- The children complete the sentences. Elicit answers.

Answers

1 going to, isn't going to **2** 's going to, isn't going to **3** isn't going to, 's going to

Grammar Central

I'm going to go snorkeling. ...

Ask *Are we talking about the present or the future?* (*the future*) Write on the board *I'm going to go swimming.* Ask a child to draw a check or a cross by it. (✔) Elicit the verb form for future plans. (*'m going to*) Repeat with *I'm not going to go swimming.* (**✘** – *'m not going to*)

For extra practice, try the **Grammar Booster** section in the Student Book (p. 130).

Answers p. 130

Activity 1: **1** going to **2** not going to **3** going to **4** isn't going to **5** going to **6** isn't going to **7** going to **8** going to

Activity 2: **1** I'm going to visit my cousins this weekend. **2** I'm going to swim in their pool. **3** Uncle Tony is going to do a barbecue. **4** Cousin Jane isn't going to be there.

Activity 3: Children's own answers.

3 Choose three things you plan to do at summer camp. Tell a friend.

- Have two children read out the example.
- Divide the class into pairs. The children take turns talking about what they are/aren't going to do at summer camp, and responding. (They can make up their answers.)

Optional activity: Draw and label

Have the children draw a picture of themselves doing three different things at summer camp. They draw a cross through one thing, to show that they're not going to do it. Then they label their picture. Have children present their pictures to the class.

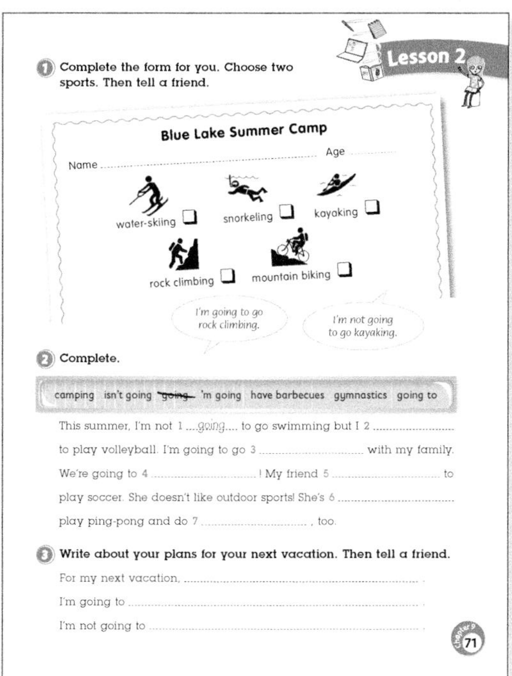

Lesson 2

1 Complete the form for you. Choose two sports. Then tell a friend.

Blue Lake Summer Camp

Name .... Age ....

water-skiing ☐ snorkeling ☐ kayaking ☐

rock climbing ☐ mountain biking ☐

I'm going to go rock climbing.

I'm not going to go kayaking.

2 Complete.

camping isn't going ~~going~~ 'm going have barbecues gymnastics going to

This summer, I'm not 1 ....*going*.... to go swimming but I 2 .... to play volleyball. I'm going to go 3 .... with my family. We're going to 4 .... ! My friend 5 .... to play soccer. She doesn't like outdoor sports! She's 6 .... play ping-pong and do 7 .... , too.

3 Write about your plans for your next vacation. Then tell a friend.

For my next vacation, ...

I'm going to ....

I'm not going to ....

Chapter 9 71

1 Complete the form for you. Choose two sports. Then tell a friend.

The children complete the form with their details and choices. Have two children read the example aloud. The children then work in pairs, saying what they are going to do/not going to do.

Answers

Children's own answers.

2 Complete.

The children complete the text using the words supplied. Elicit answers.

Answers

1 going **2** 'm going **3** camping **4** have barbecues **5** isn't going **6** going to **7** gymnastics

3 Write about your plans for your next vacation. Then tell a friend.

The children complete their vacation plans, then tell a friend about them.

Answers

Children's own answers.

Cooler: Play "Change the Text"

Do this activity with the completed paragraph from Activity Book Activity 2 (see Games Bank p. 19).

Competency Focus

Learn

The children use previously acquired vocabulary in a different context with new grammatical structures.

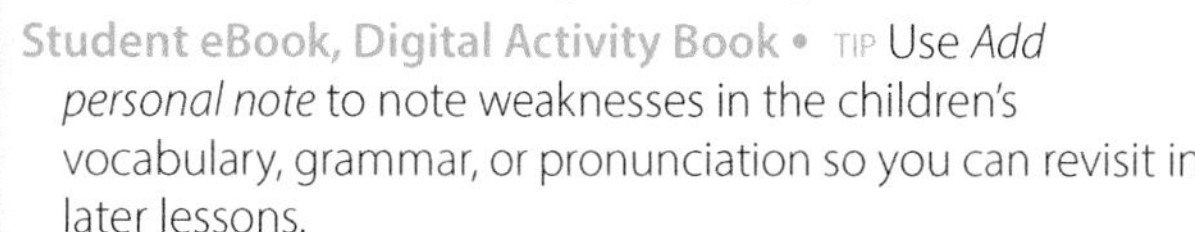

Digital Resources

Digital Activity Book • A child chooses a sport in AB Activity 1. Have them tell the class what they are going to do and one thing they are not going to do. Repeat with different children choosing different options.

Student eBook, Digital Activity Book • TIP Use *Add personal note* to note weaknesses in the children's vocabulary, grammar, or pronunciation so you can revisit in later lessons.

Teacher Resource Center • For extra grammar practice, print out Grammar Worksheet 9A.

Reading: Story Extract

Lesson objectives: remind people to take things; predict story content from title and pictures; read the extract from *Holly's Vacation* (beginning)
Functional language: *I'm going to … this weekend. Don't forget your … !*
Secondary language: *gift, pack a suitcase, take pictures, try new activities*
Materials: Tracks 9.3 and 9.4

Lesson 3

1 Listen and read. Then use the words to make new dialogue.

I'm going to…this weekend.
We're going to…tonight.

Remember to bring your bag!
Make sure to take pictures!

2 Look at the story on page 123. What do you think the title is? Check (✓).

Holly's Camera ☐
Holly's Vacation ☐
Holly's Grandparents ☐

3 Listen and read. What do Holly's grandparents give her? Why?

4 What do you think Holly is going to do at camp? Check (✓).

mountain biking ☐ soccer ☐ kayaking ☐

122

Holly's

Holly is excited. School vacation starts in two days, and she's going to go to summer camp. She packs her suitcase

1

Holly's grandparents have a surprise for her.

2

Reader Read the story in your Reader on pages 28–31.

123

Warmer: Vacation pictures

Ask *Do you take pictures when you're on vacation? What type of pictures?* Elicit ideas.

Functional language

1 9.3 Listen and read. Then use the words to make new dialogue.

- Have the children look at the pictures and dialogue. Ask *What are the children talking about?* (*their plans for the weekend*)
- Play Track 9.3. The children listen and read along.
- Play Track 9.3 again, pausing for the children to repeat.
- The children act out the dialogue in pairs, substituting different weekend activities and things to take.
- Have pairs perform their dialogue for the class.
- Elicit uses of *"Don't forget to take …"* for school things.

Before reading

2 Look at the story on page 123. What do you think the title is? Check (✓).

- Point out the beginning of the title is shown but not the end. Have the children use the pictures to get ideas, then choose and check one of the three options. Ask *What do you think the title is?* Elicit ideas, with reasons. Confirm the answer. (*Holly's Vacation*)

3 9.4 Listen and read. What do Holly's grandparents give her? Why?

- Play Track 9.4. The children listen and read along.
- Play Track 9.4 again. Ask *What do Holly's grandparents give her? Why?* Elicit answers.

Answers

Holly's grandparents give her a camera. They want Holly to take pictures for them.

4 What do you think Holly is going to do at camp? Check (✓).

- Have the children check their prediction. Elicit ideas including reasons, but do not confirm. Say they will have to read the story to find out.

Answers

Children's own answers.

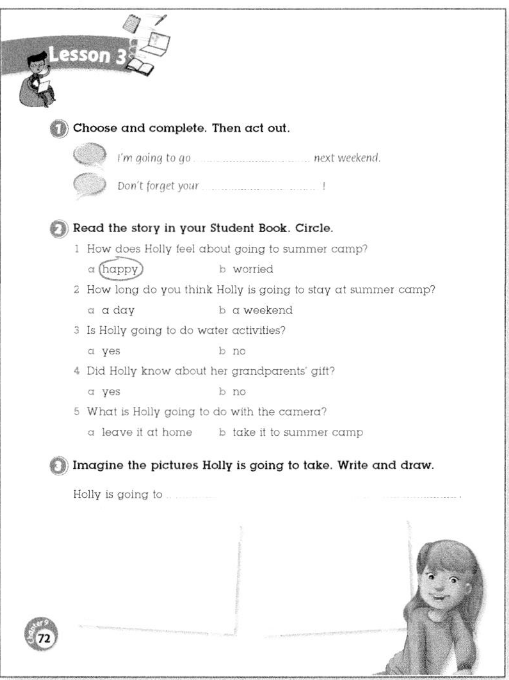
Lesson 3

1 Choose and complete. Then act out.

I'm going to go .... next weekend.

Don't forget your .... !

2 Read the story in your Student Book. Circle.

1 How does Holly feel about going to summer camp?
a (happy) b worried
2 How long do you think Holly is going to stay at summer camp?
a a day b a weekend
3 Is Holly going to do water activities?
a yes b no
4 Did Holly know about her grandparents' gift?
a yes b no
5 What is Holly going to do with the camera?
a leave it at home b take it to summer camp

3 Imagine the pictures Holly is going to take. Write and draw.

Holly is going to ....

72

1 Choose and complete. Then act out.

The children complete the dialogue with their own ideas. Then they act out the dialogue with a friend. Have pairs act out for the class.

2 Read the story in your Student Book. Circle.

The children read the Student Book story extract again and answer the questions by circling the correct option in each pair. Elicit answers.

Answers

1 a **2** b **3** a **4** b **5** b

3 Imagine the pictures Holly is going to take. Write and draw.

Elicit suggestions for the pictures Holly is going to take. The children draw and label their pictures, then swap with a friend to check.

Answers

Children's own answers.

Cooler: Play "Disappearing Text"

Play the game with *I'm going to go to summer camp. I'm going to go mountain biking but I'm not going to have barbecues.* (see Games Bank p. 19).

Competency Focus

Collaborate and Communicate

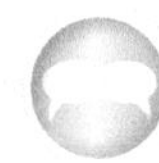

The children act out an authentic dialogue together, putting into practice new functional language.

Think! Critical Thinking

The children apply reading skills (exploiting pictures and text clues) to understand the story context.

Digital Resources

Digital Activity Book • Display the AB page for Activity 3. Have children use *Pen* to draw a picture they imagine Holly will take. Elicit who in the class had the same picture.

Student eBook, Digital Activity Book • TIP Choose an assistant! Ask a child to be responsible for choosing the relevant buttons (e.g. the answer key).

• TIP With the answer key, you can show the answers all at once or one by one to customize feedback.

Holly's Vacation

1
Holly is excited. School vacation starts in two days, and she's going to go to summer camp. She packs her suitcase.

Mom: Don't forget your bathing suit and sunblock.

Holly: What am I going to do at camp?

Mom: You're going to try a lot of new activities. Grandma and Grandpa are going to come and say goodbye.

2
Holly's grandparents have a surprise for her.

Grandpa: We have a gift for you. It's a camera.

Grandma: You can take a lot of pictures for us.

Holly: Thanks! I'm going to send you a lot of pictures.

3
At summer camp, all the children go kayaking. It's hard, and Holly falls into the lake. Her friend takes a picture. Holly sends it to her grandparents.

4
After lunch, the children go mountain biking. It's Holly's first time on a mountain bike. The children are going to make a jump for the bikes. The jump is very tricky. A lot of children fall over. Holly also falls. Holly takes a picture. Everyone laughs. Holly sends that picture to her grandparents, too.

5
Later on, the children have a barbecue. They sing around the camp fire, and make plans.

Group Leader: What are you going to do tomorrow, Holly?

Holly: Well, so far I'm not very good at kayaking, or mountain biking! Whatever we do though, I'm going to take my camera. I'm not going to miss any pictures.

6
That night, there's a noise outside the tent. Hoo-hoo! What is it? It's an owl, a very big owl. Holly gets her camera and takes a picture. The next day, she sends the picture to her grandparents.

7
Holly has a great time at summer camp. When she sees her grandparents again, they have another surprise for her.

Grandma: We sent that owl picture to a competition.

Grandpa: You won first prize, Holly.

8
The prize is a vacation. So now, Holly is planning another trip.

Mom: What are you going to do this time, Holly?

Holly: I don't know, but I know I'm going to take a lot of pictures!

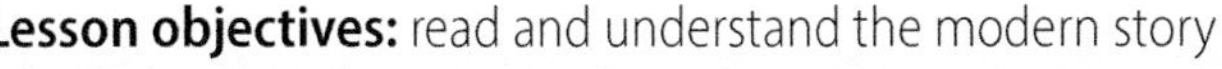

Lesson objectives: read and understand the modern story *Holly's Vacation* in the Reader
Materials: Track 9.5; Reader; Oral Storytelling Video Worksheet 9 [TRC printout] (optional)

Warmer: Take imaginary pictures

Show the children an imaginary camera and say *I'm going to take a picture of the class!* Mime taking a picture and turning the camera to show the class. Then say *I'm going to take a picture of . . . the window!* Again, mime and show the imaginary picture, then pass the "camera" to another child. Have the children continue in pairs, announcing what they are going to photograph, showing and sharing the camera.

Story Summary

When Holly goes to summer camp, she takes a camera, a gift from her grandparents. She has fun taking part in different activities. She takes a lot of pictures, and her picture of an owl wins a photography competition.

Value: Taking part is what counts. 

9.5 While reading

- Have the children look at the pictures in the Reader. Ask *What fun activities can you see? What does Holly pack in her suitcase?*
- Play Track 9.5. The children listen and read along. Ask *Did Holly have a good time at summer camp?* (*yes*)
- Play Track 9.5 again, pausing to ask questions to check comprehension (see below), e.g. *What was her best activity at the camp?* (*taking pictures*) *Which picture of hers wins a competition?* (*the picture of the owl*) *What's the prize?* (*a vacation*) *Is Holly happy?* (*yes*)

After reading: Reflect

- Ask questions to give the children the opportunity to think about the issues raised by the story: *Was Holly good at all the activities? How do you feel when things go wrong? Do you try again? Is it important to look on the positive side of things?*

Optional activity: Who said that?

Read out dialogue from the story to elicit who said it.

Story Time

Keeping focus

It is sometimes easy for children's attention to wander during a long story. When you play Track 9.5, tell the children you will stop the track sometimes and ask a question. This helps them keep focused on the story, and also lets them play a part in the storytelling.

Reading Strategy

List-Group-Label

When using the List–Group–Label strategy, the children brainstorm words related to the story before they read it. This helps them engage with the story before reading it and build up their vocabulary. In addition, they practice their critical thinking and communication skills.

For additional explanation and activities, see the Literacy Handbook on the Teacher Resource Center.

Cooler: Holly's new vacation

Ask the children to decide where Holly's second vacation is. They choose a place and draw a picture Holly took there. Children then present their drawings.

Ask the children to bring a picture they have taken for a class photo exhibition in the next lesson.

Digital Resources

Reader eBook • Minimize the story. Show random points and elicit what the children can see. Have the children revise their predictions from AB Lesson 3 Activity 3.

• Watch Oral Storytelling Video 9.1 (the story with a different ending) together at the end of the lesson, then discuss the differences.

Teacher Resource Center • Print out Oral Storytelling Video Worksheet 9 to help you get the most out of the video.

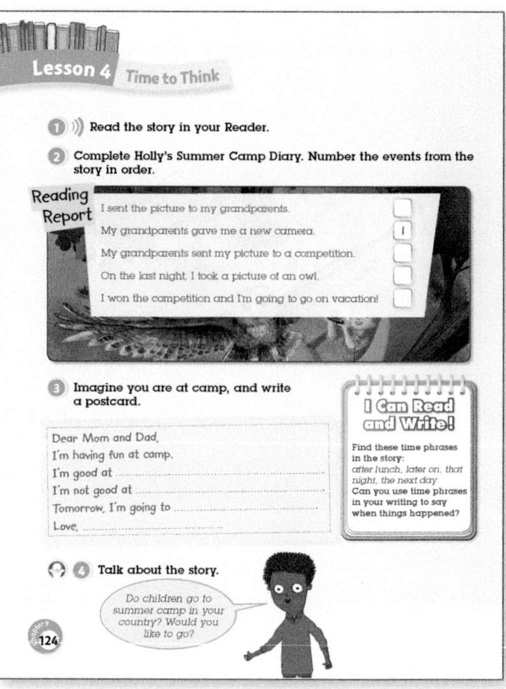

Lesson 4 Time to Think

1 Read the story in your Reader.

2 Complete Holly's Summer Camp Diary. Number the events from the story in order.

Reading Report

I sent the picture to my grandparents.

My grandparents gave me a new camera. 1

My grandparents sent my picture to a competition.

On the last night, I took a picture of an owl.

I won the competition and I'm going to go on vacation!

3 Imagine you are at camp, and write a postcard.

Dear Mom and Dad,
I'm having fun at camp.
I'm good at
I'm not good at
Tomorrow, I'm going to
Love,

I Can Read and Write!

Find these time phrases in the story:
after lunch, later on, that night, the next day
Can you use time phrases in your writing to say when things happened?

4 Talk about the story.

Do children go to summer camp in your country? Would you like to go?

124

Reading Comprehension and Critical Literacy

Lesson objectives: focus on the use of time phrases in stories to provide structure; reflect on the story theme and relate it to personal behavior
Materials: Track 9.5; Reader; photos brought by the children (optional); Oral Storytelling Video Worksheet 9 [TRC printout] (optional)

Note: Please ensure that your class has read the Reader story before you do this lesson.

Warmer: Visualization

Have the children close their eyes and imagine they are at a summer camp. Ask *What can you see? What different activities are the people doing? Do they look happy? Where are they living? What are they eating?* Ask children to say what they imagined.

1 9.5 Read the story in your Reader.

- Have the children read the story. (Alternatively, play Track 9.5 and have them read along.) Elicit whether they were correct in their predictions in Lesson 3 Activity 4.
- Check comprehension by asking *What activities did Holly do at camp? Was she good at them? (kayaking and mountain biking—no) What did Hollie's grandparents do with her picture? (They sent it to a competition.)*

2 Complete Holly's Summer Camp Diary. Number the events from the story in order.

- Do the example. Have the children number the events in the order they happen in the story.
- Elicit answers, with the children pointing to the pictures in the story.

Answers

3, 1, 4, 2, 5

I Can Read and Write!

Point out that time phrases are a useful way of structuring a story and showing the sequence of events clearly. Have the children find the time phrases in the story. Then elicit sentences about what they did yesterday, using these time phrases.

3 Imagine you are at a camp, and write a postcard.

- Ask children to read out the postcard line by line. For each blank, elicit a suggestion of what the answer might be.
- Have the children complete the postcard with their own ideas, and then exchange in pairs. Ask *Did you write about the same things?* Elicit answers and check with the class.

Answers

Children's own answers.

4 Talk about the story. 

- Have a child read out Jason's questions. Ask *Do children in your country usually go to summer camps? Have you ever been to one? If not, would you like to go?* Elicit answers.
- Divide the class into pairs and have them make a list of positive things about summer camps, e.g. *have fun, learn new things, make friends,* etc.

Optional activity: Photo exhibition

Give each child a small piece of paper and have them write a label for the picture they brought in, saying where and when they took it. Display the pictures and their labels, then have the class look at them all. Take a class vote on the best three pictures.

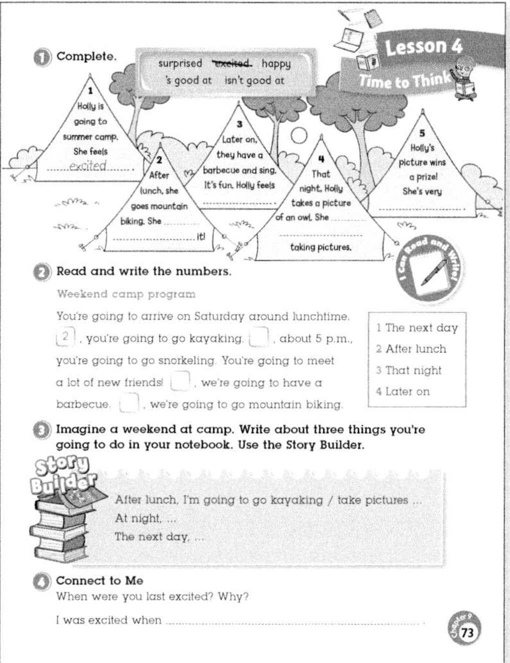

Lesson 4
Time to Think

1 Complete.

surprised ~~excited~~ happy
's good at isn't good at

1 Holly is going to summer camp. She feels ......excited......
2 After lunch, she goes mountain biking. She .... it!
3 Later on, they have a barbecue and sing. It's fun. Holly feels ....
4 That night, Holly takes a picture of an owl. She .... taking pictures.
5 Holly's picture wins a prize! She's very ....

2 Read and write the numbers.

I Can Read and Write!

Weekend camp program

You're going to arrive on Saturday around lunchtime. [2], you're going to go kayaking. [ ], about 5 p.m., you're going to go snorkeling. You're going to meet a lot of new friends! [ ], we're going to have a barbecue. [ ], we're going to go mountain biking.

1 The next day
2 After lunch
3 That night
4 Later on

3 Imagine a weekend at camp. Write about three things you're going to do in your notebook. Use the Story Builder.

Story Builder

After lunch, I'm going to go kayaking / take pictures ...
At night, ...
The next day, ...

4 Connect to Me
When were you last excited? Why?

I was excited when ....

Chapter 9 73

1 Complete.

The children complete the sentences using the words.

Answers

1 excited **2** isn't good at **3** happy **4** is good at
5 surprised

2 Read and write the numbers.

The children practice the **I Can Read and Write!** feature by writing in the number of the time phrases to complete the text. Elicit answers.

Answers

2, 4, 3, 1

3 Imagine a weekend at camp. Write about three things you're going to do in your notebook. Use the Story Builder.

Use the **Story Builder** prompts to elicit ideas. The children write a text in their notebook, then swap with a friend to check.

Answers

Children's own answers.

4 Connect to Me

Elicit ideas on when the children were last excited. The children write their own response, then compare with a friend. Elicit responses.

Answers

Children's own answers.

Cooler: Mime and guess

Divide the class into pairs. One child mimes an activity from the story and the other says what is happening, e.g. *Holly is falling in the lake. The grandparents are giving Holly a camera.*

Competency Focus

Me: Critical Literacy

The children use critical literacy skills to reflect on the story and think of similarities to their own culture and wishes.

Digital Resources

Reader eBook • Show the Reader story picture by picture without commenting on it. Minimize the screen and use *Timer* to give the children two minutes to recall the main events of the story in pairs. Elicit answers.

• Have children use *Highlighter* to identify the time phrases in the Reader story.

Teacher Resource Center • If you haven't already, print out Oral Storytelling Video Worksheet 9 to do the support activities.

Lesson 5

Song

1 Listen and number. Then sing.

We're Going to Go on Vacation
I'm going to go on vacation,
To somewhere hot and sunny.
Pack your suitcase 4, bring your camera,
And come with me!
I'm going to go to the beach,
Put your sandals on.
Bring your bathing suit and towel,
Let's play games in the sun!
The sun is getting hot,
It's really very bright,
But with our sunglasses and sunblock,
We're going to be all right.

2 Play the "I'm going to go to the beach" game.

I'm going to go to the beach. I'm going to take my sunblock.

I'm going to go to the beach. I'm going to take my sunblock and my bathing suit.

3 Write a list of things you're going to take on vacation.

4 Listen and say the chant.

Hot and bright, sunny and light; go straight to the pool, the weather is just right!

5 Find it!
How many can you find on the page? words with ending in –ght

Spelling Central
You don't hear the –gh in the word. Learn from sight and you can get it right!

125

Vocabulary, Song, and Spelling

Lesson objectives: identify and name vacation items; practice spelling words with *gh*
Key vocabulary: *bathing suit, camera, sandals, suitcase, sunblock, sunglasses, towel*
Secondary language: *bright, pack, put sandals on*
Materials: Tracks 9.6 and 9.7; pictures for Key vocabulary (Warmer) Phonics Worksheet 9 [TRC] (optional)

Warmer: Pre-teach vocabulary

Pre-teach the vocabulary using pictures of the vacation items. Then tell the class to look away. Remove one of the pictures. Elicit which item is missing. Repeat with different items.

1 9.6 Listen and number. Then sing. 

- Have the children look at the pictures next to the song. Ask *What can you see?*
- Play Track 9.6. The children listen and write the picture numbers next to the correct word in the song.
- Play Track 9.6 again. The children complete and check their answers. Elicit answers.
- Play Track 9.6 again for the children to sing along.

Answers

suitcase 4, camera 3, beach 7, sandals 8, bathing suit 5, towel 6, sunglasses 1, sunblock 2

2 Play the "I'm going to go to the beach" game.

- Model the activity. Read out the first example, have a child read out the second, and then ask another child to continue by adding one more item.
- Divide the class into groups of seven or eight and have them play the chain game.

3 Write a list of things you're going to take on vacation.

- Elicit the beginning of the sentence to answer the question. (*I'm going to take …*)
- Have the children continue the activity individually. Remind them to use some words from the song, but allow them to include other ideas.
- Ask children to read out their lists. Encourage careful listening by having the class respond *Me, too!* or *Not me!*

Answers

Children's own answers.

Spelling Central

Words with gh

Point out that *gh* in a word is often not pronounced. Say the sentence for the children to repeat after you.

4 9.7 Listen and say the chant.

- Play Track 9.7. The children listen and read along. Elicit the words with silent *gh* in *ght*.
- Play Track 9.7 again, pausing for the children to repeat.
- Have the children practice the chant in pairs. Invite pairs to perform for the class.

5 Find it!

- Set a time limit for the children to find words ending in *–ght* on the page. Elicit answers.

Answers

5—bright, light, straight, right, sight

Optional activity: Play "Ready, Set, Draw!"

Play the game with items of vocabulary from the lesson (see Games Bank p. 19).

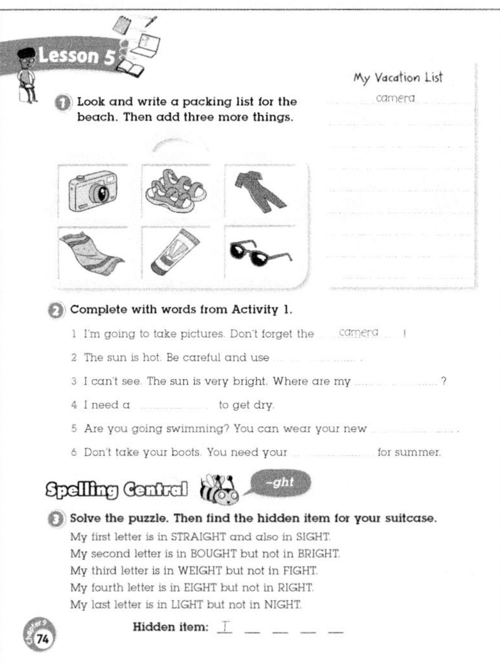

Lesson 5

1 Look and write a packing list for the beach. Then add three more things.

My Vacation List

camera

2 Complete with words from Activity 1.

1 I'm going to take pictures. Don't forget the camera !

2 The sun is hot. Be careful and use ______ .

3 I can't see. The sun is very bright. Where are my ______ ?

4 I need a ______ to get dry.

5 Are you going swimming? You can wear your new ______ .

6 Don't take your boots. You need your ______ for summer.

Spelling Central –ght

3 Solve the puzzle. Then find the hidden item for your suitcase.

My first letter is in STRAIGHT and also in SIGHT.

My second letter is in BOUGHT but not in BRIGHT.

My third letter is in WEIGHT but not in FIGHT.

My fourth letter is in EIGHT but not in RIGHT.

My last letter is in LIGHT but not in NIGHT.

Hidden item: T _ _ _ _

Chapter 9 74

1 Look and write a packing list for the beach. Then add three more things.

The children write a packing list using the items supplied and add more things they would like to take. Then they compare lists with a friend. Elicit responses.

Answers

camera, sandals, bathing suit, towel, sunblock, sunglasses + *any three other vacation items*

2 Complete with words from Activity 1.

The children complete the sentences with words for the pictures supplied in Activity 1. Elicit answers.

Answers

1 camera **2** sunblock **3** sunglasses **4** towel **5** bathing suit **6** sandals

3 Solve the puzzle. Then find the hidden item for your suitcase.

The children solve the puzzle by comparing each pair of words to identify the correct letter. Explain that there will sometimes be more than one correct option, so they may need to use some educated guessing. They write the letters in order to identify the hidden item. Elicit the answer.

Answer

Hidden item: towel

Cooler: Sing and mime

 9.6

Play the song again. The children sing along and mime along.

Competency Focus

Think! Critical Thinking

The children use critical thinking skills to identify vacation items by processing the written and spoken forms.

Digital Resources

Student eBook • Use *Add personal note* to store links to key vocabulary pictures to use in the Warmer.

- TIP Display the SB on the board for "heads-up" singing. This will enable you to check the children are participating and identify any who are struggling.
- TIP Use *Timer* to set a time limit for SB Activity 5.

Student's App • Encourage the children to play the games on their smartphone/tablet. (*The Inks* Apps are free and available on the App Store and Google Play.)

Teacher Resource Center • For phonics practice, print out Phonics Worksheet 9.

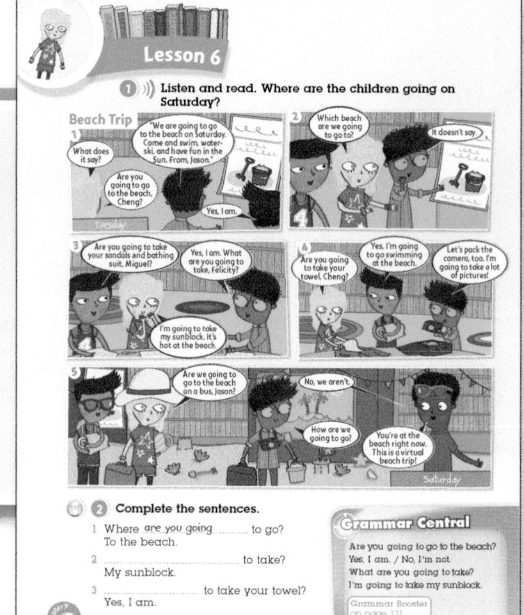
Lesson 6

1 Listen and read. Where are the children going on Saturday?

2 Complete the sentences.

1 Where are you going .... to go?
To the beach.

2 .... to take?
My sunblock.

3 .... to take your towel?
Yes, I am.

Grammar Central

Are you going to go to the beach?
Yes, I am. / No, I'm not.
What are you going to take?
I'm going to take my sunblock.

Grammar Booster on page 131

Grammar and Reading

Lesson objectives: ask and answer about plans using *Wh–* and *yes/no* questions with *going to*
Key grammar: *Are you going to (go to the beach)? Yes, I am. / No, I'm not. What are you going to (take)? I'm going to (take my sunblock).*
Secondary language: *It doesn't say, virtual*
Materials: Track 9.8; Grammar Worksheet 9B [TRC printout] (optional)

Warmer: What's in the "feely bag?"

Write scrambled versions of the key words from Lesson 5 on the board. As soon as a child finds an answer, invite them to write the correct version on the board.

1 9.8 Listen and read. Where are the children going on Saturday?

- Have the children look at the story. Ask *What are the children talking about?* (*a trip*)
- Play Track 9.8. The children listen and read along. Ask *Where are the children going on Saturday?* (*nowhere— they're staying at Story Central*) Check the meaning of *a virtual beach trip*.
- Play Track 9.8 again, pausing after phrases which feature a *going to* question or answer. Have the children repeat.

2 Look at the answers and complete the questions.

- Elicit the question for the first answer. Ask *Why is it correct?* (*We use* going to *for definite plans.*)
- Have the children complete the activity individually. Remind them they can check in the dialogue.
- Ask pairs to read out the complete questions and answers. Ask for class agreement.

Answers

1 are you going **2** What are you going **3** Are you going **4** Is, going

Grammar Central

Are you going to go to the beach? …

Have the children look at the patterns. Elicit how to form a question with *be going to*. (*be + subject + going to + verb*) Ask *How do you answer a question like this?* (*Yes, I'm going to go … / No, I'm not going to go …*) Have the children repeat the sentences after you. Elicit questions and answers with this structure in the story.

For extra practice, try the **Grammar Booster** section in the Student Book (p. 131–133).

Answers p. 131

Activity 1: **1** going to **2** am **3** not **4** going to **5** is **6** What are **7** going to **8** What are

Activity 2: **1** Are you going to take sunblock?; d **2** What are you going to pack?; c **3** Is Dad going to take his bike?; b **4** What are we going to do on the first day?; a

p. 132

Activity 1: **1** are **2** going **3** Are **4** am **5** isn't **6** to **7** going

Activity 2: **1** is going to go **2** is going to take **3** Is; going to **4** is going to play **5** isn't going to

p. 133

Activity 1: **1** going to **2** going to **3** going to **4** most **5** are going **6** are you **7** isn't **8** What **9** going to **10** are going **11** play

Activity 2: Children's own answers.

Optional activity: Play "The Chain Game"

Play the game to practice vacation vocabulary (see Games Bank p. 19). Start the chain with *I'm going to the beach and I'm going to take my sunblock.*

Lesson 6

1 **Unscramble the questions about your next vacation. Then write answers.**

1 going / to / you / beach? / to / the / Are / go

Are you going to go to the beach ? ....

2 take? / going / you / to / are / What

.... ? ....

3 going / take / camera? / you / Are / to / your

.... ? ....

4 do / going / there? / are / to / What / you

.... ? ....

2 **Complete using the correct form of *going to*, *I'm*, or *I'm not*.**

Friend: 1 Are you going to go on the trip to the forest?

You: Yes, I am.

Friend: What 2 .... take?

You: I'm going to take my bathing suit.

Friend: I'm 3 .... take my bathing suit – I can't swim!

You: 4 .... take a packed lunch?

Friend: No, 5 .... We're going to have a barbecue.

You: Okay, that's cool.

3 **Write questions for a friend about his/her school trip. Then ask and answer.**

1 .... ?

2 .... ?

3 .... ?

Chapter 9 75

1 Unscramble the questions about your next vacation. Then write answers.

The children unscramble the questions and write their own answers. Elicit answers.

Answers

1 Are you going to go to the beach? **2** What are you going to take? **3** Are you going to take your camera? **4** What are you going to do there?
Children's own answers.

2 Complete using the correct form of going to, I'm, or I'm not.

The children complete the dialogue. Elicit answers.

Answers

1 Are you going **2** are you going to **3** not going to **4** Are you going to **5** I'm not

3 Write questions for a friend about his/her school trip. Then ask and answer.

Elicit school trip ideas. The children write their questions, then ask and answer them in pairs.

Answers

Children's own answers.

Cooler: Guess the vacation

Tell the children you are thinking of a place for your next vacation and three things to take with you. Have the children first guess where you are going (e.g. *the mountains*), and then what you are going to take with you. (e.g. *sunglasses, camera, hat*)

Competency Focus

Learn

The children demonstrate and consolidate their understanding of the new language by completing the activity.

Digital Resources

Student eBook, Digital Activity Book • TIP With the answer key, you can reveal the answers all at once or one by one to customize feedback.

Teacher Resource Center • For extra grammar practice, print out Grammar Worksheet 9B.

CLIL: Science—Sun safety

Lesson objective: find out about the benefits/dangers of exposure to the Sun
Materials: CLIL Graphic Organizer 9 [TRC printout] (optional)

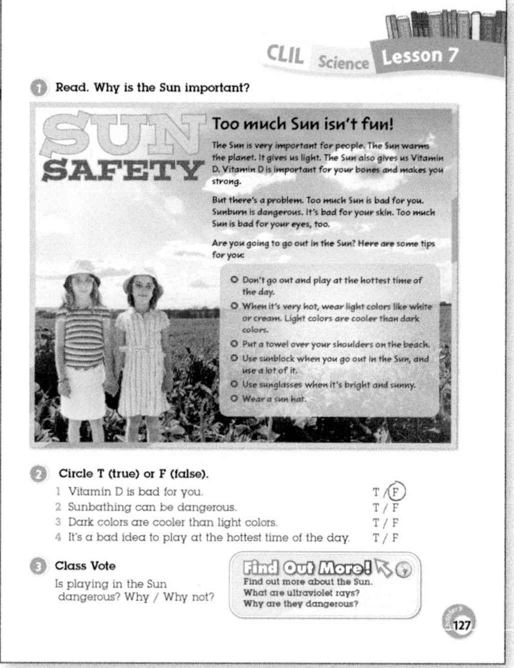

CLIL Science Lesson 7

1 Read. Why is the Sun important?

SUN SAFETY

Too much Sun isn't fun!

The Sun is very important for people. The Sun warms the planet. It gives us light. The Sun also gives us Vitamin D. Vitamin D is important for your bones and makes you strong.

But there's a problem. Too much Sun is bad for you. Sunburn is dangerous. It's bad for your skin. Too much Sun is bad for your eyes, too.

Are you going to go out in the Sun? Here are some tips for you:

- Don't go out and play at the hottest time of the day.
- When it's very hot, wear light colors like white or cream. Light colors are cooler than dark colors.
- Put a towel over your shoulders on the beach.
- Use sunblock when you go out in the Sun, and use a lot of it.
- Use sunglasses when it's bright and sunny.
- Wear a sun hat.

2 Circle T (true) or F (false).

1 Vitamin D is bad for you. T / F
2 Sunbathing can be dangerous. T / F
3 Dark colors are cooler than light colors. T / F
4 It's a bad idea to play at the hottest time of the day. T / F

3 Class Vote

Is playing in the Sun dangerous? Why / Why not?

Find Out More!
Find out more about the Sun.
What are ultraviolet rays?
Why are they dangerous?

127

Warmer: Class discussion

Write on the board *What's your favorite season / month of the year?* Give your own answers and reasons as a model, then have the children discuss in pairs. Elicit opinions. If children mention *sunny*, take the opportunity to talk about the Sun. Ask *Who likes sunny weather? Why?* Elicit responses.

1 Read. Why is the Sun important?

- Have the children look at the pictures. Ask *What can you see?*
- Ask *Why is the Sun important?* Have the children read the text to find the answer. (*Because it warms the planet, gives us light, and also gives us Vitamin D.*)
- Elicit what months the Sun is the hottest in the children's country.

2 Circle T (true) or F (false).

- Ask why the example answer is false. (*Vitamin D is important for your bones and makes you strong.*)
- The children circle true or false for each sentence.
- Elicit answers, including the correct version of the false sentences. Check with the class.

Answers

1 F **2** T **3** F **4** T

3 Class Vote

- Ask *Is playing in the Sun dangerous?* Give the children time to think and discuss with a friend. Take a vote with a show of hands for yes or no. Have one child come to the front of the class and count the votes to write them on the board. Ask some children why they answered yes or no (they may need help or to use L1 to explain this).

Find Out More!  

Elicit appropriate resources for finding out about ultraviolet rays, e.g. Internet, library books, family, etc. The children will need to complete this research before doing the follow-up activity in the Activity Book. (It could be set as homework.)

Optional activity: Play "Disappearing Text"

Do this activity with *Don't go out and play at the hottest time of the day. Put a towel over your shoulders on the beach.* (see Games Bank, p. 19).

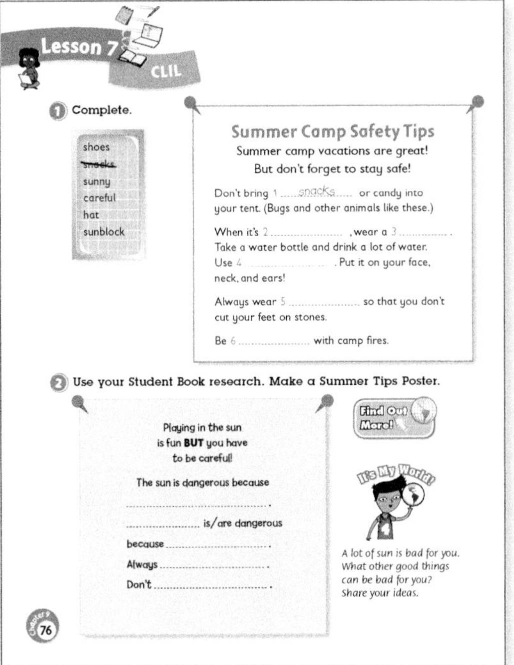

Lesson 7 CLIL

1 Complete.

shoes
~~snacks~~
sunny
careful
hat
sunblock

Summer Camp Safety Tips
Summer camp vacations are great!
But don't forget to stay safe!

Don't bring 1 snacks or candy into your tent. (Bugs and other animals like these.)

When it's 2 .... , wear a 3 .... Take a water bottle and drink a lot of water.
Use 4 .... Put it on your face, neck, and ears!

Always wear 5 .... so that you don't cut your feet on stones.

Be 6 .... with camp fires.

2 Use your Student Book research. Make a Summer Tips Poster.

Playing in the sun is fun **BUT** you have to be careful!

The sun is dangerous because ....

.... is/are dangerous because ....

Always ....

Don't ....

Find Out More!

It's My World!

A lot of sun is bad for you. What other good things can be bad for you? Share your ideas.

76

1 Complete.

The children complete the text using the words supplied. Elicit answers in the form of complete sentences.

Answers

1 snacks **2** sunny **3** hat **4** sunblock **5** shoes **6** careful

2 Use your Student Book research. Make a Summer Tips Poster.

Divide the class into groups of four. The children pool the information they learned from their research in the Student Book and the Activity Book. They make their Summer Tips Poster individually. Invite children to present their posters to the class.

It's My World!

Elicit examples of good things that can be bad for you in excess, e.g. *too much chocolate, too much TV,* etc. Create a mind map with the children's ideas on the board.

Cooler: Stay safe!

Brainstorm with the children a list of things that help us stay safe from the Sun and ultraviolet rays, e.g. *long-sleeved shirts, hats, sunglasses, sunblock, beach umbrella.* Write the ideas on the board and have the children copy them in their notebook in order of importance. They compare in small groups.

Competency Focus

Act

The children carry out research to find out about the Sun and ultraviolet rays. They relate what they learn to their world, both inside and outside the classroom.

Digital Resources

Student eBook • TIP Remember—you can use *Add personal note* to log the results of the class vote.

Teacher Resource Center • Print out CLIL Graphic Organizer 9 for the children to collate their Find Out More! research.

CLIL eBook • The children can use the CLIL eBook to expand their knowledge of the lesson topic.

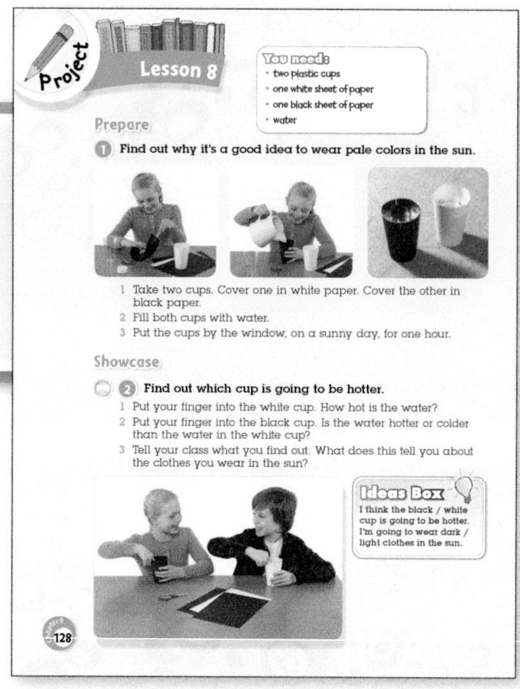

Project

Lesson 8

You need:
- two plastic cups
- one white sheet of paper
- one black sheet of paper
- water

Prepare

1 Find out why it's a good idea to wear pale colors in the sun.

1 Take two cups. Cover one in white paper. Cover the other in black paper.
2 Fill both cups with water.
3 Put the cups by the window, on a sunny day, for one hour.

Showcase

2 Find out which cup is going to be hotter.

1 Put your finger into the white cup. How hot is the water?
2 Put your finger into the black cup. Is the water hotter or colder than the water in the white cup?
3 Tell your class what you find out. What does this tell you about the clothes you wear in the sun?

Ideas Box
I think the black / white cup is going to be hotter.
I'm going to wear dark / light clothes in the sun.

Chapter 9 128

Project

Lesson objectives: review language from Chapter 9; complete a craft project—making a magic picture; act out the story from the Reader
Materials: Reader; paper/cardboard, paint, paintbrushes, jars of water, white wax crayons; simple props (optional)

Warmer: Play "Sentences Builders"

Play the game with four or five key sentences from the text in Student Book Lesson 7 (see Games Bank p. 19). (Suggestions: *The Sun is very important for people. Vitamin D is important for your bones. Too much Sun is bad for you. Use sunblock when you go out in the Sun.*)

Prepare

1 Find out why it's a good idea to wear pale colors in the sun.

- Distribute the materials. Read through the instructions together and ensure the children are clear on what to do.
- Have the children follow the instructions to prepare their experiment. Monitor and give help and suggestions as necessary.

Alternative craft activity

The experiment can be done on a smaller scale with just one or two pairs of cups for the whole class. Allocate roles: bring cups, cut the paper to size, wrap the cups, fill the cups, place the cups in the Sun, note classmates' opinions on the water temperature.

Showcase

2 Find out which cup is going to be hotter.

- Have the children test the temperature in the white cup. Then they predict if the water in the black cup is going to be hotter or cooler, using the **Ideas Box** for support.
- The children then test the black cup. Elicit results by a show of hands.
- Ask *What does this tell us about wearing white or dark clothes in the Sun?* (*Dark clothes make us feel hotter in the Sun.*) They might need to use L1.

Optional activity: Brainstorm keeping cool

Say *Imagine you are outside and feeling very hot. What can you do to stay cool?* Give the children time to think and then have them discuss ideas in pairs. Elicit suggestions and write them on the board, e.g. *drink something cool, go to the beach, put on a hat.*

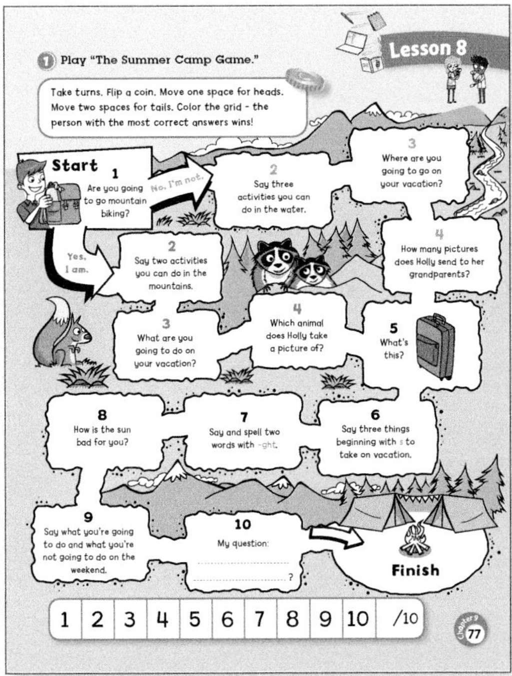
Lesson 8

1 Play "The Summer Camp Game."

Take turns. Flip a coin. Move one space for heads. Move two spaces for tails. Color the grid - the person with the most correct answers wins!

Start 1 Are you going to go mountain biking?

No, I'm not.

Yes, I am.

2 Say three activities you can do in the water.

2 Say two activities you can do in the mountains.

3 Where are you going to go on your vacation?

3 What are you going to do on your vacation?

4 How many pictures does Holly send to her grandparents?

4 Which animal does Holly take a picture of?

5 What's this?

6 Say three things beginning with s to take on vacation.

7 Say and spell two words with -ght.

8 How is the sun bad for you?

9 Say what you're going to do and what you're not going to do on the weekend.

10 My question: .... ?

Finish

1	2	3	4	5	6	7	8	9	10	/10

77

Competency Focus

Collaborate and communicate

By carrying out an experiment, the children consolidate their understanding of the topic in a challenging and engaging way. They also demonstrate their ability to work with friends and use interpersonal skills.

1 Play "The Summer Camp Game."

See p. 43 for instructions on how to play the game.

Answers

1 Yes, I am./No, I'm not. **2** *Gray path:* snorkeling, water-skiing, kayaking *Purple path:* mountain biking, rock climbing **3** *Gray path:* I'm going to go + *place Purple path:* I'm going to go + *activity* **4** *Gray path:* three *Purple path:* an owl **5** a suitcase **6** *any three of:* sunblock, shorts, sandals, sunglasses **7** *any two of:* straight, right, bought, etc. **8** You can get sunburn. / It's bad for your eyes.
9 I'm going to + *activity*. / I'm not going to + *activity*.
10 Children's own answers.

Cooler: Play "Back to the Board"

Choose ten key words from Chapter 9. Divide the class into two teams. One child from each team sits at the front, facing away from the board. Write a word on the board—they cannot look! Their teammates explain the word for the children to guess (using definitions, examples, mime, sound effects—anything except L1 or the word itself). Repeat with different children.

Digital Resources

Student eBook • Show the pictures, stage by stage, as you talk the class through the activity process.

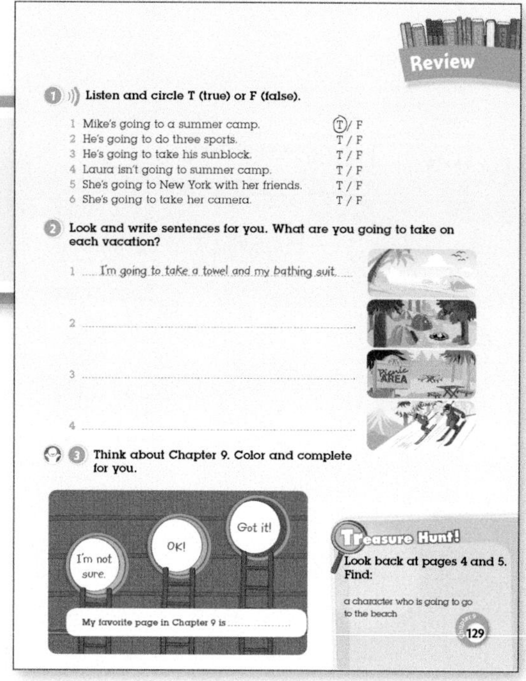
Review

1 Listen and circle T (true) or F (false).

1 Mike's going to a summer camp. T / F
2 He's going to do three sports. T / F
3 He's going to take his sunblock. T / F
4 Laura isn't going to summer camp. T / F
5 She's going to New York with her friends. T / F
6 She's going to take her camera. T / F

2 Look and write sentences for you. What are you going to take on each vacation?

1 I'm going to take a towel and my bathing suit.
2 ....
3 ....
4 ....

3 Think about Chapter 9. Color and complete for you.

My favorite page in Chapter 9 is ....

Treasure Hunt!
Look back at pages 4 and 5. Find:
a character who is going to go to the beach

129

Language Review

Lesson objective: review language from Chapter 9
Materials: Tracks 9.9, AB 9.1, AB 9.2, and AB 9.3; Reader

Warmer: Play "Disappearing Words"

Play the game with key vocabuary from Lessons 1 and 5 (see Games Bank p. 19).

1 9.9 Listen and circle T (true) or F (false).

- Have the children look at the sentences and predict what they will hear. (*a conversation about summer camp*)
- Play Track 9.9 twice. The children circle *true* or *false* for each sentence.

Audioscript

Laura: *Hi, Mike. What are you going to do on vacation?*
Mike: *Well, I'm going to a sports summer camp.*
Laura: *What sports are you going to do?*
Mike: *Well, I'm going to do two water sports—kayaking and snorkeling.*
Laura: *And water-skiing?*
Mike: *No, I'm not going to do that. I always fall in the water!*
Laura: *What are you going to take?*
Mike: *Hm, my bathing suit, my towel, and my sunblock. What about you, Laura?*
Laura: *Well, I'm going to go camping in the mountains with my family.*
Mike: *Wow, that's cool! What are you going to do there?*
Laura: *Well, we're going to visit a nature reserve. There's a big lake and a lot of birds … and I'm going to take my camera.*
Mike: *Fantastic! Have a good vacation.*

Answers

1 T **2** F **3** T **4** T **5** F **6** T

2 Look and write sentences for you. What are you going to take on each vacation?

- The children write sentences about what they are going to take on vacation.

Answers

Children's own answers.

3 Think about Chapter 9. Color and complete for you.

- Children color the circle which represents how they feel about their own progress (self-evaluation).
- Have the children complete the sentence.

Treasure Hunt!

Have the children look at pp. 4–5 to find a character who is going to the beach.

Cooler: Reader review

Give the children several minutes to look back at all the Reader stories and remember which ones they liked best. They then compare ideas with a friend. Elicit responses.

Competency Focus

Me: Self-evaluation

The children reflect on the chapter and express their opinions about their own progress.

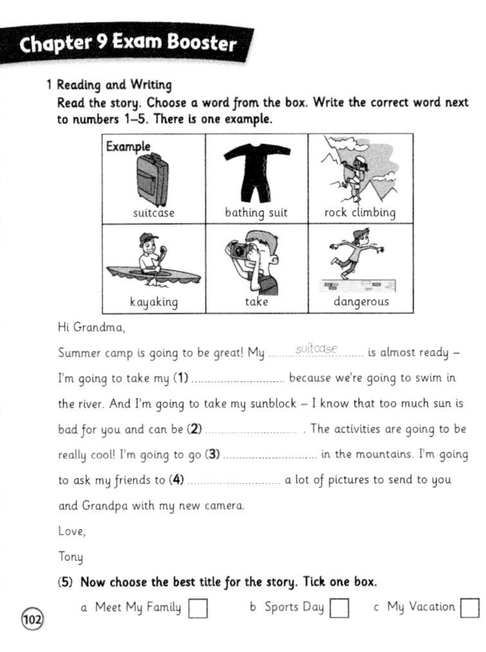

Chapter 9 Exam Booster

1 Reading and Writing

Read the story. Choose a word from the box. Write the correct word next to numbers 1–5. There is one example.

Example suitcase	bathing suit	rock climbing
kayaking	take	dangerous

Hi Grandma,

Summer camp is going to be great! My ..suitcase.. is almost ready – I'm going to take my (1) .... because we're going to swim in the river. And I'm going to take my sunblock – I know that too much sun is bad for you and can be (2) .... The activities are going to be really cool! I'm going to go (3) .... in the mountains. I'm going to ask my friends to (4) .... a lot of pictures to send to you and Grandpa with my new camera.

Love,

Tony

(5) **Now choose the best title for the story. Tick one box.**

a Meet My Family ☐ b Sports Day ☐ c My Vacation ☐

102

2 Listening

Listen and color and write. There is one example.

103

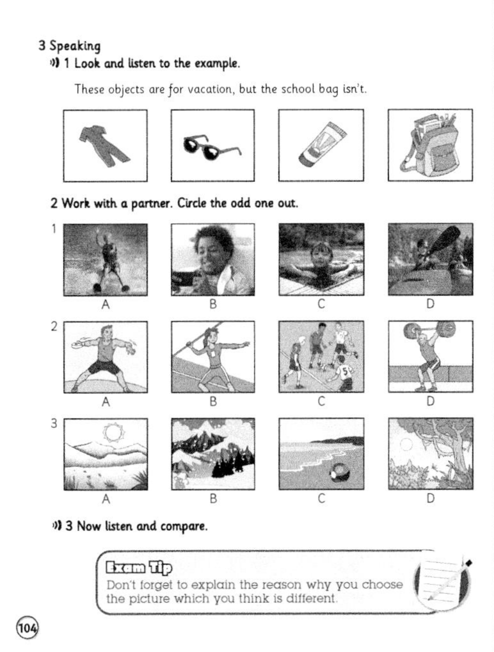

3 Speaking

1 Look and listen to the example.

These objects are for vacation, but the school bag isn't.

2 Work with a partner. Circle the odd one out.

1 A B C D

2 A B C D

3 A B C D

3 Now listen and compare.

Exam Tip

Don't forget to explain the reason why you choose the picture which you think is different.

104

1 Reading and Writing. Read the story. Choose a word from the box. Write the correct word next to numbers 1-5. There is one example.

Children complete the text and choose the best title.

Answers

1 bathing suit **2** dangerous **3** rock climbing **4** take **5** c

2)) AB 9.1 Listening. Listen and color and write. There is one example.

Play Track AB 9.1 twice. The children listen and color and write according to the recording. Check answers.

Answers (Audioscript on p. 224)

Picture colored as follows: suitcase—brown, T-shirt—red, bathing suit—orange, towel—blue

Written on sign: Blue Lake

3.1)) AB 9.2 Speaking. Look and listen to the example.

The children listen and look at the pictures.

(Audioscript on p. 224)

3.2 Speaking. Work with a partner. Circle the odd one out.

Children choose the item that is the odd one out.

3.3)) AB 9.3 Speaking. Now listen and compare.

Ask the children to listen and compare their answers.

(Audioscript on p. 224)

Digital Resources

Digital Activity Book • Use the answer key to give feedback on AB Exam Booster activities. You can show the answers all at once or one by one to customize feedback. Alternatively, you can use the interactive digital activities.

Teacher Resource Center • Print out Test Chapter 9 and End-of-year Test to use at the end of this lesson. The Test Generator also allows you to create customized tests.

Exam Booster Audioscripts

AB 1.1

N: *Example*
W: *Okay, now. Is everyone ready?*
G1: *Yes, Miss Brown. Here's my slip. We always have to get our parents' permission for a school trip. I have my water bottle too.*
W: *That's right, Sally. Thank you.*
N: *Can you see the line? This is an example. Now you listen and draw lines.*
N: *One*
W: *Now, we're almost ready. I just have to check your names. Oh, who's that boy looking out of the window? He isn't listening to me.*
G1: *The boy at the back? That's Ben.*
W: *Ben, listen please.*
B1: *Yes, Miss Brown.*
N: *Two*
W: *Now, what about lunch? Does everyone have a packed lunch?*
G2: *Yes, Miss Brown. Look, here's mine.*
W: *What do you have today, Anna?*
G2: *A cheese sandwich, an apple, and some juice.*
W: *Great!*
N: *Three*
W: *Who's that boy wearing his school uniform?*
B1: *That's Tom.*
W: *But you don't have to wear your school uniform today!*
B1: *I know. He has his bag, too! Tom is the only one. He never listens in class.*
N: *Four*
W: *Look at that boy with the ball! Who is he?*
G1: *That's Paul. He loves soccer …*
W: *Paul, don't throw that ball! Give it to me.*
B2: *But, Miss Brown, we can play in the picnic area.*
W: *No, you can't.*
N: *Five*
W: *Now, what about bathing suits?*
G3: *I have mine, Miss Brown.*
W: *Where, Lucy? Oh, in your bag?*
G3: *Yes.*
W: *Good. You need your bathing suit to swim in the river.*

AB 2.1

N: *Example*
W: *Happy Birthday, Billy.*
B: *Thanks, Mom. I can't wait for my party tomorrow!*
W: *Yes, it's tomorrow. You can go shopping for the food today after school.*
N: *Can you see the answer? Now you listen and write.*
N: *One*
W: *Billy, how many of your friends are coming?*
B: *12 from my class … and my three cousins. Fifteen people.*
W: *Fifteen. Good.*
N: *Two*
W: *I'm making an apple cake for the party. I have some eggs … Are there any apples?*
B: *No, there aren't. I can buy some.*
N: *Three*
W: *How about the sandwiches? We have some turkey and some mayonnaise.*
B: *Okay—we need cheese. How much is it?*
W: *$1.25.*
B: *Let me write it down on the list—cheese $1.25.*
N: *Four*
W: *How about melons?*
B: *My friends don't like melons …*
W: *What fruit do they like?*
B: *They love strawberries.*
W: *There aren't any strawberries at home—so buy some of those.*
N: *Five*
B: *Mom, I need some money to go shopping.*
W: *How much do you need?*
B: *Apples, cheese, strawberries … I need $5.50.*
W: *$5.50. Here's the money, Billy.*

AB 2.2

N: *Listen and look. There is one example.*
N: *Example*
W: *Now Charlie. Let's make Banana Surprise today.*
B: *Yes, great! I love bananas.*
W: *And you like ice cream, too!*
B: *Who's coming?*
W: *Well … everybody! Eight people.*
N: *Can you see the answer? Now listen and write.*
N: *One*
B: *Okay, Mom. Is this a new recipe?*
W: *Yes, it is. It's from my friend. Make a note for my book, Charlie.*
B: *What's your friend's name?*
W: *Mrs. Robinson—R-O-B-I-N-S-O-N.*
B: *Okay. Mrs. Robinson.*
N: *Two*
B: *So what do we need, Mom?*
W: *Well, we have bananas, so we don't have to buy those.*
B: *Do we need strawberries?*
W: *Yes, we do. Can you go to the store for me?*
B: *Okay.*
N: *Three*
B: *Where's the store?*
W: *Well, first, go to the park.*
B: *Okay.*
W: *The store is next to the playground.*
N: *Four*
W: *This recipe is easy! You don't have to cook.*
B: *So, eight bananas … and here's the ice cream.*
W: *And here are the strawberries.*
B: *Is it ready now?*
W: *No, put it in the fridge and wait. It'll be ready in 30 minutes.*
N: *Five*
B: *Mm, Mom, this is delicious!*
W: *Yes, and it's fast and easy.*
B: *Is it expensive?*
W: *No, it's only four fifty.*
B: *Great. Let's make it again tomorrow!*

AB 3.1

N: *One*
M: *Hello, Susie. How was your week?*
G: *Friday was good. I went to the movie theater.*
M: *How was the movie?*
G: *It was great! I was really excited!*
N: *Can you see the letter G? Now you listen and write a letter in each box.*
N: *Two*
M: *And what about the next day?*
G: *Saturday was cool. It was our school show.*
M: *Were you in it?*
G: *No, I wasn't. But my brother was. He was a musician. He played the recorder.*
N: *Three*
M: *You were very busy last weekend. Were you tired?*
G: *No! On Sunday afternoon, I went to the zoo with my parents.*
N: *Four*
M: *I called you on Wednesday, but no one was home.*
G: *I was at the circus! Julie was there, too.*
M: *Oh, I love the circus. Was it good?*
G: *Yes, it was cool! There were a lot of acrobats and clowns.*
N: *Five*
M: *What about the puppet show? Did you go?*
G: *Yes. My friend Sam was really excited.*
M: *Was it a good show?*
G: *Yes, it was great. There were two dancing puppets.*
N: *Six*
M: *That's a busy week! Were you home on Monday?*
G: *No, I wasn't. You know I have ballet class. Daisy and I go together.*
M: *Oh, yes. That's right.*

AB 3.2

G: *In this picture, there is a tree.*
B: *And in this picture, there isn't a tree.*
B: *Here, there are some flowers.*
G: *And here, there aren't any flowers.*

AB 3.3

G: *In this picture, there is a tree.*
B: *And in this picture, there isn't a tree.*

B: *Here, there are some flowers.*
G: *And here, there aren't any flowers.*

G: *In this picture, there is a musician.*
B: *In this picture, there isn't a musician.*

B: *Here, there are two dancers.*
G: *Here, there aren't any dancers.*

G: *In this picture, the singer is happy.*
B: *In this picture, the singer is sad.*

B: *Here, the children are eating sandwiches.*
G: *Here, the children are eating ice cream.*

AB 4.1

N: *Example*
W: *Joe, look at your bedroom! You never clean it.*
B1: *Sorry, Mom.*
W: *Just pick those up off the floor!*
B1: *What—these toys?*
W: *No … The socks and pants. And let me make the bed.*
N: *One*
G1: *I'd like a drink.*
W: *I'm putting the kettle on. We can have a cup of coffee.*
G1: *Can I have hot chocolate, please?*
W: *Yes. Can you get the milk from the fridge?*
G1: *OK.*
N: *Two*
W: *Look at this kitchen floor—it's really messy.*
G2: *Sorry, Mom—we had cookies. I'll get the broom and sweep up the mess.*
W: *I think you need the vacuum cleaner. It's in the closet next to the washing machine.*
G2: *OK.*
N: *Three*
G3: *Hi, Ben. What are you doing?*
B2: *I'm cleaning up.*
G3: *Really? In your bedroom?*
B2: *No, I'm in the living room.*
G3: *Where's your mom?*
B2: *She's in the kitchen. She's doing the dishes.*

AB 5.1

N: *Example*
M: *Hello, everybody. How was the activity day?*
B1: *It was great, Mr. Robson!*
M: *Were there some fun activities, Paul?*
B1: *Yes, I painted a picture. Look! It's an elephant.*
M: *That's a great elephant!*
N: *Can you see the line? This is an example. Now you listen and draw lines.*
N: *One*
M: *That's a good poem, Vicky.*
G1: *Yes, I wrote it yesterday at the activity day.*
M: *Was it difficult to write?*
G1: *Yes. I looked out of the window for ideas.*
N: *Two*
M: *And what's this?*
B2: *It's a model of an Egyptian house.*
M: *That's really interesting, Tony.*
B2: *Yes, I built it and painted the walls.*
N: *Three*
M: *What did you do in the afternoon, Daisy?*
G2: *I watched a movie.*
M: *Was it good?*
G2: *Yes, it was funny. I laughed a lot.*
N: *Four*
M: *Do you wear your school uniform at the club, Alex?*
B3: *No, we don't. Yesterday, I wore my jeans and a T-shirt with a tiger on it.*
M: *That's cool!*
N: *Five*
M: *Mm! This cake looks delicious! Who made it?*
G3: *Me! I made it with apples.*
M: *Good job, Mary! Can we have some?*
G3: *Yes, of course.*
N: *Now listen again.*

AB 5.2

N: *Example*
W: *Hello, Jane. Are you ready for the birthday party?*
G: *Yes. Look — there's a lot of food.*
W: *Oh? Who prepared it?*
G: *Me! I prepared all the sandwiches — they're turkey and tomato.*
Can you see the line? This is an example. Now you listen and draw lines.

N: *One*
W: *And who prepared the cake, Vicky?*
G: *Well, Mom prepared it yesterday—but I put the candles on the cake today.*
W: *It looks delicious!*
N: *Two*
W: *The house is very clean, Peter.*
B: *Yes, it is. I cleaned the kitchen this morning.*
W: *And the floor? Is it finished?*
B: *No, I can sweep the kitchen floor with the broom.*
N: *Three*
W: *The living room looks fantastic. Look at that Happy Birthday sign in the living room.*
G: *Yes, I wrote the sign and painted it. I often paint signs.*
W: *It's great! Good job, Sally!*
N: *Four*
W: *Do you have a birthday card?*
B: *No, there weren't any good ones at the mall, but I wasn't worried.*
W: *Why not?*
B:*Well, I often use my phone for videos. So, I used it to make some funny birthday messages. We can watch them later.*
W: *That's a good idea, Nick!*
N: *Five*
W: *Is there any music for the party?*
B: *Yes, there is. I'm a good musician. I played my guitar and sang at the school show last week. I was really excited.*
W: *That's cool, John!*
B: *I have to practice "Happy Birthday" now. I always play that song at birthday parties.*

AB 6.1

N: *Example*
G: *Hi, Tom. What are you doing?*
B: *A project for my English class.*
G: *What's it about?*
B: *My vacation last summer. I have English tomorrow. I need to finish it today.*
N: *Can you see the answer? Now you listen and write.*
N: *One*
G: *What kind of place did you go to on vacation?*
B: *We went to an island.*
G: *Wow. Was it a big island?*
B: *No, pretty small.*
N: *Two*
G: *Was it beautiful?*
B: *Yes! There were some cool beaches.*
G: *I love beaches!*
B: *Me, too, but my favorite thing was the waterfalls.*
G: *The waterfalls were your favorite?*
B: *Yes—they were great!*
N: *Three*
G: *So did you have good weather?*
B: *Well, usually it's hot in the summer, but when we were there it rained!*
G: *Did it rain every day?*
B: *Yes!*
N: *Four*
G: *How long were you on the island?*
B: *Two weeks.*
G: *When did you go?*
B: *We went in August. We always go on vacation in August.*
N: *Five*
G: *And where did you stay?*
B: *We stayed at a place called Bear Farm.*
G: *How do you spell that?*
B: *B-E-A-R F-A-R-M.*
G: *I'll look for it on the map!*

AB 6.2

N: *In picture A, Kim and Tony are walking next to South Lake. They are going to the mountains. The sun is shining. It's warm. They are wearing T-shirts and jeans.*

AB 6.3

G: *In picture A, Kim and Tony are walking next to South Lake. They are going to the mountains. The sun is shining. It's warm. The children are wearing T-shirts and jeans.*
B: *In picture B, Kim and Tony are walking in the mountains. It's not sunny. It's colder now. They are putting on sweaters.*
B: *In picture C they are going higher up the mountain. It's foggy. They can't see. They are worried and scared.*
B: *In picture D they are coming down the mountain. They can see their friend – they are surprised! They have a picnic. There is some fruit. And there are sandwiches, too!*

AB 7.1

N: *Look at the pictures. Listen and look. There is one example.*
N: *Example*
G: *Hi, Jim. Did you see the sports show yesterday?*
B: *Yes, I did.*
G: *Did you watch the weightlifting?*
B: *No, the boxing.*
G: *Oh, yes, you're on the school team, aren't you?*
B: *Yes, I am, but I like watching it on TV more.*
N: *Can you see the tick? Now you listen and tick the box.*

N: *One*
B: *How was Sports Day at school, Anna?*
G: *Well, it was OK, but I didn't win anything.*
B: *Did you run in any of the races?*
G: *No, I didn't.*
B: *Did you do the long jump?*
G: *No, the high jump—I was second.*
B: *That's great!*
N: *Two*

B: *So, how's your brother, Paul? Did he have a good Sports Day?*
G: *He did weightlifting and he won a prize!*
B: *Wow! Was it a cup? Or some money?*
G: *No—it was a gold medal.*
B: *Just like the Olympics!*
N: *Three*
B: *I remember you won something last year at Sports Day. The javelin, wasn't it?*
G: *No, it wasn't. I won a race.*
B: *Oh, yes. Did you compete in the 100 meter race?*

AB 8.1

N: *What did Pat do with her friends and family?*
N: *One*
M: *Hi, Pat. What are you doing today?*
G: *I'm going to cousin Kim's house. I always go there on Fridays.*
M: *What do you do there?*
G: *We play video games. My favorite is called Sneaky Snake!*
N: *Can you see the letter E? Now you listen and write a letter in each box.*
N: *Two*
M: *And what did you do yesterday?*
Pat Well, my friend Jack arrived after school.
M: *What did you do? Did you study?*
Pat Yes, we did our math homework together.
N: *Three*
M: *And what did you do on Monday?*
G: *I played soccer with my brother, Ben.*
M: *Did you play well?*
G: *Not really. Ben won!*
N: *Four*
G: *I had a bad day on Wednesday.*
M: *What happened?*
G: *I went to visit grandma. I played with my ball. I broke a window.*
M: *Oh, no!*
G: *And grandma shouted at me—very loudly!*
N: *Five*
M: *And tomorrow?*
G: *Well, it's Saturday. Sometimes, I go to the park with my friends Sally and Katie.*
M: *What do you do there?*
G: *I ride my bike. It's fun.*
N: *Six*
M: *Which was your favorite day?*
G: *Sunday, I think.*
M: *Why?*
G: *We had a party!*
M: *That's cool.*

G: *It was my dad's birthday. We had a lot of fun!*

AB 8.2

N: *One. Mrs. Brown is talking to Tom about the people in her family. What did each person do last weekend?*
B: *Hello, Mrs. Brown. How was your weekend?*
W: *Hi, Tom! It was good—my family visited last weekend. They all like to do different things! My dad went down to the river and fished. So, we had fish for dinner!*
N: *Can you see the letter D? Now listen and write a letter in each box.*
N: *Two*
B: *I know your son Paul. He goes to my school. What did he do on the weekend?*
W: *Well, he has a new video game. His grandma gave it to him for his birthday. He played it all weekend.*
B: *Cool! What's it about?*
W: *I think it's an adventure game about animals in the desert.*
N: *Three*
W: *I have a daughter, too.*
B: *Oh, really? I don't know her.*
W: *Well, she's older than you. She likes sports like you. But she can't throw the javelin or discus. On the weekend, she ran a race. We all watched her.*
B: *Did she win the race?*
W: *Yes, she did. She got a gold medal.*
N: *Four*
B: *What about your friend Jim? Did you see him?*
W: *Yes, I did. He worked in the yard all weekend. He likes working outside. When he was younger, he grew vegetables and sold them.*
B: *Great!*
N: *Five*
W: *My sister came, too, but she didn't stay home.*
B: *Where did she go? Did she go to the lake? It's beautiful there.*
W: *No, she didn't go there. She went walking by the ocean. But it was much colder there. The weather wasn't very good—it was freezing and damp.*
N: *Six*
B: *Do you have a brother?*
W: *Yes, I do. He was here on the weekend, too. Paul has a new skateboard like yours, and he wanted to try it. But he fell off the board. Now, he can't walk very well.*
B: *Oh, no. I have to go now. Mom is shouting for me.*
W: *Bye, Tom.*

AB 9.1

N: *Example*
W: *Can you see the girl riding a bike?*
B: *Yes, she's wearing a sunhat.*
W: *Right. Color the hat purple.*
B: *OK.*
N: *Can you see the purple hat? This is an example. Now you listen and color and write.*
N: *One*
W: *Can you see the girl arriving at summer camp?*
B: *Yes—she has a suitcase. Can I color the suitcase?*
W: *Yes. What color?*
B: *Brown.*
N: *Two*
W: *Can you see the boy near the tents?*
B: *Yes, he's wearing a T-shirt and jeans.*
W: *Yes. Color his T-shirt red.*
B: *OK.*
N: *Three*
W: *Look at the girl who's kayaking.*
B: *She's on the river?*
W: *Yes, that's right. Color her bathing suit.*
B: *What color?*
W: *Color her bathing suit orange.*
N: *Four*
W: *There's a boy next to the river.*
B: *Yes, he's going to go swimming.*
W: *Can you see his towel?*
B: *Yes.*
W: *Color the towel blue.*
B: *OK.*
N: *Five*
W: *Now, can you write something for me?*
B: *Yes. What is it?*
W: *Can you see the sign next to the lake?*
B: *Yes.*
W: *Write the words "Blue Lake" on the sign.*
B: *OK. I'm writing that now. Is that B-L-U-E L-A-K-E?*
W: *That's right.*

AB 9.2

B: *These objects are for vacation, but the school bag isn't.*
G: *Yes, the bag is different. The bathing suit, sunglasses, and the sunblock are for a vacation, but the bag is for school.*

AB 9.3

N: *One.*
G: *Picture B is different. He's playing a video game. It isn't a sport.*
B: *Yes, this is different. Pictures A, C, and D show kids doing water sports. But here he's playing a video game. It's not in the water.*
N: *Two*
G: *Picture C is different. There are four people in that picture.*
B: *Yes, that's right. Discus, javelin, and weightlifting are for only one person. Soccer is a team sport.*
N: *Three*
G: *Picture B is different. The mountain is in a cold place.*
B: *Yes, in picture A, the desert is hot. In pictures D and C, the jungle and ocean are hot, too. The mountain is different. It's snowy. It's the coldest place.*